FREE DVD   FREE   FREE DVD

From Stress to Success DVD from Trivium Test Prep

Dear Customer,

Thank you for purchasing from Trivium Test Prep! Whether you're looking to join the military, get into college, or advance your career, we're honored to be a part of your journey.

To show our appreciation (and to help you relieve a little of that test-prep stress), we're offering a **FREE *GED Essential Test Tips DVD*** by Trivium Test Prep. Our DVD includes 35 test preparation strategies that will help keep you calm and collected before and during your big exam. All we ask is that you email us your feedback and describe your experience with our product. Amazing, awful, or just so-so: we want to hear what you have to say!

To receive your **FREE *GED Essential Test Tips DVD***, please email us at 5star@triviumtestprep. com. Include "Free 5 Star" in the subject line and the following information in your email:

1. The title of the product you purchased.
2. Your rating from 1 – 5 (with 5 being the best).
3. Your feedback about the product, including how our materials helped you meet your goals and ways in which we can improve our products.
4. Your full name and shipping address so we can send your **FREE *GED Essential Test Tips DVD***.

If you have any questions or concerns please feel free to contact us directly at 5star@triviumtestprep.com.

Thank you, and good luck with your studies!

GED Preparation 2018–2019

GED Study Guide and Strategies with Practice Test Questions for the GED Test

TABLE OF CONTENTS

INTRODUCTION

Congratulations on choosing to take the GED! By purchasing this book, you've taken the first step toward getting your high-school equivalency, which will greatly expand your career options.

This guide will provide you with a detailed overview of the GED so you know exactly what to expect on test day. We'll take you through all the concepts covered on the test and give you the opportunity to test your knowledge with practice questions. Even if it's been a while since you last took a major test, don't worry; we'll make sure you're more than ready!

WHAT IS THE GED?

The General Educational Development test, or GED, is a high-school equivalency assessment. It measures whether test-takers have a high-school level understanding of four basic subjects: math, science, social studies, and language arts. In short, it tests everything taught in high school, so that if you didn't earn a diploma, you can still prove you have the equivalent knowledge.

There are several types of selected-response questions throughout the test, including multiple choice, drag and drop, fill in the blank, and hot spot. Multiple-choice questions ask a question and offer four to five responses for selection, while hot-spot questions offer ranges of space on the screen for selection. Drag-and-drop questions list answer choices to be moved, "dragged," to various places on the screen; fill-in-the-blank questions offer an area for you to type in your answer choice. In the science section you will encounter two short-answer questions that will require you to briefly respond to a question. The social studies and language arts sections contain extended-response questions, where you will be given historical and literary texts and must analyze and glean evidence from those texts to support your answer to the question.

What's on the GED?

SECTION	CONCEPTS	SELECTED-RESPONSE QUESTIONS	EXTENDED- OR SHORT-RESPONSE QUESTIONS	TIME
Math	basic operations, algebra, geometry, trigonometry, statistics, and probability	No calculator: 5	Calculator: 41	1 hour 55 minutes

SECTION	CONCEPTS	SELECTED-RESPONSE QUESTIONS	EXTENDED- OR SHORT-RESPONSE QUESTIONS	TIME
Science	physical sciences (chemistry and physics), life science (biology), Earth sciences (geology and meteorology), and space science (astronomy)	32	2	1 hour 30 minutes
Social Studies	U.S. and world history, economics, government, geography, and behavioral sciences	34	1	1 hour 30 minutes
Language Arts	interpreting informational and fictional passages	45	1	2 hours 30 minutes (10 minute break)
Total				**7 hours 25 minutes**

HOW IS THE GED SCORED?

Various questions on the GED are worth different points. For example, a multiple-choice question with one correct answer may be worth one point, but a drag-and-drop question with two correct answers may be worth two points. There is no penalty for wrong answers (so you should never leave a question blank). Other types of questions are worth a range of points depending on the difficulty of the question.

Raw scores for each section are scaled from 100 – 200, with a score of 145 needed to pass. There are three score levels: passing, college ready, and college ready + credit level. A score of 165 – 174, college ready, indicates that you likely have the skills necessary to begin college-level courses, while a score of 175 – 200 may qualify you for up to ten college credits depending on your institution. The extended-response questions in the language arts, social studies, and science sections are scored from 1 – 4, and you must earn a 2 to pass. Some states may not have updated their score practices, so be sure to check the guidelines of your individual state. Once you've passed a section, you do not need to take that section again (even if you need to retake other sections).

HOW IS THE GED ADMINISTERED?

The GED is only offered as a computer-based test. You do not need to take the test all at once—when registering, you can choose which sections you wish to take on a given day. An onscreen calculator is available during the test, but you are also welcome to bring a TI-30XS Multiview scientific calculator.

The GED is administered at private testing facilities. Each location may administer the exam slightly differently, so ask at your particular location about the details of test administration. You'll want to ask when the test begins, when breaks are offered, and what materials you're allowed to bring with you to the test.

ABOUT TRIVIUM TEST PREP

Trivium Test Prep uses industry professionals with decades' worth of knowledge in their fields, proven with degrees and honors in law, medicine, business, education, the military, and more, to produce high-quality test prep books for students.

Our study guides are specifically designed to increase any student's score, regardless of his or her current skill level. Our books are also shorter and more concise than typical study guides, so you can increase your score while significantly decreasing your study time.

HOW TO USE THIS GUIDE

This guide is not meant to waste your time on superfluous information or concepts you've already learned. Instead, we hope you use this guide to focus on the concepts YOU need to master for the test and to develop critical test-taking skills. To support this effort, the guide provides:

- organized concepts with detailed explanations
- practice questions with worked-through solutions
- key test-taking strategies
- simulated one-on-one tutor experience
- tips, tricks, and test secrets

Because we have eliminated "filler" or "fluff," you'll be able to work through the guide at a significantly faster pace than you would with other test prep books. By allowing you to focus only on those concepts that will increase your score, we'll make your study time shorter and more effective.

Now that you have a firm understanding of the exam and what is included in our book, don't forget that learning how to study, as well as how to successfully pass an exam, is just as important as the content. Trivium Test Prep would like to remind you as you begin your studies that we are offering a **FREE *From Stress to Success* DVD**. Our DVD includes 35 test preparation strategies that will help keep you calm and collected before and during your big exam. All we ask is that you email us your feedback and describe your experience with our product. Amazing, awful, or just so-so: we want to hear what you have to say!

To receive your **FREE *From Stress to Success* DVD**, please email us at 5star@triviumtestprep.com. Include "Free 5 Star" in the subject line and the following information in your email:

1. The title of the product you purchased.
2. Your rating from 1 – 5 (with 5 being the best).
3. Your feedback about the product, including how our materials helped you meet your goals and ways in which we can improve our products.
4. Your full name and shipping address so we can send you your **FREE *From Stress to Success* DVD**.

We hope you find the rest of this study guide helpful.

PART I: MATHEMATICS

THE MOST COMMON MISTAKES

People make little mistakes all the time, but during a test, those tiny mistakes can make the difference between a good score and a poor one. Watch out for these common mistakes that people make on the math section of the GED:

- answering with the wrong sign (positive/negative)
- mixing up the order of operations
- misplacing a decimal
- not reading the question thoroughly (and therefore providing an answer that was not asked for)
- circling the wrong letter or filling in the wrong circle choice

If you're thinking, *Those ideas are just common sense*, that's exactly the point. Most of the mistakes made on the GED are simple ones. But no matter how silly the mistake, a wrong answer still means a lost point on the test.

STRATEGIES FOR THE MATHEMATICS SECTION

Go Back to the Basics

First and foremost, practice your basic skills: sign changes, order of operations, simplifying fractions, and equation manipulation. These are the skills used most on the GED, though they are applied in different contexts. Remember that when it comes down to it, all math problems rely on the four basic skills of addition, subtraction, multiplication, and division. All you need to figure out is the order in which they're used to solve a problem.

Don't Rely on Mental Math

Using mental math is great for eliminating answer choices, but ALWAYS WRITE DOWN YOUR WORK! This cannot be stressed enough. Use whatever paper is provided; by writing and/or drawing out the problem, you are more likely to catch any mistakes. The act of writing things down also forces you to organize your calculations, leading to an improvement in your GED score.

The Three-Times Rule

You should read each question at least three times to ensure you're using the correct information and answering the right question:

Step one: Read the question and write out the given information.

Step two: Read the question, set up your equation(s), and solve.

Step three: Read the question and check that your answer makes sense. (Is the amount too large or small? Is the answer in the correct unit of measure?)

Make an Educated Guess

Eliminate those answer choices that you are relatively sure are incorrect, and then guess from the remaining choices. Educated guessing is critical to increasing your score.

NUMBERS AND OPERATIONS

TYPES OF NUMBERS

INTEGERS are whole numbers, including the counting numbers, the negative counting numbers, and zero. 3, 2, 1, 0, –1, –2, –3 are examples of integers. **RATIONAL NUMBERS** are made by dividing one integer by another integer. They can be expressed as fractions or as decimals. 3 divided by 4 makes the rational number $\frac{3}{4}$ or 0.75. **IRRATIONAL NUMBERS** are numbers that cannot be written as fractions; they are decimals that go on forever without repeating. The number π (3.14159…) is an example of an irrational number.

IMAGINARY NUMBERS are numbers that, when squared, give a negative result. Imaginary numbers use the symbol i to represent $\sqrt{(-1)}$, so $3i = 3\sqrt{(-1)}$ and $(3i)^2 = -9$. **COMPLEX NUMBERS** are combinations of real and imaginary numbers, written in the form $a + bi$, where a is the real number and b is the imaginary number. An example of a complex number is $4 + 2i$. When adding complex numbers, add the real and imaginary numbers separately: $(4 + 2i) + (3 + i) = 7 + 3i$.

Examples

1. Is $\sqrt{5}$ a rational or irrational number?

   $\sqrt{5}$ is an irrational number because it cannot be written as a fraction of two integers. It's a decimal that goes on forever without repeating.

2. What kind of number is $-\sqrt{64}$?

   $-\sqrt{64}$ can be rewritten as the negative whole number –8, so **it's an integer**.

3. Solve $(3 + 5i) - (1 - 2i)$

Subtract the real and imaginary numbers separately.

$3 - 1 = 2$

$5i - (-2i) = 5i + 2i = 7i$

So $(3 + 5i) - (1 - 2i) = \mathbf{2 + 7i}$

POSITIVE AND NEGATIVE NUMBER RULES

Adding, multiplying, and dividing numbers can yield positive or negative values depending on the signs of the original numbers. Knowing these rules can help determine if your answer is correct.

$(+) + (-)$ = the sign of the larger number

$(-) + (-)$ = negative number

$(-) \times (-)$ = positive number

$(-) \times (+)$ = negative number

$(-) \div (-)$ = positive number

$(-) \div (+)$ = negative number

Examples

1. Find the product of -10 and 47.

$(-) \times (+) = (-)$

$-10 \times 47 = \mathbf{-470}$

2. What is the sum of -65 and -32?

$(-) + (-) = (-)$

$-65 + -32 = \mathbf{-97}$

3. Is the product of -7 and 4 less than -7, between -7 and 4, or greater than 4?

$(-) \times (+) = (-)$

$-7 \times 4 = -28$, which is **less than -7**

4. What is the value of -16 divided by 2.5?

$(-) \div (+) = (-)$

$-16 \div 2.5 = \mathbf{-6.4}$

ORDER OF OPERATIONS

Operations in a mathematical expression are always performed in a specific order, which is described by the acronym PEMDAS:

1. Parentheses
2. Exponents
3. Multiplication
4. Division
5. Addition
6. Subtraction

✔

Can you come up with a mnemonic device to help yourself remember the order of operations?

Perform the operations within parentheses first, and then address any exponents. After those steps, perform all multiplication and division. These are carried out from left to right as they appear in the problem.

Finally, do all required addition and subtraction, also from left to right as each operation appears in the problem.

Examples

1. Solve: $[-(2)^2 - (4 + 7)]$

   First, complete operations within parentheses:

   $-(2)^2 - (11)$

   Second, calculate the value of exponential numbers:

   $-(4) - (11)$

   Finally, do addition and subtraction:

   $-4 - 11 = \mathbf{-15}$

2. Solve: $(5)^2 \div 5 + 4 \times 2$

   First, calculate the value of exponential numbers:

   $(25) \div 5 + 4 \times 2$

   Second, calculate division and multiplication from left to right:

   $5 + 8$

   Finally, do addition and subtraction:

   $5 + 8 = \mathbf{13}$

3. Solve the expression: $15 \times (4 + 8) - 3^3$

   First, complete operations within parentheses:

   $15 \times (12) - 3^3$

   Second, calculate the value of exponential numbers:

   $15 \times (12) - 27$

   Third, calculate division and multiplication from left to right:

   $180 - 27$

   Finally, do addition and subtraction from left to right:

   $180 - 27 = \mathbf{153}$

4. Solve the expression: $\left(\frac{5}{2} \times 4\right) + 23 - 4^2$

First, complete operations within parentheses:

$(10) + 23 - 4^2$

Second, calculate the value of exponential numbers:

$(10) + 23 - 16$

Finally, do addition and subtraction from left to right:

$(10) + 23 - 16$

$33 - 16 = \textbf{17}$

GREATEST COMMON FACTOR

The greatest common factor (GCF) of a set of numbers is the largest number that can evenly divide into all the numbers in the set. To find the GCF of a set, find all the factors of each number in the set. A factor is a whole number that can be multiplied by another whole number to result in the original number. For example, the number 10 has four factors: 1, 2, 5, and 10. (When listing the factors of a number, remember to include 1 and the number itself.) The largest number that is a factor for each number in the set is the GCF.

Examples

1. Find the greatest common factor of 24 and 18.

Factors of 24: 1, 2, 3, 4, 6, 8, 12, 24

Factors of 18: 1, 2, 3, 6, 9, 18

The greatest common factor is 6.

2. Find the greatest common factor of 121 and 44.

Since these numbers are larger, it's easier to start with the smaller number when listing factors.

Factors of 44: 1, 2, 4, 11, 22, 44

Now it's not necessary to list all the factors of 121. Instead, we can eliminate those factors of 44 that do not divide evenly into 121:

121 is not evenly divisible by 2, 4, 22, or 44 because it's an odd number. This leaves only 1 and 11 as common factors, so the **GCF is 11.**

3. First aid kits are being assembled at a summer camp. A complete first aid kit requires bandages, sutures, and sterilizing swabs, and each of the kits must be identical to other kits. If the camp's total supplies include 52 bandages, 13 sutures, and 39 sterilizing swabs, how many complete first aid kits can be assembled without having any leftover materials?

This problem is asking for the greatest common factor of 52, 13, and 39. The first step is to find all the factors of the smallest number, 13.

Factors of 13: 1, 13

13 is a prime number, meaning that its only factors are 1 and itself. Next we check to see if 13 is also a factor of 39 and 52:

$13 \times 2 = 26$

$13 \times 3 = 39$

$13 \times 4 = 52$

We can see that 39 and 52 are both multiples of 13. This means that **13 first aid kits can be made without having any leftover materials.**

4. Elena is making sundaes for her friends. She has 20 scoops of chocolate ice cream and 16 scoops of strawberry. If she wants to make identical sundaes and use all of her ice cream, how many sundaes can she make?

Arranging things into identical groups with no leftovers is always a tip that the problem calls for finding the greatest common factor. To find the GCF of 16 and 20, the first step is to factor both numbers:

Factors of 16: 1, 2, 4, 8, 16

Factors of 20: 1, 2, 4, 5, 10, 20

From these lists, we see that **4 is the GCF**. Elena can make 4 sundaes, each with 5 scoops of chocolate ice cream and 4 scoops of strawberry. Any other combination would result in leftover ice cream or sundaes that are not identical.

COMPARISON OF RATIONAL NUMBERS

Number comparison problems present numbers in different formats and ask which is larger or smaller or whether the numbers are equivalent. The important step in solving these problems is to convert the numbers to the same format so that it's easier to see how they compare. If numbers are given in the same format, or after they have been converted, determine which number is smaller or if the numbers are equal. Remember that for negative numbers, higher numbers are actually smaller.

The strategies for comparing numbers can also be used to put numbers in order from least to greatest (or vice versa).

Examples

1. Is $4\frac{3}{4}$ greater than, equal to, or less than $\frac{18}{4}$?

These numbers are in different formats—one is a mixed fraction and the other is just a fraction. So the first step is to convert the mixed fraction to a fraction:

$$4\frac{3}{4} = 4 \times \frac{4}{4} + \frac{3}{4} = \frac{19}{4}$$

Once the mixed number is converted, it's easier to see that $\frac{19}{4}$ **is greater than** $\frac{18}{4}$.

2. Which of the following numbers has the greatest value: 104.56, 104.5, or 104.6?

These numbers are already in the same format, so the decimal values just need to be compared. Remember that zeros can be added after the decimal without changing the value, so the three numbers can be rewritten as:

104.56

104.50

104.60

From this list, it's clearer to see that **104.60 is the greatest** because 0.60 is larger than 0.50 and 0.56.

3. Is 65% greater than, less than, or equal to $\frac{13}{20}$?

The first step is to convert the numbers into the same format. 65% is the same as $\frac{65}{100}$.

Next the fractions need to be converted to have the same denominator. It's difficult to compare fractions with different denominators. Using a factor of $\frac{5}{5}$ on the second fraction will give common denominators:

$$\frac{13}{20} \times \frac{5}{5} = \frac{65}{100}$$

Now it's easy to see that **the numbers are equivalent**.

UNITS OF MEASUREMENT

You are expected to memorize some units of measurement. These are given below. When doing unit conversion problems (i.e., when converting one unit to another), find the conversion factor, then apply that factor to the given measurement to find the new units.

You'll be given conversion factors if they're needed for a problem, but it's still good to familiarize yourself with common ones before the test.

Table 1.1. Unit prefixes

PREFIX	SYMBOL	MULTIPLICATION FACTOR
tera	T	1,000,000,000,000
giga	G	1,000,000,000
mega	M	1,000,000
kilo	k	1,000
hecto	h	100
deca	da	10
base unit	--	--
deci	d	0.1
centi	c	0.01
milli	m	0.001
micro	μ	0.0000001
nano	n	0.0000000001
pico	p	0.0000000000001

Table 1.2. Units and conversion factors

DIMENSION	AMERICAN	SI
length	inch/foot/yard/mile	meter
mass	ounce/pound/ton	gram
volume	cup/pint/quart/gallon	liter
force	pound-force	newton
pressure	pound-force per square inch	pascal
work and energy	cal/British thermal unit	joule
temperature	Fahrenheit	kelvin
charge	faraday	coulomb

CONVERSION FACTORS

1 in. = 2.54 cm	1 lb. = 0.454 kg
1 yd. = 0.914 m	1 cal = 4.19 J
1 mi. = 1.61 km	$1°F = \frac{5}{9}(°F - 32°C)$
1 gal. = 3.785 L	$1 cm^3 = 1 mL$
1 oz. = 28.35 g	1 hr = 3600 s

Examples

1. A fence measures 15 ft. long. How many yards long is the fence?

   1 yd. = 3 ft.

   $\frac{15}{3} =$ **5 yd.**

2. A pitcher can hold 24 cups. How many gallons can it hold?

   1 gal. = 16 cups

   $\frac{24}{16} =$ **1.5 gallons**

3. A spool of wire holds 144 in. of wire. If Mario has 3 spools, how many feet of wire does he have?

   12 in. = 1 ft.

   $\frac{144}{12} = 12$ ft.

   12 ft. × 3 spools = **36 ft. of wire**

4. A ball rolling across a table travels 6 inches per second. How many feet will it travel in 1 minute?

   This problem can be worked in two steps: finding how many inches are covered in 1 minute and then converting that value to feet. It can also be worked the opposite way, by finding how many feet it travels in 1 second and then converting that to feet traveled per minute. The first method is shown below.

   1 min. = 60 sec.

   (6 in.)/(sec.) × 60 s = 360 in.

   1 ft. = 12 in.

   (360 in.)/(12 in.) = **30 ft.**

5. How many millimeters are in 0.5 m?

1 meter = 1000 mm

0.5 meters = **500 mm**

6. A lead ball weighs 38 g. How many kilograms does it weigh?

1 kg = 1000 g

$\frac{38}{1000}$ g = **0.038 kg**

7. How many cubic centimeters are in 10 L?

1 L = 1000 ml

10 L = 1000 ml × 10

10 L = **10,000 ml or cm³**

8. Jennifer's pencil was initially 10 centimeters long. After she sharpened it, it was 9.6 centimeters long. How many millimeters did she lose from her pencil by sharpening it?

1 cm = 10 mm

10 cm − 9.6 cm = 0.4 cm lost

0.4 cm = 10 × .4 mm = **4 mm were lost**

DECIMALS AND FRACTIONS

Adding and Subtracting Decimals

When adding and subtracting decimals, line up the numbers so that the decimals are aligned. You want to subtract the ones place from the ones place, the tenths place from the tenths place, etc.

Examples

1. Find the sum of 17.07 and 2.52.

```
  17.07
+  2.52
= 19.59
```

2. Jeannette has 7.4 gallons of gas in her tank. After driving, she has 6.8 gallons. How many gallons of gas did she use?

```
  7.4
− 6.8
= 0.6 gal.
```

Multiplying and Dividing Decimals

When multiplying decimals, start by multiplying the numbers normally. You can then determine the placement of the decimal point in the result by adding the number of digits after the decimal in each of the numbers you multiplied together.

When dividing decimals, you should move the decimal point in the divisor (the number you're dividing by) until it's a whole. You can then move the decimal in the dividend (the number you're dividing into) the same number of places in the same direction. Finally, divide the new numbers normally to get the correct answer.

Examples

1. What is the product of 0.25 and 1.4?

25 × 14 = 350

There are 2 digits after the decimal in 0.25 and one digit after the decimal in 1.4. Therefore, the product should have 3 digits after the decimal: **0.350** is the correct answer.

2. Find 0.8 ÷ 0.2.

Change 0.2 to 2 by moving the decimal one space to the right.

Next move the decimal one space to the right on the dividend. 0.8 becomes 8.

Now divide 8 by 2. 8 ÷ 2 = **4**

3. Find the quotient when 40 is divided by 0.25.

First, change the divisor to a whole number: 0.25 becomes 25.

Next change the dividend to match the divisor by moving the decimal two spaces to the right, so 40 becomes 4000.

Now divide: 4000 ÷ 25 = **160**

Working with Fractions

FRACTIONS are made up of two parts: the NUMERATOR, which appears above the bar, and the DENOMINATOR, which is below it. If a fraction is in its SIMPLEST FORM, the numerator and the denominator share no common factors. A fraction with a numerator larger than its denominator is an IMPROPER FRACTION; when the denominator is larger, it's a PROPER FRACTION.

Improper fractions can be converted into proper fractions by dividing the numerator by the denominator. The resulting whole number is placed to the left of the fraction, and the remainder becomes the new numerator; the denominator does not change. The new number is called a MIXED NUMBER because it contains a whole number and a fraction. Mixed numbers can be turned into improper fractions through the reverse process: multiply the whole number by the denominator, and add the numerator to get the new numerator.

CONTINUE

Examples

1. Simplify the fraction $\frac{121}{77}$.

121 and 77 share a common factor of 11. So if we divide each by 11, we can simplify the fraction:

$$\frac{121}{77} = \frac{11}{11} \times \frac{11}{7} = \mathbf{\frac{11}{7}}$$

2. Convert $\frac{37}{5}$ into a proper fraction.

Start by dividing the numerator by the denominator:

$37 \div 5 = 7$ with a remainder of 2

Now build a mixed number with the whole number and the new numerator:

$$\frac{37}{5} = \mathbf{7\frac{2}{5}}$$

Multiplying and Dividing Fractions

To multiply fractions, convert any mixed numbers into improper fractions, and multiply the numerators together and the denominators together. Reduce to lowest terms if needed.

To divide fractions, first convert any mixed fractions into single fractions. Then, invert the second fraction so that the denominator and numerator are switched. Finally, multiply the numerators together and the denominators together.

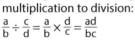

Inverting a fraction changes multiplication to division:
$$\frac{a}{b} \div \frac{c}{d} = \frac{a}{b} \times \frac{d}{c} = \frac{ad}{bc}$$

Examples

1. What is the product of $\frac{1}{12}$ and $\frac{6}{8}$?

Simply multiply the numerators together and the denominators together, then reduce:

$$\frac{1}{12} \times \frac{6}{8} = \frac{6}{96} = \mathbf{\frac{1}{16}}$$

Sometimes, it's easier to reduce fractions before multiplying if you can:

$$\frac{1}{12} \times \frac{6}{8} = \frac{1}{12} \times \frac{3}{4} = \frac{3}{48} = \mathbf{\frac{1}{16}}$$

2. Find $\frac{7}{8} \div \frac{1}{4}$.

For a fraction division problem, invert the second fraction and then multiply and reduce:

$$\frac{7}{8} \div \frac{1}{4} = \frac{7}{8} \times \frac{4}{1} = \frac{28}{8} = \mathbf{\frac{7}{2}}$$

The quotient is the result you get when you divide two numbers.

3. What is the quotient of $\frac{2}{5} \div 1\frac{1}{5}$?

This is a fraction division problem, so the first step is to convert the mixed number to an improper fraction:

$$1\frac{1}{5} = \frac{5 \times 1}{5} + \frac{1}{5} = \frac{6}{5}$$

Now, divide the fractions. Remember to invert the second fraction, and then multiply normally:

$$\frac{2}{5} \div \frac{6}{5} = \frac{2}{5} \times \frac{5}{6} = \frac{10}{30} = \mathbf{\frac{1}{3}}$$

4. A recipe calls for $\frac{1}{4}$ cup of sugar. If 8.5 batches of the recipe are needed, how many cups of sugar will be used?

This is a fraction multiplication problem: $\frac{1}{4} \times 8\frac{1}{2}$.

First, we need to convert the mixed number into a proper fraction:

$$8\frac{1}{2} = \frac{8 \times 2}{2} + \frac{1}{2} = \frac{17}{2}$$

Now multiply the fractions across the numerators and denominators, and then reduce:

$$\frac{1}{4} \times 8\frac{1}{2} = \frac{1}{4} \times \frac{17}{2} = \mathbf{\frac{17}{8}} \textbf{ cups of sugar}$$

Adding and Subtracting Fractions

Adding and subtracting fractions requires a COMMON DENOMINATOR. To find the common denominator, you can multiply each fraction by the number 1. With fractions, any number over itself (e.g., $\frac{5}{5}, \frac{12}{12}$, etc.) is equivalent to 1, so multiplying by such a fraction can change the denominator without changing the value of the fraction. Once the denominators are the same, the numerators can be added or subtracted.

To add mixed numbers, you can first add the whole numbers and then the fractions. To subtract mixed numbers, convert each number to an improper fraction, then subtract the numerators.

Examples

1. Simplify the expression $\frac{2}{3} - \frac{1}{5}$.

First, multiply each fraction by a factor of 1 to get a common denominator. How do you know which factor of 1 to use? Look at the other fraction, and use the number found in that denominator:

$$\frac{2}{3} - \frac{1}{5} = \frac{2}{3}\left(\frac{5}{5}\right) - \frac{1}{5}\left(\frac{3}{3}\right) = \frac{10}{15} - \frac{3}{15}$$

Once the fractions have a common denominator, simply subtract the numerators:

$$\frac{10}{15} - \frac{3}{15} = \mathbf{\frac{7}{15}}$$

2. Find $2\frac{1}{3} - \frac{3}{2}$.

This is a fraction subtraction problem with a mixed number, so the first step is to convert the mixed number to an improper fraction:

$$2\frac{1}{3} = \frac{2 \times 3}{3} + \frac{1}{3} = \frac{7}{3}$$

The phrase *simplify the expression* just means you need to perform all the operations in the expression.

Next, convert each fraction so they share a common denominator:

$$\frac{7}{3} \times \frac{2}{2} = \frac{14}{6}$$

$$\frac{3}{2} \times \frac{3}{3} = \frac{9}{6}$$

Now subtract the fractions by subtracting the numerators:

$$\frac{14}{6} - \frac{9}{6} = \mathbf{\frac{5}{6}}$$

3. Find the sum of $\frac{9}{16}$, $\frac{1}{2}$, and $\frac{7}{4}$.

For this fraction addition problem, we need to find a common denominator. Notice that 2 and 4 are both factors of 16, so 16 can be the common denominator:

$$\frac{1}{2} \times \frac{8}{8} = \frac{8}{16}$$

$$\frac{7}{4} \times \frac{4}{4} = \frac{28}{16}$$

$$\frac{9}{16} + \frac{8}{16} + \frac{28}{16} = \mathbf{\frac{45}{16}}$$

4. Sabrina has $\frac{2}{3}$ of a can of red paint. Her friend Amos has $\frac{1}{6}$ of a can. How much red paint do they have combined?

To add fractions, make sure that they have a common denominator. Since 3 is a factor of 6, 6 can be the common denominator:

$$\frac{2}{3} \times \frac{2}{2} = \frac{4}{6}$$

Now add the numerators:

$$\frac{4}{6} + \frac{1}{6} = \mathbf{\frac{5}{6}} \textbf{ of a can}$$

Converting Fractions to Decimals

Calculators are not allowed on part two of the math section on the GED, which can make handling fractions and decimals intimidating for many test takers. However, there are several techniques you can use to help you convert between the two forms.

The first thing to do is simply memorize common decimals and their fractional equivalents; a list of these is given in Table 1.3. With these values, it's possible to convert more complicated fractions as well. For example, $\frac{2}{5}$ is just $\frac{1}{5}$ multiplied by 2, so $\frac{2}{5} = 0.2 \times 2 = 0.4$.

Table 1.3. Common decimals and fractions

FRACTION	DECIMAL
$\frac{1}{2}$	0.5
$\frac{1}{3}$	$0.\overline{33}$
$\frac{1}{4}$	0.25
$\frac{1}{5}$	0.2
$\frac{1}{6}$	$0.1\overline{66}$
$\frac{1}{7}$	$0.\overline{142857}$
$\frac{1}{8}$	0.125
$\frac{1}{9}$	$0.\overline{11}$
$\frac{1}{10}$	0.1

Knowledge of common decimal equivalents to fractions can also help you estimate. This skill can be particularly helpful on multiple-choice tests like the GED, where excluding incorrect answers can be just as helpful as knowing how to find the right one. For example, to find $\frac{5}{8}$ in decimal form for an answer, you can eliminate any answers less than 0.5 because $\frac{4}{8} = 0.5$. You may also know that $\frac{6}{8}$ is the same as $\frac{3}{4}$ or 0.75, so anything above 0.75 can be eliminated as well.

Another helpful trick can be used if the denominator is easily divisible by 100: in the fraction $\frac{9}{20}$, you know 20 goes into 100 five times, so you can multiply the top and bottom by 5 to get $\frac{45}{100}$ or 0.45.

If none of these techniques work, you'll need to find the decimal by dividing the denominator by the numerator using long division.

Examples

1. Write $\frac{8}{18}$ as a decimal.

   The first step here is to simplify the fraction:
   $\frac{8}{18} = \frac{4}{9}$
   Now it's clear that the fraction is a multiple of $\frac{1}{9}$, so you can easily find the decimal using a value you already know:
   $\frac{4}{9} = \frac{1}{9} \times 4 = 0.\overline{11} \times 4 = \mathbf{0.\overline{44}}$

2. Write the fraction $\frac{3}{16}$ as a decimal.

   None of the tricks above will work for this fraction, so you need to do long division:

→
CONTINUE

```
         0.1875
   16 | 3.0000
       − 1 6
          1 40
        − 1 28
            120
          −  112
               80
          −    80
                0
```

The decimal will go in front of the answer, so now you know that $\frac{3}{16} =$ **0.1875**.

Converting Decimals to Fractions

Converting a decimal into a fraction is more straightforward than the reverse process is. To convert a decimal, simply use the numbers that come after the decimal as the numerator in the fraction. The denominator will be a power of 10 that matches the place value for the original decimal. For example, the numerator for 0.46 would be 100 because the last number is in the tenths place; likewise, the denominator for 0.657 would be 1000 because the last number is in the thousandths place. Once this fraction has been set up, all that's left is to simplify it.

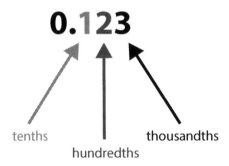

Figure 1.1. Simplified decimal

Example

Convert 0.45 into a fraction.

The last number in the decimal is in the hundredths place, so we can easily set up a fraction:

$0.45 = \frac{45}{100}$

The next step is to simply reduce the fraction down to the lowest common denominator. Here, both 45 and 100 are divisible by 5: 45 divided by 5 is 9, and 100 divided by 5 is 20. Therefore, you're left with:

$\frac{45}{100} = \mathbf{\frac{9}{20}}$

RATIOS

A **RATIO** tells you how many of one thing exists in relation to the number of another thing. Unlike fractions, ratios do not give a part relative to a whole; instead, they compare two values. For example, if you have 3 apples and 4 oranges, the ratio of apples to oranges is 3 to 4. Ratios can be written using words (3 to 4), fractions $\left(\frac{3}{4}\right)$, or colons (3:4).

In order to work with ratios, it's helpful to rewrite them as a fraction expressing a part to a whole. For instance, in the example above, you have 7 total pieces of fruit, so the fraction of your fruit that are apples is $\frac{3}{7}$, and oranges make up $\frac{4}{7}$ of your fruit collection.

One last important thing to consider when working with ratios is the units of the values being compared. On the GED, you may be asked to rewrite a ratio using the same units on both sides. For example, you might have to rewrite the ratio 3 minutes to 7 seconds as 180 seconds to 7 seconds.

Examples

1. There are 90 voters in a room, and each is either a Democrat or a Republican. The ratio of Democrats to Republicans is 5:4. How many Republicans are there?

   We know that there are 5 Democrats for every 4 Republicans in the room, which means for every 9 people, 4 are Republicans.

   $5 + 4 = 9$

   Fraction of Democrats: $\frac{5}{9}$

   Fraction of Republicans: $\frac{4}{9}$

   If $\frac{4}{9}$ of the 90 voters are Republicans, then:

   $\frac{4}{9} \times 90 =$ **40 voters are Republicans**

2. The ratio of students to teachers in a school is 15:1. If there are 38 teachers, how many students attend the school?

   To solve this ratio problem, we can simply multiply both sides of the ratio by the desired value to find the number of students that correspond to having 38 teachers:

   $\frac{15 \text{ students}}{1 \text{ teacher}} \times 38 \text{ teachers} = 570 \text{ students}$

   The school has **570 students**.

PROPORTIONS

A **PROPORTION** is an equation that states that two ratios are equal. Proportions are usually written as two fractions joined by an equal sign $\left(\frac{a}{b} = \frac{c}{d}\right)$, but they can also be written using colons ($a : b :: c : d$). Note that in a proportion, the units must be the same in both numerators and in both denominators.

Often, you will be given three of the values in a proportion and asked to find the fourth. In these types of problems, you can solve for the missing variable by cross-multiplying—multiply the numerator of each fraction by the denominator of the other to get an equation with no fractions as shown below. You can then solve the equation using basic algebra. (For more on solving basic equations, see *Algebraic Expressions and Equations*.)

$$\frac{a}{b} = \frac{c}{d} \rightarrow ad = bc$$

You'll see ratios written using fractions and colons on the test.

Examples

1. A train traveling 120 miles takes 3 hours to get to its destination. How long will it take for the train to travel 180 miles?

   Start by setting up the proportion:

   $$\frac{120 \text{ miles}}{3 \text{ hours}} = \frac{180 \text{ miles}}{x \text{ hours}}$$

   Note that it doesn't matter which value is placed in the numerator or denominator, as long as it's the same on both sides. Now solve for the missing quantity through cross-multiplication:

   120 miles × x hours = 3 hours × 180 miles

   Now solve the equation:

   $$x \text{ hours} = \frac{(3 \text{ hours}) \times (180 \text{ miles})}{120 \text{ miles}}$$

   $x = 4.5$ hours

2. One acre of wheat requires 500 gallons of water. How many acres can be watered with 2600 gallons?

   Set up the equation:

   $$\frac{1 \text{ acre}}{500 \text{ gal.}} = \frac{x \text{ acres}}{2600 \text{ gal.}}$$

   Then, solve for x:

   $$x \text{ acres} = \frac{1 \text{ acre} \times 2600 \text{ gal.}}{500 \text{ gal.}}$$

   $x = \frac{26}{5}$ or **5.2 acres**

3. If $35 : 5 :: 49 : x$, find x.

   This problem presents two equivalent ratios that can be set up in a fraction equation:

   $$\frac{35}{5} = \frac{49}{x}$$

   You can then cross-multiply to solve for x:

   $35x = 49 \times 5$

   $x = 7$

PERCENTAGES

A **PERCENT** is the ratio of a part to the whole. Questions may give the part and the whole and ask for the percent, or give the percent and the whole and ask for the part, or give the part and the percent and ask for the value of the whole. The equation for percentages can be rearranged to solve for any of these:

$$percent = \frac{part}{whole}$$

$$part = whole \times percent$$

$$whole = \frac{part}{percent}$$

In the equations above, the percent should always be expressed as a decimal. To convert a decimal into a percentage value, simply multiply it by 100. So if you've read 5 pages (the part) of a 10-page article (the whole), you've read $\frac{5}{10} = 0.5$ or 50%. (The percent sign [%] is used once the decimal has been multiplied by 100.)

Note that when you solve these problems, the units for the part and the whole should be the same. If you're reading a book, saying you've read 5 pages out of 15 chapters doesn't make any sense.

The word *of* usually indicates what the whole is in a problem. For example, the problem might say *Ella ate two slices of the pizza*, which means the pizza is the whole.

Examples

1. 45 is 15% of what number?

   Set up the appropriate equation and solve. Don't forget to change 15% to a decimal value:

   $$whole = \frac{part}{percent} = \frac{45}{0.15} = \textbf{300}$$

2. Jim spent 30% of his paycheck at the fair. He spent $15 for a hat, $30 for a shirt, and $20 playing games. How much was his check? (Round to nearest dollar.)

   Set up the appropriate equation and solve:

   $$whole = \frac{part}{percent} = \frac{15 + 30 + 20}{.30} = \textbf{\$217.00}$$

3. What percent of 65 is 39?

   Set up the equation and solve:

   $$percent = \frac{part}{whole} = \frac{39}{65} = \textbf{0.6 or 60\%}$$

4. Greta and Max sell cable subscriptions. In a given month, Greta sells 45 subscriptions and Max sells 51. If 240 total subscriptions were sold in that month, what percent were not sold by Greta or Max?

   You can use the information in the question to figure out what percentage of subscriptions were sold by Max and Greta:

   $$percent = \frac{part}{whole} = \frac{(51 + 45)}{240} = \frac{96}{240} = 0.4 \text{ or } 40\%$$

However, the question asks how many subscriptions weren't sold by Max or Greta. If they sold 40%, then the other salespeople sold 100% − 40% = **60%**.

5. Grant needs to score 75% on an exam. If the exam has 45 questions, at least how many does he need to answer correctly?

Set up the equation and solve. Remember to convert 75% to a decimal value:

part = whole × percent = 45 × 0.75 = 33.75, so he needs to answer at least **34 questions correctly**.

Words that indicate a percent change problem:
- discount
- markup
- sale
- increase
- decrease

PERCENT CHANGE

PERCENT CHANGE problems will ask you to calculate how much a given quantity changed. The problems are solved in a similar way to regular percent problems, except that instead of using the *part*, you'll use the *amount of change*. Note that the sign of the *amount of change* is important: if the original amount has increased, the change will be positive, and if it has decreased, the change will be negative. Again, in the equations below, the percent is a decimal value; you need to multiply by 100 to get the actual percentage.

$$percent\ change = \frac{amount\ of\ change}{original\ amount}$$

$$amount\ of\ change = original\ amount \times percent\ change$$

$$original\ amount = \frac{amount\ of\ change}{percent\ change}$$

The same steps shown here can be used to find percent change for problems that don't involve money as well.

Examples

1. A computer software retailer marks up its games by 40% above the wholesale price when it sells them to customers. Find the price of a game for a customer if the game costs the retailer $25.

Set up the appropriate equation and solve:

amount of change = original amount x percent change = 25 × 0.4 = 10

If the amount of change is 10, that means the store adds a markup of $10, so the game costs:

$25 + $10 = **$35**

2. A golf shop pays its wholesaler $40 for a certain club and then sells it to a golfer for $75. What is the markup rate?

First, calculate the amount of change:

75 − 40 = 35

Now you can set up the equation and solve (note that *markup rate* is another way of saying *percent change*):

$$percent\ change = \frac{amount\ of\ change}{original\ amount} = \frac{35}{40} = 0.875 = \textbf{87.5\%}$$

3. A store charges a 40% markup on the shoes it sells. How much did the store pay for a pair of shoes purchased by a customer for $63?

You're solving for the original price, but it's going to be tricky because you don't know the amount of change; you only know the new price. To solve, you need to create an expression for the amount of change:

If *original amount* $= x$

Then, *amount of change* $= 63 - x$

Now you can plug these values into your equation:

$$original\ amount = \frac{amount\ of\ change}{percent\ change}$$

$$x = \frac{63 - x}{0.4}$$

The last step is to solve for x:

$0.4x = 63 - x$

$1.4x = 63$

$x = 45$

The store paid **$45 for the shoes**.

4. An item originally priced at $55 is marked 25% off. What is the sale price?

You've been asked to find the sale price, which means you need to solve for the amount of change first:

amount of change $=$ *original amount* $\times$ *percent change* $\rightarrow$
$55 \times 0.25 = 13.75$

Using this amount, you can find the new price. Because it's on sale, we know the item will cost less than the original price:

$55 - 13.75 = 41.25$

The sale price is $41.25.

5. James wants to put in an 18 foot by 51 foot garden in his backyard. If he does, it will reduce the size of this yard by 24%. What will be the area of the remaining yard?

This problem is tricky because you need to figure out what each number in the problem stands for. 24% is obviously the percent change, but what about the measurements in feet? If you multiply these values you get the area of the garden (for more on area, see *Area and Perimeter*):

18 ft. $\times$ 51 ft. $= 918$ ft.^{2}

This 918 ft.^{2} is the amount of change—it's how much smaller the lawn is. Now we can set up an equation:

$$original\ amount = \frac{amount\ of\ change}{percent\ change} = \frac{918}{.24} = 3825$$

If the original lawn was 3825 ft.^{2} and the garden is 918 ft.^{2}, then the remaining area is

$3825 - 918 = 2907$

The remaining lawn covers **2907 ft.^{2}**

EXPONENTS AND RADICALS

EXPONENTS tell us how many times to multiply a base number by itself. In the example 2^4, 2 is the base number and 4 is the exponent. $2^4 = 2 \times 2 \times 2 \times 2 = 16$. Exponents are also called powers: 5 to the third power $= 5^3 = 5 \times 5 \times 5 = 125$. Some exponents have special names: x to the second power is also called "x squared," and x to the third power is also called "x cubed." The number 3 squared $= 3^2 = 3 \times 3 = 9$.

RADICALS are expressions that use roots. Radicals are written in the form $\sqrt[a]{x}$, where $a =$ the **RADICAL POWER** and $x =$ the **RADICAND**. The solution to the radical $\sqrt[3]{8}$ is the number that, when multiplied by itself 3 times, equals 8. $\sqrt[3]{8} = 2$ because $2 \times 2 \times 2 = 8$. When the radical power is not written, we assume it's 2, so $\sqrt{9} = 3$ because $3 \times 3 = 9$. Radicals can also be written as exponents, where the power is a fraction. For example, $x^{\frac{1}{3}} = \sqrt[3]{x}$.

Review more of the rules for working with exponents and radicals in the table below.

Table 1.4. Exponents and radicals rules

RULE	EXAMPLE
$x^0 = 1$	$5^0 = 1$
$x^1 = x$	$5^1 = 5$
$x^a \times x^b = x^{a+b}$	$5^2 \times 5^3 = 5^5 = 3125$
$(xy)^a = x^a y^a$	$(5 \times 6)^2 = 5^2 \times 6^2 = 900$
$(x^a)^b = x^{ab}$	$(5^2)^3 = 5^6 = 15{,}625$
$\left(\dfrac{x}{y}\right)^a = \dfrac{x^a}{y^a}$	$\left(\dfrac{5}{6}\right)^2 = \dfrac{5^2}{6^2} = \dfrac{25}{36}$
$\dfrac{x^a}{x^b} = x^{a-b} \; (x \neq 0)$	$\dfrac{5^4}{5^3} = 5^1 = 5$
$x^{-a} = \dfrac{1}{x^a} \; (x \neq 0)$	$5^{-2} = \dfrac{1}{5^2} = \dfrac{1}{25}$
$x^{\frac{1}{a}} = \sqrt[a]{x}$	$25^{\frac{1}{2}} = \sqrt[2]{25} = 5$
$\sqrt[a]{x \times y} = \sqrt[a]{x} \times \sqrt[a]{y}$	$\sqrt[3]{8 \times 27} = \sqrt[3]{8} \times \sqrt[3]{27} = 2 \times 3 = 6$
$\sqrt[a]{\dfrac{x}{y}} = \dfrac{\sqrt[a]{x}}{\sqrt[a]{y}}$	$\sqrt[3]{\dfrac{27}{8}} = \dfrac{\sqrt[3]{27}}{\sqrt[3]{8}} = \dfrac{3}{2}$
$\sqrt[a]{x^b} = x^{\frac{b}{a}}$	$\sqrt[2]{5^4} = 5^{\frac{4}{2}} = 5^2 = 25$

Examples

1. Simplify the expression $2^4 \times 2^2$.

   When multiplying exponents in which the base number is the same, simply add the powers:

   $$2^4 \times 2^2 = 2^{(4+2)} = 2^6$$
   $$2^6 = 2 \times 2 \times 2 \times 2 \times 2 \times 2 = \mathbf{64}$$

2. Simplify the expression $(3^4)^{-1}$.

   When an exponent is raised to a power, multiply the powers:

   $$(3^4)^{-1} = 3^{-4}$$

   When the exponent is a negative number, rewrite as the reciprocal of the positive exponent:

   $$3^{-4} = \frac{1}{3^4}$$
   $$\frac{1}{3^4} = \frac{1}{3 \times 3 \times 3 \times 3} = \mathbf{\frac{1}{81}}$$

3. Simplify the expression $\left(\frac{9}{4}\right)^{\frac{1}{2}}$.

   When the power is a fraction, rewrite as a radical:

   $$\left(\frac{9}{4}\right)^{\frac{1}{2}} = \sqrt{\frac{9}{4}}$$

   Next distribute the radical to the numerator and denominator:

   $$\sqrt{\frac{9}{4}} = \frac{\sqrt{9}}{\sqrt{4}} = \mathbf{\frac{3}{2}}$$

PROBABILITIES

A **PROBABILITY** is found by dividing the number of desired outcomes by the number of total possible outcomes. As with percentages, a probability is the ratio of a part to a whole, with the whole being the total number of things that could happen, and the part being the number of those things that would be considered a success. Probabilities can be written using percentages (40%), decimals (0.4), fractions $\left(\frac{2}{5}\right)$, or in words (probability is 2 in 5).

$$probability = \frac{desired\ outcomes}{total\ possible\ outcomes}$$

Examples

1. A bag holds 3 blue marbles, 5 green marbles, and 7 red marbles. If you pick one marble from the bag, what is the probability it will be blue?

   Because there are 15 marbles in the bag (3 + 5 + 7), the total number of possible outcomes is 15. Of those outcomes, 3 would be blue marbles, which is the desired outcome. With that information, you can set up an equation:

   $$probability = \frac{desired\ outcomes}{total\ possible\ outcomes} = \frac{3}{15} = \frac{1}{5}$$

   The probability is **1 in 5 or 0.2 that a blue marble is picked.**

2. A bag contains 75 balls. If the probability that a ball selected from the bag will be red is 0.6, how many red balls are in the bag?

Because you're solving for desired outcomes (the number of red balls), first you need to rearrange the equation:

$$probability = \frac{desired\ outcomes}{total\ possible\ outcomes} \rightarrow$$
$$desired\ outcomes = probability \times total\ possible\ outcomes$$

In this problem, the desired outcome is choosing a red ball, and the total possible outcomes are represented by the 75 total balls.

$$desired\ outcomes = 0.6 \times 75 = 45$$

There are **45 red balls in the bag.**

3. A theater has 230 seats: 75 seats are in the orchestra area, 100 seats are in the mezzanine, and 55 seats are in the balcony. If a ticket is selected at random, what is the probability that it will be for either a mezzanine or balcony seat?

In this problem, the desired outcome is a seat in either the mezzanine or balcony area, and the total possible outcomes are represented by the 230 total seats, so the equation should be written as:

$$probability = \frac{desired\ outcomes}{total\ possible\ outcomes} = \frac{100 + 55}{230} = \textbf{0.67}$$

4. The probability of selecting a student whose name begins with the letter *s* from a school attendance log is 7%. If there are 42 students whose names begin with *s* enrolled at the school, how many students attend the school?

Because you're solving for total possible outcomes (total number of students), first you need to rearrange the equation:

$$total\ possible\ outcomes = \frac{desired\ outcomes}{probability}$$

In this problem, you are given a probability (7% or 0.07) and the number of desired outcomes (42). These can be plugged into the equation to solve:

$$total\ possible\ outcomes = \frac{42}{0.07} = \textbf{600 students}$$

2

ALGEBRA

ALGEBRAIC EXPRESSIONS

Algebraic expressions and equations include a **VARIABLE**, which is a letter standing for a number. These expressions and equations are made up of **TERMS**, which are groups of numbers and variables (e.g., $2xy$). An **EXPRESSION** is simply a set of terms (e.g., $3x + 2xy$), while an **EQUATION** includes an equal sign (e.g., $3x + 2xy = 17$). When simplifying expressions or solving algebraic equations, you'll need to use many different mathematical properties and operations, including addition, subtraction, multiplication, division, exponents, roots, distribution, and the order of operations.

Evaluating Algebraic Expressions

To evaluate an algebraic expression, simply plug the given value(s) in for the appropriate variable(s) in the expression.

Example

Evaluate $2x + 6y - 3z$, if $x = 2$, $y = 4$, and $z = -3$.

Plug in each number for the correct variable and simplify:

$2x + 6y - 3z = 2(2) + 6(4) - 3(-3) = 4 + 24 + 9 = \mathbf{37}$

Adding and Subtracting Terms

Only **LIKE TERMS**, which have the exact same variable(s), can be added or subtracted. **CONSTANTS** are numbers without variables attached, and those can be added and subtracted together as well. When you simplify an expression, like terms should be added or subtracted so that no individual group of variables occurs in more than one term. For example, the expression $5x + 6xy$ is in its simplest form, while $5x + 6xy - 11xy$ is not because the term xy appears more than once.

Example

Simplify the expression $5xy + 7y + 2yz + 11xy - 5yz$.

Start by grouping together like terms:

$(5xy + 11xy) + (2yz - 5yz) + 7y$

Now you can add together each set of like terms:

$16xy + 7y - 3yz$

Multiplying and Dividing Terms

To multiply a single term by another, simply multiply the coefficients and then multiply the variables. Remember that when you multiply variables with exponents, those exponents are added together. For example, $(x^5 y)(x^3 y^4) = x^8 y^5$.

When multiplying a term by a set of terms inside parentheses, you need to DISTRIBUTE to each term inside the parentheses as shown below:

$$a(b+c) = ab + ac$$

Figure 2.1. Distribution

When variables occur in both the numerator and denominator of a fraction, they cancel each other out. So a fraction with variables in its simplest form will not have the same variable on the top and bottom.

Examples

1. Simplify the expression $(3x^4 y^2 z)(2y^4 z^5)$.

   Multiply the coefficients and variables together:

   $3 \times 2 = 6$

   $y^2 \times y^4 = y^6$

   $z \times z^5 = z^6$

   Now put all the terms back together:

   $6x^4 y^6 z^6$

2. Simplify the expression: $(2y^2)(y^3 + 2xy^2 z + 4z)$.

   Multiply each term inside the parentheses by the term $2y^2$:

   $(2y^2)(y^3 + 2xy^2 z + 4z)$

   $(2y^2 \times y^3) + (2y^2 \times 2xy^2 z) \times (2y^2 \times 4z)$

   $2y^5 + 4xy^4 z + 8y^2 z$

3. Simplify the expression: $(5x + 2)(3x + 3)$.

   Use the acronym FOIL—First, Outer, Inner, Last—to multiply the terms:

   First: $5x \times 3x = 15x^2$

   Outer: $5x \times 3 = 15x$

Inner: $2 \times 3x = 6x$

Last: $2 \times 3 = 6$

Now combine like terms:

$15x^2 + 21x + 6$

4. Simplify the expression: $\frac{2x^4y^3z}{8x^2z^2}$.

   Simplify by looking at each variable and crossing out those that appear in the numerator and denominator:

   $\frac{2}{8} = \frac{1}{4}$

   $\frac{x^4}{x^2} = \frac{x^2}{1}$

   $\frac{z}{z^2} = \frac{1}{z}$

   $\frac{2x^4y^3z}{8x^2z^2} = \frac{x^2y^3}{4z}$

When multiplying terms, add the exponents. When dividing, subtract the exponents.

Factoring Expressions

FACTORING is splitting one expression into the multiplication of two (or more) expressions. It requires finding the HIGHEST COMMON FACTOR and dividing terms by that number. For example, in the expression $15x + 10$, the highest common factor is 5 because both terms are divisible by 5: $\frac{15x}{5} = 3x$ and $\frac{10}{5} = 2$. When you factor the expression, you get $5(3x + 2)$.

Sometimes, it's difficult to find the highest common factor. In these cases, consider whether the expression fits a polynomial identity. A polynomial is an expression with more than one term. If you can recognize the common polynomials listed below, you can easily factor the expression.

$a^2 - b^2 = (a + b)(a - b)$

$a^2 + 2ab + b^2 = (a + b)(a + b) = (a + b)^2$

$a^2 - 2ab + b^2 = (a - b)(a - b) = (a - b)^2$

$a^3 + b^3 = (a + b)(a^2 - ab - b^2)$

$a^3 - b^3 = (a - b)(a^2 + ab + b^2)$

Examples

1. Factor the expression $27x^2 - 9x$.

   First, find the highest common factor. Both terms are divisible by 9:

   $\frac{27x^2}{9} = 3x^2$ and $\frac{9x}{9} = x$

   Now the expression is $9(3x^2 - x)$—but wait, you're not done! Both terms can be divided by x:

   $\frac{3x^2}{x} = 3x$ and $\frac{x}{x} = 1$.

   The final factored expression is **$9x(3x - 1)$**.

CONTINUE

2. Factor the expression $25x^2 - 16$.

Since there is no obvious factor by which you can divide terms, you should consider whether this expression fits one of your polynomial identities.

This expression is a difference of squares $a^2 - b^2$, where $a^2 = 25x^2$ and $b^2 = 16$.

Recall that $a^2 - b^2 = (a + b)(a - b)$. Now solve for a and b:

$a = \sqrt{25x^2} = 5x$

$b = \sqrt{16} = 4$

$(a + b)(a - b) = (5x + 4)(5x - 4)$

You can check your work by using the FOIL acronym to expand your answer back to the original expression:

First: $5x \times 5x = 25x^2$

Outer: $5x \times -4 = -20x$

Inner: $4 \times 5x = 20x$

Last: $4 \times -4 = -16$

$25x^2 - 20x + 20x - 16 = 25x^2 - 16$

3. Factor the expression $100x^2 + 60x + 9$.

This is another polynomial identity, $a^2 + 2ab + b^2$. (The more you practice these problems, the faster you will recognize polynomial identities.)

$a^2 = 100x^2$, $2ab = 60x$, and $b^2 = 9$

Recall that $a^2 + 2ab + b^2 = (a + b)^2$. Now solve for a and b:

$a = \sqrt{100x^2} = 10x$

$b = \sqrt{9} = 3$

$(a + b)^2 = \mathbf{(10x + 3)^2}$

You can check your work by confirming that $2ab = 2 \times 10x \times 3 = 60x$.

LINEAR EQUATIONS

Solving Linear Equations

To solve an equation, you need to manipulate the terms on each side to isolate the variable, meaning if you want to find x, you have to get the x alone on one side of the equal sign. To do this, you'll need to use many of the tools discussed above: you might need to distribute, divide, add, or subtract like terms, or find common denominators.

Think of each side of the equation as the two sides of a seesaw. As long as the two people on each end weigh the same amount, the seesaw will be balanced: if you have a 120-pound person on each end, the seesaw is balanced. Giving each of them a 10-pound rock to hold changes the weight on each end, but the seesaw itself stays balanced. Equations work the same way: you can add, subtract, multiply, or divide whatever you want as long as you do the same thing to both sides.

Most equations you'll see on the GED can be solved using the same basic steps:

1. Distribute to get rid of parentheses.
2. Use the least common denominator to get rid of fractions.
3. Add/subtract like terms on either side.
4. Add/subtract so that constants appear on only one side of the equation.
5. Multiply/divide to isolate the variable.

Examples

1. Solve for x: $25x + 12 = 62$.

   This equation has no parentheses, fractions, or like terms on the same side, so you can start by subtracting 12 from both sides of the equation:

   $25x + 12 = 62$

   $(25x + 12) - 12 = 62 - 12$

   $25x = 50$

   Now divide by 25 to isolate the variable:

   $\frac{25x}{25} = \frac{50}{25}$

   $\textbf{\textit{x} = 2}$

2. Solve the following equation for x: $2x - 4(2x + 3) = 24$.

   Start by distributing to get rid of the parentheses (don't forget to distribute the negative):

   $2x - 4(2x + 3) = 24 \rightarrow$

   $2x - 8x - 12 = 24$

   There are no fractions, so now you can join like terms:

   $2x - 8x - 12 = 24 \rightarrow$

   $-6x - 12 = 24$

   Now add 12 to both sides and divide by −6.

   $-6x - 12 = 24$

   $(-6x - 12) + 12 = 24 + 12 \rightarrow$

   $-6x = 36 \rightarrow$

   $\frac{-6x}{-6} = \frac{36}{-6}$

   $\textbf{\textit{x} = −6}$

3. Solve the following equation for x: $\frac{x}{3} + \frac{1}{2} = \frac{x}{6} - \frac{5}{12}$.

   Start by multiplying by the least common denominator to get rid of the fractions:

   $\frac{x}{3} + \frac{1}{2} = \frac{x}{6} - \frac{5}{12} \rightarrow$

$$12\left(\frac{x}{3}+\frac{1}{2}\right)=12\left(\frac{x}{6}-\frac{5}{12}\right)\rightarrow$$

$$4x+6=2x-5$$

Now you can isolate x:

$$(4x+6)-6=(2x-5)-6\rightarrow$$

$$4x=2x-11\rightarrow$$

$$(4x)-2x=(2x-11)-2x\rightarrow$$

$$2x=-11$$

$$x=-\frac{11}{2}$$

4. Find the value of x: $2(x+y)-7x=14x+3$.

This equation looks more difficult because it has 2 variables, but you can use the same steps to solve for x. First, distribute to get rid of the parentheses and combine like terms:

$$2(x+y)-7x=14x+3\rightarrow$$

$$2x+2y-7x=14x+3\rightarrow$$

$$-5x+2y=14x+3$$

Now you can move the x terms to one side and everything else to the other and then divide to isolate x:

$$-5x+2y=14x+3\rightarrow$$

$$-19x=-2y+3\rightarrow$$

$$x=\frac{2y-3}{19}$$

Graphing Linear Equations

Linear equations can be plotted as straight lines on a coordinate plane. The x-AXIS is always the horizontal axis, and the y-AXIS is always the vertical axis. The x-axis is positive to the right of the y-axis and negative to the left. The y-axis is positive above the x-axis and negative below. To describe the location of any point on the graph, write the coordinates in the form (x,y). The origin, the point where the x- and y-axes cross, is $(0,0)$.

The y-INTERCEPT is the y coordinate where the line crosses the y-axis. The SLOPE is a measure of how steep the line is. Slope is calculated by dividing the change along the y-axis by the change along the x-axis between any two points on the line.

Linear equations are easiest to graph when they are written in POINT-SLOPE FORM: $y = mx + b$. The constant m represents slope, and the constant b represents y-intercept. If you know two points along the line $(x1,y1)$ and $(x2,y2)$, you can calculate slope using the following equation: $m=\frac{y_2-y_1}{x_2-x_1}$. If you know the slope and one other point along the line, you can calculate the y-intercept by plugging the number 0 in for x_2 and solving for y_2.

When graphing a linear equation, first plot the y-intercept. Next plug in values for x to solve for y, and plot additional points. Connect the points with a straight line.

Examples

1. Find the slope of the line: $\frac{3y}{2} + 3 = x$.

Slope is easiest to find when the equation is in point-slope form ($y = mx + b$). Rearrange the equation to isolate y:

$\frac{3y}{2} + 3 = x$

$3y + 6 = 2x$

$y + 2 = \frac{2x}{3}$

$y = \frac{2x}{3} - 2$

Finally, identify the term m to find the slope of the line:

$\boldsymbol{m = \frac{2}{3}}$

2. Plot the linear equation $2y - 4x = 6$.

First, rearrange the linear equation to point-slope form ($y = mx + b$):

$2y - 4x = 6$

$y = 2x + 3$

Next identify the y-intercept (b) and the slope (m):

$b = 3, m = 2$

Now plot the y-intercept:

$(0, b) = (0, 3)$

Next plug in values for x and solve for y:

$y = 2(1) + 3 = 5 \rightarrow (1, 5)$

$y = 2(-1) + 3 = 1 \rightarrow (-1, 1)$

Plot these points on the graph, and connect the points with a straight line:

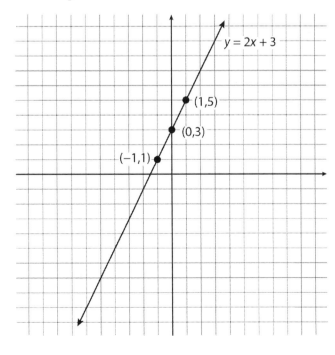

SYSTEMS OF EQUATIONS

A system of equations is a group of related questions each of which has the same variable. The problems you see on the GED will most likely involve two equations that each have two variables, although you can also solve sets of equations with any number of variables as long as there are a corresponding number of equations (e.g., to solve a system with four variables, you need four equations).

There are two main methods used to solve systems of equations. In **SUBSTITUTION**, one equation is solved for a single variable, and the resulting expression is substituted into the second equation for the correct variable. In **ELIMINATION**, equations are added together so that variables cancel and one variable can be solved for.

Examples

1. Solve the following system of equations: $3y - 4 + x = 0$ and $5x + 6y = 11$.

   To solve this system using substitution, first solve one equation for a single variable:

   $3y - 4 + x = 0$

   $3y + x = 4$

   $x = 4 - 3y$

   Next substitute the expression to the right of the equal sign for x in the second equation:

   $5x + 6y = 11$

   $5(4 - 3y) + 6y = 11$

   $20 - 15y + 6y = 11$

   $20 - 9y = 11$

   $-9y = -9$

   $y = 1$

   Finally, plug the value for y back into the first equation to find the value of x:

   $3y - 4 + x = 0$

   $3(1) - 4 + x = 0$

   $-1 + x = 0$

   $x = 1$

   The solution is $x = 1$ and $y = 1$, or the point (1, 1).

2. Solve the system: $2x + 4y = 8$ and $4x + 2y = 10$.

   To solve this system using elimination, start by manipulating one equation so that a variable (in this case x) will cancel when the equations are added together:

   $2x + 4y = 8$

   $-2(2x + 4y = 8)$

   $-4x - 8y = -16$

Now you can add the two equations together, and the *x* variable will drop out:

$-4x - 8y = -16$

$4x + 2y = 10$

$-6y = -6$

$y = 1$

Lastly, plug the *y* value into one of the equations to find the value of *x*:

$2x + 4y = 8$

$2x + 4(1) = 8$

$2x + 4 = 8$

$2x = 4$

$x = 2$

The solution is *x* = 2 and *y* = 1, or the point (2, 1).

INEQUALITIES

SOLVING LINEAR INEQUALITIES

INEQUALITIES look like equations, except that instead of having an equal sign, they have one of the following symbols:

> Greater than: The expression left of the symbol is larger than the expression on the right.

< Less than: The expression left of the symbol is smaller than the expression on the right.

≥ Greater than or equal to: The expression left of the symbol is larger than or equal to the expression on the right.

≤ Less than or equal to: The expression left of the symbol is less than or equal to the expression on the right.

Inequalities are solved like linear and algebraic equations. The only difference is that the symbol must be reversed when both sides of the equation are multiplied by a negative number.

Example

Solve for *x*: $-7x + 2 < 6 - 5x$.

Collect like terms on each side as you would for a regular equation:

$-7x + 2 < 6 - 5x \rightarrow$

$-2x < 4$

The direction of the sign switches when you divide by a negative number:

$-2x < 4 \rightarrow$

$x > -2$

See *Solving Equations* for step-by-step instructions on solving basic equations.

Graphing Linear Inequalities

Graphing a linear inequality is just like graphing a linear equation, except that you shade the area on one side of the line. To graph a linear inequality, first rearrange the inequality expression into $y = mx + b$ form. Then, treat the inequality symbol like an equal sign, and plot the line. If the inequality symbol is < or >, make a dashed line; for ≤ or ≥, make a solid line. Finally, shade the correct side of the graph:

For $y < mx + b$ or $y \leq mx + b$, shade the side below the line.

For $y > mx + b$ or $y \geq mx + b$, shade the side above the line.

Example

Plot the inequality $3x \geq 4 - y$.

To rearrange the inequality into $y = mx + b$ form, first subtract 4 from both sides:

$3x - 4 \geq -y$

Next divide both sides by −1 to get positive y; remember to switch the direction of the inequality symbol:

$-3x + 4 \leq y$

Now plot the line $y = -3x + 4$, making a solid line, and then shade the side above the line:

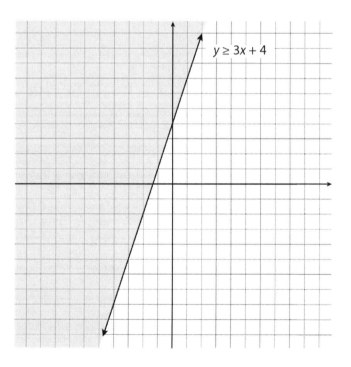

$y \geq 3x + 4$

QUADRATIC EQUATIONS

Quadratic equations include terms where the variable has been raised to the second power. A quadratic equation is often in the form $ax^2 + bx + c = 0$. In quadratic equations, x is the variable, and a, b, and c are all constants (a cannot be 0).

Solving Quadratic Equations

There is more than one way to solve a quadratic equation. The first method is to simply take the square root of both sides. For example, the equation $x^2 = 64$ can be solved by taking the square root of both sides ($x = \pm 8$).

For more difficult quadratic equations, it's often possible to factor the equation. By rearranging the expression $ax^2 + bx + c$ into one factor multiplied by another factor, you can easily solve for the ROOTS, that is, the values of x for which the quadratic expression equals 0. For example, the equation $x^2 - 5x + 6 = 0$ can be factored to $(x - 3)(x - 2) = 0$. From here, each factor can be set equal to 0 and solved ($x = 3$ and $x = 2$).

The last resort to solve a quadratic equation is by using the QUADRATIC FORMULA: $x = \dfrac{-b \pm \sqrt{b^2 - 4ac}}{2a}$. The expression $b^2 - 4ac$ is called the discriminant. When it's positive, you will get two real numbers for x; when it's negative, you will get one real number and one imaginary number for x; when it's zero, you will get one real number for x.

Examples

1. Factor the quadratic equation $-2x^2 = 14x$, and find the roots.

   Not every quadratic equation you see will be presented in the standard form. Rearrange terms to set one side equal to 0:

   $2x^2 + 14x = 0$

   Note that $a = 2$, $b = 14$, and $c = 0$ because there is no third term.

   Now divide the expression on the left by the common factor:

   $(2x)(x + 7) = 0$

   To find the roots, set each of the factors equal to 0:

   $2x = 0 \rightarrow x = 0$

   $x + 7 = 0 \rightarrow \mathbf{x = -7}$

2. Use the quadratic formula to solve for x: $3x^2 = 7x - 2$.

   First, rearrange the equation to set one side equal to 0:

   $3x^2 - 7x + 2 = 0$

   Next identify the terms a, b, and c:

   $a = 3, b = -7, c = 2$

   Now plug those terms into the quadratic formula:

   $x = \dfrac{-b \pm \sqrt{b^2 - 4ac}}{2a}$

   $x = \dfrac{7 \pm \sqrt{(-7)^2 - 4(3)(2)}}{2(3)}$

   $x = \dfrac{7 \pm \sqrt{25}}{6}$

$$x = \frac{7 \pm 5}{6}$$

Since the determinant is positive, we expect two real numbers for x. Solve for the two possible answers:

$$x = \frac{7 + 5}{6} \rightarrow \boldsymbol{x = 2}$$

$$x = \frac{7 - 5}{6} \rightarrow \boldsymbol{x = \frac{1}{3}}$$

Graphing Quadratic Equations

Graphing a quadratic equation forms a **PARABOLA**. A parabola is a horseshoe-shaped curve that is symmetrical about a vertical axis passing through the **VERTEX** (the highest or lowest point on the parabola). Each term in the equation $ax^2 + bx + c = 0$ affects the shape of the parabola. A bigger value for a makes the curve narrower, while a smaller value makes the curve wider. A negative value for a flips the parabola upside down. The axis of symmetry is the vertical line $x = \frac{-b}{2a}$. To find the y coordinate for the vertex, plug this value for x into the expression $ax^2 + bx + c$.

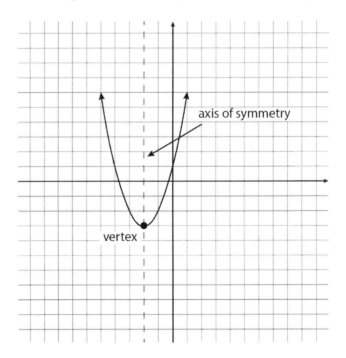

Figure 2.1. Parabola

The easiest way to graph a quadratic equation is to find the axis of symmetry, solve for the vertex, then create a table of points by plugging in other numbers for x and solving for y. Plot these points and trace the parabola.

Example

Graph the equation $x^2 + 4x + 1 = 0$.

First, find the axis of symmetry. The equation for the line of symmetry is $x = \frac{-b}{2a}$.

$x = \frac{-4}{2(1)} = -2$

Next plug in -2 for x to find the y coordinate of the vertex:

$y = (-2)^2 + 4(-2) + 1 = -3$

The vertex is $(-2, -3)$.

Now make a table of points on either side of the vertex by plugging in numbers for x and solving for y:

x	$y = x^2 + 4x + 1$	(x,y)
−3	$y = (-3)2 + 4(-3) + 1 = -2$	$(-3, -2)$
−1	$y = (-3)^2 + 4(-3)\ 1 = -2$	$(-1, -2)$
−4	$y = (-1)^2 + 4(-1) + 1 = -2$	$(-4, 1)$
0	$y = (0)^2 + 4(0) + 1 = 1$	$(0, 1)$

Finally, draw the axis of symmetry, plot the vertex and your table of points, and trace the parabola:

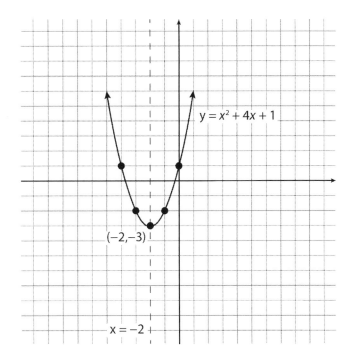

FUNCTIONS

FUNCTIONS describe how an input relates to an output. Linear equations, sine, and cosine are examples of functions. In a function, there must be one and only one output for each input. $\sqrt{x}$ is not a function because there are two outputs for any one input: $\sqrt{4} = 2, -2$.

Describing Functions

Functions are often written in $f(x)$ form: $f(x) = x^2$ means that for input x, the output is x^2. In relating functions to linear equations, you can think of $f(x)$ as equivalent to y. The domain of a function is all the possible inputs of that function. The range of a function includes the outputs of the inputs. For example, for the function $f(x) = x^2$, if the domain includes all positive and negative integers, the range will include 0 and only positive integers. When you graph a function, the domain is plotted on the x-axis, and the range is plotted on the y-axis.

Examples

1. Given $f(x) = 2x - 10$, find $f(9)$.

   Plug in 9 for x:

   $f(9) = 2(9) - 10$

   $f(9) = 8$

2. Given $f(x) = \frac{4}{x}$ with a domain of all positive integers except 0, and $g(x) = \frac{4}{x}$ with a domain of all positive and negative integers except 0, which function has a range that includes the number −2?

   The function $f(x)$ has a range of only positive numbers, since x cannot be negative. The function $g(x)$ has a range of positive and negative numbers, since x can be either positive or negative. **The number −2, therefore, must be in the range for $g(x)$ but not for $f(x)$.**

Exponential Functions

An exponential function is in the form $f(x) = a^x$, where $a > 0$. When $a > 1$, $f(x)$ approaches infinity as x increases and 0 as x decreases. When $0 < a < 1$, $f(x)$ approaches 0 as x increases and infinity as x increases. When $a = 1$, $f(x) = 1$. The graph of an exponential function where $a \neq 1$ will have a horizontal asymptote along the x-axis; the graph will never cross below the x-axis. The graph of an exponential function where $a = 1$ will be a horizontal line at $y = 1$. All graphs of exponential functions include the points $(0, 1)$ and $(1, a)$.

Examples

1. Graph the function $f(x) = 3^x$.

   First, estimate the shape and direction of the graph based on the value of a. Since $a > 1$, you know that $f(x)$ will approach infinity as x increases and there will be a horizontal asymptote along the negative x-axis.

   Next plot the points $(0, 1)$ and $(1, a)$.

   Finally, plug in one or two more values for x, plot those points, and trace the graph:

   $f(2) = 3^2 = 9 \rightarrow (2, 9)$

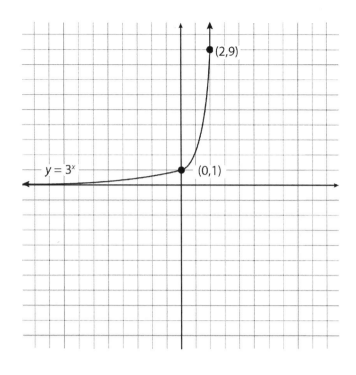

$y = 3^x$

(2,9)

(0,1)

2. Given $f(x) = 2^x$, solve for x when $f(x) = 64$.

$64 = 2^x$

The inverse of an exponent is a log. Take the log of both sides to solve for x:

$\log_2 64 = x$

$\boldsymbol{x = 6}$

Logarithmic Functions

A LOGARITHMIC FUNCTION is the inverse of an exponential function. Recall the definition of a log: if $\log_a x = b$, then $a^b = x$. Logarithmic functions are written in the form $f(x) = \log_a x$, where a is any number greater than 0, except for 1. If a is not shown, it's assumed that $a = 10$. The function $\ln x$ is called a NATURAL LOG, equal to $\log_e x$. When $0 < a < 1$, $f(x)$ approaches infinity as x approaches 0 and negative infinity as x increases. When $a > 1$, $f(x)$ approaches negative infinity as x approaches 0 and infinity as x increases. In either case, the graph of a logarithmic function has a vertical asymptote along the y-axis; the graph will never cross to the left of the y-axis. All graphs of logarithmic functions include the points $(1, 0)$ and $(a, 1)$.

Examples

1. Graph the function $f(x) = \log_4 x$.

First, estimate the shape and direction of the graph based on the value of a. Since $a > 1$, you know that $f(x)$ will approach infinity as x increases and there will be a vertical asymptote along the negative y-axis.

Next, plot the points $(1, 0)$ and $(a, 1)$.

Finally, it's easier to plug in a value for $f(x)$ and solve for x rather than attempting to solve for $f(x)$. Plug in one or two values for $f(x)$, plot those points, and trace the graph:

$$2 = \log_4 x$$

$$4^2 = x$$

$$16 = x \rightarrow (16, 2)$$

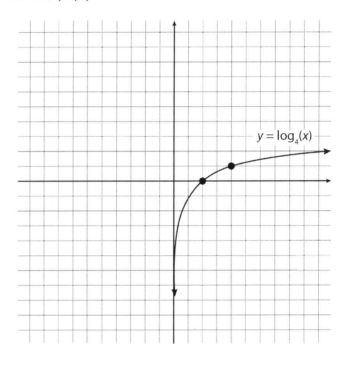

2. Given $f(x) = \log_{\frac{1}{3}} x$, solve for $f(81)$.

Rewrite the function in exponent form:

$$x = \frac{1}{3}^{f(x)}$$

$$81 = \frac{1}{3}^{f(x)}$$

The question is asking: to what power must you raise $\frac{1}{3}$ to get 81?

Recognize that $3^4 = 81$, so $\frac{1}{3}^4 = \frac{1}{81}$.

Switch the sign of the exponent to flip the numerator and denominator:

$$\frac{1}{3}^{-4} = \frac{81}{1}$$

$$f(81) = -4$$

Arithmetic and Geometric Sequences

Sequences are patterns of numbers. Most questions about sequences require you to figure out the pattern. In an **arithmetic sequence**, you add or subtract the same number between terms. In a **geometric sequence**, you multiply or divide by the same number between terms. For example, 2, 6, 10, 14, 18 and 11, 4, –3, –10, –17 are arithmetic sequences because you add 4 to each term in the first example and you subtract 7 from each term in the second example. The sequence 5, 15, 45, 135 is a geometric sequence because you multiply each term by 3. In arithmetic sequences, the number you add or subtract between terms is called the COMMON DIFFERENCE. In geometric sequences, the number by which you multiply or divide is called the COMMON RATIO.

In an arithmetic sequence, the nth term (a_n) can be found by calculating $a_n = a_1 + (n-1)d$, where d is the common difference and a_1 is the first term in the sequence. In a geometric sequence, $a_n = a_1(r^n)$, where r is the common ratio.

Examples

1. Find the common difference and the next term of the following sequence: 5, −1, −7, −13.

Find the difference between two terms that are next to each other:

$5 - (-1) = -6$

The common difference is −6. (It must be negative to show the difference is subtracted, not added.)

Now subtract 6 from the last term to find the next term:

$-13 - 6 = -19$

The next term is −19.

2. Find the 12th term of the following sequence: 2, 6, 18, 54.

First, decide whether this is an arithmetic or geometric sequence. Since the numbers are getting farther and farther apart, we know this must be a geometric sequence.

Divide one term by the term before it to find the common ratio:

$18 \div 6 = 3$

Next plug in the common ratio and the first term to the equation $a_n = a_1(r^n)$:

$a_{12} = 2(3^{12})$

$a_{12} = 1{,}062{,}882$

Notice that it would have taken a very long time to multiply each term by 3 until we got the 12th term—this is where that equation comes in handy!

3. The 4th term of a sequence is 9. The common difference is 11. What is the 10th term?

To answer this question, we can simply add $9 + 11 = 20$ to get the 5th term, $20 + 11 = 31$ to get the 6th term, and so on until we get the 10th term. Or we can plug the information we know into our equation $a_n = a_1 + (n-1)d$. In this case, we do not know the first term. If we use the fourth term instead, we must replace $(n-1)$ with $(n-4)$:

$a_{10} = 9 + (10-4)11$

$a_{10} = 75$

ABSOLUTE VALUE

The **ABSOLUTE VALUE** of a number (represented by the symbol $|x|$) is its distance from zero, not its value. For example, $|3| = 3$ and $|-3| = 3$ because both 3 and –3 are three units from zero. The absolute value of a number is always positive.

Equations with absolute values will have two answers, so you need to set up two equations. The first is simply the equation with the absolute value symbol removed. For the second equation, isolate the absolute value on one side of the equation, and multiply the other side of the equation by –1.

Examples

1. Solve for x: $|2x - 3| = x + 1$.

   Set up the first equation by removing the absolute value symbol, then solve for x:

   $|2x - 3| = x + 1$

   $2x - 3 = x + 1$

   $x = 4$

   For the second equation, remove the absolute value and multiply by –1:

   $|2x - 3| = x + 1 \rightarrow$

   $2x - 3 = -(x + 1) \rightarrow$

   $2x - 3 = -x - 1 \rightarrow$

   $3x = 2$

   $x = \frac{2}{3}$

   Both answers are correct, so the complete answer is $x = 4$ or $\frac{2}{3}$.

2. Solve for y: $2|y + 4| = 10$.

   Set up the first equation:

   $2(y + 4) = 10 \rightarrow$

   $y + 4 = 5 \rightarrow$

   $y = 1$

   Set up the second equation. Remember to isolate the absolute value before multiplying by –1:

   $2|y + 4| = 10 \rightarrow$

   $|y + 4| = 5 \rightarrow$

   $y + 4 = -5$

   $y = -9$

   $y = 1$ or -9

SOLVING WORD PROBLEMS

Any of the math concepts discussed here can be turned into a word problem, and you'll likely see word problems in various forms throughout the test. (In fact, you may have noticed that several examples in the ratio and proportion sections were word problems.)

The most important step in solving any word problem is to read the entire problem before beginning to solve it: one of the most commonly made mistakes on word problems is providing an answer to a question that wasn't asked. Also, remember that not all the information given in a problem is always needed to solve it.

When you work multiple-choice word problems like those on the GED, it's important to check your answer. Many of the incorrect choices will be answers that test takers arrive at by making common mistakes. So even if an answer you calculated is given as an answer choice, that doesn't necessarily mean you've worked the problem correctly—you have to check your own work to make sure.

General Steps for Word Problem Solving

Step 1: Read the entire problem, and determine what the question is asking for.

Step 2: List all the given data and define the variables.

Step 3: Determine the formula(s) needed, or set up equations from the information in the problem.

Step 4: Solve.

Step 5: Check your answer. (Is the amount too large or small? Are the answers in the correct unit of measure?)

Key Words

Word problems generally contain key words that can help you determine what math processes may be required to solve them.

- Addition: added, combined, increased by, in all, total, perimeter, sum, and more than
- Subtraction: how much more, less than, fewer than, exceeds, difference, and decreased
- Multiplication: of, times, area, and product
- Division: distribute, share, average, per, out of, percent, and quotient
- Equals: is, was, are, amounts to, and were

Basic Word Problems

A word problem in algebra is just an equation or a set of equations described using words. Your task when solving these problems is to turn the "story" of the problem into mathematical equations.

⟶
CONTINUE

Examples

1. A store owner bought a case of 48 backpacks for $476.00. He sold 17 of the backpacks in his store for $18 each, and the rest were sold to a school for $15 each. What was the salesman's profit?

   Start by listing all the data and defining the variable:

   total number of backpacks = 48

   cost of backpacks = $476.00

   backpacks sold in store at price of $18 = 17

   backpacks sold to school at a price of $15 = 48 − 17 = 31

   total profit = x

   Now set up an equation:

   total profit = income − cost = (306 + 465) − 476 = 295

   The store owner made a profit of **$295**.

2. Thirty students in Mr. Joyce's room are working on projects over two days. The first day, he gave them $\frac{3}{5}$ hour to work. On the second day, he gave them half as much time as the first day. How much time did each student have to work on the project?

   Start by listing all the data and defining your variables. Note that the number of students, while given in the problem, is not needed to find the answer:

   time on 1st day = $\frac{3}{5}$ hr. = 36 min.

   time on 2nd day = $\frac{1}{2}$(36) = 18 min.

   total time = x

   Now set up the equation and solve:

   total time = time on 1st day + time on 2nd day

   $x = 36 + 18 = 54$

   The students had **54 minutes** to work on the projects.

Converting units can often help you avoid operations with fractions when dealing with time.

Distance Word Problems

Distance word problems involve something traveling at a constant or average speed. Whenever you read a problem that involves *how fast*, *how far*, or *for how long*, you should think of the distance equation, $d = rt$, where *d* stands for distance, *r* for rate (speed), and *t* for time.

These problems can be solved by setting up a grid with *d*, *r*, and *t* along the top and each moving object on the left. When setting up the grid, make sure the units are consistent. For example, if the distance is in meters and the time is in seconds, the rate should be meters per second.

Examples

1. Will drove from his home to the airport at an average speed of 30 mph. He then boarded a helicopter and flew to the hospital with an average speed of 60 mph. The entire distance was 150 miles, and the trip took 3 hours. Find the distance from the airport to the hospital.

   The first step is to set up a table and fill in a value for each variable:

   Table 2.1. Drive time

	d	r	t
driving	d	30	t
flying	$150 - d$	60	$3 - t$

   You can now set up equations for driving and flying. The first row gives the equation $d = 30t$, and the second row gives the equation $150 - d = 60(3 - t)$.

   Next you can solve this system of equations. Start by substituting for d in the second equation:

   $d = 30t$

   $150 - d = 60(3 - t) \rightarrow 150 - 30t = 60(3 - t)$

   Now solve for t:

   $150 - 30t = 180 - 60t$

   $-30 = -30t$

   $1 = t$

   Although you've solved for t, you're not done yet. Notice that the problem asks for distance. So you need to solve for d: what the problem asked for. It does not ask for time, but the time is needed to solve the problem.

   Driving: $30t = 30$ miles

   Flying: $150 - d = 120$ miles

   The distance from the airport to the hospital is **120 miles**.

2. Two cyclists start at the same time from opposite ends of a course that is 45 miles long. One cyclist is riding at 14 mph, and the second cyclist is riding at 16 mph. How long after they begin will they meet?

   First, set up the table. The variable for time will be the same for each, because they will have been on the road for the same amount of time when they meet:

   Table 2.2. Cyclist times

	d	r	t
Cyclist #1	d	14	t
Cyclist #2	$45 - d$	16	t

   Next set up two equations:

   Cyclist #1: $d = 14t$

   Cyclist #2: $45 - d = 16t$

   Now substitute and solve:

$d = 14t$

$45 - d = 16t \rightarrow 45 - 14t = 16t$

$45 = 30t$

$t = 1.5$

They will meet **1.5 hr.** after they begin.

Work Problems

WORK PROBLEMS involve situations where several people or machines are doing work at different rates. Your task is usually to figure out how long it will take these people or machines to complete a task while working together. The trick to doing work problems is to figure out how much of the project each person or machine completes in the same unit of time. For example, you might calculate how much of a wall a person can paint in one hour or how many boxes an assembly line can pack in one minute.

Once you know that, you can set up an equation to solve for the total time. This equation usually has a form similar to the equation for distance, but here *work = rate × time*.

See *Adding and Subtracting Fractions* for step-by-step instruction on operations with fractions.

Examples

1. Bridget can clean an entire house in 12 hours while her brother Tom takes 8 hours. How long would it take for Bridget and Tom to clean two houses together?

   Start by figuring out how much of a house each sibling can clean on his or her own. Bridget can clean the house in 12 hours, so she can clean $\frac{1}{12}$ of the house in an hour. You know that Tom can clean $\frac{1}{8}$ of a house in an hour.

   By adding these values together, you get the fraction of the house they can clean together in an hour:

   $$\frac{1}{12} + \frac{1}{8} = \frac{5}{24}$$

   They can do $\frac{5}{24}$ of the job per hour.

   Now set up variables and an equation to solve:

   t = time spent cleaning (in hours)

   h = number of houses cleaned = 2

   work = rate × time

   $h = \frac{5}{24}t \rightarrow$

   $2 = \frac{5}{24}t \rightarrow$

   $t = \frac{48}{5} = 9\frac{3}{5}$ **hours**

2. Farmer Dan needs to water his cornfield. One hose can water a field 1.25 times faster than a second hose. When both hoses are opened, they water the field in 5 hours. How long would it take to water the field if only the second hose is used?

   In this problem, you don't know the exact time, but you can still find the hourly rate as a variable:

The first hose completes the job in f hours, so it waters $\frac{1}{f}$ field per hour. The slower hose waters the field in $1.25f$, so it waters the field in $\frac{1}{1.25f}$ hours. Together, they take 5 hours to water the field, so they water $\frac{1}{5}$ of the field per hour.

Now you can set up the equations and solve:

$$\frac{1}{f} + \frac{1}{1.25f} = \frac{1}{5} \rightarrow$$

$$1.25f\left(\frac{1}{f} + \frac{1}{1.25f}\right) = 1.25f\left(\frac{1}{5}\right) \rightarrow$$

$$1.25 + 1 = 0.25f$$

$$2.25 = 0.25f$$

$$f = 9$$

The fast hose takes 9 hours to water the cornfield. The slower hose takes $1.25(9) = $ **11.25 hours**.

3. Alex takes 2 hours to shine 500 silver spoons, and Julian takes 3 hours to shine 450 silver spoons. How long will they take, working together, to shine 1000 silver spoons?

Calculate how many spoons each man can shine per hour:

Alex: $\dfrac{500 \text{ spoons}}{2 \text{ hours}} = \dfrac{250 \text{ spoons}}{\text{hour}}$

Julian: $\dfrac{450 \text{ spoons}}{3 \text{ hours}} = \dfrac{150 \text{ spoons}}{\text{hour}}$

Together: $\dfrac{(250 + 150) \text{ spoons}}{\text{hour}} = \dfrac{400 \text{ spoons}}{\text{hour}}$

Now set up an equation to find the time it takes to shine 1000 spoons:

total time $= \dfrac{1 \text{ hour}}{400 \text{ spoons}} \times 1000 \text{ spoons} = \dfrac{1000}{400} \text{ hours} =$

2.5 hours

3

GEOMETRY

Geometry is the study of shapes. On the GED, you'll need to be able to find the perimeter and area of two-dimensional shapes and the volume of three-dimensional shapes. You will also need to have a basic understanding of congruency and trigonometry.

PROPERTIES OF SHAPES

Area and Perimeter

AREA and PERIMETER problems will require you to use the equations shown in the table below to find either the area inside a shape or the distance around it (the perimeter). These equations will not be given on the test, so you need to have them memorized on test day.

Table 3.1. Equations

SHAPE	AREA	PERIMETER
circle	$A = \pi r^2$	$C = 2\pi r = \pi d$
triangle	$A = \frac{b \times h}{2}$	$P = s_1 + s_2 + s_3$
square	$A = s^2$	$P = 4s$
rectangle	$A = l \times w$	$P = 2l + 2w$

These equations aren't given to you on test day—you need to have them memorized.

Examples

1. A farmer has purchased 100 m of fencing to put around his rectangular garden. If one side of the garden is 20 m long and the other is 28 m, how much fencing will the farmer have left over?

   The perimeter of a rectangle is equal to twice its length plus twice its width:

   $P = 2(20) + 2(28) = 96$ m

   The farmer has 100 m of fencing, so he'll have
   100 – 96 = **4 m left.**

2. Taylor is going to paint a square wall that is 3.5 m tall. What is the total area that Taylor will be painting?

Each side of the square wall is 3.5 m:

$A = 3.5^2 = $ **12.25 m²**

Volume

Volume is the amount of space taken up by a three-dimensional object. Different shapes have different formulas to find the volume.

Table 3.2. Volume formulas

SHAPE	VOLUME
cylinder	$V = \pi r^2 h$
pyramid	$V = \frac{l \times w \times h}{3}$
cone	$V = \pi r^2 \frac{h}{3}$
sphere	$V = \frac{4}{3} \pi r^3$

Examples

1. Charlotte wants to fill her circular swimming pool with water. The pool has a diameter of 6 meters and is 1 meter high. How many cubic meters of water will she need to fill the pool?

This question is asking about the volume of Charlotte's pool. The circular pool is actually a cylinder, so use the formula for a cylinder: $V = \pi r^2 h$.

The diameter is 6 meters. The radius is half the diameter, so $r = 6 \div 2 = 3$ meters.

Now solve for the volume:

$V = \pi r^2 h$

$V = \pi (3 \text{ m})^2 (1 \text{ m})$

$V = 28.3 \text{ m}^3$

Charlotte will need approximately 28.3 cubic meters of water to fill her pool.

2. Danny keeps his goldfish in a fishbowl that is filled to the brim with water. One day he brought home some spherical glass marbles that he thought would look nice in the bottom of the fishbowl. He dropped in four marbles, and water spilled out of the fishbowl. If the radius of each marble is 1 cm, how much water spilled out?

Since the fishbowl was filled to the brim, the volume of the water that spilled out is equal to the volume of the marbles that Danny dropped in. First, find the volume of one marble using the equation for a sphere:

$V = \frac{4}{3} \pi r^3$

$V = \frac{4}{3} \pi (1 \text{ cm})^3$

$V = 4.2 \text{ cm}^3$

Since Danny dropped in 4 marbles, multiply this volume by 4 to find the total volume:

$4.2 \text{ cm}^3 \times 4 = 16.8 \text{ cm}^3$

Approximately 16.8 cubic centimeters of water spilled out of the fishbowl.

Circles

The definition of a circle is the set of points that are equal distance from a center point. The distance from the center to any given point on the circle is the RADIUS. If you draw a straight line segment across the circle going through the center, the distance along the line segment from one side of the circle to the other is called the DIAMETER. The radius is always equal to half the diameter:

$d = 2r$

A CENTRAL ANGLE is formed by drawing radii out from the center to two points A and B along the circle. The INTERCEPTED ARC is the portion of the circle (the arc length) between points A and B. You can find the intercepted arc length l if you know the central angle θ and vice versa:

$l = 2\pi r \dfrac{\theta}{360°}$

A CHORD is a line segment that connects two points on a circle. Unlike the diameter, a chord does not have to go through the center. You can find the chord length if you know either the central angle θ or the radius of the circle r and the distance from the center of the circle to the chord d (d must be at a right angle to the chord):

If you know the central angle, chord length = $2r \sin \dfrac{\theta}{2}$.

If you know the radius and distance, chord length = $2\sqrt{r^2 - d^{\wedge 2}}$.

A SECANT is similar to a chord; it connects two points on a circle. The difference is that a secant is a line, not a line segment, so it extends outside the circle on either side.

A TANGENT is a straight line that touches a circle at only one point.

A SECTOR is the area within a circle that is enclosed by a central angle; if a circle is a pie, a sector is the piece of pie cut by two radii. You can find the AREA OF A SECTOR if you know either the central angle θ or the arc length l.

If you know the central angle, the area of the sector = $\pi r^2 \dfrac{\theta}{360°}$.

If you know the arc length, the area of a sector = $\dfrac{1}{2} rl$.

There are two other types of angles you can create in or around a circle. INSCRIBED ANGLES are <u>inside</u> the circle: the vertex is a point P on the circle, and the rays extend to two other points on the circle (A and B). As long as A and B remain constant, you can move the vertex P anywhere along the circle, and the inscribed angle will be the same. **CIRCUMSCRIBED ANGLES** are outside the circle: the rays are formed by two tangent lines that touch the circle at points A and B.

You can find the inscribed angle if you know the radius of the circle r and the arc length l between A and B:

inscribed angle $= \frac{90°l}{\pi r}$

To find the circumscribed angle, find the central angle formed by the same points A and B, and subtract that angle from 180°.

Examples

1. A circle has a diameter of 10 cm. What is the intercepted arc length between points A and B if the central angle between those points measures 46°?

   First divide the diameter by two to find the radius:

   $r = 10 \text{ cm} \div 2 = 5 \text{ cm}$

   Now use the formula for intercepted arc length:

   $l = 2\pi r \frac{\theta}{360°}$

   $l = 2\pi(5 \text{ cm}) \frac{46°}{360°}$

   $l = 4.0$ cm

2. A chord is formed by line segment $\overline{QP}$. The radius of the circle is 5 cm and the chord length is 6 cm. Find the distance from center C to the chord.

   Use the formula for chord length:

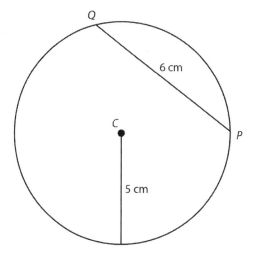

   chord length $= 2\sqrt{r^2 - d^2}$

   In this example, we are told the chord length and the radius, and we need to solve for d:

   $6 \text{ cm} = 2\sqrt{(5 \text{ cm})^2 - d^2}$

   $3 \text{ cm} = \sqrt{(5 \text{ cm})^2 - d^2}$

   $9 \text{ cm}^2 = 25 \text{ cm}^2 - d^2$

   $d^2 = 16 \text{ cm}^2$

   $d = 4$ cm

3. Points A and B are located on a circle. The arc length between A and B is 2 cm. The diameter of the circle is 8 cm. Find the inscribed angle.

First, divide the diameter by two to find the radius:

$r = \frac{1}{2}(8 \text{ cm})$

$r = 4 \text{ cm}$

Now use the formula for an inscribed angle:

inscribed angle $= \frac{90°l}{\pi r}$

inscribed angle $= \frac{90°(2 \text{ cm})}{\pi(4 \text{ cm})}$

inscribed angle = 14.3°

CONGRUENCE

CONGRUENCE means having the same size and shape. Two shapes are congruent if you can turn (rotate), flip (reflect), and/or slide (translate) one to fit perfectly on top of the other. Two angles are congruent if they measure the same number of degrees; they do not have to be facing the same direction, nor must they necessarily have rays of equal length.

If two triangles have one of the combinations of congruent sides and/or angles listed below, then those triangles are congruent:

SSS – "side, side, side"

ASA – "angle, side, angle"

SAS – "side, angle, side"

AAS – "angle, angle, side"

An ISOSCELES TRIANGLE has two sides of equal length. The sides of equal length are called the legs, and the third side is called the base. If you bisect an isosceles triangle by drawing a line perpendicular to the base, you will form two congruent right triangles.

Where two lines cross and form an X, the opposite angles are congruent and are called VERTICAL ANGLES.

PARALLEL LINES are lines that never cross. If you cut two parallel lines by a transversal, you will form four pairs of congruent COR-RESPONDING ANGLES.

A PARALLELOGRAM is a quadrilateral in which both pairs of opposite sides are parallel and congruent (equal length). In a parallelogram, the two pairs of opposite angles are also congruent. If you divide a parallelogram by either of the diagonals, you will form two congruent triangles.

$\longrightarrow$
CONTINUE

Examples

1. Kate and Emily set out for a bike ride together from their house. They ride 6 miles north, then Kate turns 30° to the west and Emily turns 30° to the east. They both ride another 8 miles. If Kate rides 12 miles to return home, how far must Emily ride to get home?

Draw out Kate's and Emily's trips to see that they form triangles.

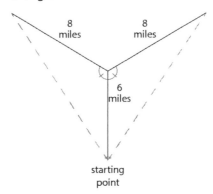

The triangles have corresponding sides with lengths of 6 miles and 8 miles with a corresponding angle of 120° in between. This fits the "SAS" rule, so the triangles must be congruent. The length Kate has to ride home corresponds to the length Emily has to ride home, so **Emily must ride 12 miles.**

2. Angle A measures 53°. Find angle H.

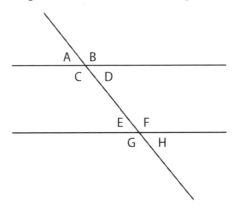

For parallel lines cut by a transversal, look for vertical and corresponding angles.

Angles A and D are vertical angles, so angle D must be congruent to angle A. Angle D = 53°.

Angles D and H are corresponding angles, so angle H must be congruent to angle D. **Angle H = 53°.**

RIGHT TRIANGLES AND TRIGONOMETRY

Pythagorean Theorem

Shapes with three sides are known as TRIANGLES. In addition to knowing the formulas for their area and perimeter, you should also know the Pythagorean theorem, which describes the relationship between the three sides (*a*, *b*, and *c*) of a right triangle:

$$a^2 + b^2 = c^2$$

Example

Erica is going to run a race in which she'll run 3 miles due north and 4 miles due east. She'll then run back to the starting line. How far will she run during this race?

Start by drawing a picture of Erica's route. You'll see it forms a triangle:

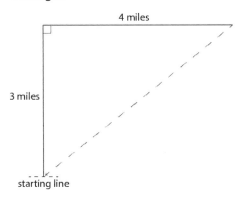

One leg of her route (the triangle) is missing, but you can find its length using the Pythagorean theorem:

$$a^2 + b^2 = c^2$$

$$3^2 + 4^2 = c^2$$

$$25 = c^2$$

$$c = 5$$

Adding all 3 sides gives the length of the whole race:

$$3 + 4 + 5 = \textbf{12 miles}$$

Trigonometry

Using TRIGONOMETRY, you can calculate an angle in a right triangle based on the ratio of two sides of that triangle. You can also calculate one of the side lengths using the measure of an angle and another side. SINE (SIN), COSINE (COS), and TANGENT (TAN) correspond to the three possible ratios of side lengths. They are defined below:

$$\sin \theta = \frac{opposite}{hypotenuse}$$

$$\cos \theta = \frac{adjacent}{hypotenuse}$$

$$\tan \theta = \frac{opposite}{adjacent}$$

Opposite is the side opposite from the angle θ, *adjacent* is the side adjacent to the angle θ, and *hypotenuse* is the longest side of the triangle, opposite from the right angle. SOH-CAH-TOA is an acronym to help you remember which ratio goes with which function.

When solving for a side or an angle in a right triangle, first identify which function to use based on the known lengths or angle.

Examples

1. Phil is hanging holiday lights on the outside of his house. He leans a 20-foot ladder against the house. For safety, he knows to keep the top of the ladder at an angle of 15° or less against the house. At what maximum distance from the house should he place the base of the ladder?

   Draw a triangle with the known length and angle labeled.

   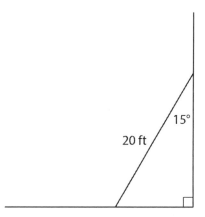

   The known side (the length of the ladder) is the hypotenuse of the triangle, and the unknown distance is the side opposite the angle. Therefore, you can use sine:

   $$\sin \theta = \frac{opposite}{hypotenuse}$$

   $$\sin 15° = \frac{opposite}{20 \text{ feet}}$$

   Now solve for the opposite side:

   $$opposite = \sin 15° \, (15 \text{ feet})$$

   $opposite = 5.2$ feet

2. Grace is practicing shooting hoops. She is 5 feet 4 inches tall, and her basketball hoop is 10 feet off the ground. When she stands 8 feet away from the basket, at what angle does she have to look up to see the hoop? Assume that her eyes are 4 inches lower than the top of her head.

   Draw a diagram. Notice that the line from Grace's eyes to the hoop of the basket forms the hypotenuse of a right triangle. The side adjacent to the angle of her eyes is the distance from the basket: 8 feet. The side opposite to Grace's eyes is the difference between the height of her eyes and the height of the basket: 10 feet − 5 feet = 5 feet.

Next, use the formula for tangent to solve for the angle:

$$\tan \theta = \frac{opposite}{adjacent}$$

$$\tan \theta = \frac{5\ feet}{8\ feet}$$

Now take the inverse tangent of both sides to solve for the angle:

$$\theta = \tan^{-1} \frac{5}{8}$$

$$\boldsymbol{\theta = 32°}$$

COORDINATE GEOMETRY

Coordinate geometry is the study of points, lines, and shapes that have been graphed on a set of axes.

Points, Lines, and Planes

In coordinate geometry, points are plotted on a **COORDINATE PLANE**. The coordinate plane is a two-dimensional plane in which the horizontal direction is represented by the *x*-**AXIS**, and the vertical direction is represented by the *y*-**AXIS**. The intersection of these two axes is called the **ORIGIN**. Points are defined by their distance and direction along the horizontal and vertical axes. The coordinates of a point are written **(*x, y*)**. The coordinates of the origin are $(0, 0)$. Moving right, the *x* coordinates become more positive, and moving left, the *x* coordinates become more negative. Moving up, the *y* coordinates become more positive, and moving down, the *y* coordinates become more negative.

A **LINE** is formed by connecting any two points on a coordinate plane and is continuous in both directions. Lines can be defined by their **SLOPE**, or steepness, and *Y*-**INTERCEPT**, or the point at which they intersect the *y*-axis. A line is represented by the equation $y = mx + b$. The constant *m* represents slope and the constant *b* represents *y*-intercept.

Examples

1. Matt parks his car near a forest where he goes hiking. From his car he hikes 1 mile north, 2 miles east, then 3 miles west. If his car is represented as the origin, find the coordinates of Matt's current location.

   To find the coordinates, you must find Matt's displacement along the *x*- and *y*-axes. Matt hiked 1 mile north and 0 miles south, so his displacement along the *y*-axis is +1 mile. Matt hiked 2 miles east and 3 miles west, so his displacement along the *x*-axis is +2 miles − 3 miles = −1 mile.

   Matt's coordinates are (−1, 1).

CONTINUE

2. A square is drawn on a coordinate plane. The bottom corners are located at $(-2, 3)$ and $(4, 3)$. What are the coordinates for the top right corner?

Draw the coordinate plane and plot the given points. If you connect these points, you will see that the bottom side is 6 units long. Since it's a square, all sides must be 6 units long. Count 6 units up from the point $(4, 3)$ to find the top right corner.

The coordinates for the top right corner are (4, 9).

The Distance and Midpoint Formulas

To determine the distance between the points (x_1, y_1) and (x_2, y_2) from a grid, use the formula: $d = \sqrt{(x_2 - x_1)^2 + (y_2 - y_1)^2}$. The midpoint, which is halfway between the 2 points, is the point $\left(\frac{x_1 + x_2}{2}\right), \left(\frac{y_1 + y_2}{2}\right)$.

Examples

1. What is the distance between points $(3, -6)$ and $(-5, 2)$?

Plug the values for x_1, x_2, y_1, and y_2 into the distance formula and simplify:

$d = \sqrt{(-5 - 3)^2 + (2 - (-6))^2}$

$\sqrt{64 + 64} = \sqrt{64 \times 2} = $

$\mathbf{8\sqrt{2}}$

2. What is the midpoint between points $(3, -6)$ and $(-5, 2)$?

Plug the values for x_1, x_2, y_1, and y_2 into the midpoint formula and simplify:

$midpoint = \left(\frac{3 + (-5)}{2}\right), \left(\frac{(-6) + 2}{2}\right) = \left(\frac{-2}{2}\right), \left(\frac{-4}{2}\right)$

$\mathbf{(-1, -2)}$

4

STATISTICS

DESCRIBING SETS OF DATA

STATISTICS is the study of sets of data. The goal of statistics is to take a group of values—numerical answers from a survey, for example—and look for patterns of how that data is distributed.

When you look at a set of data, it's often helpful to look at the MEASURES OF CENTRAL TENDENCY, which are a group of values that describe the central or typical data point from the set. The GED covers three measures of central tendency: mean, median, and mode.

MEAN is the mathematical term for average. To find the mean, total all the terms and divide by the number of terms. The MEDIAN is the middle number of a given set. To find the median, put the terms in numerical order; the middle number will be the median. In the case of a set of even numbers, the middle two numbers are averaged. MODE is the number that occurs most frequently within a given set. If two different numbers both appear with the highest frequency, they are both the mode.

When you examine a data set, it's also possible to look at MEASURES OF VARIABILITY, which describe how the data is dispersed around the central data point. The GED covers two measures of variability: range and standard deviation. RANGE is simply the difference between the largest and smallest values in the set. STANDARD DEVIATION is a measure of how dispersed the data is; in other words, it describes how far from the mean the data is. To find standard deviation, find the square root of the average of the squared differences from the mean.

Examples

1. Find the mean of 24, 27, and 18.

   Add the terms, then divide by the number of terms:

   $$mean = \frac{24 + 27 + 18}{3} = 23$$

2. The mean of three numbers is 45. If two of the numbers are 38 and 43, what is the third number?

   Set up the equation for mean with x representing the third number, then solve:

   $$mean = \frac{38 + 43 + x}{3} = 45$$

   $$\frac{38 + 43 + x}{3} = 45$$

   $$38 + 43 + x = 135$$

   $$x = 54$$

3. What is the median of 24, 27, and 18?

   Place the terms in order, then pick the middle term:

   18, 24, 27

   The median is 24.

4. What is the median of 24, 27, 18, and 19?

   Place the terms in order. Because there are an even number of terms, the median will be the average of the middle two terms:

   18, 19, 24, 27

   $$median = \frac{(19 + 24)}{2} = 21.5$$

5. What is the mode of 2, 5, 4, 4, 3, 2, 8, 9, 2, 7, 2, and 2?

   The mode is 2 because it appears the most within the set.

6. What is the standard deviation of 62, 63, 61, and 66?

   To find the standard deviation, first find the mean:

   $$mean = \frac{62 + 63 + 61 + 66}{4} = 63$$

   Next, find the difference between each term and the mean, and square that number:

   $$63 - 62 = 1 \rightarrow 1^2 = 1$$

   $$63 - 63 = 0 \rightarrow 0^2 = 0$$

   $$63 - 61 = 2 \rightarrow 2^2 = 4$$

   $$63 - 66 = -3 \rightarrow (-3)^2 = 9$$

   Now, find the mean of the squares:

   $$mean = \frac{1 + 0 + 4 + 9}{4} = 3.5$$

   Finally, find the square root of the mean:

   $$\sqrt{3.5} = 1.87$$

   The standard deviation is 1.87.

PROBABILITY

PROBABILITY is the likelihood that an event will take place. This likelihood is expressed as a value between 0 and 1. The closer the probability is to 0, the less likely the event is to occur; the closer the probability is to 1, the more likely it is to occur.

Probability of a Single Event

A **PROBABILITY** is found by dividing the number of desired outcomes by the number of total possible outcomes. As with percentages, a probability is the ratio of a part to a whole, with the whole being the total number of things that could happen, and the part being the number of those things that would be considered a success. Probabilities can be written using percentages (40%), decimals (0.4), fractions ($\frac{2}{5}$), or in words (probability is 2 in 5).

$$probability = \frac{desired\ outcomes}{total\ possible\ outcomes}$$

Examples

1. A bag holds 3 blue marbles, 5 green marbles, and 7 red marbles. If you pick one marble from the bag, what is the probability it will be blue?

   Because there are 15 marbles in the bag (3 + 5 + 7), the total number of possible outcomes is 15. Of those outcomes, 3 would be blue marbles, which is the desired outcome. With that information, you can set up an equation:

   $$probability = \frac{desired\ outcomes}{total\ possible\ outcomes} = \frac{3}{15} = \frac{1}{5}$$

   The probability is 1 in 5 or 0.2 that a blue marble is picked.

2. A bag contains 75 balls. If the probability that a ball selected from the bag will be red is 0.6, how many red balls are in the bag?

   Because you're solving for desired outcomes (the number of red balls), first you need to rearrange the equation:

   $$probability = \frac{desired\ outcomes}{total\ possible\ outcomes} \rightarrow$$

   $$desired\ outcomes = probability \times total\ possible\ outcomes$$

   In this problem, the desired outcome is choosing a red ball, and the total possible outcomes are represented by the 75 total balls.

   $$desired\ outcomes = 0.6 \times 75 = 45$$

   There are 45 red balls in the bag.

CONTINUE

3. A theater has 230 seats: 75 seats are in the orchestra area, 100 seats are in the mezzanine, and 55 seats are in the balcony. If a ticket is selected at random, what is the probability that it will be for either a mezzanine or balcony seat?

In this problem, the desired outcome is a seat in either the mezzanine or balcony area, and the total possible outcomes are represented by the 230 total seats, so the equation should be written as:

$$probability = \frac{desired\ outcomes}{total\ possible\ outcomes}$$

$$\frac{100+55}{230} = 0.67$$

4. The probability of selecting a student whose name begins with the letter *S* from a school attendance log is 7%. If there are 42 students whose names begin with *S* enrolled at the school, how many students attend the school?

Because you're solving for total possible outcomes (total number of students), first you need to rearrange the equation:

$$total\ possible\ outcomes = \frac{desired\ outcomes}{probability}$$

In this problem, you are given a probability (7% or 0.07) and the number of desired outcomes (42). These can be plugged into the equation to solve:

$$\textbf{total possible outcomes} = \frac{42}{0.07} = \textbf{600 students}$$

Conditional Probability

CONDITIONAL PROBABILITY refers to the chances of one event occurring, given that another event has occurred. INDEPENDENT EVENTS are events that have no effect on one another. The classic example is flipping a coin: whether you flip heads or tails this time has no bearing on how you might flip the next time. Your chance of flipping heads is always 50/50. DEPENDENT EVENTS, on the other hand, have an effect on the next event's probability. If you have a bag full of red and blue marbles, removing a red marble the first time will decrease the probability of picking a red marble the second time, since now there are fewer red marbles in the bag. The probability of event B occurring, given that event A has occurred, is written $P(B|A)$.

The probability of either event A or event B occurring is called the union of events A and B, written $A \cap B$. The probability of $A \cap B$ is equal to the <u>sum</u> of the probability of A occurring and the probability of B occurring, minus the probability of both A and B occurring. The probability of both A and B occurring is called the intersection of events A and B, written $A \cap B$. The probability of $A \cap B$ is equal to the <u>product</u> of the probability of A and the probability of B, given A. Review the equations for the probabilities of unions and intersections below:

$$P(A \cup B) = P(A) + P(B) - P(A \cap B)$$

$$P(A \cap B) = P(A) \times P(B|A)$$

The complement of an event is when the event does not occur. The probability of the complement of event A, written $P(A')$, is equal to $1 - P(A)$.

Examples

1. A bag contains 5 red marbles and 11 blue marbles. What is the probability of pulling out a blue marble, followed by a red marble?

   This question is asking about an intersection of events. The equation for an intersection of events is

   $P(A \cap B) = P(A) \times P(B|A)$.

   The first event, event A, is picking out a blue marble. Find $P(A)$:

   $$P(A) = \frac{11 \text{ blue marbles}}{16 \text{ total marbles}} = \frac{11}{16}$$

   The second event, event B, is picking out a red marble now that there are 15 marbles left. Find $P(B|A)$:

   $$P(B|A) = \frac{5 \text{ red marbles}}{15 \text{ total marbles}} = \frac{5}{15} = \frac{1}{3}$$

   $$P(A \cap B) = P(A) \times P(B|A) = \frac{11}{16} \times \frac{1}{3} = \mathbf{\frac{11}{48}}$$

2. Caroline randomly draws a playing card from a full deck. What is the chance she will select either a queen or a diamond?

   This question is asking about a union of events. The equation for a union of events is

   $P(A \cup B) = P(A) + P(B) - P(A \cap B)$.

   The first event, event A, is selecting a queen. Find $P(A)$:

   $$P(A) = \frac{4 \text{ queens}}{52 \text{ total cards}} = \frac{4}{52}$$

   The second event, event B, is selecting a diamond. Find $P(B)$:

   $$P(B) = \frac{13 \text{ diamonds}}{52 \text{ total cards}} = \frac{13}{52}$$

   Now, find the probability of selecting a queen that is also a diamond:

   $$P(A \cap B) = \frac{1 \text{ diamond queen}}{52 \text{ total cards}} = \frac{1}{52}$$

   $$P(A \cup B) = P(A) + P(B) - P(A \cap B)$$

   $$\frac{4}{52} + \frac{13}{52} - \frac{1}{52} = \frac{16}{52} = \mathbf{\frac{4}{13}}$$

PART II: REASONING THROUGH LANGUAGE ARTS

The Language Arts section will test your understanding of the basic rules of grammar. The first step in getting ready for this section of the test is to review parts of speech and the rules that accompany them. The good news is that you have been using these rules since you first began to speak; even if you don't know a lot of the technical terms, many of these rules may be familiar to you. Some of the topics you might see include:

- matching pronouns with their antecedents
- matching verbs with their subjects
- ensuring that verbs are in the correct tense
- spelling irregular, hyphenated, and commonly misspelled words
- using correct capitalization
- distinguishing between types of sentences
- correcting sentence structure
- changing passive to active voice

5

WRITING: GRAMMAR

NOUNS AND PRONOUNS

NOUNS are people, places, or things. They are typically the subject of a sentence. For example, in the sentence *The hospital was very clean*, the noun is *hospital*; it's a place. PRONOUNS replace nouns and make sentences sound less repetitive. Take the sentence *Sam stayed home from school because Sam was not feeling well*. The word *Sam* appears twice in the same sentence. Instead, you can use a pronoun and say *Sam stayed at home because he did not feel well*. Sounds much better, right?

Because pronouns take the place of nouns, they need to agree both in number and gender with the noun they replace. So a plural noun needs a plural pronoun, and a feminine noun needs a feminine pronoun. In the previous sentence, for example, the plural pronoun *they* replaced the plural noun *pronouns*. There will usually be several questions on the English and Language Usage section that cover pronoun agreement, so it's good to get comfortable spotting pronouns.

SINGULAR PRONOUNS
- I, me, mine, my
- you, your, yours
- he, him, his
- she, her, hers
- it, its

PLURAL PRONOUNS
- we, us, our, ours
- they, them, their, theirs

Examples

Wrong: If a student forgets their homework, it's considered incomplete.

Correct: If a student forgets his or her homework, it's considered incomplete.

Student is a singular noun, but *their* is a plural pronoun. So this first sentence is grammatically incorrect. **To correct it, replace *their* with the singular pronoun *his* or *her*.**

Wrong: Everybody will receive their paychecks promptly.

Correct: Everybody will receive his or her paycheck promptly.

Everybody is a singular noun, but *their* is a plural pronoun. So this sentence is grammatically incorrect. **To correct it, replace *their* with the singular pronoun *his* or *her*.**

Wrong: When a nurse begins work at a hospital, you should wash your hands.

Correct: When a nurse begins work at a hospital, he or she should wash his or her hands.

This sentence begins in third-person perspective and finishes in second-person perspective. So this sentence is grammatically incorrect. **To correct it, ensure the sentence finishes in third-person perspective.**

Wrong: After the teacher spoke to the student, she realized her mistake.

Correct: After Mr. White spoke to his student, she realized her mistake (*she* and *her* referring to student).

Correct: After speaking to the student, the teacher realized her own mistake (*her* referring to teacher).

This sentence refers to a teacher and a student. But whom does *she* refer to, the teacher or the student? **To improve clarity, use specific names, or state more specifically who spotted the mistake.**

VERBS

Remember the old commercial, *Verb: It's what you do?* That sums up verbs in a nutshell. A *verb* is the action of a sentence; verbs *do* things. Verbs must be conjugated to match the context of the sentence; this can sometimes be tricky because English has many irregular verbs. For example, *runs* is an action verb in the present tense that becomes *ran* in the past tense; the linking verb *is* (which describes a state of being) becomes *was* in the past tense.

Table 5.1. Conjugations of the verb *to be*

	PAST	PRESENT	FUTURE
SINGULAR	was	is	will be
PLURAL	were	are	will be

As mentioned, verbs must use the correct tense, and that tense must make sense in the context of the sentence. For example, the sentence *I was baking cookies and eat some dough* sounds strange, right? That's because the two verbs *was baking* and *eat* are in different tenses. *Was baking* occurred in the past; *eat*, on the other hand, occurs in the present. Instead, it should be *ate some dough*.

Like pronouns, verbs must agree in number with the noun they refer back to. In the example above, the verb *was* refers back to the singular *I*. If the subject of the sentence was plural, it would need to be modified to read *They were baking cookies and ate some dough.*

Note that the verb *ate* does not change form; this is common for verbs in the past tense.

Examples

Wrong: The cat chase the ball while the dogs runs in the yard.

Correct: The cat chases the ball while the dogs run in the yard.

Cat is singular, so it takes a singular verb (which confusingly ends with an s); dogs is plural, so it needs a plural verb.

Wrong: The cars that had been recalled by the manufacturer was returned within a few months.

Correct: The cars that had been recalled by the manufacturer were returned within a few months.

Sometimes, the subject and verb are separated by clauses or phrases. Here, the subject cars is separated from the verb phrase were returned, making it more difficult to conjugate the verb.

Correct: The deer hid in the trees.

Correct: The deer are not all the same size.

The subject of these sentences is a collective noun, which describes a group of people or items. This noun can be singular if it's referring to the group as a whole or plural if it refers to each item in the group as a separate entity.

Correct: The doctor and nurse work in the hospital.

Correct: Neither the nurse nor her boss was scheduled to take a vacation.

Correct: Either the patient or her parents need to sign the release forms.

When the subject contains two or more nouns connected by and, that subject is plural and requires a plural verb. Singular subjects joined by or, either/or, neither/nor, or not only/ but also remain singular; when these words join plural and singular subjects, the verb should match the closest subject.

Wrong: Because it will rain during the party last night, we had to move the tables inside.

Correct: Because it rained during the party last night, we had to move the tables inside.

All the verb tenses in a sentence need to agree both with each other and with the other information in the sentence. In the first sentence above, the tense doesn't match the other information in the sentence: last night indicates the past (rained), not the future (will rain).

Think of the subject and the verb as sharing a single *s*. If the noun ends with an *s*, the verb shouldn't, and vice versa.

If the subject is separated from the verb, cross out the phrases between them to make conjugation easier.

ADJECTIVES AND ADVERBS

ADJECTIVES are words that describe a noun. Take the sentence *The boy hit the ball*. If you want to know more about the noun *boy*, then you could use an adjective to describe him: *The little boy hit the ball*. An adjective simply provides more information about a noun or subject in a sentence.

For some reason, many people have a difficult time with adverbs, but don't worry! They are really quite simple. **ADVERBS** and adjectives are similar because they provide more information about a part of a sentence; however, adverbs do not describe nouns—that's an adjective's job. Instead, adverbs describe verbs, adjectives, and even other adverbs. For example, in the sentence *The doctor had recently hired a new employee,* the adverb *recently* tells us more about how the action *hired* took place.

Adjectives, adverbs, and **MODIFYING PHRASES** (groups of words that together modify another word) should always be placed as close as possible to the word they modify. Separating words from their modifiers can create incorrect or confusing sentences.

Examples

Wrong: Running through the hall, the bell rang and the student knew she was late.

Correct: Running through the hall, the student heard the bell ring and knew she was late.

The phrase *running through the hall* should be placed next to *student*, the noun it modifies.

Wrong: Of my two friends, Clara is the most smartest.

Correct: Of my two friends, Clara is more smart.

The first sentence above has two mistakes. First, the word *most* should only be used when comparing three or more things. Second, the adjective should only be modified with *more/most* or the suffix *-er/-est*, not both.

OTHER PARTS OF SPEECH

PREPOSITIONS express the location of a noun or pronoun in relation to other words and phrases in a sentence. For example, in the sentence *The nurse parked her car in a parking garage*, the preposition *in* describes the position of the car in relation to the garage. Together, the preposition and the noun that follow it are called a **PREPOSITIONAL PHRASE**. In the example above, the prepositional phrase is *in a parking garage*.

CONJUNCTIONS connect words, phrases, and clauses. The conjunctions summarized in the acronym FANBOYS—For, And, Nor, But, Or, Yet, So—are called **COORDINATING CONJUNCTIONS** and are used to join **INDEPENDENT CLAUSES** (clauses that can stand alone as a complete sentence). For example, in the sentence *The nurse prepared the patient for surgery, and the doctor performed the surgery*, the conjunction *and* joins the two independent clauses. Other conjunctions, like *although*, *because*, and *if*, join an independent and DEPENDENT CLAUSE (which cannot stand on its own). In the sentence *She had to ride the subway because her car was broken*, the conjunction *because* joins the two clauses.

INTERJECTIONS, like *wow* and *hey*, express emotion and are most commonly used in conversation and casual writing.

⚠ An independent (or main) clause can stand alone as its own sentence. A dependent (or subordinate) clause must be attached to an independent clause to make a complete sentence.

Examples

Choose the word that best completes the sentence.

1. Her love _____ blueberry muffins kept her coming back to the bakery every week.

   A) to

   B) with

   C) of

   D) about

   The correct preposition is *of* (choice C).

2. Christine left her house early on Monday morning, _____ she was still late for work.

   A) but

   B) and

   C) for

   D) or

   In this sentence, the conjunction is joining two contrasting ideas, so **the correct answer is *but* (choice A).**

CONSTRUCTING SENTENCES

Phrases and Clauses

A PHRASE is a group of words acting together that contain either a subject or a verb, but not both. Phrases can be made from many different parts of speech. For example, a prepositional phrase includes a preposition and the object of that preposition (e.g., *under the table*), and a verb phrase includes the main verb and any helping verbs (e.g., *had been running*). Phrases cannot stand alone as a sentence.

A CLAUSE is a group of words that contains both a subject and a verb. There are two types of clauses: INDEPENDENT CLAUSES can stand alone as a sentence, and DEPENDENT CLAUSES cannot stand alone. Dependent clauses begin with a subordinating conjunction.

Examples

Classify each of the following as a phrase, an independent clause, or a dependent clause:

1. I have always wanted to drive a bright red sports car

2. under the bright sky filled with stars

3. because my sister is running late

Number 1 is an independent clause—it has a subject (*I*) and a verb (*have wanted*) and has no subordinating conjunction. **Number 2 is a phrase** made up of a preposition (*under*), its object (*sky*), and words that modify sky (*bright, filled with stars*). **Number 3 is a dependent clause**—it has a subject (*sister*), a verb (*is running*), and a subordinating conjunction (*because*).

Types of Sentences

A sentence can be classified as simple, compound, complex, or compound-complex based on the type and number of clauses it has.

Table 5.2. Types of sentences

SENTENCE TYPE	NUMBER OF INDEPENDENT CLAUSES	NUMBER OF DEPENDENT CLAUSES
simple	1	0
compound	2+	0
complex	1	1+
compound-complex	2+	1+

A SIMPLE SENTENCE consists of only one independent clause. Because there are no dependent clauses in a simple sentence, it can simply be a two-word sentence, with one word being the subject and the other word being the verb (e.g., *I ran*). However, a simple sentence can also contain prepositions, adjectives, and adverbs. Even though these additions can extend the length of a simple sentence, it's still considered a simple sentence as long as it doesn't contain any dependent clauses.

COMPOUND SENTENCES have two or more independent clauses and no dependent clauses. Usually a comma and a coordinating conjunction (*and, or, but, nor, for, so,* and *yet*) join the independent clauses, though semicolons can be used as well. For example, the sentence *My computer broke, so I took it to be repaired* is compound.

COMPLEX SENTENCES have one independent clause and at least one dependent clause. In the complex sentence *If you lie down with dogs, you'll wake up with fleas*, the first clause is dependent (because of the subordinating conjunction *If*), and the second is independent.

COMPOUND-COMPLEX SENTENCES have two or more independent clauses and at least one subordinate clause. For example, the sentence *Even though David was a vegetarian, he went with his friends to steakhouses, but he focused on the conversation instead of the food* is compound-complex.

Examples

Classify: San Francisco in the springtime is one of my favorite places to visit.

Although the sentence is lengthy, **it's simple** because it contains only one subject and verb (*San Francisco... is*) modified by additional phrases.

Classify: I love listening to the radio in the car because I can sing along as loud as I want.

The sentence has one independent clause (*I love... car*) and one dependent clause (*because I... want*), so **it's complex**.

Classify: I wanted to get a dog, but I have a fish because my roommate is allergic to pet dander.

This sentence has three clauses: two independent (*I wanted... dog and I have a fish*) and one dependent (*because my... dander*), so **it's compound-complex**.

Classify: The game was canceled, but we will still practice on Saturday.

This sentence is made up of two independent clauses joined by a conjunction (*but*), so **it's compound**.

PUNCTUATION

The basic rules for using the major punctuation marks are given in the table below.

Table 5.3. Using punctuation

PUNCTUATION	USED FOR ...	EXAMPLE
period	ending sentences	Periods go at the end of complete sentences.
question mark	ending questions	What's the best way to end a sentence?
exclamation point	ending sentences that show extreme emotion	I'll never understand how to use commas!
comma	joining two independent clauses (always with a coordinating conjunction)	Commas can be used to join clauses, but they must always be followed by a coordinating conjunction.
	setting apart introductory and nonessential words and phrases	Commas, when used properly, set apart extra information in a sentence.

	separating items in a list	My favorite punctuation marks include the colon, semicolon, and period.
semicolon	joining together two independent clauses (never with a conjunction)	I love exclamation points; they make sentences seem so exciting!
colon	introducing a list, explanation, or definition	When I see a colon I know what to expect: more information.
apostrophe	form contractions	It's amazing how many people can't use apostrophes correctly.
	show possession	Parentheses are my sister's favorite punctuation; she finds comma rules confusing.
quotation marks	indicate a direct quote	I said to her, "Tell me more about parentheses."

CAPITALIZATION

- The first word of a sentence is always capitalized.
- The first letter of a proper noun is always capitalized. (We're going to Chicago on Wednesday.)
- Titles are capitalized if they precede the name they modify. (President Obama met with Joe Biden, his vice president.)
- Months are capitalized, but not the names of the seasons. (Snow fell in March even though winter was over.)

ACTIVE AND PASSIVE VOICE

Sentences can be written in active voice or passive voice. **ACTIVE VOICE** means that the subjects of the sentences are performing the action of the sentence. In a sentence in **PASSIVE VOICE**, the subjects are being acted on. So the sentence *Justin wrecked my car* is in the active voice because the subject (*Justin*) is doing the action (*wrecked*). The sentence can be rewritten in passive voice by using a *to be* verb: *My car was wrecked by Justin*. Now the subject of the sentence (*car*) is being acted on. Notice that it's possible to write the sentence so that the person performing the action is not identified: *My car was wrecked*.

Generally, good writing will make more use of the active than passive voice. However, passive voice can sometimes be the better choice. For example, if it's not known who or what performed the action of the sentence, it's necessary to use passive voice.

Examples

1. Rewrite the following sentence in active voice: *I was hit with a stick by my brother.*

   To rewrite a sentence in active voice, first take the person or object performing the action (usually given in a prepositional phrase) and make it the subject. Then, the subject of the original sentence becomes the object and the *to be* verb disappears: **My brother hit me with a stick.**

2. Rewrite the following sentence in passive voice: *My roommate made coffee this morning.*

   To rewrite a sentence in passive voice, you make the object (*coffee*) the subject, and then move the subject to a prepositional phrase at the end of the sentence. Lastly, the *to be* verb is added: **The coffee was made this morning by my roommate.**

POINT OF VIEW

A sentence's **POINT OF VIEW** is the perspective from which it's written. Point of view is described as either first, second, or third person.

Table 5.4. Point of view

PERSON	PRONOUNS USED	WHO'S ACTING?	EXAMPLE
first	I, we	the writer	I take my time when shopping for shoes.
second	you	the reader	You prefer to shop online.
third	he, she, it, they	the subject	She buys shoes from her cousin's store.

Using first person is best for writing in which the writer's personal experiences, feelings, and opinions are an important element. Second person is best for writing in which the author directly addresses the reader. Third person is most common in formal and academic writing; it creates distance between the writer and the reader. A sentence's point of view has to remain consistent throughout the sentence.

Look for pronouns to help you identify which point of view a sentence is using.

Example

Wrong: If someone wants to be a professional athlete, you have to practice often.

Correct: If you want to be a professional athlete, you have to practice often.

Correct: If someone wants to be a professional athlete, he or she has to practice often.

In the first sentence, the person shifts from third (*someone*) to second (*you*). It needs to be rewritten to be consistent.

TRANSITIONS

TRANSITIONS join two ideas and also explain the logical relationship between those ideas. For example, the transition *because* tells you that two things have a cause and effect relationship, while the transitional phrase *on the other hand* introduces a contradictory idea. On the GED Writing section, you may be asked to identify the best transition for a particular sentence, and you will definitely need to make good use of transitions in your essay.

Table 5.5. Common transitions

CAUSE AND EFFECT	as a result, because, consequently, due to, if/then, so, therefore, thus
SIMILARITY	also, likewise, similarly
CONTRAST	but, however, in contrast, on the other hand, nevertheless, on the contrary, yet
CONCLUDING	briefly, finally, in conclusion, in summary, thus, to conclude
ADDITION	additionally, also, as well, further, furthermore, in addition, moreover
EXAMPLES	in other words, for example, for instance
TIME	after, before, currently, later, recently, subsequently, since, then, while

Examples

Choose the transition that would best fit in the blank.

1. Clara's car breaks down frequently. _____, she decided to buy a new one.

2. Chad scored more points than any other player on his team. _____, he is often late to practice, so his coach won't let him play in the game Saturday.

3. Miguel will often eat his lunch outside. _____, on Wednesday, he took his sandwich to the park across from his office.

4. Alex set the table _____ the lasagna finished baking in the oven.

    A) however

    B) for example

    C) while

    D) therefore

Sentence 1 is describing a cause (her car breaks down) and an effect (she'll buy a new one), **so the correct transition is therefore.**

Sentence 2 includes a contrast: it would make sense for Chad to play in the game, but he isn't, so **the best transition is however.**

In Sentence 3, the clause after the transition is an example, so **the best transition is for example.**

In Sentence 4, two things are occurring at the same time, so **the best transition is while.**

WORDINESS AND REDUNDANCY

Sometimes sentences can be grammatically correct but still be confusing or poorly written. Often this problem arises when sentences are wordy or contain redundant phrasing (i.e., when several words with similar meanings are used). Often such phrases are used to make the writing seem more serious or academic when actually they can confuse the reader. On the test, you might be asked to clarify or even remove such phrases.

Some examples of excessive wordiness and redundancy are included in the table below:

Table 5.6. Wordiness examples

WORDY	IMPROVED
I'll meet you in the <u>place where I parked my car</u>.	I'll meet you in the <u>parking lot</u>.
<u>The point I am trying to make is that</u> the study was flawed.	The study was flawed.
A memo was sent out <u>concerning the matter of</u> dishes left in the sink.	A memo was sent out <u>about</u> dishes left in the sink.
The email was <u>brief and to the point</u>.	The email was <u>terse</u>.
I don't think I'll ever <u>understand or comprehend</u> Italian operas.	I don't think I'll ever <u>understand</u> Italian operas.

Examples

Rewrite each of the following sentences to eliminate wordiness and redundancy.

1. The game was canceled due to the fact that a bad storm was predicted.

   The game was canceled because a bad storm was predicted.

   Replace the long phrase *due to the fact that* with the much shorter *because*.

2. The possibility exists that we will have a party for my mother's birthday.

   We might have a party for my mother's birthday.

   By rearranging the sentence, we can replace the phrase *the possibility exists that* with the word *might*.

3. With the exception of our new puppy, all of our dogs have received their vaccinations.

   All of our dogs have been vaccinated except our new puppy.

   The sentence can be rearranged to replace *with the exception of* with *except*. The phrase *receive their vaccinations* has also been shortened to *been vaccinated*.

4. We threw away the broken microwave that didn't work.

   We threw away the broken microwave.

   If something is broken that means it doesn't work, so the phrase *that didn't work* can be removed.

5. It was an unexpected surprise when we won the raffle.

   It was a surprise when we won the raffle.

   By definition, a surprise is always unexpected, so the word *unexpected* can be removed.

6

WRITING: THE ESSAY

On the Writing section of the GED, you will need to write an essay. A strong essay takes a position on an issue, addresses its complexities, presents specific ideas and examples that explain and support the position, and maintains an organized, logical structure. A good essay also includes strong vocabulary and varied sentence structure. Bear this in mind as you prepare for the GED. The following sections walk through these steps and provide examples.

WRITING A THESIS STATEMENT

The thesis, or THESIS STATEMENT, is central to the structure and meaning of an essay. It presents the writer's argument or position on an issue; in other words, it tells readers specifically what you think and what you will discuss. A strong, direct thesis statement is key to the organization of any essay.

Writing a good thesis statement is as simple as stating your idea and why you think it's true or correct.

Example

Take a position on the following topic in your essay. You can choose to write about either of the two viewpoints discussed in the prompt, or you may argue for a third point of view.

Many high schools have begun to adopt 1:1 technology programs, meaning that each school provides every student with a computing device such as a laptop or tablet. Educators who support these initiatives say that the technology allows for more dynamic collaboration and that students need to learn technology skills to compete in the job market. On the other hand, opponents cite increased distraction and the dangers of cyber-bullying or unsupervised internet use as reasons not to provide students with such devices.

Possible thesis statements:

> **Providing technology to every student is good for education because it allows students to learn important skills such as typing, web design, and video editing; it also gives students more opportunities to work cooperatively with their classmates and teachers.**
>
> **I disagree with the idea that schools should provide technology to students because most students will simply be distracted by the free access to games and websites when they should be studying or doing homework.**
>
> **In a world where technology is improving and changing at a phenomenal rate, schools have a responsibility to teach students how to navigate that technology safely and effectively; providing each student with a laptop or tablet is one way to help them do that.**

STRUCTURING THE ESSAY

There are a few different ways to organize an essay, but some basics apply no matter what the style.

Essays may differ in how they present an idea, but they all have the same basic parts—introduction, body, and conclusion. The most common essay types are **PERSUASIVE** essays and **EXPOSITORY** essays. A persuasive essay takes a position on an issue and attempts to show the reader why it's correct. An expository essay explains different aspects of an issue without necessarily taking a side.

Introductions

Present your argument or idea in the introduction. Usually, the introductory paragraph ends with a thesis statement, which clearly sets forth the position or point the essay will prove. The introduction is a good place to bring up complexities, counterarguments, and context, all of which will help the reader understand the reasoning behind your position on the issue at hand. Later, revisit those issues and wrap all of them up in the conclusion.

Example

Below is an example of an introduction. Note that it provides some context for the argument, acknowledges an opposing perspective, and gives the reader a good idea of the issue's complexities. Pay attention to the thesis statement in the last few lines, which clearly states the author's position.

> **Technology has changed massively in recent years, but today's generation barely notices—high school students are already experienced with the internet, computers, apps, cameras, cell phones, and more. Teenagers must learn to use these tools safely and responsibly. Opponents of 1:1 technology programs might argue that students will be distracted or misuse the technology,**

but that is exactly why schools must teach them to use it. By providing technology to students, schools can help them apply it positively by creating great projects with other students, communicating with teachers and classmates, and conducting research for class projects. In a world where technology is improving and changing at a phenomenal rate, schools have a responsibility to teach students how to navigate that technology safely and effectively; providing each student with a laptop or tablet is one way to help them do that.

The Body Paragraphs

The body of an essay consists of a series of structured paragraphs. You may organize the body of your essay by creating paragraphs that describe or explain each reason you give in your thesis; addressing the issue as a problem and offering a solution in a separate paragraph; telling a story that demonstrates your point (make sure to break it into paragraphs around related ideas); or comparing and contrasting the merits of two opposing sides of the issue (make sure to draw a conclusion about which is better at the end).

Make sure that each paragraph is structurally consistent, beginning with a topic sentence to introduce the main idea, followed by supporting ideas and examples. No extra ideas unrelated to the paragraph's focus should appear. Use transition words and phrases to connect body paragraphs, and improve the flow and readability of your essay.

In the following section, you will find an example of a paragraph that is internally consistent and explains one of the main reasons given in one of the sample thesis statements above. Your essay should have one or more paragraphs like this to form the main body.

Conclusions

To end your essay smoothly, write a conclusion that reminds the reader why you were talking about these topics in the first place. Go back to the ideas in the introduction and thesis statement, but be careful not to simply restate your ideas; rather, reinforce your argument.

Example

Here is a sample conclusion paragraph that could go with the introduction above. Notice that this conclusion talks about the same topics as the introduction (changing technology and the responsibility of schools), but it does not simply rewrite the thesis.

As technology continues to change, teens will need to adapt to it. Schools already teach young people myriad academic and life skills, so it makes sense that

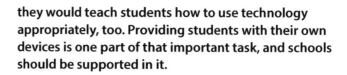

they would teach students how to use technology appropriately, too. Providing students with their own devices is one part of that important task, and schools should be supported in it.

PROVIDING SUPPORTING EVIDENCE

Your essay requires not only structured, organized paragraphs; it must also provide specific evidence supporting your arguments. Whenever you make a general statement, follow it with specific examples that will help to convince the reader that your argument has merit. These specific examples do not bring new ideas to the paragraph; rather, they explain or defend the general ideas that have already been stated.

The following are some examples of general statements and specific statements that provide more detailed support:

General: Students may get distracted online or access harmful websites.

Specific: Some students spend too much time using chat features or social media, or they get caught up in online games. Others spend time reading websites that have nothing to do with an assignment.

Specific: Teens often think they are hidden behind their computer screens. If teenagers give out personal information such as age or location on a website, it can lead to dangerous strangers seeking them out.

General: Schools can teach students how to use technology appropriately and expose them to new tools.

Specific: Schools can help students learn to use technology to work on class projects, communicate with classmates and teachers, and carry out research for classwork.

Specific: Providing students with laptops or tablets will allow them to get lots of practice using technology and programs at home, and only school districts can ensure that these tools are distributed widely, especially to students who may not have them at home.

Example

The following is an example of a structured paragraph that uses specific supporting ideas. This paragraph supports the thesis introduced above (see Introductions).

Providing students with their own laptop or tablet will allow them to explore new programs and software in class with teachers and classmates and to practice using it at home. In schools without laptops for students, classes have to visit computer labs where they share old computers often missing keys or that run so slowly they are hardly powered on before class ends. When a teacher tries to show students how to use a new tool or website, students must scramble to follow along and have no time to explore the new feature. If they can take laptops home instead, students can do things like practice editing video clips or photographs until they are perfect. They can email classmates or use shared files to collaborate even after school. If schools expect students to learn these skills, it is the schools' responsibility to provide students with enough opportunities to practice them.

This paragraph has some general statements:

… their own laptop or tablet will allow them to explore new programs and software… and to practice…

…it is the schools' responsibility to provide… enough opportunities…

It also has some specific examples to back them up:

…computers… run so slowly they are hardly powered on… students must scramble to follow along and have no time to explore…

They can email classmates or use shared files to collaborate…

WRITING WELL

Pay attention to the following details to ensure the clarity of your argument and to help readers understand the complexity and depth of your writing.

Transitions

Transitions are words, phrases, and ideas that help connect ideas throughout a text. You should use them between sentences and between paragraphs. Some common transitions include *then*, *next*, *in other words*, *as well*, and *in addition to*. Be creative with your transitions, and make sure you understand what the transition you are using shows about the relationship between the ideas. For instance, the transition *although* implies that there is some contradiction between the first idea and the second.

See *Transitions* in Chapter Five for more information and examples.

Syntax

The way you write sentences is important to maintaining the reader's interest. Try to begin sentences differently. Make some sentences long and some sentences short. Write simple sentences. Write complex sentences that have complex ideas in them. Readers appreciate variety.

See *Types of Sentences* in Chapter Five for more information and examples.

There are four basic types of sentences: simple, compound, complex, and compound-complex. Try to use some of each type. Be sure that your sentences make sense, though—it's better to have clear and simple writing that a reader can understand than to have complex, confusing syntax that does not clearly express the idea.

Word Choice and Tone

The words you choose influence the impression you make on readers. Use words that are specific, direct, and appropriate to the task. For instance, a formal text may benefit from complex sentences and impressive vocabulary, while it may be more appropriate to use simple vocabulary and sentences in writing intended for a young audience. Make use of strong vocabulary; avoid using vague, general words such as *good, bad, very,* or *a lot.* However, make sure that you are comfortable with the vocabulary you choose; if you are unsure about the word's meaning or its use in the context of your essay, don't use it at all.

Editing, Revising, and Proofreading

When writing a timed essay, you will not have very much time for these steps; spend any time you have left after writing the essay looking over it and checking for spelling and grammar mistakes that may interfere with a reader's understanding. Common mistakes to look out for include: subject/verb disagreement, pronoun/antecedent disagreement, comma splices and run-ons, and sentence fragments (phrases or dependent clauses unconnected to an independent clause).

7

READING

The GED Reading section will require you to read both non-fiction and fiction passages and then answer questions about them. These questions will fall into three main categories:

ABOUT THE AUTHOR: The question will ask about the author's attitude, thoughts, and opinions. When encountering a question asking specifically about the author, pay attention to context clues in the article. The answer may not be explicitly stated, but instead conveyed in the overall message.

PASSAGE FACTS: You must distinguish between facts and opinions presented in the passage. You may also be asked to identify specific information supplied by the author of the passage.

ADDITIONAL INFORMATION: These questions will have you look at what kind of information could be added to or was missing from the passage. They may also ask in what direction the passage was going. Questions may ask what statement could be added to strengthen the author's statement, or weaken it; they may also provide a fill-in-the-blank option to include a statement that is missing from, but fits with, the rest of the passage.

STRATEGIES

Despite the different types of questions you will face, there are some strategies for reading comprehension that apply across the board:

- Read the answer choices first, then read the passage. This will save you time, as you will know what to look out for as you read.

- Use the process of elimination. Some answer choices are obviously incorrect and are relatively easy to detect. After reading the passage, eliminate those blatantly incorrect answer choices; this increases your chance of finding the correct answer much more quickly.

- Avoid negative statements. Generally, test makers will not make negative statements about anyone or anything. Statements will be either neutral or positive, so if it seems like an answer choice has a negative connotation, it's very likely that the answer is false.

THE MAIN IDEA

The main idea of a text is the purpose behind why a writer would choose to write a book, article, story, etc. Being able to find and understand the main idea is a critical skill necessary to comprehend and appreciate what you're reading.

Consider a political election. A candidate is running for office and plans to deliver a speech asserting her position on tax reform. The topic of the speech—tax reform—is clear to voters and probably of interest to many. However, imagine that the candidate believes that taxes should be lowered. She is likely to assert this argument in her speech, supporting it with examples proving why lowering taxes would benefit the public and how it could be accomplished. While the topic of the speech would be tax reform, the benefit of lowering taxes would be the main idea. Other candidates may have different perspectives on the topic; they may believe that higher taxes are necessary or that current taxes are adequate. It's likely that their speeches, while on the same topic of tax reform, would have different main ideas: different arguments likewise supported by different examples. Determining what a speaker, writer, or text is asserting about a specific issue will reveal the MAIN IDEA.

One more quick note: the GED may also ask about a passage's THEME, which is similar to, but distinct from its topic. While a TOPIC is usually a specific *person, place, thing,* or *issue,* the theme is an *idea* or *concept* that the author refers back to frequently. Examples of common themes include ideas like the importance of family, the dangers of technology, and the beauty of nature.

There will be many questions on the GED that require you to differentiate between the topic, theme, and main idea of a passage. Let's look at an example passage to see how you would answer these questions:

Topic: The subject of the passage.
Theme: An idea or concept the author refers to repeatedly.
Main idea: The argument the writer is making about the topic.

Babe Didrikson Zaharias, one of the most decorated female athletes of the twentieth century, is an inspiration for everyone. Born in 1911 in Beaumont, Texas, Zaharias lived in a time when women were considered second-class to men, but she never let that stop her from becoming a champion. Babe was one of seven children in a poor immigrant family and was competitive from an early age. As a child she excelled at most things she tried, especially sports, which continued into high school and beyond. After high school, Babe played amateur basketball for two years, and soon after began training in track and field. Despite the fact that women were only allowed to enter in three events, Babe represented the United States in the 1932 Los Angeles Olympics and won two gold medals and one silver for track and field events.

In the early 1930s, Babe began playing golf, which earned her a legacy. The first tournament she entered was a men's only tournament; however, she did not make the cut to play. Playing golf as an amateur was the only option for a woman at this time, since there was no professional women's league. Babe played as an amateur for a little over a decade, until she turned pro in 1947 for the Ladies Professional Golf Association (LPGA), of which she was a founding member. During her career as a golfer, Babe won eighty-two tournaments, amateur and professional, including the U.S. Women's Open, All-American Open, and British Women's Open Golf Tournament. In 1953, Babe was diagnosed with cancer, but fourteen weeks later, she played in a tournament. That year, she won her third U.S. Women's Open. However, by 1955 she didn't have the physicality to compete anymore, and she died of the disease in 1956.

The topic of this paragraph is obviously Babe Zaharias—the whole passage describes events from her life. Determining the main idea, however, requires a little more analysis. The passage describes Babe Zaharias' life, but the main idea of the paragraph is what it says about her life. To figure out the main idea, consider what the writer is saying about Babe Zaharias. The writer is saying that she's someone to admire—that's the main idea and what unites all the information in the paragraph. Lastly, what might the theme of the passage be? The writer refers to several broad concepts, including never giving up and overcoming the odds, both of which could be themes for the passage.

Two major indicators of the main idea of a paragraph or passage follow:

- It's a general idea; it applies to the more specific ideas in the passage. Every other sentence in a paragraph should be able to relate in some way to the main idea.

- It asserts a specific viewpoint that the author supports with facts, opinions, or other details. In other words, the main idea takes a stand.

Example

From so far away, it's easy to imagine the surface of our solar system's planets as enigmas—how could we ever know what those far-flung planets really look like? It turns out, however, that scientists have a number of tools at their disposal that allow them to paint detailed pictures of many planets' surfaces. The topography of Venus, for example, has been explored by several space probes, including the Russian Venera landers and NASA's Magellan orbiter. These craft used imaging and radar to map the surface of the planet, identifying a whole host of features, including volcanoes, craters, and a complex system of channels. Mars has similarly been mapped by space probes, including the famous Mars Rovers, which are automated vehicles that actually landed on the surface of Mars. These rovers have been used by NASA and other space agencies to study the geology, climate, and possible biology of the planet.

In addition to these long-range probes, NASA has also used its series of orbiting telescopes to study distant planets. These four massively powerful telescopes include the famous Hubble Space Telescope as well as the Compton Gamma Ray Observatory, Chandra X-Ray Observatory, and the Spitzer Space Telescope. Scientists can use these telescopes to examine planets using not only visible light but also infrared and near-infrared light, ultraviolet light, x-rays, and gamma rays.

Powerful telescopes aren't just found in space: NASA makes use of Earth-bound telescopes as well. Scientists at the National Radio Astronomy Observatory in Charlottesville, VA, have spent decades using radio imaging to build an incredibly detailed portrait of Venus' surface. In fact, Earth-bound telescopes offer a distinct advantage over orbiting telescopes because they allow scientists to capture data from a fixed point, which in turn allows them to effectively compare data collected over a long period of time.

Which of the following sentences best describes the main idea of the passage?

A) It's impossible to know what the surfaces of other planets are really like.

B) Telescopes are an important tool for scientists studying planets in our solar system.

C) Venus' surface has many of the same features as the Earth's, including volcanoes, craters, and channels.

D) Scientists use a variety of advanced technologies to study the surface of the planets in our solar system.

Answer A) can be eliminated because it directly contradicts the rest of the passage. Answers B) and C) can also be eliminated because they offer only specific details from the passage—while both choices contain details from the passage, neither is general enough to encompass the passage as a whole. **Only answer D) provides an assertion that is both backed up by the passage's content and general enough to cover the entire passage.**

Topic and Summary Sentences

The main idea of a paragraph usually appears within the topic sentence. The TOPIC SENTENCE introduces the main idea to readers; it indicates not only the topic of a passage but also the writer's perspective on the topic.

Notice, for example, how the first sentence in the example paragraph about Babe Zaharias states the main idea: *Babe Didrikson Zaharias, one of the most decorated female athletes of the twentieth century, is an inspiration for everyone.*

Even though paragraphs generally begin with topic sentences due to their introductory nature, on occasion writers build up to the topic sentence by using supporting details to generate interest or build an argument. Be alert for paragraphs when writers do not include a clear topic sentence at all; even without a clear topic sentence, a paragraph will still have a main idea. You may also see a SUMMARY SENTENCE at the end of a passage. As its name suggests, this sentence sums up the passage, often by restating the main idea and the author's key evidence supporting it.

Example

In the following paragraph, what are the topic and summary sentences?

The Constitution of the United States establishes a series of limits to rein in centralized power. Separation of powers distributes federal authority among three competing branches: the executive, the legislative, and the judicial. Checks and balances allow the branches to check the usurpation of power by any one branch. States' rights are protected under the Constitution from too much encroachment by the federal government. Enumeration of powers names the specific and few powers the federal government has. These four restrictions have helped sustain the American republic for over two centuries.

The topic sentence is the first sentence in the paragraph. It introduces the topic of discussion, in this case the constitutional limits aimed at restricting centralized power. **The summary sentence is the last sentence in the paragraph.** It sums up the information that was just presented: here, that constitutional limits have helped sustain the United States of America for over two hundred years.

Implied Main Idea

A paragraph without a clear topic sentence still has a main idea; rather than clearly stated, it's implied. Determining the IMPLIED MAIN IDEA requires some detective work: you will need to look at the author's word choice and tone in addition to the content of the passage to find his or her main idea. Let's look at a few example paragraphs.

Examples

One of my summer reading books was *Mockingjay*. I was captivated by the adventures of the main character and the complicated plot of the book. However, I felt that the ending didn't reflect the excitement of the story. Given what a powerful personality the main character has, I felt that the ending didn't do her justice.

1. Even without a clear topic sentence, this paragraph has a main idea. What is the writer's perspective on the book—what is the writer saying about it?

   A) *Mockingjay* is a terrific novel.

   B) *Mockingjay* is disappointing.

   C) *Mockingjay* is full of suspense.

   D) *Mockingjay* is a lousy novel.

   The correct answer is B): the novel is disappointing.
   How can you tell that this is the main idea? First, you can eliminate choice C) because it's too specific to be a main idea. It only deals with one specific aspect of the novel (its suspense).

   Sentences A), B), and D), on the other hand, all express a larger idea about the quality of the novel. However, only one of these statements can actually serve as a "net" for the whole paragraph. Notice that while the first few sentences praise the novel, the last two criticize it. Clearly, this is a mixed review.

   Therefore, the best answer is B). Sentence A) is too positive and doesn't account for the *letdown* of an ending. Sentence D), on the other hand, is too negative and doesn't account for the reader's sense of suspense and interest in the main character. But sentence B) allows for both positive and negative aspects—when a good thing turns bad, we often feel disappointed.

Fortunately, none of Alyssa's coworkers have ever seen inside the large filing drawer in her desk. Disguised by the meticulous neatness of the rest of her workspace, there was no sign of the chaos beneath. To even open it, she had to struggle for several minutes with the enormous pile of junk jamming the drawer, until it would suddenly give way, and papers, folders, and candy wrappers spilled out of the top and onto the floor. It was an organizational nightmare, with torn notes and spreadsheets haphazardly thrown on top of each other, and melted candy smeared across pages. She was worried the odor would soon permeate to her coworkers' desks, revealing her secret.

2. Which sentence best describes the main idea of the paragraph above?

A) Alyssa wishes she could move to a new desk.

B) Alyssa wishes she had her own office.

C) Alyssa is glad none of her coworkers know about her messy drawer.

D) Alyssa is sad because she doesn't have any coworkers.

Clearly, Alyssa has a messy drawer, and C) is the right answer. The paragraph begins by indicating her gratitude that her coworkers do not know about her drawer (*Fortunately, none of Alyssa's coworkers have ever seen inside the large filing drawer in her desk.*) Plus, notice how the drawer is described: *it was an organizational nightmare,* and it apparently doesn't even function properly: *to even open the drawer, she had to struggle for several minutes.* The writer reveals that it has an odor, with melted candy inside. Alyssa is clearly ashamed of her drawer and fearful of being judged by her coworkers about it.

SUPPORTING DETAILS

SUPPORTING DETAILS provide more support for the author's main idea. For instance, in the Babe Zaharias example, the writer makes the general assertion that *Babe Didrikson Zaharias, one of the most decorated female athletes of the twentieth century, is an inspiration for everyone.* The rest of the paragraph provides supporting details with facts showing why she is an inspiration: the names of the illnesses she overcame and the specific years she competed in the Olympics.

Be alert for SIGNAL WORDS, which can be helpful in identifying supporting details. These signal words tell you that a supporting fact or idea will follow and so can be helpful in identifying supporting details. Signal words can also help you rule out sentences that are not the main idea or topic sentence: if a sentence begins with one of these phrases, it will likely be too specific to be a main idea.

SIGNAL WORDS
- for example
- specifically
- in addition
- furthermore
- for instance
- others
- in particular
- some

Examples

From so far away, it's easy to imagine the surface of our solar system's planets as enigmas—how could we ever know what those far-flung planets really look like? It turns out, however, that scientists have a number of tools at their disposal that allow them to paint detailed pictures of many planets' surfaces. The topography of Venus, for example, has been explored by several space probes, including the Russian Venera landers and NASA's Magellan orbiter. These craft used imaging and radar to map the surface of the planet, identifying a whole host of features, including volcanoes, craters, and a complex system of channels. Mars has similarly been mapped by space probes, including the famous Mars Rovers, which are automated vehicles that actually landed on the surface of Mars. These rovers have been used by NASA and other space agencies to study the geology, climate, and possible biology of the planet.

In addition to these long-range probes, NASA has also used its series of orbiting telescopes to study distant planets. These four massively powerful telescopes include the famous Hubble Space Telescope as well as the Compton Gamma Ray Observatory, Chandra X-Ray Observatory, and the Spitzer Space Telescope. Scientists can use these telescopes to examine planets using not only visible light but also infrared and near-infrared light, ultraviolet light, x-rays, and gamma rays.

Powerful telescopes aren't just found in space: NASA makes use of Earth-bound telescopes as well. Scientists at the National Radio Astronomy Observatory in Charlottesville, VA, have spent decades using radio imaging to build an incredibly detailed portrait of Venus' surface. In fact, Earth-bound telescopes offer a distinct advantage over orbiting telescopes because they allow scientists to capture data from a fixed point, which in turn allows them to effectively compare data collected over a long period of time.

1. Which sentence from the text best develops the idea that scientists make use of many different technologies to study the surfaces of other planets?

    A) These rovers have been used by NASA and other space agencies to study the geology, climate, and possible biology of the planet.

    B) From so far away, it's easy to imagine the surface of our solar system's planets as enigmas—how could we ever know what those far-flung planets really look like?

    C) In addition to these long-range probes, NASA has also used its series of orbiting telescopes to study distant planets.

    D) These craft used imaging and radar to map the surface of the planet, identifying a whole host of features, including volcanoes, craters, and a complex system of channels.

    You're looking for details from the passage that supports the main idea—scientists make use of many different technologies to study the surfaces of other planets. Answer A) includes a specific detail about rovers but does not offer any details that support the idea of multiple technologies being used. Similarly, answer D) provides another specific detail about space probes. Answer B) doesn't provide any supporting details; it simply introduces the topic of the passage. **Only answer C) provides a detail that directly supports the author's assertion that scientists use multiple technologies to study the planets.**

2. If true, which detail could be added to the passage above to support the author's argument that scientists use many different technologies to study the surface of planets?

   A) Because the Earth's atmosphere blocks x-rays, gamma rays, and infrared radiation, NASA needed to put telescopes in orbit above the atmosphere.

   B) In 2015, NASA released a map of Venus that was created by compiling images from orbiting telescopes and long-range space probes.

   C) NASA is currently using the Curiosity and Opportunity rovers to look for signs of ancient life on Mars.

   D) NASA has spent over $2.5 billion to build, launch, and repair the Hubble Space Telescope.

   You can eliminate answers C) and D) because they don't address the topic of studying the surface of planets. Answer A) can also be eliminated because it only addresses a single technology. **Only choice B) would add support to the author's claim about the importance of using multiple technologies.**

3. The author likely included the detail *Earth-bound telescopes offer a distinct advantage over orbiting telescopes because they allow scientists to capture data from a fixed point* in order to:

   A) explain why it has taken scientists so long to map the surface of Venus

   B) suggest that Earth-bound telescopes are the most important equipment used by NASA scientists

   C) prove that orbiting telescopes will soon be replaced by Earth-bound telescopes

   D) demonstrate why NASA scientists rely on many different types of scientific equipment

   Only answer D) speaks directly to the author's main argument. The author doesn't mention how long it has taken to map the surface of Venus (answer A), nor does he say that one technology is more important than the others (answer B). And while this detail does highlight the advantages of using Earth-bound telescopes, the author's argument is that many technologies are being used at the same time, so there's no reason to think that orbiting telescopes will be replaced (answer C).

FACTS VS. OPINIONS

On GED reading passages, you might be asked to identify a statement in a passage as either a fact or an opinion, so you'll need to know the difference between the two. A FACT is a statement or thought that can be proven to be true. The statement *Wednesday comes after Tuesday* is a fact—you can point to a calendar to prove it. In contrast, an OPINION is an assumption that is not based in fact and cannot be proven to be true. The assertion that *television is more*

Which of the following words would be associated with opinions?

- for example
- studies have shown
- I believe
- in fact
- the best/worst
- it's possible that

entertaining than feature films is an opinion—people will disagree on this, and there's no reference you can use to prove or disprove it.

Example

Exercise is critical for healthy development in children. Today, there is an epidemic of unhealthy children in the United States who will face health problems in adulthood due to poor diet and lack of exercise as children. This is a problem for all Americans, especially with the rising cost of health care.

It is vital that school systems and parents encourage their children to engage in a minimum of thirty minutes of cardiovascular exercise each day, mildly increasing their heart rate for a sustained period. This is proven to decrease the likelihood of developmental diabetes, obesity, and a multitude of other health problems. Also, children need a proper diet rich in fruits and vegetables so that they can grow and develop physically, as well as learn healthy eating habits early on.

Which of the following is a fact in the passage, not an opinion?

A) Fruits and vegetables are the best way to help children be healthy.

B) Children today are lazier than they were in previous generations.

C) The risk of diabetes in children is reduced by physical activity.

D) Children should engage in thirty minutes of exercise a day.

Answer C) is a simple fact stated by the author; it's introduced by the word *proven* **to indicate that you don't need to just take the author's word for it.** Choice B) can be discarded immediately because it is not discussed anywhere in the passage and also because it is negative. Answers A) and D) are both opinions—the author is promoting exercise, fruits, and vegetables as a way to make children healthy. (Notice that these incorrect answers contain words that hint at being an opinion such as *best, should*, or other comparisons.)

DRAWING CONCLUSIONS

In addition to understanding the main idea and factual content of a passage, you'll also be asked to take your analysis one step further and anticipate what other information could logically be added to the passage. In a non-fiction passage, for example, you might be asked which statement the author of the passage would agree with. In an excerpt from a fictional work, you might be asked to anticipate what the character would do next.

To answer these questions, you need to have a solid understanding of the topic, theme, and main idea of the passage; armed with this information, you can figure out which of the answer choices best fits within those criteria (or alternatively, which ones do not). For example, if the author of the passage is advocating for safer working conditions in textile factories, any supporting details that would be added to the passage should support that idea. You might add sentences that contain information about the number of accidents that occur in textile factories or that outline a new plan for fire safety.

Example

Exercise is critical for healthy development in children. Today, there is an epidemic of unhealthy children in the United States who will face health problems in adulthood due to poor diet and lack of exercise as children. This is a problem for all Americans, especially with the rising cost of health care.

It is vital that school systems and parents encourage their children to engage in a minimum of thirty minutes of cardiovascular exercise each day, mildly increasing their heart rate for a sustained period. This is proven to decrease the likelihood of developmental diabetes, obesity, and a multitude of other health problems. Also, children need a proper diet rich in fruits and vegetables so that they can grow and develop physically, as well as learn healthy eating habits early on.

What other information might the author have provided to strengthen the argument?

A) an example of how fruits and vegetables can improve a child's development

B) how much health insurance costs today versus ten years ago

C) a detailed explanation of how diabetes affects the endocrine and digestive systems

D) how many calories the average person burns during thirty minutes of exercise

All the choices would provide additional information, but only one pertains specifically to the improvement of health in children: **choice A).**

COMPARING PASSAGES

In addition to analyzing single passages, the GED will also require you to compare two passages. Usually these passage will discuss the same topic, and it will be your task to identify the similarities and differences between the authors' main ideas, supporting details, and tone.

CONTINUE

Examples

Read the two passages below and answer the following questions.

Passage 1

Today, there is an epidemic of unhealthy children in the United States who will face health problems in adulthood due to poor diet and lack of exercise during their childhood: in 2012, the Centers for Disease Control found that 18 percent of students aged 6 – 11 were obese. This is a problem for all Americans, as adults with chronic health issues are adding to the rising cost of health care. A child who grows up living an unhealthy lifestyle is likely to become an adult who does the same.

Because exercise is critical for healthy development in children, it is vital that school systems and parents encourage their children to engage in a minimum of thirty minutes of cardiovascular exercise each day. Even this small amount of exercise has been proven to decrease the likelihood that young people will develop diabetes, obesity, and other health issues as adults. In addition to exercise, children need a proper diet rich in fruits and vegetables so that they can grow and develop physically. Starting a good diet early also teaches children healthy eating habits they will carry into adulthood.

Passage 2

When was the last time you took a good, hard look at a school lunch? For many adults, it's probably been years—decades even—since they last thought about students' midday meals. If they did stop to ponder, they might picture something reasonably wholesome if not very exciting: a peanut butter and jelly sandwich paired with an apple or a traditional meat-potatoes-and-veggies plate. At worst, they may think, kids are making due with some pizza and a carton of milk.

The truth, though, is that many students aren't even getting the meager nutrients offered up by a simple slice of pizza. Instead, schools are serving up heaping helpings of previously frozen, recently fried delicacies like french fries and chicken nuggets. These high-carb, low-protein options are usually paired with a limp, flavorless, straight-from-the-freezer vegetable that quickly gets tossed in the trash. And that carton of milk? It's probably a sugar-filled chocolate sludge, or it's been replaced with a student's favorite high-calorie soda.

So what, you might ask. Kids like to eat junk food—it's a habit they'll grow out of soon enough. Besides, parents can always pack lunches for students looking for something better. But is that really the lesson we want to be teaching our kids? Many of those children aren't going to grow out of bad habits; they're going to reach adulthood thinking that ketchup is a vegetable. And students in low-income families are particularly impacted by the sad state of school food. These parents rely on schools to provide a warm, nutritious meal because they don't have the time or money to prepare food at home. Do we really want to be punishing these children with soggy meat patties and salt-soaked potato chips?

1. Both authors are arguing for the important of improving childhood nutrition. How do the authors' strategies differ?

   A) Passage 1 presents several competing viewpoints while Passage 2 offers a single argument.

   B) Passage 1 uses scientific data while Passage 2 uses figurative language.

   C) Passage 1 is descriptive while Passage 2 uses a cause-and-effect structure.

   D) Passage 1 has a friendly tone while the tone of Passage 2 is angry.

   The first author uses scientific facts (*the Centers for Disease Control found...* and *Even this small amount of exercise has been proven...*) to back up his argument, while the second uses figurative language (the ironic *delicacies* and the metaphor *sugar-filled chocolate sludge*), so **the correct answer is B)**. Answer A) is incorrect because the first author does not present any opposing viewpoints. Answer C) is incorrect because Passage 2 does not have a cause-and-effect structure. And while the author of the second passage could be described as angry, the first author is not particularly friendly, so you can eliminate answer D) as well.

2. Both authors argue that

   A) Children should learn healthy eating habits at a young age.

   B) Low-income students are disproportionately affected by the low-quality food offered in schools.

   C) Teaching children about good nutrition will lower their chances of developing diabetes as adults.

   D) Schools should provide children an opportunity to exercise every day.

   Both authors argue children should learn healthy eating habits at a young age (answer A). The author of Passage 1 states that a child who grows up living an unhealthy lifestyle is likely to become an adult who does the same, and the author of Passage 2 states that many of those children aren't going to grow out of bad habits— both of these sentences argue that it's necessary to teach children about nutrition early in life. Answers C) and D) are mentioned only by the author of Passage 1, and answer B) is only discussed in Passage 2.

UNDERSTANDING THE AUTHOR

Author's Purpose

Whenever an author writes a text, she or he always has a purpose, whether that's to entertain, inform, explain, or persuade. A short story, for example, is meant to entertain, while an online news article would be designed to inform the public about a current event. Each of these different types of writing has a specific name:

- Narrative writing tells a story (novel, short story, play).
- Expository writing informs people (newspaper and magazine articles).
- Technical writing explains something (product manual, directions).
- Persuasive writing tries to convince the reader of something (opinion column on a blog).

On the exam, you may be asked to categorize a passage as one of these types, either by specifically naming it as such or by identifying its general purpose.

You may also be asked about primary and secondary sources. These terms describe not the writing itself but the author's relationship to what's being written about. A **PRIMARY SOURCE** is an unaltered piece of writing that was composed during the time when the events being described took place; these texts are often written by the people directly involved. A **SECONDARY SOURCE** might address the same topic but provide extra commentary or analysis. These texts are written by outside observers and may even be composed after the event. For example, a book written by a political candidate to inform people about his or her stand on an issue is a primary source. An online article written by a journalist analyzing how that position will affect the election is a secondary source; a book by a historian about that election would be a secondary source, too.

Example

Elizabeth closed her eyes and braced herself on the armrests that divided her from her fellow passengers. Takeoff was always the worst part for her. The revving of the engines, the way her stomach dropped as the plane lurched upward; it made her feel sick. Then, she had to watch the world fade away beneath her, getting smaller and smaller until it was just her and the clouds hurtling through the sky. Sometimes (but only sometimes) it just had to be endured, though. She focused on the thought of her sister's smiling face and her new baby nephew as the plane slowly pulled onto the runway.

The passage above is reflective of which type of writing?

A) narrative

B) expository

C) technical

D) persuasive

The passage is telling a story—we meet Elizabeth and learn about her fear of flying—**so it's a narrative text, answer choice A).** There is no factual information presented or explained, nor is the author trying to persuade the reader of anything.

The Audience

A good author will write with a specific audience in mind. For example, an opinion column on a website might be specifically targeted toward undecided voters, or a brochure for an upcoming art exhibit might address people who have donated money to the museum in the past. The author's audience can influence what information is included in the text, the tone the author uses, and the structure of the text.

The easiest way to identify the intended audience of a text is simply to ask yourself who would benefit the most from the information in the passage. A passage about how often to change the oil in a car would provide useful information to new drivers, but likely wouldn't tell an experienced driver something she didn't already know. Thus, the audience is likely new drivers who are learning to take care of cars.

The author may also directly or indirectly refer to his audience. The author of an article on oil changes might say something like *new drivers will want to keep an eye on their mileage when deciding how often to get an oil change*, which tells the reader who the intended audience is.

Example

The museum's newest exhibit opens today! *The Ecology of the Columbia River Basin* is an exciting collaboration between the New Valley Museum of Natural Science and the U.S. Department of the Interior. The exhibit includes plants, insects, birds, and mammals that are unique to the Columbia River Basin and explores the changes that have occurred in this delicate ecosystem over the last century. The exhibit is kid friendly, with interactive, hands-on exhibits and exciting audio-visual presentations. Individual tickets are available on the museum's website, and groups may apply for special ticket prices by calling the museum directly.

The intended audience for this passage likely includes all of the following except

A) a middle school biology teacher

B) employees of the U.S. Department of the Interior

C) parents of young children

D) naturalists with an interest in local birds

The passage provides information to anyone who might be interested in an exhibit on the ecology of the Columbia River Basin. This includes biology teachers (who can get special group ticket prices), parents of young children (who now know the exhibit is kid friendly), and naturalists (who will want to see the unique birds). **The only people who would not learn anything new from reading the passage are employees of the U.S. Department of the Interior (answer B),** who likely already know about the exhibit since they helped create it.

Tone

The author of a text expresses how she or he feels about the subject and audience through the tone of the text. For example, a newspaper article about a prominent philanthropist might have to be serious and appreciative, while a website blurb about an upcoming sale could be playful and relaxed.

Table 7.1. Tone words

POSITIVE	admiring, approving, celebratory, comforting, confident, earnest, encouraging, excited, forthright, funny, hopeful, humorous, modest, nostalgic, optimistic, playful, poignant, proud, relaxed, respectful, sentimental, silly, sympathetic
NEUTRAL	casual, detached, formal, impartial, informal, objective, questioning, unconcerned
NEGATIVE	angry, annoyed, belligerent, bitter, condescending, confused, cynical, depressed, derisive, despairing, disrespectful, embarrassed, fearful, gloomy, melancholy, mournful, ominous, pessimistic, skeptical, solemn, suspicious, unsympathetic

Authors signify tone in a number of ways. The main clue to look for is the author's DICTION, or word choice. Obviously, if the author is choosing words that have a negative connotation, then the overall tone of the text is negative, while words with a positive connotation will convey a positive tone. For example, the author of a biographical article may choose to describe his subject as *determined* or *pigheaded*; both mean similar things, but the first has a more positive connotation than the second. Literary devices such as imagery and metaphors can likewise generate a specific tone by evoking a particular feeling in the reader.

Tone is also developed by the structure of the text. Long, complicated sentences will make a passage seem formal, while short, pithy writing is more informal. Similarly, a text that cites statistical figures to support a logical argument will have a different tone than a text structured as a casual conversation between author and reader.

Example

It could be said that the great battle between the North and South we call the Civil War was a battle for individual identity. The states of the South had their own culture, one based on farming, independence, and the rights of both man and state to determine their own paths. Similarly, the North had forged its own identity as a center of centralized commerce and manufacturing. This clash of lifestyles was bound to create tension, and this tension was bound to lead to war. But people who try to sell you this narrative are wrong.

The tone of the passage above can best be described as

A) formal and forthright

B) casual and mournful

C) detached and solemn

D) objective and skeptical

The author of this passage is using a formal tone as indicated by his use of academic-sounding phrases like *rights of both man and state* and *centralized commerce*. He is also very forthright in his final sentence, when he directly and strongly states his opinion to the reader, so **the correct answer is A)**. Because of the formal language, the tone isn't casual, and the author's obvious strong feelings about the topic eliminate detached and objective as answer choices. The author's tone could be described as skeptical; however answer D) has already been eliminated.

TEXT STRUCTURE

Authors can structure passages in a number of different ways. These distinct organizational patterns, referred to as TEXT STRUCTURE, use the logical relationships between ideas to improve the readability and coherence of a text. The most common ways passages are organized include:

- **PROBLEM-SOLUTION**: the author presents a problem and then discusses a solution.

- **COMPARISON-CONTRAST**: the author presents two situations and then discusses the similarities and differences.

- **CAUSE-EFFECT**: the author presents an action and then discusses the resulting effects.

- **DESCRIPTIVE**: an idea, object, person, or other item is described in detail.

Example

The issue of public transportation has begun to haunt the fast-growing cities of the southern United States. Unlike their northern counterparts, cities like Atlanta, Dallas, and Houston have long promoted growth out and not up—these are cities full of sprawling suburbs and single-family homes, not densely concentrated skyscrapers and apartments. What to do then, when all those suburbanites need to get into the central business districts for work? For a long time, it seemed highways were the answer: twenty-lane wide expanses of concrete that would allow commuters to move from home to work and back again. But these modern miracles have become time-sucking, pollution-spewing nightmares. They may not like it, but it's time for these cities to turn toward public transport like trains and buses if they want their cities to remain livable.

The organization of this passage can best be described as:

A) a comparison of two similar ideas

B) a description of a place

C) a discussion of several effects all related to the same cause

D) a discussion of a problem followed by the suggestion of a solution

You can exclude answer choice C) because the author provides no root cause or a list of effects. From there this question gets tricky, because the passage contains structures similar to those described above. For example, it compares two things (cities in the North and South) and describes a place (a sprawling city). However, if you look at the overall organization of the passage, you can see that it starts by presenting a problem (transportation) and then presents a solution (trains and buses), **making answer D) the only choice that encompasses the entire passage.**

VOCABULARY

On the Reading section, you may also be asked to provide definitions or intended meanings for words within passages. You may have never encountered some of these words before the test, but there are tricks you can use to figure out what they mean.

Context Clues

The most fundamental vocabulary skill is using the context in which a word is used to determine its meaning. Your ability to observe sentences closely is extremely useful when it comes to understanding new vocabulary words.

There are two types of context that can help you understand the meaning of unfamiliar words: situational context and sentence context. Regardless of which context is present, these types of questions are not really testing your knowledge of vocabulary; rather, they test your ability to comprehend the meaning of a word through its usage.

SITUATIONAL CONTEXT is context that is presented by the setting or circumstances in which a word or phrase occurs. SENTENCE CONTEXT occurs within the specific sentence that contains the vocabulary word. To figure out words using sentence context clues, you should first determine the most important words in the sentence.

There are four types of clues that can help you understand the context and therefore the meaning of a word:

- RESTATEMENT clues occur when the definition of the word is clearly stated in the sentence.
- POSITIVE/NEGATIVE CLUES can tell you whether a word has a positive or negative meaning.

- **CONTRAST CLUES** include the opposite meaning of a word. Words like *but, on the other hand,* and *however* are tip offs that a sentence contains a contrast clue.
- **SPECIFIC DETAIL CLUES** provide a precise detail that can help you understand the meaning of the word.

It's important to remember that more than one of these clues can be present in the same sentence. The more there are, the easier it will be to determine the meaning of the word. For example, the following sentence uses both restatement and positive/negative clues: *Janet suddenly found herself destitute, so poor she could barely afford to eat.* The second part of the sentence clearly indicates that *destitute* is a negative word. It also restates the meaning: very poor.

Examples

Select the answer that most closely matches the definition of the underlined word or phrase as it is used in the sentence.

1. I had a hard time reading her <u>illegible</u> handwriting.

    A) neat

    B) unsafe

    C) sloppy

    D) educated

    Already, you know that this sentence is discussing something that is hard to read. Look at the word that *illegible* is describing: handwriting. Based on context clues, you can tell that *illegible* means that her handwriting is hard to read.

    Next, look at the answer choices. Choice A), *neat,* is obviously a wrong answer because neat handwriting would not be difficult to read. Choices B) and D), *unsafe* and *educated,* don't make sense. **Therefore, choice C), *sloppy*, is the best answer.**

2. The dog was <u>dauntless</u> in the face of danger, braving the fire to save the girl trapped inside the building.

    A) difficult

    B) fearless

    C) imaginative

    D) startled

    Demonstrating bravery in the face of danger would be B) *fearless.* In this case, the restatement clue (*braving the fire*) tells you exactly what the word means.

→
CONTINUE

3. Beth did not spend any time preparing for the test, but Tyrone kept a <u>rigorous</u> study schedule.

    A) strict

    B) loose

    C) boring

    D) strange

In this case, the contrast word *but* tells us that Tyrone studied in a different way than Beth, which means it's a contrast clue. If Beth did not study hard, then Tyrone did. **The best answer, therefore, is choice A).**

Analyzing Words

As you no doubt know, determining the meaning of a word can be more complicated than just looking in a dictionary. A word might have more than one DENOTATION, or definition; which one the author intends can only be judged by looking at the surrounding text. For example, the word *quack* can refer to the sound a duck makes or to a person who publicly pretends to have a qualification that he or she does not actually possess.

A word may also have different CONNOTATIONS, which are the implied meanings and emotion a word evokes in the reader. For example, a cubicle is simply a walled desk in an office, but for many, the word implies a constrictive, uninspiring workplace. Connotations can vary greatly between cultures and even between individuals.

Lastly, authors might make use of FIGURATIVE LANGUAGE, which is the use of a word to imply something other than the word's literal definition. This is often done by comparing two things. If you say *I felt like a butterfly when I got a new haircut*, the listener knows you don't resemble an insect but instead felt beautiful and transformed.

Examples

Select the answer that most closely matches the definition of the underlined word or phrase as it is used in the sentence.

1. The uneven <u>pupils</u> suggested that brain damage was possible.

    A) part of the eye

    B) student in a classroom

    C) walking pace

    D) breathing sounds

Only answer choice A (part of the eye) matches both the definition of the word and context of the sentence. Choice B is an alternative definition for pupil but does not make sense in the sentence. Both C and D could be correct in the context of the sentence, but neither is a definition of pupil.

2. Aiden examined the antique lamp and worried that he had been <u>taken for a ride</u>. He had paid a lot for the vintage lamp, but it looked as if it was worthless.

    A) transported

    B) forgotten

    C) deceived

    D) hindered

It's clear from the context of the sentence that Aiden was not literally taken for a ride. Instead, this phrase is an example of figurative language. From context clues, it can be figured out that Aiden paid too much for the lamp, **so he was deceived (answer choice C).**

Word Structure

Although you are not expected to know every word in the English language for your test, you will need the ability to use deductive reasoning to find the choice that is the best match for the word in question, which is why we are going to explain how to break a word into its parts to determine its meaning. Many words can be broken down into three main parts:

PREFIX — ROOT — SUFFIX

ROOTS are the building blocks of all words. Every word is either a root itself or has a root. Just as a plant cannot grow without roots, neither can vocabulary, because a word must have a root to give it meaning. The root is what is left when you strip away all the prefixes and suffixes from a word. For example, in the word *unclear*, if you take away the prefix *un-*, you have the root *clear*.

Roots are not always recognizable words, because they generally come from Latin or Greek words, such as *nat*, a Latin root meaning born. The word *native*, which means a person born in a referenced place, comes from this root; so does the word *prenatal*, meaning *before birth*. It's important to keep in mind, however, that roots do not always match the exact definitions of words, and they can have several different spellings.

PREFIXES are syllables added to the beginning of a word, and **SUFFIXES** are syllables added to the end of the word. Both carry assigned meanings and can be attached to a word to completely change the word's meaning or to enhance the word's original meaning.

Let's use the word *prefix* itself as an example: *fix* means to place something securely, and *pre-* means before. Therefore, *prefix* means to place something before or in front of. Now let's look at a suffix: in the word *feminism*, *femin* is a root that means female. The suffix *-ism* means act, practice, or process. Thus, *feminism* is the process of establishing equal rights for women.

Check out chapter ten, *Human Body Science*, for a list of medical roots and prefixes that are commonly tested on the GED.

Can you figure out the definitions of the following words using their parts?

- ambidextrous
- anthropology
- diagram
- egocentric
- hemisphere
- homicide
- metamorphosis
- nonsense
- portable
- rewind
- submarine
- triangle
- unicycle

Although you cannot determine the meaning of a word by a prefix or suffix alone, you can use this knowledge to eliminate answer choices; understanding whether the word is positive or negative can give you the partial meaning of the word.

Table 7.2. Common roots and affixes

ROOT	DEFINITION	EXAMPLE
ast(er)	star	asteroid, astronomy
audi	hear	audience, audible
auto	self	automatic, autograph
bene	good	beneficent, benign
bio	life	biology, biorhythm
cap	take	capture
ced	yield	secede
chrono	time	chronometer, chronic
corp	body	corporeal
crac or crat	rule	autocrat
demo	people	democracy
dict	say	dictionary, dictation
duc	lead or make	ductile, produce
gen	give birth	generation, genetics
geo	earth	geography, geometry
grad	step	graduate
graph	write	graphical, autograph
ject	throw	eject
jur or jus	law	justice, jurisdiction
log or logue	thought	logic, logarithm
luc	light	lucidity
man	hand	manual
mand	order	remand
mis	send	transmission
mono	one	monotone
omni	all	omnivore
path	feel	pathology
phil	love	philanthropy
phon	sound	phonograph
port	carry	export
qui	rest	quiet
scrib or script	write	scribe, transcript
sense or sent	feel	sentiment
tele	far away	telephone
terr	earth	terrace
uni	single	unicode
vac	empty	vacant
vid	see	video

Table 7.3. Common prefixes

PREFIX	DEFINITION	EXAMPLE
a- (also an-)	not, without; to, toward; of, completely	atheist, anemic, aside, aback, anew, abashed
ante-	before, preceding	antecedent, ante-room
anti-	opposing, against	antibiotic, anticlimax
com- (also co-, col-, con-, cor-)	with, jointly, completely	combat, codriver, collude, confide
dis- (also di-)	negation, removal	disadvantage, disbar
en- (also em-)	put into or on; bring into the condition of; intensify	engulf, entomb
hypo-	under	hypoglycemic, hypothermia
in- (also il-, im-, ir-)	not, without; in, into, toward, inside	infertile, impossible, influence, include
intra-	inside, within	intravenous, intrapersonal
out-	surpassing, exceeding; external, away from	outperform, outdoor
over-	excessively, completely; upper, outer, over, above	overconfident, overcast
pre-	before	precondition, pre-adolescent, prelude
re-	again	reapply, remake
semi-	half, partly	semicircle, semi-conscious
syn- (also sym-)	in union, acting together	synthesis, symbiotic
trans-	across, beyond	transatlantic
trans-	into a different state	translate
under-	beneath, below	underarm, undersecretary
under-	not enough	underdeveloped

Examples

Select the answer that most closely matches the definition of the underlined word or phrase as it is used in the sentence.

1. The <u>bellicose</u> dog will be sent to training school next week.

   A) misbehaved

   B) friendly

   C) scared

   D) aggressive

Both misbehaved and aggressive look like possible answers given the context of the sentence. **However, the prefix *belli*, which means warlike, can be used to confirm that aggressive (choice D) is the right answer.**

2. The new menu <u>rejuvenated</u> the restaurant and made it one of the most popular spots in town.

   A) established

   B) invigorated

   C) improved

   D) motivated

   All the answer choices could make sense in the context of the sentence, so it's necessary to use word structure to find the definition. The root *juven* means young and the prefix *re* means again, so *rejuvenate* means to be made young again. **The answer choice with the most similar meaning is *invigorated*, which means to give something energy.**

PART III: SCIENCE

8

SCIENTIFIC REASONING

SYSTEMS

A **SYSTEM** is a set of interacting parts that work together to form an integrated whole. Many scientific disciplines study systems: doctors, for example, study organ systems like the respiratory system, which is made up of interacting parts that allow animals to breathe. Similarly, ecologists might look at all the plants and animals that interact in a specific area, and chemists might look at a set of chemicals interacting in a beaker.

While obviously different, all these systems share some common traits. We'll use the respiratory system to look at the important characteristics of systems.

- All systems have a structure. (The respiratory system is highly organized.)
- All systems perform an action. (The respiratory system allows animals to breathe.)
- All systems have interacting parts. (The respiratory system is made up of many interacting parts, including the lungs, blood vessels, and bronchial tubes.)
- All systems have boundaries. (We can separate structures that are part of the respiratory system from those that are not.)
- Systems may receive input and produce output. (The respiratory system brings oxygen into the body and gets rid of carbon dioxide.)
- The processes in a system may be controlled by feedback. (The action of breathing is controlled in part by how much oxygen and carbon dioxide are in the body.)

Sometimes larger systems are made of smaller, independent systems called SUBSYSTEMS. For example, a body cell is made of many organelles.

These organelles each perform their own tasks, which together support the system of the cell.

SCIENTIFIC INVESTIGATIONS

A theory and a hypothesis are both important aspects of science. There is a common misconception that they are one and the same, which is not true; however the two are very similar. A HYPOTHESIS is a proposed explanation for a phenomenon; it's usually based on observations or previous research. A THEORY is an explanation for a phenomenon that has been thoroughly tested and is generally accepted to be true by the scientific community.

Although science can never really prove something, it does provide a means to answering many questions about our natural world. Scientists use different types of investigations, each providing different types of results, based upon what they are trying to find. There are three main types of scientific investigations: descriptive, experimental, and comparative.

DESCRIPTIVE INVESTIGATIONS start with observations. A model is then constructed to provide a visual of what was seen: a description. Descriptive investigations do not generally require hypotheses, as they usually just attempt to find more information about a relatively unknown topic. EXPERIMENTAL INVESTIGATIONS, on the other hand, usually involve a hypothesis. These experiments are sometimes referred to as controlled experiments because they are performed in a controlled environment. During experimental investigations, all variables are controlled except for one: the dependent variable, which is part of the hypothesis being tested. Often, there are many tests involved in this process. Lastly, COMPARATIVE INVESTIGATIONS involve manipulating different groups to compare them with each other. There is no control during comparative investigations.

THE SCIENTIFIC METHOD

To ensure that experimental and comparative investigations are thorough and accurate, scientists use the scientific method, which has five main steps:

1. Observe and ask questions: look at the natural world to observe and ask questions about patterns and anomalies you see.

2. Gather information: look at what other scientists have done to see where your questions fit in with current research.

3. Construct a hypothesis: make a proposal that explains why or how something happens.

4. Experiment and test your hypothesis: set up an experimental investigation that allows you to test your hypothesis.

5. Analyze results and draw conclusions: examine your results and see whether they disprove your hypothesis. Note that you can't actually *prove* a hypothesis; you can only provide evidence to support it.

9

LIFE SCIENCE

BIOLOGICAL MOLECULES

ORGANIC compounds are those that contain carbon. These compounds, such as glucose, triacylglycerol, and guanine, are used in day-to-day metabolic processes. Many of these molecules are POLYMERS formed from repeated smaller units called MONOMERS. INORGANIC compounds are those that do not contain carbon. These make up a very small fraction of mass in living organisms, and are usually minerals such as potassium, sodium, and iron.

There are several classes of organic compounds commonly found in living organisms. These biological molecules include carbohydrates, proteins, lipids, and nucleic acids, which combined make up more than 95 percent of non-water material in living organisms.

Carbohydrates

CARBOHYDRATES, also called sugars, are molecules made of carbon, hydrogen, and oxygen. Sugars are primarily used in organisms as a source of energy: they can be catabolized (broken down) to create energy molecules such as adenosine triphosphate (ATP) or nicotinamide adenine dinucleotide (NAD+), providing a source of electrons to drive cellular processes.

The basic formula for a carbohydrate is CH_2O, and the majority of carbohydrates are multiples of this empirical formula. For example, GLUCOSE is $C_6H_{12}O_6$. Carbohydrates can also bond together to form polymeric compounds. Some polymers of glucose include starch, which is used to store excess sugar, and cellulose, which is a support fiber responsible in part for the strength of plants.

HYDROCARBONS AND CARBOHYDRATES
alkanes:
C_nH_{2n+2}

alkenes:
C_nH_{2n}

alkynes:
C_nH_{2n-2}

monosaccharides:
$(CH_2O)_n$

Lipids

LIPIDS are compounds primarily composed of carbon and hydrogen with only a small percentage of oxygen. Lipids contain a **HEAD**, usually formed of glycerol or phosphate, and a **TAIL**, which is a hydrocarbon chain. The composition of the head, whether it's a carboxylic acid functional group, a phosphate group, or some other functional group, is usually polar, meaning it's hydrophilic. The tail is composed of carbon and hydrogen and is usually nonpolar, meaning it's hydrophobic.

The combined polarity of the lipid head and the nonpolarity of the lipid tail is a unique feature of lipids critical to the formation of the phospholipid bilayer in the cell membrane. The fatty acid tails are all pointed inward, and the heads are pointed outward. This provides a semipermeable membrane that allows a cell to separate its contents from the environment.

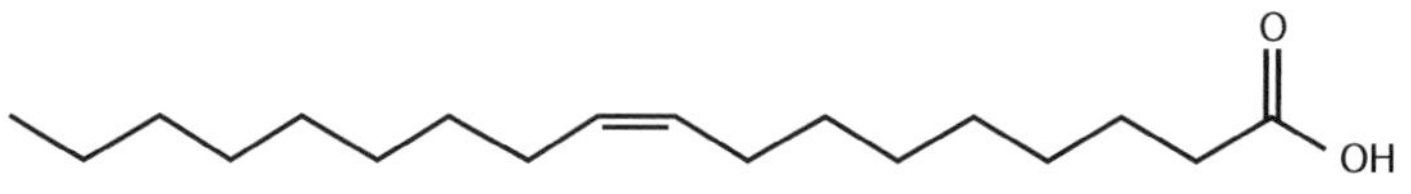

Figure 9.1. Free fatty acid lipid

The **SATURATION** of a lipid describes the number of double bonds in the tail of the lipid. The more double bonds a lipid tail has, the more unsaturated the molecule is, and the more bends there are in its structure. As a result, unsaturated fats (like oils) tend to be liquid at room temperature, whereas saturated fats (like lard or butter) are solid at room temperature.

Proteins

PROTEINS are large molecules composed of a chain of **AMINO ACIDS**. The sequence of amino acids in the chain determines the protein's structure and function. Each amino acid is composed of three parts:

- Amino group ($-NH_2$): The amino group is found on all amino acids.
- Carboxyl group ($-COOH$): The carboxyl group is found on all amino acids.
- R group: The R group is a unique functional group that is different for each amino acid. For example, in the histidine amino acid seen in Figure 9.2, the R group is a cyclic imidazole group.

Figure 9.2. The amino acid histidine

The R group determines the amino acid's physiological function.

There are twenty-two amino acids used to produce proteins. It's not necessary to know each amino acid, but it's important to know that sequences of these amino acids form proteins and that each amino acid has a unique R-functional group.

Nucleic Acids

NUCLEIC ACIDS, which include DNA and RNA, store all information necessary to produce proteins. These molecules are built using smaller molecules called NUCLEOTIDES, which are composed of a 5-carbon sugar, a phosphate group, and a nitrogenous base.

DNA is made from four nucleotides: adenine, guanine, cytosine, and thymine. Together, adenine and guanine are classified as PURINES, while thymine and cytosine are classified as PYRIMIDINES. These nucleotides bond in pairs; the pairs are then bonded in a chain to create a double helix shape with the sugar as the outside and the nitrogenous base on the inside. In DNA, adenine and thymine always bond as do guanine and cytosine. In RNA, thymine is replaced by a nucleotide called uracil, which bonds with adenine. RNA also differs from DNA in that it often exists as a single strand.

The major differences between DNA and RNA include:

- Uracil replaces thymine in RNA.
- RNA can exist as a single strand while DNA is double stranded.
- RNA contains ribose while DNA contains deoxyribose.

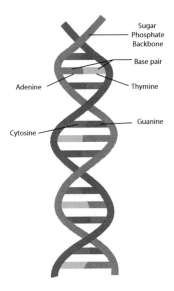

Figure 9.3. DNA

Examples

1. Match the polymer with the correct monomer.
   A) DNA; nucleic acid
   B) RNA; amino acid
   C) starch; lipid
   D) histidine; glucose

2. Which of the following is not found in DNA?
   A) adenine
   B) uracil
   C) thymine
   D) cytosine

3. Which of the following is not a compound created from sugar?
   A) glycogen
   B) starch
   C) cellulose
   D) guanine

4. An amino acid contains an R group, an amino group, and a:
   A) hydroxyl group
   B) carboxyl group
   C) phenyl group
   D) phosphate group

Answers: 1. A) 2. B) 3. D) 4. B)

THE HISTORY OF LIFE

Scientists believe life on Earth started around 3.8 billion years ago. The exact time when the first living cells appeared is unknown, but observations in geology have indicated the type of environment when living cells first appeared. It's hypothesized that life began due to a sequence of events that created biological molecules and cell-like structures:

1. synthesis of amino acid molecules and sugars, possibly from interaction of lightning and high temperatures near volcanic vents

2. joining and interaction of these molecules in something resembling modern-day proteins

3. assembly of these molecules within a membrane, which started to resemble a cell

The researchers **STANLEY MILLER** and **HAROLD UREY** had a hypothesis that the above three steps could have happened in a primordial environment in which there was no oxygen. Note that higher concentrations of oxygen did not appear until the evolution of plants, so life must have started without a significant oxygen presence.

Miller-Urey Experiment

In the MILLER-UREY EXPERIMENT, the researchers placed a mixture of ingredients that included water, methane, ammonia, and hydrogen into an enclosed reactor bulb. The conditions were modified to simulate those that were thought to exist on Earth several billion years ago. A pair of electrodes was placed into the reactor vessel, and sparks that simulated lightning were fired through the mixture every few minutes.

Miller and Urey found that their reaction mixture turned pink in color within a day, and after two weeks, the reactor vessel contained a thick solution that included a number of important molecules. Among the compounds that formed were with some amino acids, including glycine, as well as sugars. After full characterization, the scientists found that the experiment created eleven of the twenty-two known amino acids.

Fossil Record

The FOSSIL RECORD is a history of species that existed throughout time that has been unearthed by archaeologists. The fossils, if well preserved, are able to show us the bone structures and the forms of animals, plants, and even cells that existed billions of years ago. The fossils can be used to understand how species evolved through time and, in some cases, even to see what they ate and the environments in which they lived.

The age of fossils is determined through a method called RADIOMETRIC DATING, which examines the amount of radioactive carbon remaining in the sample. The radioactive carbon isotope carbon-14 has a half-life of 5,730 years, which means that this isotope can be used to reliably date fossils that are up to about ten half-lives, or 50,000 years in age. For fossils older than that, an isotope with a longer half-life is used. In some fossils, the presence of small amounts of uranium-238, with a half-life of 4.5 billion years, can aid in dating.

Timeline of Earth

- 4.6 billion years ago: formation of Earth
- 3.7 billion years ago: prokaryotes first came into existence
- 2.6 billion years ago: oxygen is believed to be present in the atmosphere
- 2.1 billion years ago: eukaryotic organisms have evolved

- 1.5 billion years ago: multicellular organisms have evolved
- 800 million years ago: the first animals exist
- 500 million years ago: Paleozoic Era
- 260 million years ago: Mesozoic Era
- 65 million years ago: Cenozoic Era
- 10,000 years ago: early humans

The three eras, the Paleozoic, Mesozoic, and Cenozoic, were each characterized by an explosion of different species. Each era was responsible for the formation of a number of different species.

PALEOZOIC: The Paleozoic era was characterized by the colonization of land, with many types of plants appearing, and the diversification of fish and reptile species.

MESOZOIC: The Mesozoic era saw the first flowering plants appearing, as well as many land animals, including the dinosaurs. However, at the end of the Mesozoic era, the extinction of the dinosaurs occurred, likely due to a catastrophic event such as a huge meteorite striking the earth.

CENOZOIC: In the Cenozoic era, many of the animals and plants that we see today started to evolve, including mammals, many different angiosperm plants, and the direct ancestors of humans.

Examples

1. A student is attempting to replicate the Miller-Urey experiment. Which of the following reagents does he *not* need?

   A) ammonia

   B) carbon dioxide

   C) oxygen

   D) water vapor

2. In the Miller-Urey experiment, which attempted to replicate conditions that were existent in early Earth, which of the following compounds was *not* created?

   A) amino acids

   B) methane

   C) lipid precursors

   D) chlorophyll

   Answers: 1. C) 2. D)

THE BASICS OF THE CELL

The CELL is the most basic unit of life; all higher organisms are composed of cells. Most cells range from 20 μm to 100 μm in size, although some can be even larger. Cells were first discovered by

---

⚠

THE BIOLOGICAL HIERARCHY
- atom
- molecule
- organelle
- cell
- tissue
- organ
- organ system
- organism
- population
- community
- ecosystem
- biome
- biosphere

the Englishman **Robert Hooke**, the inventor of the microscope, in the 1600s. However, cell theory truly began to develop when a Dutchman named **Antony van Leeuwenhoek** pioneered new developments in the field of microscopy, allowing scientists to view bacteria, protozoa, and other microorganisms.

Cell Subgroups

Cells are roughly divided into two large subgroups: prokaryotic cells and eukaryotic cells. The primary similarities and differences are listed in Table 9.1. below.

Table 9.1. Prokaryotic and eukaryotic cells

Traits unique to prokaryotic cells	Prokaryotic cells, such as bacteria, are the only types of cells that contain peptidoglycan, a sugar, and an amino acid layer that supports the cell membrane.	Prokaryotic cells do not have a nuclear membrane.	Many prokaryotic cells contain plasmids, which are circular rings of DNA that hold genetic information.
Traits shared by prokaryotic and eukaryotic cells	Both cells have cell membranes and often have cell walls.	Both types of cells contain DNA.	Both can have flagella and ribosomes.
Traits unique to eukaryotic cells	Eukaryotic cells have a nuclear membrane, and DNA is contained within the membrane.	Eukaryotic cells have a Golgi body, which is used for transport of proteins.	Some eukaryotic cells have lysosomes or peroxisomes, which are used in digestion.

Parts of the Cell

Although the cell is the smallest unit of life, there are many small bodies, called **organelles**, that exist in the cell. These organelles are required for the many processes that take place inside a cell.

- **Mitochondria:** The mitochondria are the organelles responsible for making ATP within the cell. A mitochondria has several layers of membranes used to assist the electron transport chain. This pathway uses energy provided by molecules such as glucose or fat (lipid) to generate ATP through the transfer of electrons.
- **Vacuole:** A vacuole is a small body used to transfer materials within and out of the cell. It has a membrane of its own and can carry things such as cell wastes, sugars, or proteins.
- **Nucleus:** The nucleus of a eukaryotic cell contains all of its genetic information in the form of DNA. In the nucleus, DNA replication and transcription occur. In the eukaryotic cell, after transcription, the mRNA is exported out of the nucleus into the cytosol for use.
- **Endoplasmic reticulum:** The ER, for short, is used for translation of mRNA into proteins and

for the transport of proteins out of the cell. The rough endoplasmic reticulum has many ribosomes attached to it, which function as the cell's machinery in transforming RNA into protein. The smooth endoplasmic reticulum is associated with the production of fats and steroid hormones.

- **RIBOSOME:** The ribosome is a small two-protein unit that reads mRNA and, with the assistance of transport proteins, creates an amino acid.

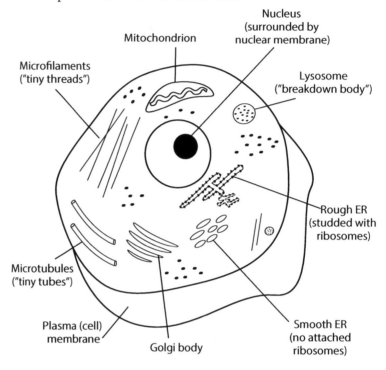

Figure 9.4. Animal cell

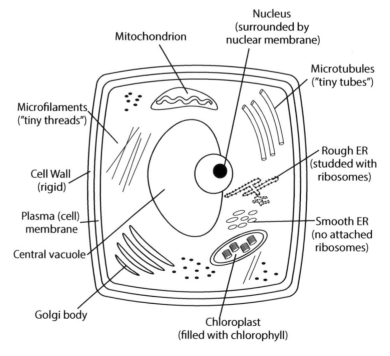

Figure 9.5. Plant cell

Cell Membrane

The **CELL MEMBRANE** is a unique layer that surrounds the cell and performs numerous functions. It's composed of compounds called **PHOSPHOLIPIDS**, which are amphipathic, and consist of an alkane tail and a phospho-group head. The alkane lipid tail is hydrophobic, meaning it will not allow water to pass through, and the phosphate group head is hydrophilic, which allows water to pass through. The arrangement of these molecules forms a bilayer, which has a hydrophobic middle layer. In this manner, the cell is able to control the import and export of various substances into the cell.

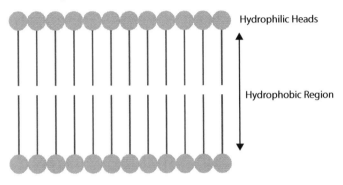

Figure 9.6. Cell membrane bilayer

In addition to the phospholipid bilayer, the cell membrane often includes proteins, which perform a variety of functions. Some proteins are used as receptors, which allow the cell to interact with its surroundings. Others are **TRANSMEMBRANE PROTEINS**, meaning that they cross the entire membrane. These types of proteins are usually channels that allow the transportation of molecules into and out of the cell.

Membrane proteins are also used in cell-to-cell interaction. This includes functions such as cell-cell joining or recognition, in which a cell membrane protein contacts a protein from another cell. A good example of this is the immune response in the human body. Due to the proteins found on the cell membrane of antigens, immune system cells can contact, recognize, and attempt to remove them.

Membrane Transport

A cell needs to be able to both import and export vital substances across the membrane while at the same time preventing harmful substances from entering the cell. Two major classes of transportation allow this process to occur: active transport and passive transport.

ACTIVE TRANSPORT uses ATP to accomplish one of two tasks: it can move a molecule against the concentration gradient (from low concentration to high), or it can be used to import or export a bulky molecule, such as a sugar or a protein, across the cell membrane. Active transport requires the use of proteins and energy in the form of ATP. The ATP produced by the cell binds to the proteins in the cell membrane and is hydrolyzed, producing the energy required to change the conformational structure of the protein. This change in the structure of the protein allows the protein to funnel molecules across the cell membrane.

PASSIVE TRANSPORT does not require energy and allows molecules such as water to passively diffuse across the cell membrane. Facilitated diffusion is a form of passive transport that does not require energy but does require the use of proteins located on the cell membrane. These transport proteins typically have a "channel" running through the core of a protein specific to a certain type of molecule. For example, a transport protein for sodium only allows sodium to flow through the channel.

Tonicity

The balance of water in the cell is one of the most important regulatory mechanisms for the cell. Water enters or exits the cell through a process called OSMOSIS. This movement of water does not usually require energy, and the movement is regulated by a factor called tonicity.

TONICITY is the concentration of solutes in the cell. Solutes can be salt ions, such as sodium or chlorine, or other molecules such as sugar, amino acids, or proteins. The difference in tonicity between the cell and its outside environment governs the transportation of water into and out of the cell. For example, if there is a higher tonicity inside the cell, then water will enter the cell. If there is a higher tonicity outside the cell, the water will leave the cell. This is due to a driving force called the CHEMIOSMOTIC POTENTIAL that attempts to make tonicity equal across a membrane.

There are three terms used to describe a cell's tonicity:

- An ISOTONIC cell has the same concentration of solutes inside and outside the cell. There will be no transport of water in this case.
- A HYPERTONIC cell has a lower concentration of solutes inside than outside the cell. The cell will lose water to the environment and shrivel. This is what happens if a cell is placed into a salty solution.
- A HYPOTONIC cell has a higher concentration of solutes inside than outside the cell. The cell will absorb water from the environment and swell, becoming turgid.

Cell Interactions

With the vast number of cells in living organisms (an estimated 100 trillion in the human body), how do they all interact and talk with one another? Cells are able to communicate with one another through cell signaling, which occurs via chemical signals excreted by the cell. It's also possible to have direct cell-to-cell communication through protein receptors located in the cell membrane. Important signaling molecules include CYCLIC AMP, which is best known for its function in the signaling cascade when epinephrine binds to a cell, and NEUROTRANSMITTERS such as glycine, aspartate, acetylcholine, dopamine, serotonin, and melatonin, among many others.

LOCAL or DIRECT SIGNALING is a signal that occurs between cells that are either right next to each other or within a few cells' distance. This communication can occur by two methods. First, GAP JUNCTIONS exist between the membranes of two cells that can allow signaling molecules to directly enter the cells. Second, the receptors on the membrane can bind with other cells that have membrane receptors to communicate.

The primary chemical used in long-range signaling is called a HORMONE. In humans and animals, hormones are produced by organs and cells in the endocrine system such as the testes, hypothalamus, and pituitary glands. These hormones, once released, can travel throughout the organism through the circulatory system (blood). The hormones can then bind to other cells that have the appropriate receptor and cause a signal to start inside the cell.

One example of long-range signaling in the human body is the production of insulin by the pancreas. Insulin spreads through the body via the blood, and when it binds to an insulin receptor on a cell, the cell begins to take in more glucose. This process is called long-range signaling because insulin is produced by cells in only one location (the pancreas) but is able to affect nearly all other cells in the body.

How do the hormones you studied in human body science act as long range signaling molecules?

An example of long-distance signaling in plants is the production of ethylene, a ripening chemical. It can be present in the air or diffuse through cell walls, and the production of ethylene by one plant can cause a chain reaction that causes nearby plants to also start ripening.

Examples

1. The Golgi body is one of the largest organelles found in the cell and is responsible for:

   A) protein synthesis

   B) intracellular and extracellular transport

   C) replication of DNA

   D) formation of ribosomes

2. In animal cell structure, the cell membrane is composed of a phospholipid bilayer that separates the cell from its surroundings. Which of the following is also present in the cell membrane?

    A) proteins

    B) ATP

    C) mitochondria

    D) vacuoles

3. A student places a cell with a 50 mM intracellular ion content into a solution containing 20 mM ion content. What will happen to the cell?

    A) The cell will shrink.

    B) The cell membrane will become porous.

    C) The cell will expand.

    D) The cell is isotonic, and nothing will occur.

4. Which of the following species cannot travel across a cell membrane without the use of energy?

    A) water

    B) potassium

    C) sodium

    D) glucose

5. Although plant cells and animal cells are roughly the same size, the volume of cytosol, or plasma, inside an animal cell is significantly larger than that seen in a plant cell. What is responsible for this difference?

    A) the presence of chlorophyll in plant cells

    B) the presence of an endoplasmic reticulum in plant cells

    C) the presence of a large storage vacuole in plant cells

    D) the presence of a cell wall in plant cells

6. The endoplasmic reticulum is broken up into the rough ER and the smooth ER. The rough ER is responsible for synthesis of proteins and some polysaccharides. What is the smooth ER responsible for?

    A) metabolism of carbohydrates and synthesis of lipids

    B) DNA replication and transcription

    C) modification of RNA after the transcription process

    D) degradation of residual amino acids and cell waste

7. Which of the following is not a type of cell connection or junction between cells?

A) tight junction

B) gap junction

C) desmosome

D) channel junction

Answers: 1. B) 2. A) 3. C) 4. D) 5. C) 6. D) 7. C)

ENZYMES

Enzymes are an important type of protein crucial for aiding various reactions in the cell. An **ENZYME** is a large protein that acts as a catalyst, which is a substance able to speed up a reaction by reducing the activation energy of a reaction or bringing reactants closer together.

All chemical reactions have something called an activation energy, which is the amount of energy required for a reaction to begin. For some reactions, this barrier is quite high, which is why enzymes are necessary. Enzymes can reduce the activation energy of a reaction through interaction with the bonds in the reactants. Many enzymes have something called an **ACTIVE SITE**, which is an area of the protein with certain functional groups that are able to bind with a reactant. This binding forms a stabilized intermediate that allows the reactant to more easily dissociate or react with another reagent.

Enzymes can also bring reactants closer together. Many reaction rates are limited by the concentration of reactants in the solution. For example, in a cell, the concentration of glucose is usually less than 0.5 mM. This means that the chance for a glucose molecule to contact another reactant is quite low. Enzymes can bind to a glucose molecule and then bind to the other reactant, forcing the reactants close enough together for the reaction to take place.

Some examples of important enzymes include:
- **DNA POLYMERASE**: the enzyme responsible for copying DNA. The enzyme binds to a single strand of DNA and assembles nucleotides to match the strand.
- **PYRUVATE KINASE**: the enzyme responsible for glycolysis, which is the initial breakdown of glucose in the human body (and other organisms).
- **ENDOGLUCANASE:** enzyme responsible for the breakdown of cellulose in fungi and bacteria. This enzyme breaks down the cellulose chain into smaller sugars.

CELLULAR METABOLISM

METABOLISM is the series of chemical reactions that produce the energy and molecules necessary for cellular activity. These processes can best be understood as a pathway. For example, a glucose molecule can be converted into an intermediate (pyruvate) which is then converted into a product (ATP). In a single cell, there are hundreds, if not thousands, of these metabolic pathways that all function to keep the cell alive.

Catabolism versus Anabolism

A major function of metabolism is **CATABOLISM**, which is the breakdown of molecules. A catabolic pathway breaks down a larger molecule into smaller ones, often releasing energy. For example, the process of breaking down fat for energy is catabolic. **ANABOLISM** is the opposite of catabolism: in an anabolic pathway, energy and smaller molecules are used by the cell to build a more complicated molecule. A good example of an anabolic pathway is the synthesis of a protein.

ATP: The Most Important Energy Molecule

ATP is short for **ADENOSINE TRIPHOSPHATE**, which is the most common molecule used for energy. The ATP molecule is formed from ribose, a sugar, and three phosphate groups (a phosphate group is written as Pi). ATP is primarily used for energy but is also used to form adenine.

ATP is able to store energy through the formation of high-energy bonds between the phosphate groups in the "tail" of the molecule. When the last phosphate bond in the group is broken through a hydrolysis reaction, a phosphate molecule is released. This exothermic reaction releases energy that can then be used to drive another cellular reaction. The product of the reaction is a phosphate molecule and a lower-energy adenosine diphosphate (ADP) molecule. When two phosphate groups are removed from ATP in a unit called a pyrophosphate (PPi), the molecule adenosine monophosphate (AMP) is produced.

Under standard state conditions, the conversion of ATP to ADP releases 30.5 kilojoules per mole of energy. In a living cell, however, that value increases to 57 kilojoules per mole.

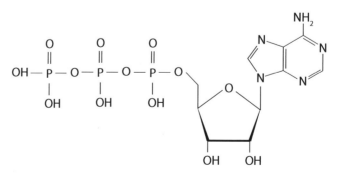

Figure 9.7. Adenosine triphosphate

Because ATP is highly reactive, it's not stored in the body in high quantities. Instead, ADP is recycled and converted to ATP by the addition of a phosphate group. This process of forming ATP is a catabolic pathway that largely occurs in the mitochondria. The energy for this process is stored in lipids, carbohydrates, and proteins.

Respiratory Pathways

ATP is produced through a catabolic process that can take place in one of two ways. The first method, in which oxygen is used, is called an AEROBIC RESPIRATORY PATHWAY. In a respiratory pathway, a food substance, such as glucose or amino acids, is broken down with the use of oxygen, and ATP is produced. The second method (addressed further below) is an anaerobic process called fermentation that does not use oxygen.

The basic overall process of aerobic cellular respiration is shown below:

$$\text{Organic compound + Oxygen} \rightarrow$$
$$\text{Carbon dioxide + Water + Energy}$$

Because the reaction requires oxygen, animals that use aerobic respiration require oxygen to live. For example, humans breathe in oxygen using our lungs for respiration and produce carbon dioxide and water as a byproduct. (Note that while the act of breathing is often called respiration, it's a different process than cellular respiration.)

The energy obtained from the breakdown of organic compounds comes from the bonds of the compound. This energy can vary widely, from about four kilocalories of energy per gram in carbohydrates to nine kilocalories per gram in lipids. The transfer of energy from the bonds breaking in these molecules occurs through an oxidation-reduction reaction, which involves the transfer of electrons from one species to another.

In respiration, there are two primary pathways that are important to know. The first is glycolysis, which breaks down glucose into two molecules of pyruvate and produces a small amount of ATP. The second is the citric acid cycle, which takes pyruvate and produces much more ATP, as well as the by-product carbon dioxide.

Glycolysis

GLYCOLYSIS is the first step in the breakdown of sugars. The overall reaction of glycolysis is as follows:

$$\text{Glucose + 2 [NAD] + 2 [ADP] + 2 [P]}_i \rightarrow$$
$$\text{2 Pyruvate + 2 [NADH] + 2H}^+ \text{ + 2 [ATP] + 2H}_2\text{O}$$

Overall, a glucose molecule is used to produce two pyruvate molecules (which are fed into the citric acid cycle), four energy

Cellular respiration is the conversion of energy into a form that can be used by cells. Physiological respiration is the exchange of oxygen and carbon dioxide between cells and the environment.

molecules (two NADH and two ATP molecules), and two molecules of water.

The conversion of glucose into these products takes place over a ten-step pathway, which involves two phases. The first phase uses energy to break apart the glucose molecule. The second phase then recovers energy in the form of ATP and NADH and results in the production of the pyruvate molecules.

As a result of these steps, there is a production of four molecules of ATP and two molecules of NADH; there is a corresponding use of two molecules of ATP. This results in the net production of two ATP, two NADH, and two pyruvate molecules.

Citric Acid Cycle

The majority of the energy in the glucose molecule has not been released by glycolysis. Under aerobic conditions, the citric acid cycle and electron transport chain, which follow glycolysis, will produce more ATP. The citric acid cycle is also known as the Krebs cycle or the tricarboxylic acid (TCA) cycle.

In eukaryotic cells, the CITRIC ACID CYCLE takes place in the matrix of the mitochondria of the cell. The same reaction can occur in the cytosol/cytoplasm of prokaryotic cells. The citric acid cycle gets its name from the production and reabsorption of citric acid during the process. During the course of the TCA cycle, a molecule of pyruvate derived from glycolysis is transformed into three molecules of CO_2 and two molecules of ATP. The TCA cycle needs to run twice for each molecule of glucose, due to the two molecules of pyruvate obtained from a molecule of glucose. Thus, at the end of two turns of the cycle, four ATP have been produced.

- In each turn of the citric acid cycle, which includes the oxidation of pyruvate (Step 1), four NADH, one $FADH_2$, one GTP, and two CO_2 are produced. NADH and $FADH_2$ are used to feed the electron transport chain, during which the bulk of ATP is produced.

- Each glucose molecule requires two turns of the citric acid cycle, yielding eight NADH, two $FADH_2$, two GTP, and four CO_2. The GTP can be converted to ATP.

- After glycolysis and the citric acid cycle have been completed, there is a net of four ATP, ten NADH, and two $FADH_2$.

The Electron Transport Chain

The ELECTRON TRANSPORT CHAIN is located in the inner membrane of the mitochondria in the eukaryotic cell. In the chain, a series of electron carriers couple the movment of electrons with the transportation of hydrogen ions (H+) across a membrane to create an electrochemical gradient. The source of these electrons is usually NADH and FADH$_2$ generated from the citric acid cycle.

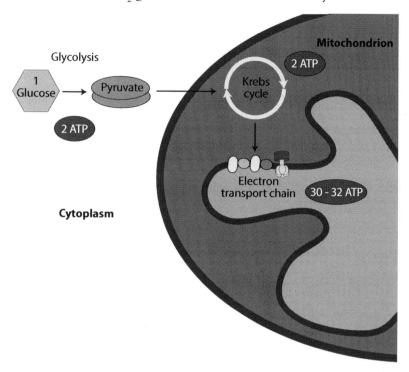

Figure 9.8. Cellular respiration

This electrochemical gradient is used by the molecule ATP synthase to create ATP from ADP: the flow of the hydrogen ions through the ATP synthase molecules provides the energy to generate ATP. Each NADH typically generates 2.5 ATP; each FADH$_2$ generates 1.5 ATP.

At the end of the Electron Transport Chain, 30 to 32 ATP have typically been produced. It's important to note, however, that this number can vary—up to 38 ATP are produced in plants—depending on what type of shuttles are used to transport the electrons from NADH across the membrane. (Plants don't spend an ATP to transport NADH into the mitochondria.)

Fermentation

Fermentation is an alternative process that can generate ATP in anaerobic conditions. Many organisms, such as yeast, can primarily use fermentation, so they do not need oxygen to live. There are two primary forms of fermentation, alcohol and lactic acid fermentation.

ALCOHOL FERMENTATION is probably the most common type of fermentation. After glycolysis occurs, the pyruvate is converted into ethanol. 2-NADH is used in the process, but as acetaldehyde is converted into ethanol, 2-NADH is produced. Yeast are known to ferment sugars, producing ethanol and carbon dioxide, which is the source of the alcohol and carbonation in beer.

LACTIC ACID FERMENTATION differs only slightly from alcohol fermentation. Instead of acetaldehyde being produced, the pyruvate is directly fermented into lactic acid. This takes place in some fungi and bacteria and can occur in the human body. When you use up your excess stores of ATP during strenuous exercise, and the citric acid cycle is unable to provide more ATP quickly, lactic acid fermentation occurs in your muscles to produce additional energy. This is what causes the "burning" feeling during exercise.

✔
What are some other conditions under which cells might need to use anaerobic respiration?

Examples

1. Which of the following processes produces the most ATP during cellular respiration?

   A) glycolysis

   B) citric acid cycle

   C) lactic acid fermentation

   D) the electron transport chain

2. Which of the following statements about the cycling of ATP is NOT true?

   A) $ATP \rightarrow ADP + P_i$

   B) $ATP \rightarrow ADP + PP_i$

   C) $ATP \rightarrow AMP + PP_i$

   D) $ADP \rightarrow AMP + P_i$

3. In the citric acid cycle, how many runs of the cycle are required to process one molecule of glucose?

   A) 1

   B) 2

   C) 3

   D) 4

4. During the process of aerobic respiration, the movement of which of these ions is responsible for the generation of a large amount of ATP?

   A) potassium

   B) hydrogen

   C) sodium

   D) chlorine

5. Which of the following compounds is not produced by the citric acid cycle?

A) NADH

B) GTP

C) ATP

D) FADH

Answers: 1. D) 2. B) 3. B) 4. B) 5. D)

THE CELL CYCLE

The cell cycle is the process cells go through as they live, grow, and divide to produce new cells. The cell cycle can be divided into four primary phases:

1. G1 phase: growth phase one
2. S phase: DNA replication
3. G2 phase: growth phase two
4. Mitotic phase: The cell undergoes mitosis and splits into two cells.

Together, the G1, S, and G2 phases are known as INTERPHASE. During these phases, which usually take up 80 to 90 percent of the total time in a cell cycle, the cell is growing and conducting normal cell functions.

Mitosis

The process of cell division is called MITOSIS. When a cell divides, it needs to make sure that each copy of the cell has a roughly equal amount of the necessary elements, including DNA, proteins, and organelles.

A cell has a lot of DNA: even the smallest human cell contains a copy of the entire human genome. In human cells, this copy of the genome is nearly two meters in length—quite long when you consider that the average cell is only 100 μm in diameter.

In the nucleus, DNA is organized around proteins called HISTONES; together, this protein and DNA complex is known as CHROMATIN. During interphase, chromatin is usually arranged loosely to allow access to DNA. During mitosis, however, DNA is tightly packaged into units called CHROMOSOMES. When DNA has replicated, the chromosome is composed of two CHROMATIDS joined at the CENTROMERE.

The mitotic phase is separated into five substages:

- Prophase: In prophase, the DNA in the cell winds into chromatin, and each pair of duplicated chromosomes becomes joined. The mitotic spindle, which pulls apart the chromosomes later, forms and drifts to each end of the cell.

THE CELL CYCLE
Go **S**ally **G**o, **M**ake **C**hildren!
- **G**rowth phase 1
- **D**NA **s**ynthesis
- **G**rowth phase 2
- **M**itosis
- **C**ytokinesis

- Prometaphase: In this phase, the nuclear membrane, which holds the DNA, dissolves, allowing the chromosomes to come free. The chromosomes now start to attach to microtubules linked to the centrioles.
- Metaphase: The centrioles, with microtubules attached to the chromosomes, are now on opposite sides of the cell. The chromosomes align in the middle of the cell, and the microtubules begin contracting.
- Anaphase: In anaphase, the chromosomes move to separate sides of the cell, and the cell structure begins to lengthen, pulling apart as it goes.
- Telophase: In this last part of the cell cycle, the cell membrane splits, and two new daughter cells are formed. The nucleolus, containing the DNA, reforms.

In this manner, cells are able to reproduce quite quickly. Many bacteria or yeast cells have a total cell cycle time of between twenty and thirty minutes, meaning they are able to double in number in that amount of time. This can lead to rapid proliferation of cells, assuming there is no food shortage. For example, a small colony of 200 *E.coli* cells can rapidly grow to more than 20 million cells in a matter of hours.

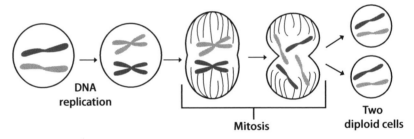

Figure 9.9. Mitosis

Meiosis

A somatic cell contains pairs of homologous chromosomes with one set of chromosomes coming from each parent. For example, humans have 23 pairs of chromosomes, for a total of 46 chromosomes. These cells are described as DIPLOID. Sex cells, on the other hand, have only one set of chromosomes (so, a human sex cell has 23 chromosomes), which is referred to as being HAPLOID. Meiosis is the process by which a diploid cell produces four haploid cells.

There are two consecutive stages of meiosis known as Meiosis I and Meiosis II. These two stages are further broken down into four stages each.

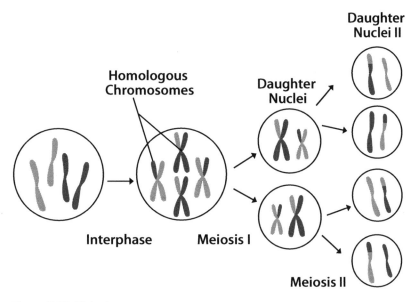

Homologous
Chromosomes

Daughter
Nuclei

Daughter
Nuclei II

Interphase

Meiosis I

Meiosis II

Figure 9.10. Meiosis

Meiosis I

1. Prophase I: In prophase, the chromosomes condense using histone proteins and become paired. The paired chromosomes will connect with each other via structures called the synaptonemal complexes. This is also known as synapsis. An important event called crossing-over occurs at this point. Genetic material is exchanged between sister chromatids, resulting in a random assembly of homologous chromosomes. After this is complete, microtubules attach to the chromosomes and centrioles and begin to align them in the middle of the cell.

2. Metaphase I: Similar to mitosis, the chromosomes align in the middle of the cell and begin to pull apart from one another.

3. Anaphase I: The sister chromatids separate and move toward opposite sides of the cell.

4. Telophase I: The cells separate, and each cell now has one copy each of a homologous chromosome.

Meiosis II

1. Prophase II: In prophase II, a spindle forms and aligns the chromosomes. No crossing-over occurs.

2. Metaphase II: In Metaphase II, the chromosomes again align at the metaphase plate. This time, however, when they are pulled apart, each daughter cell will not have the same copy of a sister chromatid. This is one of the causes of genetic variation among offspring.

3. Anaphase II: As in Anaphase I, the sister chromatids pull apart to opposite ends of the cell.

Mitosis
I Passed **M**y **A**natomy **T**est
- Interphase
- Prophase
- Metaphase
- Anaphase
- Telophase

4. Telophase II: The cell splits apart, resulting in four unique daughter cells.

Table 9.2. Mitosis versus meiosis

EVENT	MITOSIS	MEIOSIS
DNA replication	Occurs in interphase	Occurs in interphase
Number of Divisions	1	2
Synapsis	Does not occur	Occurs in prophase I
Number of Daughter Cells	2	4
Role in Animals	Cell growth and repair	Production of gametes for reproduction

Introduction of Genetic Variation in Meiosis

One of meiosis' most important roles is the introduction of genetic variation. The INDEPENDENT ASSORTMENT of chromosomes in this process gives each gamete a unique subset of genes from the parent. When the haploid gamete combines with another to form a zygote, the result is a genetically unique organism that has a different gene composition than either of the parents.

The process of meiosis also introduces genetic variation during CROSSING OVER, which occurs in prophase I when homologous chromosomes pair along their lengths. Each gene on each chromosome becomes aligned with its sister gene. Then, when crossing over occurs, the DNA sequence is broken and crisscrossed, creating a new chromatid with pieces of each of the original homologous chromosomes.

Finally, meiosis allows for RANDOM FERTILIZATION. Although the gametes produced by each gender are unique, the fact that millions of sperm are produced by the human male (and quite a bit more in other species) means that there are many different possible combinations. For this reason, even though we might cross an animal pair together hundreds of times, it's next to impossible to get two children that have the same genotype (except identical twins).

Apoptosis

APOPTOSIS is an elaborate cellular signaling mechanism that determines when a cell dies. In normal animals and cells, apoptosis is a well-regulated occurrence that prevents the overgrowth of cells. In the process of apoptosis, enzymes and other cellular agents break down materials in the cell until the membrane dissociates and nothing remains.

Apoptosis has been observed in nearly all living organisms and is an essential part of growth and regrowth. For example, humans' skin cells undergo apoptosis every day with dead skin cells shedding off and new skin cells replacing them.

The mechanism of apoptosis is one of the most studied in biology due to its link to many cancers. Cancerous tumors can develop due to a failure of the apoptosis pathway, leading to the growth of cells that never die. (Note, however, that cancer can be caused by many things, not just a lack of apoptosis.)

Examples

1. A scientist takes DNA samples from a cell culture at two different times, each sample having the same cell count. In the first sample, he finds that there is 6.5 pg of DNA, whereas in the second sample he finds that there is 13 pg of DNA. Which stage of the cell cycle is the second sample in?

   A) interphase G1

   B) interphase S

   C) interphase G2

   D) none of the above

2. Which of the following processes will take place in both mitosis and meiosis?

   A) separation of homologous chromatids

   B) formation of new nuclei that each have half the number of chromosomes that exist in the parent nuclei

   C) tightening of chromatin into chromosomes

   D) separation of duplicated sister chromatids

3. Meiosis creates genetic variation in all the following ways except:

   A) creating haploid sex cells that will be randomly fertilized

   B) allowing for the exchange of genetic material between chromosomes

   C) increasing the probability of mutations in the nucleotide sequence of DNA

   D) sorting each set of homologous chromosomes independently

   Answers: 1. C) 2. D) 3. C)

DNA REPLICATION

DNA REPLICATION is the process by which a copy of DNA is created in a cell.

The Basics of DNA

Deoxyribonucleic acid, or DNA, has a double helix structure consisting of two complementary strands of DNA. Each DNA strand has a deoxyribose sugar backbone and one of four nucleic acid bases: guanine, adenine, thymine, and cytosine (G, A, T, and C, respectively). These bases bind to create DNA's two strands: A and T form a pair, and G and C form a pair.

The individual strands of DNA are directional, meaning it matters in which direction the DNA is read. The two ends of a DNA strand are called the 3' end and the 5' end, and these names are included when describing a section of DNA, as shown below:

5'-ATGAATTGCCT-3'

For two complementary strands of DNA, one end starts at 5' and the other starts at 3':

5'-ATGAATTGCCT-3'

3'-TACTTAACGGA-5'

This naming convention is needed to understand the direction of DNA replication and where the enzymes bind during the process.

The Process of Replication

During DNA replication, three steps will occur. The first step is INITIATION, in which an initiator protein binds to regions of DNA known as origin sites. Once the initiation protein has been bound, the DNA polymerase complex will be able to attach. At this point, the DNA will unwind into two separate single strands.

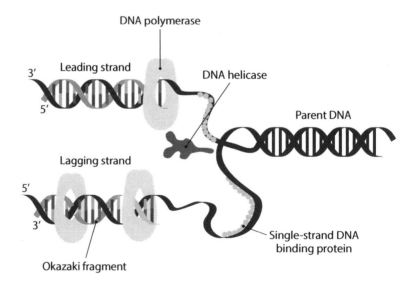

Figure 9.11. DNA replication

During the next step, ELONGATION, new strands of DNA are created. Single-strand binding proteins (SSBs) will bind to each strand of the DNA. Then, DNA polymerase will attach and start replicating the strands by synthesizing a new, complementary strand. DNA polymerase reads the DNA in the 3' to 5' direction, meaning the new strand is synthesized in the 5' to 3' direction. This creates a problem, because the DNA can only be read in the 3' to 5' direction on one strand, known as the LEADING STRAND. The LAGGING STRAND, which runs from 5' to 3', has to be synthesized piece by piece in chunks called OKAZAKI FRAGMENTS. The breaks between these fragments are later filled in by DNA ligase.

The last step in the process of DNA replication is TERMINATION. After DNA polymerase completes the copying process, the replication forks meet and the process is terminated. There is one catch to this: because the DNA polymerase enzyme can never read or replicate the very end of a strand of DNA, every time a full chromosome is replicated, a small part of DNA is lost at the end. This piece of DNA is usually noncoding and is called a TELOMERE. The shortening of the telomeres is the reason why replication can only occur a limited number of times in somatic cells before DNA replication is no longer possible.

Table 9.3. Important enzymes in DNA replication

DNA HELICASE	Unwinds a section of DNA to create a segment with two single strands.
DNA POLYMERASE	DNA polymerase I is responsible for synthesizing Okasaki fragments. DNA polymerase III is responsible for the primary replication of the 5' to 3' strand.
DNA LIGASE	Ligase fixes small breaks in the DNA strand and is used to seal the finished DNA strands.
DNA TELOMERASE	In some cells, DNA telomerase lengthens the telomeres at the end of each strand of DNA, allowing it to be copied additional times.

Polymerase Chain Reaction (PCR)

PCR, which was developed in 1983, is a method used in biology to artificially replicate DNA. This can be useful when looking at the presence or size of a gene or to get enough DNA to insert into a host organism. The PCR method uses primers, DNA polymerase, a template, and a machine called a thermocycler in to replicate the DNA. The basic steps are as follows:

1. Denaturation: The DNA is heated to 90°C to denature it and cause it to form single strands.

2. Annealing: The reaction temperature is set to between 50 and 60°C, which allows the primers to anneal to the template.

3. Elongation: The reaction temperature is set between 70 and 80°C, which is an optimal temperature for a modified DNA polymerase called Taq polymerase. DNA replication occurs.

This set of steps is then repeated up to one hundred times in the thermocycler. As a result, one hundred copies of DNA can result in 1.1×10^{14} copies of DNA in forty cycles.

Examples

1. During DNA replication, the 3' strand and the 5' strand are simultaneously replicated. Which enzyme is responsible for replicating the 3' strand?

   A) DNA polymerase III

   B) DNA ligase

   C) DNA polymerase I

   D) DNA helicase

2. Small sections of DNA are lost during replication because

   A) the sections of DNA between Okazaki fragments cannot be recovered.

   B) DNA polymerase cannot replicate the end of the DNA strand.

   C) DNA cannot be read in the 5' to 3' direction.

   D) the initiator proteins bind to only one strand of DNA.

   Answers: 1. C) 2. B)

TRANSCRIPTION AND TRANSLATION

The processing of information stored in DNA to produce a protein takes place in two stages: transcription and translation. In transcription, an mRNA copy of the DNA is created. In translation, the mRNA strand is read by a ribosome to create an amino acid chain, which is folded into a protein.

Transcription

DNA TRANSCRIPTION is the process of making messenger RNA (mRNA) from a DNA strand. The steps for DNA transcription are similar to that of DNA replication, although different enzymes are used. The DNA strand provides a template for RNA polymerase: the DNA is first unwound, and then RNA polymerase makes a complementary transcript of the DNA sequence.

After the primary transcript has been made, the mRNA is sent to SPLICEOSOMES, which remove the noncoding regions of the RNA called INTRONS. The final RNA product is then available for translation into the actual protein.

Codons

The "message" contained in DNA and RNA is encoded in the nucleotides. Each amino acid is represented by a set of three base pairs in the nucleotide sequence called a CODON. There are 64 possible codons ($4 \times 4 \times 4$), which means many of the 22 amino acids are coded for with more than one codon. There is also a stop codon, which instructs the ribosome to stop processing the mRNA.

You will not need to memorize the codons, but you will need to identify corresponding codons and amino acids from a chart like the one shown here.

Table 9.4. Codons and amino acids

1st base	2nd base								3rd base
	U		C		A		G		
U	UUU	(Phe/F) Phenylaline	UCU	(Ser/S) Serine	UAU	(Tyr/Y) Tyrosine	UGU	(Cys/C) Cysteine	U
	UUC		UCC		UAC		UGC		C
	UUA	(Leu/L) Leucine	UCA		UAA	Stop (Ochre)	UGA	Stop (Opal)	A
	UUG		UCG		UAG	Stop (Amber)	UGG	(Trp/W) Tryptophan	G
C	CUU		CCU	(Pro/P) Proline	CAU	(His/H) Histidine	CGU	(Arg/R) Arginine	U
	CUC		CCC		CAC		CGC		C
	CUA		CCA		CAA	(Gin/Q) Glutamine	CGA		A
	CUG		CCG		CAG		CGG		G
A	AUU	(Ile/I) Isoleucine	ACU	(Thr/T) Threon	AAU	(Asn/N) Asparagine	AGU	(Ser/Serine)	U
	AUC		ACC		AAC		AGC		C
	AUA		ACA		AAA	(Lys/K) Lysine	AGA	(Arg/R) Arginine	A
	AUG	(Met/M) Methionine	ACG		AAG		AGG		G
G	GUU	(Val/V) Valine	GCU	(Ala/A) Alanine	GAU	(Asp/D) Aspartic acid	GGU	(Gly/G) Glycine	U
	GUC		GCC		GAC		GGC		C
	GUA		GCA		GAA	(Glu/E) Glutamic acid	GGA		A
	GUG		GCG		GAG		GGG		G

Translation

The **TRANSLATION** process converts the mRNA transcript into a useable protein. This process occurs in a ribosome, which lines up the mRNA so it can bind to the appropriate tRNA (transfer RNA). Each tRNA includes an amino acid and an anti-codon, which matches to the complementary codon on the mRNA. When the tRNA is in place, the enzyme aminoacyl-tRNA synthetase uses a molecule of ATP to form a bond between the existing amino acid strand and the new amino acid brought in by the tRNA.

The translation process stops when a stop codon is reached in the sequence. These codons activate a protein called a release factor, which binds to the ribosome. The ribosome, which is made of two proteins, will split apart after the release factor binds. This releases the newly formed amino acid chain.

Protein Folding

After the amino acid chain has been produced, the process is still not complete: the amino acid chain needs to be folded into a protein. The polypeptide chain, now able to interact with itself due to hydrogen and disulfide bonds, will start to form a three-dimensional structure. A protein structure has four primary levels of structures:

1. The primary structure is the sequence of amino acids.
2. The secondary structure results from hydrogen bonds within the protein. These bonds create regular patterns called alpha helixes and beta sheets.
3. The tertiary structure is the overall three-dimensional structure and shape of the protein.
4. The quaternary structure results when multiple proteins interact. Not all proteins have a quarternary structure.

Mutations

The DNA or RNA sequence can sometimes undergo a MUTATION, which is a change in the base pair sequence of the DNA or RNA strand. A mutation can be benign or silent, meaning it has no effect, or it can cause a change in the protein structure.

An example of how a single POINT MUTATION can change the entire tertiary structure of a protein is sickle cell anemia. In sickle cell anemia, there is a single change in the base pair sequence from a T to an A. This results in an mRNA transcript codon change from GAA to GUA, which changes the amino acid from glutamate to valine. As a result, the protein is unable to fold properly, and the hemoglobin structure is longer than usual. When present in a red blood cell, this mutation causes the red blood cells to become elongated and sicklelike. As a result, oxygen is not carried as effectively in individuals who have sickle cell anemia.

On the other hand, many mutations will not result in any change in the protein sequence at all. For example, if the sequence CCG mutated to CCA, there would be no change, because the codon produced by both sequences corresponds to the amino acid glycine.

Gene Regulation

An important part of understanding metabolism is learning how genes are activated and deactivated. Studying gene expression and regulation is easier in bacteria due to their simple genomes and the simplicity of extracting their plasmids. Although human gene regulation is becoming more thoroughly understood, the vast complexity of the human metabolism and number of genes makes it difficult to get a full picture of all the interactions.

To understand gene regulation, you need to understand the structure of the genetic code. Proteins are not produced from a single gene; instead, a set of genes, called an OPERON, is required. The operon includes a PROMOTER, which initiates transcription; an OPERATOR, to which an enzyme can bind to regulate transcription; and the protein coding sequence.

Either negative or positive regulation is used to control the operon. In negative regulation, a gene will be expressed unless a

✔——————————

How might mutations in DNA and RNA affect fitness and, consequently, natural selection?

repressor becomes attached. In positive regulation, genes are only expressed when an activator attaches to initiate expression.

In addition to interactions with the operon, the expression of DNA can be controlled by modifications to the chromatin. Because the location of the promoters in the chromatin sequence greatly affects access to the gene, expression can be regulated by managing how tightly bound the chromatin is in the nucleus. Modifications to histone proteins, small amino acid structures found only in eukaryotic cell nuclei, can also inhibit or allow access to DNA.

Lastly, gene expression can be controlled when DNA is methylated at the cytosine group. The methylation of DNA will prevent a DNA polymerase or RNA polymerase enzyme from attaching to the DNA, in effect preventing transcription.

Examples

1. A researcher has discovered a mutation in a sequence of mRNA, which changes a codon from AUG to AAG. What effect will this have on the sequence?

   A) There will be no effect.

   B) The codon sequence will start being translated at a different location than before.

   C) The codon sequence will stop being translated at a different location than before.

   D) The protein will no longer fold at all due to the mismatched codon.

2. Which of the following DNA sequences coding for an amino acid sequence does *not* include a stop codon?

   A) TTG-GTC-TAA-AAT

   B) TTT-GGC-AGA-CTC

   C) GTA-AUG-TAG-AGC

   D) TTC-CAT-CAC-TGA

3. Which of the following removes introns from mRNA?

   A) an operon

   B) an anti-codon

   C) a ribosome

   D) a spliceosome

4. Histone proteins can be found in which of these locations?

   A) eukaryotic cell nucleus

   B) prokaryotic cell nucleus

   C) mitochondria

   D) all the above

5. Which of the following is not a method by which DNA expression can be controlled?

A) operon

B) methylation

C) promotion

D) sulfonation

Answers: 1. B) 2. B) 3. D) 4. A) 5. D)

GENETICS

GENETICS is the study of genes and how they are passed down to offspring. Before the discovery of genes, there were many theories about how traits are passed to offspring. One of the dominant theories in the 19th century was blending inheritance, which stated that the genetic material from the parents would mix to form that of the children in the same way that two colors might mix.

The idea was eventually displaced by the current theory, which is based on the concept of a **GENE**, which is a region of DNA that codes for a specific protein. Multiple versions of the same gene, called **ALLELES**, account for variation in a population.

If an organism is described as true-breeding for a specific trait, it's homozygous for that trait and will pass it on to its offspring.

During sexual reproduction, offspring receive a single copy of every gene from each parent. These two genes may be identical, making the individual **HOMOZYGOUS**, or they may be different, making the individual **HETEROZYGOUS** for that gene. In a heterozygous individual, the genes don't blend; instead they act separately, with one often being completely or partially suppressed.

Mendel's Laws

The idea that individual genes are passed down from parents to their children was conceived by **GREGOR MENDEL**. Mendel used various plants to test his ideas, but his best-known work is with pea plants.

Mendel became an Augustinian monk at the age of 21. He studied briefly at the University of Vienna and after returning to the monastery, started work on breeding plants. During the course of his work, he discovered that the plants had heritable features, meaning features that were passed from parent to offspring. Because of the short generation time of peas, Mendel started working on identifying the traits that could be passed on in the pea plant. He tracked two characteristics: pea flower color and pea shape. From this, he found that the traits were independent of one another, meaning that the pea's flower color in no way affected the pea shape.

During the course of his work, Mendel came up with three laws to describe genetic inheritance: the laws of segregation, independent assortment, and dominance. The **LAW OF SEGREGATION** states that genes come in allele pairs (if the organism is diploid, which most are) and that each parent can only pass a single allele down to its child. Thus, for a pair of alleles in a gene, one comes from the father and one comes from the mother in sexual reproduction. The law of segregation also states that the alleles must separate during the course of meiosis so that only one is given to each gamete.

The **LAW OF INDEPENDENT ASSORTMENT** states that genes responsible for different traits are passed on independently. Thus, there is not necessarily a correlation between two genes. For example, if a mother is tall and has brown hair, she might pass on her genes for tallness to her child but perhaps not the ones for brown hair. This law can be seen in the use of the Punnett square, in which gene alleles are separated to determine inheritance.

Lastly, the **LAW OF DOMINANCE** states that some alleles are dominant and some are recessive. Dominant alleles will mask the behavior of recessive ones. For example in a rose, red might be dominant and white recessive. Thus, if a homozygous red rose mates with a homozygous white rose, all of their offspring will be red. Although the white gene allele will be present, it will not be expressed.

Punnett Square

A **PUNNETT SQUARE** is a table-based diagram that can be used to predict the offspring outcome from the mating of a set of parents; it was developed by Reginald Punnett. In the square, the alleles from each parent (the P generation) are placed on the X and Y axes of the square, and the boxes are then filled in to represent the possible offspring gene combinations (F_1 for the first generation). Note that dominant genes are described with capital letters and recessive genes with lowercase letters.

Examples

1. Potatoes can be either round or oval. The dominant gene is oval. A heterozygous oval potato plant (Oo) is mated with a homozygous round potato plant (oo). What will be the distribution of this trait in the first generation of offspring?

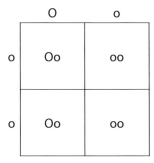

In the Punnett Square above, we have placed the parents on each side of the box. The heterozygous parent is seen on the X-axis as Oo, and the homozygous is on the Y-axis as oo. By separating the alleles (the law of segregation)

and then recombining the possible combinations from the parents, we can predict what the genotype, and thus phenotype, of the offspring will be. **In this case, half the offspring will be round (oo), and the other half will be oval (Oo).**

2. In the same plant described in problem #1, purple flowers are dominant, and pink flowers are recessive. If an OoPP parent is crossed with an ooPp parent, what would the resulting offspring look like?

	OP	OP	oP	oP
oP	OoPP	OoPP	ooPP	ooPP
oP	OoPP	OoPP	ooPP	ooPP
op	OoPp	OoPp	ooPp	ooPp
op	OoPp	OoPp	ooPp	ooPp

In this case, we separate out the alleles so that each one is matched with the other allele in all the possible combinations:

The four possible combinations for OoPP are OP, OP, oP, and oP. The four combinations for ooPp are oP, oP, op, and op. Filling in the squares gives all possible outcomes for the offpsring.

Half will be oval and purple, and half will be round and purple.

Phenotype versus Genotype

A **PHENOTYPE** is an organism's observable characteristics, such as height, eye color, skin color, and hair color. **GENOTYPE** is an organism's genetic code. Although the genotype of two different people might be different, they could have the same phenotype, depending on which alleles are dominant or recessive. For example, the two types of roses Rr and RR are both red, meaning they have the same phenotype. However, they have a different genotype, with one rose type being heterozygous and the other being homozygous.

Individuals with the same genotype may also have different phenotypes. For example, the environment can have a large effect on phenotypic traits. Someone with light brown skin will tan in the sunlight, for instance, and a malnourished child may grow up to be shorter than expected.

Examples

1. In a type of plant newly discovered in South America, the seed color is controlled by the gene R. In these plants, those having the dominant allele R have bright-red seeds, and those that have the homozygous recessive allele pair rr have pale-pink seeds. In the first generation, a scientist crosses a true-breeding RR plant with a recessive rr plant. The F1 plant is then crossed with itself, resulting in the F2 generation. In the F2 generation, what percentage of the plants will have bright-red seeds?

    A) 25%

    B) 50%

    C) 75%

    D) 100%

2. If a recessive trait is linked to the X-chromosome, it will most likely be seen in:

    A) males

    B) females

    C) both genders

    D) neither gender

3. A sex-linked trait primarily seen in males but sometimes seen in females is passed along on the:

    A) 22nd chromosome

    B) 18th chromosome

    C) X chromosome

    D) Y chromosome

4. Below are four statements regarding mutations. Which of these statements are true?

    > I.   Mutations are always harmful to the individual or species.
    >
    > II. Mutations can be beneficial.
    >
    > III. Mutations can occur randomly, without the aid of radiation or chemicals.
    >
    > IV. Mutations play an important role in evolution.

    A) I and II are true.

    B) Only II is true.

    C) II and III are true.

    D) II, III, and IV are true.

    Answers: 1. C) 2. A) 3. C) 4. D)

EVOLUTION

Evolution is best defined as descent from previous species with modification. That is, each generation changes slightly from the last until the difference is so great that a new species is formed. Evolution is why there is a diversity of life on Earth; it's the reason there are different species of animals and plants. This was what Charles Darwin meant by the title of his book *On the Origin of Species*.

Charles Darwin

CHARLES DARWIN was an Englishman with an intense interest in nature. Darwin enrolled at several universities, including Cambridge. He became interested in botany there and had a chance to accompany the HMS *Beagle* on a voyage around the world. It was during this trip that he came across numerous species and started to form the theory of evolution.

Upon his return, Darwin published a book called *On the Origin of Species*. It's worth noting that Darwin did not coin the term evolution at this time but rather called it "descent with modification." He stated that all organisms were inter-related and could be traced to a distant ancestor. He was also one of the first to describe evolution as a tree, with different species branching off at different parts of the "tree."

Based on his observations, Darwin proposed the theory of NATURAL SELECTION. Charles Darwin noticed that birds on the Galapagos Islands, while mostly similar, had unique beak shapes that allowed them to eat particular foods. Some beaks were small, some were wide and blunt, and some were needlelike. Darwin hypothesized that these different beak shapes arose due to a selection process.

A selection process, whether natural or artificial, refers to the removal of inferior organisms that cannot survive in an environment. For example, farmers use artificial selection when they plant only seeds from plants that have produced a large yield in the past. This practice creates a field of plants that only produces large yields. Natural selection works in a similar fashion, except it's the conditions in nature that determine whether a particular individual will thrive and reproduce.

Darwin proposed the theory of natural selection based on specific observations. These were:

1. The members of a population of species have varied traits. For example, one species of monkey might have fur color varying from white to brown.

2. All species produce excess offspring. For example, if left uncontrolled, rabbit populations will more than double

Natural selection acts on an organism's phenotype, not its genotype. Only alleles that affect an organism's fitness will be selected for or against.

in size every year. Secondly, not all offspring are able to survive.

3. The traits in an individual of a population that give it a higher chance of surviving also allow it to produce more offspring.

4. As a result, "more fit" individuals are more likely to pass on their traits; this will result in a change in the species over time.

This difference in reproduction is the basis of natural selection. Essentially, the traits of an individual determine whether it's "selected" by the environment. Individuals with superior traits are more likely to survive and reproduce and thus pass on their genes. Individuals with inferior traits will not survive, and their genes will be lost. Over many generations, natural selection will lead to a species being driven toward a certain set of characteristics, which is how evolution occurs.

Speciation

SPECIATION is the process by which organisms evolve and become new species. A **SPECIES** is generally defined as a group of organisms in which two hybrids are able to produce fertile offspring. However, there is often debate and uncertainty about how species are defined and identified.

Speciation can occur under a number of different conditions. In **ALLOPATRIC SPECIATION**, a population becomes geographically separated, and the separated populations evolve to the point that they can no longer interbreed. In **PERAPATRIC EVOLUTION**, a new species is formed when a small portion of the population becomes isolated. **PARAPATRIC SPECIATION** occurs when populations are mostly separated but share a small area of overlap; selection pressures prevent interbreeding and eventually result in the development of new species.

Patterns of Evolution

Evolution can follow a number of different patterns depending on environmental factors. In **DIVERGENT EVOLUTION**, two species descended from the same ancestor develop different traits. In **CONVERGENT EVOLUTION**, two unrelated species develop similar traits, usually to meet the same basic need. For example, flight developed independently in a number of groups of organisms, including insects, birds, and bats. Finally, **PARALLEL EVOLUTION** occurs when two related species independently develop the same traits.

Case Study: Drug-Resistant Bacteria

Antibiotics and other chemicals are commonly used to treat infections. This has, over the course of the last twenty to thirty years, acted as a selection pressure on bacteria.

Staphylococcus aureus is a dangerous bacteria that resides on the skin of many people. It's ordinarily harmless, but if the individual has a weakened immune system, or the bacteria are allowed to enter the body in large amounts, *S. aureus* will eat away at the flesh of that person. This is the reason it's called the flesh-eating disease, or necrotizing fasciitis.

The best drug to treat *S. aureus* infections is methicillin, which was developed in 1959. However, just several years after the use of methicillin was introduced, methicillin-resistant *S. aureus* bacteria (called MRSA) began to appear. How did this happen?

The use of antibiotics will usually kill 99.9 percent of the bacteria, but some bacteria will manage to survive, through either genetic resistance or an insufficient dose. These bacteria have been artificially selected and will reproduce. Over time, as more and more people use the antibiotic, the small proportion of bacteria able to survive will thrive and multiply, eventually creating a population of methicillin-resistant bacteria.

Today, more than half of *S. aureus* infections are methicillin-resistant, causing doctors to have to look elsewhere for an effective method of treatment. This is a present-day study of evolution in progress.

Examples

1. For genetic drift to occur, in which a gene allele drops out of the population, which of the following must be true of the population?

   A) The population is large.

   B) The population is small.

   C) The population has many food sources.

   D) The population is able to survive in many niches.

2. Charles Darwin based his theory of natural selection on a number of logical observations and premises. Which of the following is *not* one of them?

   A) Organisms have many more offspring that the environment could be expected to support.

   B) Many species are able to mutate or alter their genes to adapt to the environment.

   C) Organisms are unique, and their offspring inherit traits from their parents.

   D) In a given environment, populations of species typically remain about the same throughout time.

3. Which of the following is an example of convergent evolution?

A) The evolution of tails in both whales and sharks

B) The evolution of pine cones in both southern pine and spruce trees

C) The evolution of pincers in both ants and termites

D) The evolution of feathers in both the sparrow and finch

Answers: 1. B) 2. B) 3. A)

PHYLOGENY AND SPECIES CLASSIFICATION

PHYLOGENY is the understanding of how species evolved through time. The study of phylogeny creates charts called phylogeny trees, which show the inter-relatedness of different species. For example, humans are quite closely related to many mammals, with our DNA being 90 percent similar to that of cats.

The Phylogenetic Tree

A PHYLOGENETIC TREE, shown in the diagram below, shows how groups of organisms are related to each other. The branches represent the relative point in time when each group of species, or family, diversified. For example, we can say according to the tree below that animals and fungi are more closely related than animals and flagellates, due to their relative distances on the tree.

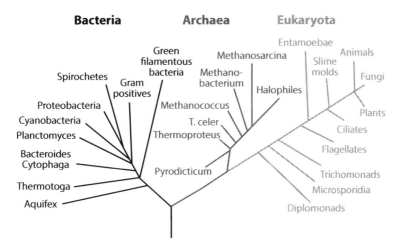

Figure 9.12. Phylogenetic tree

This type of diagram is useful for showing relationships in genetics but not necessarily actual physical similarity. It should be easy to see that although animals and fungi might share their genotype, they definitely have almost no similar phenotypic characteristics.

The diagram is also relative in nature, meaning that no absolute geologic time scale can be assigned to the branches. We know from the fossil record and DNA evidence which species are more closely related than others are; this allows us to construct the tree. However, other than a rough estimation on when the branching actually occurred, we cannot put exact numbers on the ages of the species.

Taxonomy

TAXONOMY is the science of grouping species into correct taxa, or related groups. Groups descend in nature of similarity. For example, the kingdom group is less similar than the genus group. The current classification of species is:

- domain
- kingdom
- phylum
- class
- order
- family
- genus
- species

According to this organization, two species from the same phylum are more related than two species from the same order. A good mnemonic to remember this organization scheme is: *Dear King Phillip Cried Out For Good Soup!*

Morphological Similarities Between Species

Many organisms share phenotypic similarities; these may or may not be due to shared ancestry. A **HOMOLOGOUS STRUCTURE** is a phenotype structure that is similar due to genetic relatedness, as in one species evolved from another, or two species both evolved from a common ancestor. A good example of a homologous structure is the thumb. In the fossil record and from present day analysis, the thumb bone is seen in nearly all mammalian species. This is because they were all derived from a common ancestor.

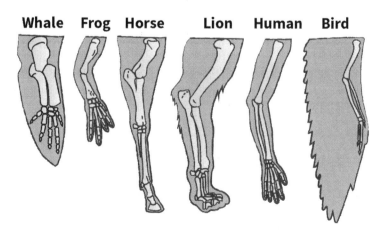

Figure 9.13. Homologous structures

> Organisms are identified by their genus and species names. For example, humans are *Homo sapiens* and grizzly bears are *Ursus arctos*.

An **ANALOGOUS STRUCTURE** is one not based on DNA similarity or shared ancestry. A good example of an analogous structure is the comparison between a bird wing and a bat wing. Upon looking at the bone structure, we see some similarities, but the two species have a completely different genetic history, having evolved independently by convergent evolution. As a result, it would be incorrect to conclude that birds and bats are closely related.

Examples

1. Which of the following is an example of an analogous structure?

   A) the fact that salmon and tuna both have gills

   B) the ability of multiple types of plants to grow in a rain forest

   C) the ability of both birds and butterflies to fly

   D) the many different species of elephants that exist

2. Which two species will likely share the greatest percentage of their genomes?

   A) those in the same family

   B) those in the same order

   C) those in the same kingdom

   D) those in the same class

3. A student proposes the idea that the modern day sparrow is a descent of the genus Archaeopteryx, an ancient bird. Which of the following findings would help support this hypothesis?

   A) The finding that Archaeopteryx and sparrows had the same diet.

   B) The finding that Archaeopteryx and sparrows lived in the same region.

   C) The finding that Archaeopteryx and sparrows were both able to fly.

   D) The finding that Archaeopteryx and sparrows share bone structure homology.

   Answers: 1. C) 2. A) 3. D)

BACTERIA

BACTERIA and **ARCHAEA** are a large subset of species that are mostly unicellular. Unlike the kingdoms Plantae and Animalia, nearly all of these species are single-celled prokaryotes, which are unicellular organisms that are quite small, usually less than 10 μm in diameter. (The smallest eukaryotic cells are usually larger than 10μm.)

Like plants, prokaryotes have a cell wall. However, unlike plants, the cell wall structural material is peptidoglycan, which is a polymer created by a mixture of cross-linked proteins and sugar. The cell wall supporting material in plants is called cellulose, which is made entirely from glucose, a sugar. The presence of the cell wall allows prokaryotes to be separated into two classes: gram-positive and gram-negative.

GRAM-POSITIVE bacteria contain peptidoglycan in their cell walls, and they turn purple-red when dyed with gram stain (a solution of crystal violet and iodine). Archaea cell walls contain a cross-linked polysaccharide but do not have any peptidoglycan. As a result, they are GRAM-NEGATIVE.

As prokaryotes, none of the bacteria or Archaea species contain nuclear membranes. All the DNA is freely arranged within the cytosol in a structure called the NUCLEOID. In addition to the chromosomal DNA contained inside the nucleoid, the cells also contain plasmids, which are ring-shaped DNA sequences that contain an active gene.

Example

Which of the following is a key difference between organisms in the domains Archaea and Bacteria?

A) Archaea cells do not contain peptidoglycan in their cell wall.

B) Archaea cells do not contain phospholipids in their cell membrane.

C) Archaea cells do not use RNA.

D) Archaea cells do not use ribosomes to produce amino acid chains.

Answer: A)

VIRUSES

A VIRUS is a special form of organism designed to be infectious. Its name is derived from the Latin word for poison. Viruses are interesting organisms that do not contain organelles or other structures usually found in living creatures. For this reason, the question of whether viruses are alive has been a subject of serious debate.

What is the Definition of Life?

Scientists debate many different definitions of life, but in general, there is agreement on the following characteristics:

1. Growth: A living organism must be able to grow, usually by converting some external material into its own mass.

2. Stimulus response: A living organism must be able to react to stimuli in its environment, such as light, other organisms, or toxins.

3. Energy use: A living organism must be able to use energy and convert energy into different forms, either as heat or as a stored energy compound.

4. Homeostasis: A living organism must be able to maintain its own organism conditions within a certain level.

5. Reproduction: Living organisms must be able to reproduce.

6. Mutation: The genetic code of living organisms must be able to change between generations.

7. Autonomous motion: Living organisms must be able to move, even if it's just a short distance.

Under these requirements, the majority of scientists do not consider viruses to be alive. This is because they do not have a metabolism of their own and cannot reproduce by themselves: they require a host.

Virus Structure and Life Cycle

A virus' structure is simple: it consists of a protein coat, known as a CAPSID, which surrounds a nucleic acid, which can be either DNA or RNA. The capsid is a tough layer of protein that is resistant to heat, moisture, and other environmental variables. It protects the genetic information inside the virus, and usually has some sort of receptor or protein that allows the virus to inject its DNA to a host organism.

Viruses can infect many types of cells, including animal somatic cells, plant cells, and bacteria. Because the capsid of a virus reacts with particular receptors on the cell's membrane, viruses usually require a specific type of host cell. For example, HIV infects human immune cells, and the cauliflower mosaic virus mostly infects members of the Brassicaceae family. A virus that infects bacteria is called a BACTERIOPHAGE.

Viruses are obligate parasites (meaning they cannot complete their life cycle outside a host) and inject their DNA or RNA into other organisms to reproduce. In most cases, a virus will enter a host and use the host cell's energy and resources to reproduce, and then lyse the host cell, releasing more virus cells. This is known as the LYTIC CYCLE. The lytic cycle of a typical virus is detailed below:

1. Attachment: the virus bonds to the host cell using proteins on the capsid.

2. Entry: the proteins inject DNA into the host cell.

3. Synthesis and reproduction: the DNA is replicated using the host cell's machinery.

4. Assembly: new viruses are assembled from the reproduced parts in the cell.

5. Lysis and release: the virus destroys the host cell, lysing the cell membrane and releasing the newly created virus cells.

Some viruses contain RNA genomes rather than DNA. Among these viruses is the human immunodeficiency virus, or HIV. These viruses inject RNA, and the RNA can be translated into proteins or enzymes directly after infection. For this method of transmission to work, the virus must carry some RNA reverse transcriptase. This protein is able to translate RNA back into DNA, so that the host organism can utilize it.

Although viruses are not "alive" per se, they are capable of evolving very quickly due to their short life cycle and their ability to use a host genome. Many viruses are capable of assimilating other pieces of DNA into their own genome, often creating a new virus. For example, what people refer to as influenza, or the flu, is actually a group of viruses that continue to change and evolve; this is why new vaccines are introduced each year.

Vaccines contain harmless versions of infectious agents that activate the body's immune system without causing illness.

Examples

1. Viruses and prokaryotes both differ from eukaryotes in that they do not have a nuclear membrane. What is one manner in which viruses are distinguished from prokaryotes?

   A) Viruses contain RNA, and prokaryotes do not.

   B) Prokaryotes have ribosomes, whereas viruses do not.

   C) Prokaryotes can form a protein shell, whereas viruses cannot.

   D) Viruses are harmful to humans, whereas prokaryotes are not.

2. Which of the following statements about viruses is not true?

   A) Viruses are only able to reproduce after infecting a host cell.

   B) Because they are obligate parasites, viruses do not evolve.

   C) Some viruses contain RNA instead of DNA inside their capsid.

   D) Bacteriophages are viruses that infect bacteria.

   Answers: 1. B) 2. B)

PLANTS

Plants make up the largest percentage of organic matter on the planet. Without plants, which are autotrophs, the majority of other living organisms could not exist. Plants act as a necessary source of both oxygen and nutrients for the organisms that consume them.

A plant is composed of three basic units: the roots, stems, and leaves. The **ROOTS** of plants usually reside in the soil and are responsible for absorbing water and minerals from the soil. There are two types of roots: a taproot, which is a central, thick root (think of a carrot), and lateral roots, which are smaller roots that branch out from the main root. Some root tubers, such as potatoes and carrots, are able to elongate and store significant amounts of nutrients.

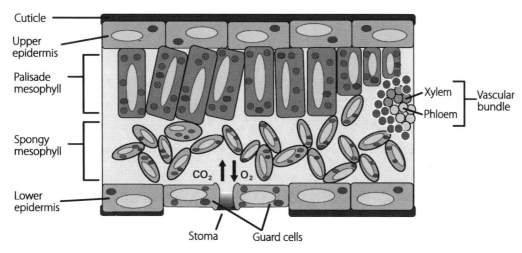

Figure 9.14. Structure of a leaf

The **STEM** of the plant provides structural stability and also moves water and nutrients from the roots to the other parts of the plant. The **LEAVES** of the plant are high in surface area and contain the majority of the plant's chlorophyll. They absorb sunlight and perform photosynthesis.

Plants are composed of three main types of cells:

- The **PARENCHYMA** cells have thin, flexible cell walls and have a large vacuole in the middle of the cell used for storage. These types of cells perform many functions, including many metabolic reactions. Root tissue, the interior of leaves, and most fruit tissue is made from parenchyma cells.
- The **COLLENCHYMA** cells are seen in parts of the stem and support the plant as it's growing. These cells remain flexible even as they get older.
- The **SCLERENCHYMA** cells are the most rigid of the cells. These cell types contain high amounts of lignin and cellulose in the secondary cell wall, making it an indigestible structural component of the plant.

The Vascular Tissue System

VASCULAR TISSUE is able to transport sugar and water to other parts of the plant. Plants contain two types of vascular tissue: xylem and phloem. **XYLEM** is commonly known as woody tissue and is very stiff. It consists of a series of hollow cell structures that move water from the roots up to the leaves or flowers. **PHLOEM** is a living tissue near the outside of the stem of the plant that transports sugars.

In plants, the movement of water from the roots to the top of the plant is an important and difficult process. Diffusion is effective over short distances, but to move water to the top of a twenty-meter tall tree, additional forces are needed. In plants, the bulk flow of water from the roots is regulated by several mechanisms. These include the capillary action of water moving up the xylem, the transpiration of water from the leaves at the top of the tree, osmotic pressure in the roots, and active transport in the plant.

Plant Growth

Plant growth takes place at **MERISTEMS**, which are groups of undifferentiated, quickly dividing cells. The roots grow starting at the **ROOT APICAL MERISTEM**, where new root cells are created and capped by a harder layer of tissue known as the **ROOT CAP**. Shoot growth occurs at the **SHOOT APICAL MERISTEM**, and flowers grow from **FLORAL MERISTEMS**.

The growth at these meristems elongates the plants and is known as **PRIMARY GROWTH**. Plant stems will also expand outward in a process called **SECONDARY GROWTH**. The majority of this growth occurs in the **CAMBIUM**, a layer of high growth cells on the outer edge of the stem. These cells increase the diameter of the stem and create the wood and bark in woody plants.

Leaves

The **EPIDERMIS** is the outer layer of leaf cells and is surrounded by the **CUTICLE**, a waxy layer that aids the plant in retaining moisture and preventing evaporation from the leaf. The epidermis also contains structures called **STOMATA** (singular: stoma). These openings in the leaf structure allow carbon dioxide and oxygen to be exchanged for photosynthesis.

The **MESOPHYLL** consists of parenchyma cells that contain large amounts of chlorophyll and are specialized for photosynthesis. In the middle of the leaf are the two types of mesophyll: the palisade and spongy mesophyll. The **PALISADE MESOPHYLL** has layers of parallel cells and is located on the upper portion of the leaf. The **SPONGY MESOPHYLL** is a collection of loosely organized cells that have many spaces in which carbon dioxide and oxygen are able to penetrate.

Plant Reproduction

Plants have a wide variety of reproductive strategies and life cycles. Some plants are able to reproduce asexually by producing genetically identical clones, but the majority of plants reproduce sexually. These plants produce seeds from female and male gametes, known respectively as eggs and pollen.

Seed-producing plants are broken down into two groups: gymnosperms and angiosperms. **GYMNOSPERMS**, which include conifers, Ginkgos, and cycads, produce "naked" seeds that grow in cones or on the surface of leaves. **ANGIOSPERMS**, or flowering plants, produce seeds that are surrounded by a fruit that provides protection and can help with seed dispersal.

The reproductive organs of angiosperms are contained in flowers. The **PETALS** of the flowers are usually colorful appendages that attract pollinators and protect the reproductive organs. At the base of the flower are the **SEPALS,** protective leaflike structures. The male and/ or female reproductive organs are contained within the petals.

The female organs include the **OVARY**, which contains egg-producing ovules. The **STYLE** is a long, slender stalk that connects the ovary to the **STIGMA**, which collects pollen. Together the ovary, style, and stigma are called the **PISTOL** (and sometimes the carpel).

The male organs include the **ANTHER**, which contains the pollen, and the **FILAMENT**, which holds the anther. Together, the anther and filament compose the **STAMEN**. The male gametophytes are known as **POLLEN** and are housed inside the anther. Inside each anther are microsporangia, which contain the cells that undergo meiosis to produce pollen.

Flowers often have colors, scents, or shapes that have evolved to attract a specific pollinator. For example, bees can see ultraviolet (UV) light, so many flowers have UV patterns in their petals that humans cannot see.

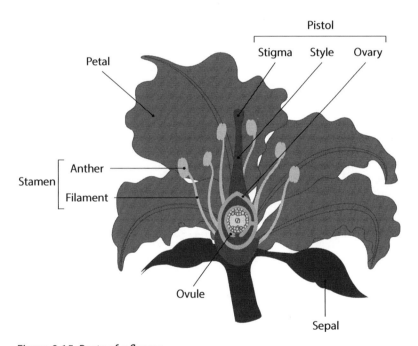

Figure 9.15. Parts of a flower

POLLINATION occurs when there is a transfer of pollen from the anther of one flower to the ovaries of another flower. Pollination can occur through many means, including wind, water, or animals.

After pollination occurs, a pollen tube starts to grow down from the stigma to the ovaries. Upon reaching the ovaries, the pollen tube will discharge two sperm cells into the embryo sac. One sperm cell will be able to fertilize the egg, creating the zygote. The other sperm is involved in the formation of the ENDOSPERM, which grows into a nutritious layer that surrounds the zygote. Examples of the endosperm include the grain of wheat and the white meat of a coconut.

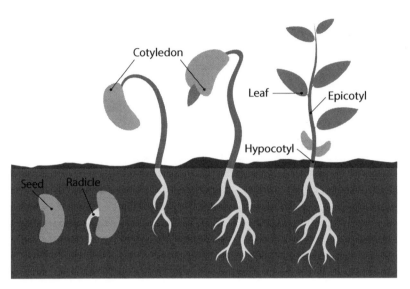

Figure 9.16. Seed germination

The embryo develops a short while after the endosperm. After it has matured, the seed will have several parts, including the epicotyl, the hypocotyl, the radicle, and the cotyledon.

Examples

1. Stomata allow for the passage of all the following except

   A) carbohydrates

   B) carbon dioxide

   C) oxygen

   D) water

2. In plants, the formation of a seed includes the creation of an endosperm. Which of the following is not true about the endosperm?

   A) It can have a triploid (3n) chromosome number.

   B) The endosperm in many plants contains fats and nutrients for the growing embryo.

   C) The endosperm is created solely from maternal tissue.

   D) The endosperm begins formation after a pollen grain contacts the maternal cell.

3. Which of the following phenomena is not a mechanism by which trees move water from the roots to the leaves?

   A) transpiration

   B) osmotic pressure

   C) capillary action

   D) sublimation

4. Both gymnosperms and angiosperms produce which of the following?

   A) seeds

   B) fruits

   C) petals

   D) endosperm

   Answers: 1. A) 2. C) 3. D) 4. A)

PHOTOSYNTHESIS

DURING PHOTOSYNTHESIS, light energy is absorbed by plants and converted via photosynthesis into sugars. This process is the energy source for nearly all the biomass on Earth. The term is derived from *photo*, meaning light, and *synthesis*, meaning construction. Organisms that are able to produce their own sustenance in this manner are known as AUTOTROPHS.

Photosynthesis takes place in CHLOROPLASTS, which are small organelles in plant tissue that contain CHLOROPHYLL, a green pigment that allows plants to capture the energy from light. Chloroplasts are contained inside the mesophyll of the plant leaf (the section sandwiched between the top and bottom layers of the leaf). Inside the chloroplast are two primary structures: the STROMA, which is the envelope of the chloroplast, and the THYLAKOIDS, which are stacks of sacs that contain the chlorophyll.

The Chemistry of Photosynthesis

The overall chemical reaction of photosynthesis is as follows:

$$6\ CO_2 + 6\ H_2O + \text{Light energy} \rightarrow C_6H_{12}O_6\ \text{(Glucose)} + 6\ O_2$$

The photosynthesis reaction uses carbon dioxide and water, in addition to energy from sunlight, to produce glucose and oxygen. In this reaction, the carbon from carbon dioxide ends up in the glucose molecule. Half the oxygen from carbon dioxide ends up in the glucose, and the other half ends up in the produced water. All the oxygen from the water molecules on the reactant side of the equation ends up in the oxygen produced.

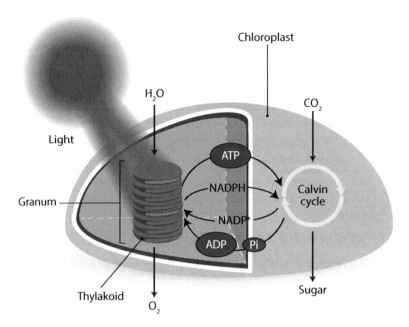

Figure 9.17. Photosynthesis

Similar to aerobic respiration, photosynthesis is an oxidation-reduction process and relies on the transfer of electrons to be effective. These reactions take place in two phases. The first is the light reactions, in which the energy from the sun is captured and translated into high-energy electrons. The second is in the Calvin cycle, where this energy is used in conjunction with carbon dioxide and water to produce a glucose molecule.

Light Reactions

The **LIGHT REACTIONS** occur in the chloroplast. They take light from the sun, which is best absorbed by chlorophyll between the wavelengths of 420 nanometers to 460 nanometers, and convert it into active electrons.

The movement of electrons in chlorophyll occurs in two systems: **PHOTOSYSTEM I** and **PHOTOSYSTEM II**. These systems work together to funnel high-energy electrons down to a terminal electron acceptor. The passage of electrons along the system is aided by molecules called quinones. At the end of the chain, the enzyme NADP+ reductase adds an electron to an NADP+ molecule, creating the energy storage molecule NADPH. The basic steps of the light reactions are as follows:

1. Light strikes PS II, energizing an electron.
2. The electron is transferred to a primary electron acceptor in P680, a compound in the chlorophyll.
3. An enzyme splits water, supplying two H+ ions and an oxygen atom. The H+ ions form a gradient across the lumen layer in the thylakoid membrane.

4. The energized electrons pass to PSI via a chain of quinone structures.

5. The transport of electrons helps to drive the gradient of H+ ions even farther onto one side of the thylakoid membrane.

6. The enzyme NADP+ reductase takes the active electrons and catalyzes the formation of NADPH. Two electrons are needed for one molecule of NADPH.

The Calvin Cycle

Now that the energy molecules of NADPH have been produced by the light-fixing reactions, they can be used to fix carbon dioxide and turn it into glucose. The **CALVIN CYCLE** is somewhat similar to the citric acid cycle, in that there is an intermediate compound (oxalo-acetate in the TCA cycle) recycled after every round of synthesis. The Calvin cycle produces a sugar precursor, known as glyceralde-hyde 3-phosphate (G3P). This 3-carbon molecule requires three cycles of the Calvin cycle for construction with each cycle fixing one molecule of carbon dioxide. Two molecules of G3P are required to create one 6-carbon glucose molecule.

The steps of the Calvin cycle are as follows:

1. Three CO_2 molecules are used by RuBisCo (Ribulose-1, 5-bisphosphate carboxylase/oxygenase), an enzyme, to produce six molecules of 3-phosphoglycerate.

2. 6-ATP is then used to convert the 3-phosphoglycerate into six molecules of 1, 3-bisphosphoglycerate, an activated compound.

3. 6-NADPH is then used to convert the 1, 3-bisphos-phoglycerate into six molecules of glyceraldehyde 3-phosphate. At this point, one molecule of the G3P is exported for conversion to glucose or other materials, and five molecules of G3P continue in the cycle.

4. The five molecules of G3P, in addition to three ATP, are used to regenerate the three molecules of ribulose bisphosphate that catalyze the CO_2 fixation reaction.

Note that this is an energy-intensive process. To make one G3P molecule, a plant has to expend nine units of ATP and six units of NADPH. These energy molecules are generated from light reactions that occur in the chloroplast.

C3 versus C4 Plants

There are two types of carbon-fixing plants, referred to as C3 or C4 plants because of the number of carbons that the fixed molecule contains. The majority of plants are C3 and fix carbon into G3P.

C4 plants are rarer and are seen in only about twenty different plant families. Instead of fixing carbon into glyceraldehyde

3-phosphate, these plants fix carbon into a 4-carbon molecule known as oxaloacetate, which becomes malate that is then transformed into pyruvate for the production of sugar or ATP.

The major difference between these plants is the manner in which they PHOTORESPIRATE. To get an adequate amount of carbon dioxide, plants need to have stomata open, which allows air to enter the leaf. This is typical in most C3 plants. However, in hot environments, such as the desert, having stomata open during the day, when the light-fixing reactions take place, can be lethal. Thus, C4 plants use a different enzyme, called PEP carboxylase, that can fix carbon dioxide even in very low concentrations. This eliminates the need to have stomata open during the day and reduces the amount of water lost due to photorespiration.

Examples

1. Which of the following is the primary feature distinguishing C3 from C4 plants?

    A) C3 plants use the Krebs cycle, and C4 plants use the citric acid cycle.

    B) C3 plants produce a 3-carbon glucose precursor, whereas C4 plants produce a 4-carbon glucose precursor.

    C) C4 plants are able to tolerate extreme cold temperatures, but C3 plants cannot.

    D) C4 plants produce four molecules of ATP per round of the citric acid cycle, whereas C3 plants only produce three molecules of ATP per round of the citric acid cycle.

2. The thylakoid membrane structures, found only in organisms with chlorophyll, are the sites that

    A) produce ATP from sugar, much like mitochondria.

    B) trap energy from the sun in the form of NADH and ATP.

    C) provide an active site for the enzyme RuBisCo to fix carbon dioxide.

    D) act as a structural platform from which the plant cell wall is generated.

3. Which of the following is correct regarding the relationship between photosystem I and II?

    A) Electrons are trapped by photosystem I and proceed to photosystem II.

    B) Photosystem I and II both trap electrons, but only photosystem II produces ATP.

    C) Photosystem II traps energy from the sun to excite electrons, which are then provided to photosystem I.

    D) Photosystem I is located in the cytosol, whereas photosystem II is located in the chloroplasts.

4. A scientist provides a growing sunflower plant with CO_2 that has been made with heavy oxygen, an isotope of normal oxygen that has a weight of 18 AMUs, rather than 16. After the carbon dioxide has been metabolized, where will the heavy oxygen show up?

A) in water secreted by the plant

B) in glucose created by the plant

C) in pyruvate created by the plant

D) in oxygen produced by the plant

Answers: 1. B) 2. B) 3. C) 4. B)

ECOLOGY

Ecology is the study of the relationships between organisms and their environment, including both the **BIOTIC** components, which are alive, and the **ABIOTIC** components, which are not alive.

Population Ecology

A **POPULATION** is a group of individuals of the same species. (As discussed above, a species is any group of organisms that can interbreed and produce fertile hybrids.) This field of study focuses on how populations grow and interact with the enviornment.

Ecologists have developed a number of mathematical models that describe how populations may grow. In theory, a population would show geometric (generational) or logarithmic (continuous) growth. In practice, population size is constrained by the enviroment and the resources available. A population's **CARRYING CAPACITY** (K) is the number of individuals the environment can support.

Species can be placed into two broad categories based on their life histories. Species that produce large amounts of offspring with low parental investment and high mortality rates are known as **R-SELECTED** species. Examples of such species include rodents and insects. Conversely, some species produce fewer offspring but invest more in each, resulting in a lower mortality rate among the young. These species, which includes humans, are **K-SELECTED**.

Community Ecology

A **COMMUNITY** is composed of populations of many species occupying the same geographic area. Much of community ecology focuses on the many types of interactions between species.

- **COMPETITION** occurs when species compete for the same resources.
- **PREDATION** occurs when one individual (the predator) consumes another (the prey) for sustenance.
- **MUTUALISM** is an interaction between species in which both benefit.

✔ Would the following species be described as R-selected or K-selected?
- mice
- elephants
- whales
- mosquitos
- wheat

The species within a community consume each other for energy and nutrients; these interactions are mapped out in a FOOD WEB. In a food web, it's possible to see which TROPHIC LEVEL a particular species occupies. Primary producers (plants) occupy the first trophic level, herbivores make up the second level, and predators comprise the remaining trophic levels.

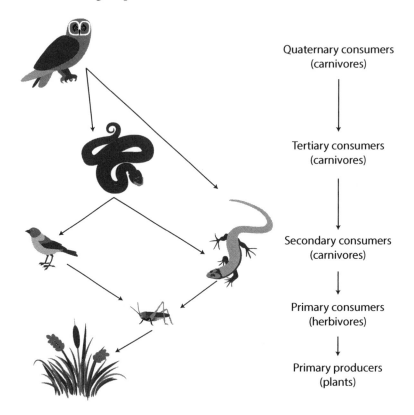

Figure 9.18. Food web

Ecosystems

An ECOSYSTEM includes all the biotic and abiotic components in a particular geographic area. Ecosystems are typically defined by their climate, which is the average temperature and precipitation in the area.

- A TROPICAL RAIN FOREST is typically moist and warm, with average temperatures year round of 25° – 29° Celsius, and receiving 150 – 200 centimeters of precipitation every year. Tropical forests have a large number of species and are the most species-dense of all the ecosystems.

- DESERTS are characterized by extreme temperatures and low rainfall. Daytime temperatures can exceed 45° Celsius, and nighttime temperatures can fall below 30° Celsius. Average precipitation is less than 30 centimeters per year.

- The **SAVANNA** is best characterized as grassland with moderate precipitation. Rainfall is usually between 30 – 50 centimeters every year, and temperatures range between 24° – 29° Celsius.

- **CHAPARRAL** is an ecosystem characterized by shrubs and low trees. A temperate ecosystem, it features rocky soil and low, rolling hills.

- **TEMPERATE GRASSLANDS** typically receive 40 – 60 centimeters of seasonal precipitation every year. There are well-defined seasons, with temperatures in the summer rising above 30° Celsius, and temperatures in the winter falling below 0° Celsius.

- **CONIFEROUS FORESTS** are the most common type of forest. They are characterized by moderately cold temperatures, with an average year-round temperature around 15° Celsius. They feature plentiful coniferous trees, such as pine, hemlock, and spruce.

- **BROADLEAF FORESTS**, containing many deciduous trees, are characterized by moderate temperatures. They receive 70 – 150 centimeters of precipitation annually.

- The **TUNDRA** is one of the world's largest land-area ecosystems, covering 20 percent of the world's existing land mass. It's quite cold, with temperatures usually no higher than 10° Celsius, even in the summer.

- **WETLANDS**, or swamps, are areas of land permeated with shallow water. They are among the most productive habitats in the world and support a high level of biodiversity.

- **ESTUARIES** are regions that flow from the river into the sea. They are characterized by low beds of silt and sand. Many invertebrate crustaceans live in this zone.

- **FRESHWATER ECOSYSTEMS** include lakes, streams, and rivers. These bodies of water have a low salt concentration and support a wide variety of wildlife.

- **MARINE ECOSYSTEMS**, which include oceans, coral reefs, and tidal zones, are bodies of water characterized by their high salt content. They cover 71 percent of the Earth's surface.

10

HUMAN BODY SCIENCE

Anatomy and physiology are the studies of body parts and body systems. This section will cover all necessary medical terms, prefixes, suffixes, and terminology as well as the anatomy and physiology of each body system.

TERMINOLOGY

Table 10.1. Directional terms

TERM	DEFINITION
superior	toward the head or toward the upper body region
inferior	toward the lower body region
anterior (ventral)	on the belly or front side of the body
posterior (dorsal)	on the buttocks or back side of the body
proximal	near the trunk or middle part of the body
distal	farthest away from the point of reference
medial	close to the midline of the body
lateral	away from the midline of the body

Table 10.2. Prefixes and suffixes

PREFIX	DEFINITION	SUFFIX	DEFINITION
epi–	on/upon	–coccus	spherical bacterium
hyper–	over	–ia	condition
hypo–	under	–ectomy	removal
intra–	within	–malacia	softening
para–	beside	–tomy	to cut
per–	through	–rrhea	discharge
peri–	surrounding	–plasty	surgical repair
sub–	under	–opsy	view of

These prefixes can help you on the *Language Arts* portions of the test.

Table 10.3. Cavities

CAVITY	CONTAINS
cranial	the brain
spinal	contains the spinal cord and extends from the brainstem in the cranial cavity to the end of the spinal cord
thoracic	contains the lungs, heart, and large blood vessels and is separated from the abdomen by the diaphragm
abdominal	contains the stomach, intestines, liver, gallbladder, pancreas, spleen, and kidneys and is separated from the thoracic cavity by the diaphragm
pelvic	contains the urinary bladder, urinary structures, and reproductive organs

THE CIRCULATORY SYSTEM

The **CIRCULATORY SYSTEM** circulates nutrients, gases, wastes, and other substances throughout the body. This system includes the blood, which carries these substances; the heart, which powers the movement of blood; and the blood vessels, which carry the blood.

The Heart

The whole system relies on the **HEART**, a cone-shaped muscular organ that is no bigger than a closed fist. The heart must pump the blood low in oxygen to the lungs; once the blood is in the lungs, it's oxygenated and returned to the heart. The heart then pumps the oxygenated blood through the whole body.

The heart is located inside the rib cage. It can be found approximately between the second and the sixth rib from the bottom of the rib cage. The heart does not sit on the body's midline. Rather, two-thirds of it is located on the left side of the body. The narrower part of the heart is called the apex, and it points downward and to the left of the body; the broader part of the heart is called the base, and it points upward.

The cavity that holds the heart is called the **PERICARDIAL CAVITY**. It's filled with serous fluid produced by the pericardium, which is the lining of the pericardial cavity. The serous fluid acts as a lubricant for the heart. It also keeps the heart in place and empties the space around the heart.

The heart wall has three layers:
- **EPICARDIUM**: the outermost layer of the heart and one of the two layers of the pericardium.
- **MYOCARDIUM**: the middle layer of the heart that contains the cardiac muscular tissue. It performs the function of pumping what is necessary for the

circulation of blood. It's the most massive part of the heart.

- **ENDOCARDIUM**: the smooth innermost layer that keeps the blood from sticking to the inside of the heart.

The heart wall is uneven because some parts of the heart—like the atria—don't need a lot of muscle power to perform their duties. Other parts, like the ventricles, require a thicker muscle to pump the blood.

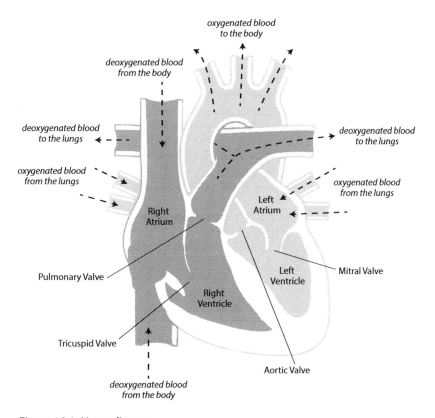

Figure 10.1. Heart diagram

There are four **CHAMBERS** in the heart: the right and left atria and the right and left ventricles. The **ATRIA** (plural for atrium) are smaller than the ventricles, and they have thin walls, as their function is to receive blood from the lungs and the body and pump it to the ventricles. The **VENTRICLES** have to pump the blood to the lungs and the rest of the body, so they are larger and have a thicker wall. The left half of the heart, which is responsible for pumping the blood through the body, has a thicker wall than the right half, which pumps the deoxygenated blood to the lungs.

The heart has one-way valves allowing the blood to flow in only one direction. The valves that keep the blood from going back into the atria from the ventricles are called the **ATRIOVENTRICULAR VALVES**, and the valves that keep the blood from going back into the ventricles from the arteries are called the **SEMILUNAR VALVES**.

The pumping function of the heart is made possible by two groups of cells that set the heart's pace and keep it well coordinated: the sinoatrial and the atrioventricular node. The **SINOATRIAL NODE** sets the pace and signals the atria to contract; the **ATRIOVENTRICULAR NODE** picks up the signal from the sinoatrial node, and this signal tells the ventricles to contract.

The Blood Vessels

The **BLOOD VESSELS** carry the blood from the heart throughout the body and then back. They vary in size depending on the amount of the blood that needs to flow through them. The hollow part in the middle, called the **LUMEN**, is where the blood actually flows. The vessels are lined with endothelium, which is made out of the same type of cells as the endocardium and serves the same purpose—to keep the blood from sticking to the walls and clotting.

ARTERIES are blood vessels that transport the blood away from the heart. They work under a lot more pressure than the other types of blood vessels; hence, they have a thicker, more muscular wall, which is also highly elastic. The smaller arteries are usually more muscular, while the larger are more elastic.

The largest artery in the body is called the **AORTA**. It ascends from the left ventricle of the heart, arches to the back left, and descends behind the heart. Narrower arteries that branch off of main arteries and carry blood to the capillaries are called **ARTERIOLES**. The descending part of the aorta carries blood to the lower parts of the body, except for the lungs. The lungs get blood through the **PULMONARY ARTERY**, which comes out of the right ventricle.

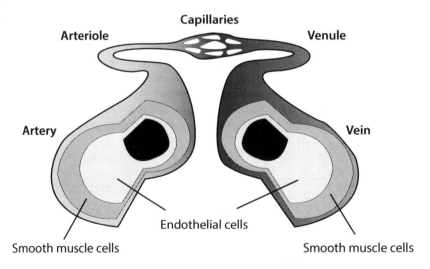

Figure 10.2. Artery and vein diagram

The arching part of the aorta (called the **AORTIC ARCH**) branches into three arteries: the brachiocephalic artery, the left common artery, and the left subclavian artery. The **BRACHIOCEPHALIC ARTERY** carries blood to the brain and head. The brachiocephalic artery divides into the right subclavian artery, which brings the blood to the right arm. The LEFT COMMON CAROTID ARTERY carries blood to the brain; the LEFT SUBCLAVIAN ARTERY carries blood to the left arm.

VEINS are blood vessels that bring the blood from the body back to the heart. As they don't work under the same pressure as the arteries, they are much thinner and not as muscular or elastic. The veins also have a number of one-way valves that stop the blood from going back through them.

Veins use inertia, muscle work, and gravity to get the blood to the heart. Thin veins that connect to the capillaries are called VENULES. The lungs have their own set of veins: the LEFT and RIGHT SUPERIOR and INFERIOR PULMONARY VEINS. These vessels enter the heart through the left atrium.

The two main veins are called the superior vena cava and the inferior vena cava. The SUPERIOR VENA CAVA ascends from the right atrium and connects to the head and neck, delivering the blood supply to these structures. The superior vena cava also connects to the arms via both subclavian and brachiocephalic veins. The INFERIOR VENA CAVA descends from the right atrium, carrying the blood from the lumbar veins, gonadal veins, hepatic veins, phrenic veins, and renal veins.

CAPILLARIES are the smallest blood vessels and the most populous in the body. They can be found in almost every tissue. They connect to arterioles on one end and the venules on the other end. Also, capillaries carry the blood very close to the cells and thus enable cells to exchange gases, nutrients, and cellular waste. The walls of capillaries have to be very thin for this exchange to happen.

The Blood

BLOOD is the medium for the transport of substances throughout the body. There are four to five liters of this liquid connective tissue in the human body. Blood is composed of red blood cells, hemoglobin, white blood cells, platelets, and plasma.

$\longrightarrow$
CONTINUE

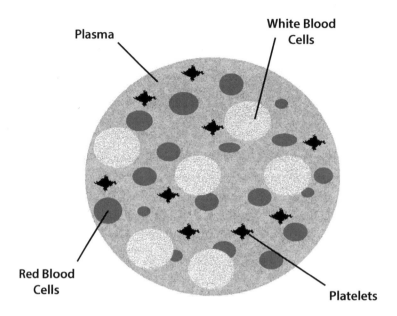

Plasma

White Blood Cells

White Blood Cells

Red Blood Cells

Platelets

Figure 10.3. Blood

Also called **ERYTHROCYTES**, **RED BLOOD CELLS** (RBCs) are produced inside the red bone marrow and transport oxygen. **HEMO-GLOBIN** (HGB) is a red pigment found in the red blood cells, and it's rich in iron and proteins, which both allow these cells to transport the oxygen. RBCs also have a biconcave shape, which means they are round and thinner in the middle. This shape gives them a larger surface area, making them more effective.

WHITE BLOOD CELLS (WBCs), also called **LEUKOCYTES**, are important for the human immune system. There are two classes of white blood cells: granular and agranular leukocytes. **GRANULAR LEUKOCYTES** are divided into three types: the neutrophils that digest bacteria, the eosinophils that digest viruses, and the basophils that release histamine. **AGRANULAR LEUKOCYTES** are divided into two classes: the lymphocytes, which fight off viral infections and produce antibodies for fighting pathogen-induced infection, and the monocytes, which play a role in removing pathogens and dead cells from wounds.

PLATELETS, also called **THROMBOCYTES**, are vital for blood clotting. They are formed in the red bone marrow and serve many functions in the body. Finally, **PLASMA** is the liquid part of blood, and it forms 55 percent of the total blood volume. Plasma consists of up to 90 percent water, as well as proteins, including antibodies and albumins. Other substances circulating in the blood plasma include glucose, nutrients, cell waste, and various gases.

The Cardiac Cycle

The heart works by shifting between two states: systole and diastole. In SYSTOLE, the cardiac muscles are contracting and moving blood from any given chamber. During DIASTOLE, the muscles are relaxing and the chamber is expanding to fill with blood. The systole and diastole are responsible for the pressure in the major arteries. This is the BLOOD PRESSURE that is measured in a regular exam. The two values are systolic and diastolic pressures, respectively, with the former being larger than the latter.

A CARDIAC CYCLE is the series of events that occur during one heartbeat. These events include:

- Atrial systole: The first phase of the cardiac cycle is atrial systole. With this, the blood is pushed by the atria through the valves into ventricles, which are in diastole during that event.

- Ventricular systole: After atrial systole, ventricular systole occurs. This pushes the blood from the ventricles to the organs, which occurs while the atria are in diastole.

- Relaxation phase: After ventricular systole, there is a pause called the relaxation phase. During this, all the chambers are in diastole, and the blood enters the atria through the veins.

- Refilling phase: When atria are at about 75 percent of their capacity, the cycle starts again. With the refilling phase, the atria are fully filled before atrial systole occurs again.

THE HEART VALVES
Try Pulling My Aorta
- Tricuspid
- Pulmonary
- Mitral
- Aorta

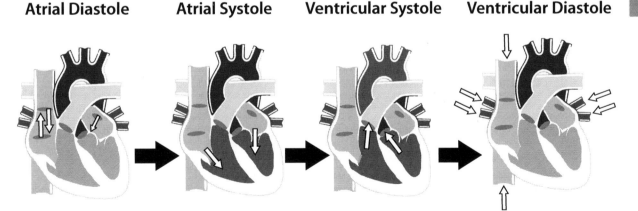

Atrial Diastole	**Atrial Systole**	**Ventricular Systole**	**Ventricular Diastole**
All heart muscle in relaxation	Atria in contraction	Ventricles in contraction	All heart muscle in relaxation
All heart valves are closed	AV valves are open	Semilunar valves are open	All heart valves are closed
Blood returning to atria	Blood to ventricles	Blood passing to the arteries	Blood returning to atria

Figure 10.4. Cardiac cycle

Oxygenating the Blood

There are four steps to blood cell oxygenation:

1. The poorly oxygenated blood comes into the right atrium through the superior and inferior vena cava.

2. The blood is then passed to the right ventricle, which sends it through the pulmonary artery into the lungs, where oxygenation occurs.

3. The oxygen-rich blood then comes to the left atrium through the pulmonary veins and gets moved from the left atrium to the left ventricle.

4. By way of blood pressure, the blood is then sent from the left ventricle through the aorta and the aortic arch into the arteries in the whole body.

After leaving the left ventricle, the blood passes from the arteries to the arterioles and on to the capillaries, where the exchange of gases, nutrients, wastes, and hormones occur. The blood then passes into venules and gets back to the heart through the veins. A healthy resting heart can pump around five liters per minute through this cycle.

The veins of the stomach and intestines don't carry the blood directly to the heart. Rather, they divert it to the liver first, through the hepatic portal vein, so that the liver can store sugar, remove toxins, and process the products of digestion. The blood then goes to the heart through the inferior vena cava.

Examples

1. At what rate does a healthy heart pump blood while resting?

   A) around 3 liters per minute

   B) around 5 liters per minute

   C) around 8 liters per minute

   D) around 10 liters per minute

2. Which of the layers of the wall of the heart contains cardiac muscles?

   A) myocardium

   B) epicardium

   C) endocardium

   D) all layers of the heart

3. The heart chamber with the thickest wall is:

   A) the left atrium

   B) the right ventricle

   C) the right atrium

   D) the left ventricle

4. The blood from the left ventricle goes to:

A) the right ventricle

B) the vena cava

C) the aorta and aortic arch

D) the lungs

5. The blood vessels that carry the blood from the heart are called:

A) veins

B) venules

C) capillaries

D) arteries

Answers: 1. B) 2. A) 3. D) 4. C) 5. D)

THE RESPIRATORY SYSTEM

The human body needs oxygen in order to function. The system that is responsible for intake of this gas is called the **RESPIRATORY SYSTEM**. It's also in charge of removing carbon dioxide from the body, which is equally important. The respiratory system can be divided into two sections: the upper respiratory tract and the lower respiratory tract.

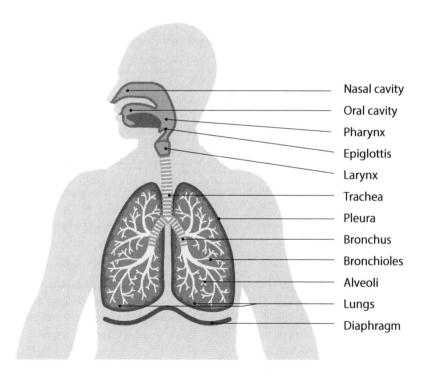

Figure 10.5. Respiratory tract

CONTINUE

The Upper Respiratory Tract

The UPPER RESPIRATORY TRACT consists of the nose, nasal cavity, olfactory membranes, mouth, pharynx, epiglottis, and the larynx.

The NOSE is the primary body part for air intake and removing carbon dioxide. The nose itself is made out of bone, cartilage, muscle, and skin, and it serves as a protector of the hollow space behind it called the NASAL CAVITY. The nasal cavity is covered with hair and mucus, which together serve an important function—they stop contaminants from the outside. Common contaminants include dust, mold, and other particles. The nasal cavity prevents the contaminants from entering further into the respiratory system; it also warms and moisturizes air.

The nose and the nasal cavity also contain OLFACTORY MEMBRANES, which are small organs responsible for our sense of smell. They are located on the top of the nasal cavity, just under the bridge of the nose.

We can also breathe through the MOUTH, although it's not the primary breathing opening. The mouth doesn't perform as well when it comes to the three functions of the primary opening (filtering, moisturizing, and warming of air). However, the mouth does have advantages over the nose when it comes to breathing, including its larger size and proximity to the lungs.

The next part of the respiratory system is the THROAT, which is also called the PHARYNX. The pharynx is a smooth, muscular structure lined with mucus and divided into three regions: the nasopharynx, the oropharynx, and the laryngopharynx.

Air comes in through the nose and then passes through the NASOPHARYNX, which is also where the Eustachian tubes from the middle ears connect with the pharynx. The air then enters the ORO- PHARYNX, which is where air from the mouth enters the pharynx; this is the same passageway used for transporting food when eating. Both air and food also pass through the LARYNGOPHARYNX, where these substances are diverted into different systems.

The EPIGLOTTIS is responsible for ensuring that air enters the trachea and food enters the esophagus. The epiglottis is a flap made of elastic cartilage, which covers the opening of one passageway to allow the air or food to go into the other one. When you breathe, the epiglottis covers the opening of the esophagus, and when you swallow, it protects the opening of the trachea.

The LARYNX is the part of the airway that sits between the pharynx and the trachea. It's also called the voice box, because it contains mucus membrane folds (vocal folds) that vibrate when air passes through them to produce sounds. The larynx is made out of three cartilage structures: the epiglottis, the thyroid cartilage (also called the Adam's apple), and the cricoid cartilage, a ring-shaped structure that keeps the larynx open.

The Lower Respiratory Tract

The LOWER RESPIRATORY TRACT consists of the trachea, bronchi, lungs, and the muscles that help with breathing.

The lower respiratory tract begins with the TRACHEA, also known as the windpipe. The trachea is the part of the respiratory system between the larynx and the bronchi. As its name suggests, the windpipe resembles a pipe, and it's really flexible so it can follow various head and neck movements. The trachea is made out of fibrous and elastic tissues, smooth muscle, and about twenty cartilage rings.

The interior of the windpipe is lined with mucus-producing cells called GOBLET CELLS, as well as cells that have small fringes that resemble hair. These hairlike structures, called CILIA, allow air to pass through the windpipe, where it's further filtered by the mucus. The fringes also help to move mucus up the airways and out, keeping the air passage free.

Connecting to the trachea are the BRONCHI. The PRIMARY BRONCHI, consisting of many C-shaped cartilage rings, branch into the secondary bronchi. Two extend from the left primary bronchi, and three branch from the right, corresponding to the number of lobes in the lungs.

The SECONDARY BRONCHI contain less cartilage and have more space between the rings. The same goes for the TERTIARY BRONCHI, which are extensions of the secondary bronchi as they divide throughout the lobes of the lungs. Like the trachea, the bronchi are lined with epithelium that contains goblet cells and cilia.

BRONCHIOLES branch from the tertiary bronchi. They contain no cartilage at all; rather, they are made of smooth muscle and elastic fiber tissue, which allows them to be quite small yet still able to change their diameter. For example, when the body needs more oxygen, they expand, and when there is a danger of pollutants entering the lungs, they constrict.

Bronchioles end with TERMINAL BRONCHIOLES, which connect them with ALVEOLI, which is where the gas exchange happens. Alveoli are small cavities located in alveolar sacs and surrounded by capillaries. The inner surface of alveoli is coated with ALVEOLAR FLUID, which plays a vital role in keeping the alveoli moist, the lungs elastic, and the thin wall of the alveoli stable. The wall of the alveoli is made out of alveolar cells and the connective tissue that forms the respiratory membrane where it comes into contact with the wall of the capillaries.

The LUNGS themselves are two spongy organs that contain the bronchi, bronchioles, alveoli, and blood vessels. The lungs are contained in the rib cage and are surrounded by the pleura, a double-layered membrane consisting of the outer PARIETAL PLEURA and the inner VISCERAL PLEURA. Between the layers of the pleura is a hollow space called the PLEURAL CAVITY, which allows the lungs to expand.

The lungs are wider at the bottom, which is referred to as the BASE, and they are narrower at the top, which is called the APEX. The lungs are divided into LOBES, with the larger lung (the right one) consisting of three lobes, and the smaller lung (the left lung) consisting of two lobes.

Respiration

The muscles that play a major role in respiration are the diaphragm and the intercostal muscles. The DIAPHRAGM is a structure made of skeletal muscle, and it's located under the lungs, forming the floor of the thorax. The INTERCOSTAL MUSCLES are located between the ribs. The INTERNAL INTERCOSTAL MUSCLES help with breathing out (expiration) by depressing the ribs and compressing the thoracic cavity; the EXTERNAL INTERCOSTAL MUSCLES help with breathing in (inspiration).

Breathing in and out is also called PULMONARY VENTILATION. The two types of pulmonary ventilation are inhalation and exhalation.

During INHALATION (also called inspiration), the diaphragm contracts and moves a few inches toward the stomach, making more space for the lungs to expand, and this movement pulls the air into the lungs. The external intercostal muscles also contract to expand the rib cage and pull more air into the lungs. The lungs are now at a lower pressure than the atmosphere (called negative pressure), which causes air to come into the lungs until the pressure inside the lungs and the atmospheric pressure are the same.

During EXHALATION (or expiration), the diaphragm and the external intercostal muscles relax, and the internal intercostal muscles contract. This causes the thoracic cavity to become smaller, and the pressure in the lungs to climb higher than the atmospheric pressure, which moves air out of the lungs.

Types of Breathing

In shallow breathing, around 0.5 liters of air are circulated, a capacity called TIDAL VOLUME. During deep breathing, a larger amount of air is moved, usually three to five liters, a volume known as VITAL CAPACITY. The abdominal, as well as other muscles, is also involved in breathing in and out during deep breathing.

EUPNEA is a term for the breathing our body does when resting, which consists of mostly shallow breaths with an occasional deep breath. The lungs are never completely without air—around a liter of air is always present in the lungs.

Examples

1. The primary opening for breathing in and out is:
   A) the nose
   B) the mouth
   C) the skin pores
   D) the pharynx

2. The air that we breathe in through the mouth enters the throat at the:
   A) nasopharynx
   B) oropharynx
   C) laryngopharynx
   D) larynx

3. For air to go to the lungs, the epiglottis needs to close the:
   A) bronchi
   B) pharynx
   C) larynx
   D) esophagus

4. How many lobes does the left lung have?
   A) 1
   B) 2
   C) 3
   D) 4

5. Bronchioles branch from the:
   A) primary bronchi
   B) secondary bronchi
   C) tertiary bronchi
   D) quaternary bronchi

Answers: 1. A) 2. B) 3. D) 4. B) 5. C)

THE SKELETAL SYSTEM

There are a number of roles the skeletal system plays in the body. The bones and joints that make up the skeletal system are responsible for:

- providing support and protection
- allowing movement

- generating blood cells
- storing fat, iron, and calcium
- guiding the growth of the entire body

Generally, the skeleton can be divided into two parts: the axial skeleton and the appendicular skeleton. The **AXIAL SKELETON** consists of eighty bones placed along the body's midline axis and grouped into the skull, ribs, sternum, and vertebral column. The **APPENDICULAR SKELETON** consists of 126 bones grouped into the upper and lower limbs and the pelvic and pectoral girdles. These bones anchor muscles and allow for movement.

Bone Components

On the cellular level, the bone consists of two distinctively different parts: the matrix and living bone cells. The **BONE MATRIX** is the nonliving part of the bone, which is made out of water, collagen, protein, calcium phosphate, and calcium carbonate crystals. The **LIVING BONE CELLS (OSTEOCYTES)** are found at the edges of the bones and throughout the bone matrix in small cavities. Bone cells play a vital part in the growth, development, and repair of bones and can be used for the minerals they store.

Looking at a cross section of a bone, you can see that it's made out of layers. These include the **PERIOSTEUM**, which is the topmost layer of the bone, acting as a layer of connective tissue. The periosteum contains collagen fibers that anchor the tendons and the muscles; it also holds the stem and the osteoblast cells that are necessary for growth and repair of the bones. Nervous tissue, nerve endings, and blood vessels are also present in the periosteum.

Under the periosteum is a layer of **COMPACT BONE**, which gives the bone its strength. Made out of mineral salts and collagen fibers, it also contains many cavities where osteocytes can be found. Under the compact bone is a layer where the bone tissue grows in columns called **TRABECULAE**. The bone tissue forms space that contains the red bone marrow. The trabeculae provide structural strength, even while keeping the bones light.

Hematopoiesis and Calcification

Inside the red bone marrow, which is located in the medullar cavity of the bones, a process called **HEMATOPOIESIS** occurs. In the process, white and red blood cells are made from stem cells. The amount of the red bone marrow declines at the end of puberty, as a significant part of it is replaced by the yellow bone marrow.

When we are born, we have 300 bones. As we grow, the structure of the bones changes. In **CALCIFICATION,** bones transform from mostly hyaline cartilage and connective tissue to osseous tissue. They also fuse, which is why adults have 206 instead of 300 bones.

The Five Types of Bones

The LONG BONES make up the major bones of the limbs. They are longer than they are wide, and they are responsible for most of our height. The long bones can be divided into two regions: the EPIPHYSES, located at the ends of the bone, and DIAPHYSIS, located in the middle. The middle of the diaphysis contains a hollow medullary cavity, which serves as a storage for bone marrow.

The SHORT BONES are roughly as long as they are wide and are generally cube shaped or round. Short bones in the body include the carpal bones of the wrist and tarsal bones of the foot. The FLAT BONES do not have the medullary cavity because they are thin and usually thinner on one end region. Flat bones in the body include the ribs and the hip bones, as well as the frontal, the parietal, and the occipital bones of the skull. The IRREGULAR BONES are those bones that do not fit the criteria to be the long, the short, or the flat bones. The vertebrae and the sacrum, among others, are irregular bones.

There are only two SESAMOID BONES that are actually counted as proper bones: the patella and the pisiform bone. Sesamoid bones are formed inside the tendons located across the joints, and apart from the two mentioned, they are not present in all people.

The Skull

Made out of twenty-two bones, the SKULL protects the brain and the sense organs for vision, hearing, smell, taste and balance. The skull has only one movable joint that connects it with the mandible—the jaw bone, which is the only movable bone of the skull. The other twenty-one are fused.

The upper part of the skull is known as the CRANIUM, which is the part that protects the brain, while the lower and frontal parts of the skull form the facial bones. Located just under the mandible, and not a part of the skull, is the HYOID BONE. The hyoid is the only bone in the body that is not attached to any other bone. It helps keep the trachea open and is where the tongue muscles are anchored.

Other bones closely connected to, but not part of the skull, are the AUDITORY OSSICLES: the malleus, incus, and stapes. These bones play an important role in hearing.

The Vertebral Column

The VERTEBRAL COLUMN, or the spine, begins at the base of the skull and stretches through the trunk down the middle of the back to the coccyx; it provides support for the weight of the upper body and protects the spinal cord. It's made up of twenty-four vertebrae, plus the SACRUM and the COCCYX (the tailbone). These twenty-four vertebrae are divided into three groups:

- the **CERVICAL**, or the neck vertebrae (seven bones)
- the **THORACIC**, or the chest vertebrae (twelve bones)
- the **LUMBAR**, or the lower back vertebrae (five bones)

Furthermore, each vertebra has its own name, which is derived from the first letter of the group to which it belongs (for example, *L* for lumbar vertebrae). The letter is placed first, followed by a number (the first of the lumbar vertebrae is thus called *L1*).

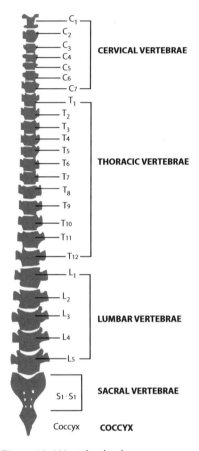

Figure 10.6 Vertebral column

The Ribs and the Sternum

The ribs and the sternum are the bones that form the rib cage of the thoracic region. The **STERNUM**, also known as the breastbone, is a thin bone that goes along the midline of the thoracic region. Most of the ribs are connected to this bone via the **COSTAL CARTILAGE**, a thin band of cartilage.

The human skeleton has twelve **RIBS**. On the back side, they are attached to the thoracic vertebrae. On the front, the first seven of them attach directly to the sternum, the next three attach to the cartilage between the seventh rib and the sternum, and the remaining two do not attach to the sternum at all. Rather, they protect the kidneys, not the lungs and heart. The first seven ribs are known as the true ribs, and the rest are known as false ribs. Together, these bones form the **THORACIC CAGE**, which supports and protects the heart and lungs.

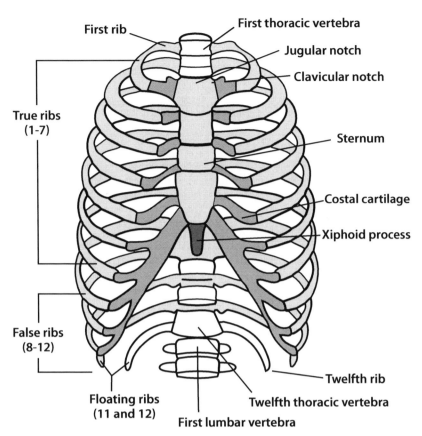

First rib

First thoracic vertebra

Jugular notch

Clavicular notch

True ribs
(1-7)

Sternum

Costal cartilage

Xiphoid process

False ribs
(8-12)

Twelfth rib

Twelfth thoracic vertebra

Floating ribs
(11 and 12)

First lumbar vertebra

Figure 10.7. Ribs

The Appendicular Skeleton

The upper limbs, which belong to the APPENDICULAR SKELETON, are connected with the axial skeleton by the PECTORAL GIRDLE. The pectoral girdle is formed from the left and right CLAVICLE and SCAPULA. The scapula and the HUMERUS, the bones of the upper arm, form the ball and socket of the shoulder joint. The upper limbs also include the ULNA, which forms the elbow joint with the humerus, and the RADIUS, which allows the turning movement at the wrist.

The WRIST JOINT is formed out of the forearm bones and the eight CARPAL bones, which themselves are connected with the five METACARPALS. Together, these structures form the bones of the hand. The metacarpals connect with the fingers, each made out of three bones called PHALANGES, except the thumb, which only has two phalanges.

The lower limbs are connected to the axial skeleton by the PELVIC GIRDLE, which includes the left and right hip bones. The hip joint is formed by the hip bone and the FEMUR, which is the largest bone in the body. On its other end, the femur forms the knee joint with the PATELLA (the kneecap) and the TIBIA, which is one of the bones of the lower leg.

Of the two lower leg bones, the TIBIA is the larger, and it carries the weight of the body. The FIBULA, the other leg bone, serves mostly to anchor the muscle. Together, these two bones form the ankle joint with a foot bone called the TALUS. The talus is one of seven tarsal bones that form the back part of the foot and the heel. They connect to the five long METATARSALS, which form the foot itself and connect to the toes. Each toe is made out of three phalanges, except the big toe, which has only two phalanges.

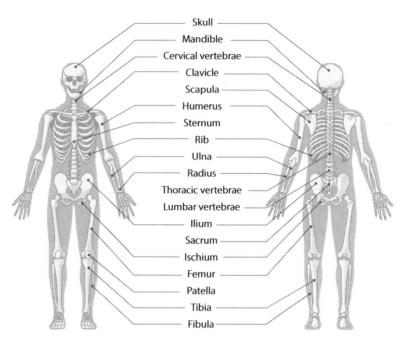

Figure 10.8. Skeletal system

The Joints

The JOINTS, also known as articulations, are where the bones come into contact with each other, with cartilage, or with teeth. There are three types of joints: synovial, fibrous, and cartilaginous joints.

The SYNOVIAL JOINTS feature a small gap between the bones that is filled with synovial fluid, which lubricates the joint. They are the most common joints in the body, and they allow the most movement. FIBROUS JOINTS, found where bones fit tightly together, permit little to no movement. These joints also hold teeth in their sockets. In a CARTILAGINOUS JOINT, two bones are held together by cartilage; these joints allow more movement than fibrous joints but less than synovial ones.

Examples

1. How many bones do adults have?

   A) 201

   B) 206

   C) 222

   D) 300

2. Stem cells can be found in the:

A) red bone marrow

B) periosteum

C) compact bones

D) cartilaginous joints

3. The long bones are the main bones of the:

A) limbs

B) thoracic cage

C) skull

D) vertebral column

4. The jawbone is called the:

A) mandible

B) cranium

C) hyoid

D) ulna

5. The second vertebra in the chest region is called:

A) L2

B) L3

C) T2

D) T3

Answers: 1. B) 2. A) 3. A) 4. A) 5. C)

THE MUSCULAR SYSTEM

Movement is the main function of the MUSCULAR SYSTEM; muscles are found attached to the bones in our bodies and allow us to move our limbs. They also work in the heart, blood vessels, and digestive organs, where they facilitate movement of substances through the body. In addition to movement, muscles also help support the body's posture and create heat. There are three types of muscle: visceral, cardiac, and skeletal.

Visceral Muscle

VISCERAL MUSCLE is the weakest type of muscle. It can be found in the stomach, intestines, and blood vessels, where it helps contract and move substances through them. We cannot consciously control visceral muscle—it's controlled by the unconscious part of the brain. That's why it's sometimes referred to as *involuntary muscle*.

Visceral muscle is also called SMOOTH MUSCLE because of its appearance under the microscope. The cells of the visceral muscle form a smooth surface, unlike the other two types of muscle.

Cardiac Muscle

CARDIAC MUSCLE is only found in the heart; it makes the heart contract and pump blood through the body. Like visceral muscle, cardiac muscle cannot be voluntarily controlled. Unlike visceral muscle, however, the cardiac muscle is quite strong.

Cardiac muscle is composed of individual muscle cells called CARDIOMYOCYTES that are joined by INTERCALATED DISCS. These discs allow the cells in cardiac muscle to contract in sync. When observed under a microscope, light and dark stripes are visible in the muscle: this pattern is caused by the arrangement of proteins.

Skeletal Muscle

The last type of muscle is SKELETAL MUSCLE, which is the only type of muscle that contracts and relaxes by voluntary action. Skeletal muscle is attached to the bone by tendons. Tendons are formed out of connective tissue rich in collagen fibers.

Skeletal muscle is made out of cells that are lumped together to form fiber structures. These fibers are covered by a cell membrane called the SARCOLEMMA, which serves as a conductor for electro-chemical signals that tell the muscle to contract or expand. The TRANSVERSE TUBES, which are connected to the sarcolemma, transfer the signals deeper into the middle of the muscle fiber.

CALCIUM IONS, which are necessary for muscle contraction, are stored in the SARCOPLASMIC RETICULUM. The fibers are also rich in MITOCHONDRIA, which act as power stations fueled by sugars and provide the energy necessary for the muscle to work. Muscle fibers are mostly made out of MYOFIBRILS, which do the actual contracting. Myofibrils are made out of protein fibers arranged into small subunits called SARCOMERES.

Skeletal muscle can be divided into two types, according to the way it produces and uses energy. TYPE I fibers contract slowly and are used for stamina and posture. They produce energy from sugar using aerobic respiration, making them resistant to fatigue. TYPE II muscle fibers contract more quickly. Type IIA fibers are found in the legs and are weaker and show more endurance than Type IIB fibers, which are found mostly in the arms.

Skeletal muscles work by contracting. This shortens the length in their middle part, called the muscle belly, which in turn pulls one bone closer to another. The bone that remains stationary is called the ORIGIN. The other bone, the one that is actually moving toward the other, is called the INSERTION.

Skeletal muscles usually work in groups. The muscle mainly responsible for the action is called the AGONIST, and it's always paired with another muscle that does the opposite action, called the ANTAGONIST. If the two were to contract together at the same time, they would cancel each other out and produce no movement.

Other muscles that support the agonist include **SYNERGISTS**, which are found near the agonist, attach to the same bones, stabilize the movement, and reduce unnecessary movement. **FIXATORS** are other support muscles that keep the origin stable.

There are several different ways to name the more than 600 skeletal muscles found in the human body. Muscles can be named according to:

- the region of the body in which they're located (e.g., transverse abdominis)
- number of origins (e.g., biceps)
- bones to which they are attached (e.g., occipitofrontalis)
- function (e.g., flexor)
- relative size (e.g., gluteus maximus)

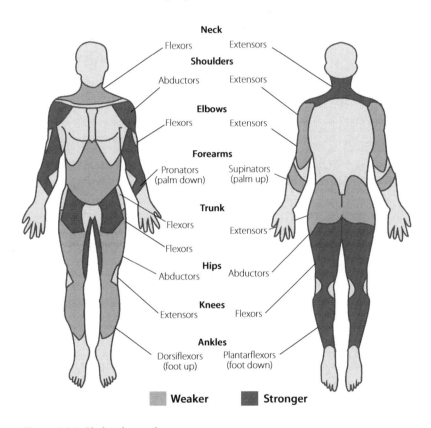

Figure 10.9. Skeletal muscles

Motor Neurons and Contractions

The neurons that control muscles are called **MOTOR NEURONS**. Motor neurons control a number of muscle cells that together are called the **MOTOR UNIT**. The number of cells in the motor unit is larger in big muscles that need more strength, like those in the arms and legs. In small muscles where precision is more important than strength, like the muscles in fingers and around the eyes, the number of cells in motor units is smaller.

When signaled by motor neurons, muscles can contract in several different ways:

- Isotonic muscle contractions produce movement.
- Isometric muscle contractions maintain posture and stillness.
- Muscle tone is naturally occurring constant semi-contraction of the muscle.
- Twitch contraction is a short contraction caused by a single, short nerve impulse.
- Temporal summation is a phenomenon in which a few short impulses delivered over time build up the muscle contraction in strength and duration.
- Tetanus is a state of constant contraction caused by many rapid short impulses.

Muscle Metabolism

There are two ways muscles get energy: through aerobic respiration, which is most effective, and through LACTIC ACID FERMENTATION, which is a type of anaerobic respiration. The latter is less effective, and it only happens when blood cannot get into the muscle due to very strong or prolonged contraction.

In both these methods, the goal is to produce ADENOSINE TRI-PHOSPHATE (**ATP**) from glucose. ATP is the most important energy molecule for our bodies. During its conversion to ADENOSINE DI-PHOSPHATE (**ADP**), energy is released.

Muscles also use other molecules to help in the production of energy. MYOGLOBIN stores oxygen, allowing muscles to use aerobic respiration even when there is no blood coming into the muscles. CREATINE PHOSPHATE creates ATP by giving its phosphate group to the energy-depleted adenosine di-phosphate. Lastly, muscles use GLYCOGEN, a large molecule made out of several glucose molecules, which helps muscles make ATP.

When it runs out of energy, a muscle goes into a state called MUSCLE FATIGUE. This means it contains little to no oxygen, ATP, or glucose, and that it has high levels of lactic acid and ADP. When a muscle is fatigued, it needs more oxygen to replace the oxygen used up from myoglobin sources and to rebuild its other energy supplies.

Examples

1. Which type of muscle is found in the blood vessels?
   A) cardiac muscle
   B) skeletal muscle
   C) visceral muscle
   D) Type IIA

2. Cardiac muscle is:

   A) involuntary muscle

   B) voluntary muscle

   C) both

   D) neither

3. Tendons always attach skeletal muscle to bone:

   A) along the entire length of the bone

   B) at one end only

   C) at both ends

   D) on at least one end

4. Myofibrils:

   A) store sugars

   B) are found only in smooth muscle

   C) make up the sarcolemma

   D) cause muscle contractions

5. Which is the strongest type of skeletal muscle?

   A) Type I

   B) Type II A

   C) Type II B

   D) Type III

Answers: 1. C) 2. A) 3. D) 4. D) 5. C)

THE NERVOUS SYSTEM

The NERVOUS SYSTEM consists of the brain, the spinal cord, the nerves, and the sensory organs. This system is responsible for gathering, processing, and reacting to information from both inside and outside the body. It's divided into two parts: the central nervous system and the peripheral nervous system. The CENTRAL NERVOUS SYSTEM (CNS) is made up of the brain and spinal cord and is responsible for processing and storing information, as well as deciding on the appropriate action and issuing commands.

The PERIPHERAL NERVOUS SYSTEM (PNS) is responsible for gathering information, transporting it to the CNS, and then transporting commands from the CNS to the appropriate organs. Sensory organs and nerves do the gathering and transporting of information, while the efferent nerves transport the commands.

Nervous System Cells

The nervous system is mostly made out of nervous tissue, which in turn consists of two classes of cells: neurons and neuralgia. NEURONS are the nerve cells. They can be divided into several distinct parts.

The SOMA is the body of the neuron; it contains most of the cellular organelles. DENDRITES are small, treelike structures that extend from the soma. Their main responsibility is to carry information to the soma and sometimes away from it. Also extending from the soma is the long, thin AXON. There is usually one axon per soma, but the axon can branch out farther. It's responsible for sending information from the soma, rarely to it. Lastly, the places where two neurons meet, or where they meet other types of cells, are called SYNAPSES.

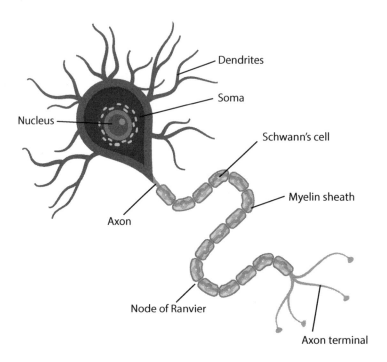

Figure 10.10. Neuron

Neurons can be divided into three classes. EFFERENT NEURONS are motor neurons responsible for transmitting signals from the CNS to the effectors in the body, while AFFERENT NEURONS transmit signals from receptors in the body to the CNS. The third type of neuron—INTERNEURONS—form complex networks in the CNS. They integrate the signals received from the afferent neurons and control the body by sending signals through the efferent neurons.

Together, these three types of neurons perform the three main tasks of the nervous system:

1. Efferent neurons (also called motor neurons) signal effector cells in muscles and glands to react to stimuli.

2. Afferent neurons (also called sensory neurons) take in information from inside and outside the body through the sensory organs and receptors.

3. Interneurons transmit information to the CNS where it's evaluated, compared to previously stored information, stored or discarded, and used to make a decision (a process called integration).

NEUROGLIA are the maintenance cells for neurons. Neurons are so specialized that they almost never reproduce. Therefore, they need the neuroglial cells, a number of which surround every neuron, to protect and feed them. Neuroglia are also called the GLIAL CELLS.

Protecting the Central Nervous System (CNS)

The **CNS** consists of the brain and spinal cord. Both are placed within cavities in protective skeletal structures: the brain is housed in the cranial cavity of the skull, and the spinal cord is enclosed in the vertebral cavity in the spine.

Since the organs that form the CNS are vital to our survival, they are also protected by two other important structures: the meninges and the cerebrospinal fluid. The MENINGES are a protective covering of the CNS made up of three distinct layers. The first is the DURA MATER, which, as its name suggests, is the most durable, outer part of the meninges. It's made out of collagen fibers—rich and thick connective tissue—and it forms a space for the cerebrospinal fluid around the CNS.

Next is the ARACHNOID MATER, which is the thin lining on the inner side of the dura mater. It forms many tiny fibers that connect the dura mater with the next layer, the PIA MATER, which is separated from the arachnoid mater by the SUBARACHNOID SPACE. The pia mater directly covers the surface of the brain and spinal cord, and it provides sustenance to the nervous tissue through its many blood vessels.

The subarachnoid space is filled with CEREBROSPINAL FLUID (**CSF**), a clear fluid formed from blood plasma. CSF can also be found in the ventricles (the hollow spaces in the brain) and in the central canal (a cavity found in the middle of the spinal cord).

As the CNS floats in the cerebrospinal fluid, it appears lighter than it really is. This is especially important for the brain, because the fluid keeps it from being crushed by its own weight. The floating also protects the brain and the spinal cord from shock—like sudden movements and trauma. Additionally, the CSF contains the necessary chemical substance for the normal functioning of the nervous tissue, and it serves to remove the cellular waste from the neurons.

The Brain

The nervous tissue that makes up the brain is divided into two classes. The GRAY MATTER, which consists mostly of interneurons that are unmyelinated, is the tissue where the actual processing of signals happens. It's also where the connections between neurons are made. The WHITE MATTER, which consists mostly of myelinated neurons, is the tissue that conducts signals to, from, and between the gray matter regions.

The brain can be divided into three distinct parts: the prosencephalon (forebrain), the mesencephalon (midbrain), and the rhombencephalon (hindbrain).

The **PROSENCEPHALON** is further broken down into two more regions: the cerebrum and the diencephalon. The outermost and the largest part of the brain, the **CEREBRUM** is divided through the middle by the longitudinal fissure into the left and the right hemispheres, each of which is further divided into four lobes: the frontal, parietal, temporal, and occipital.

The surface of the cerebrum, called the **CEREBRAL CORTEX**, is made out of gray matter with characteristic grooves (**SULCI**) and bulges (**GYRI**). The cerebral cortex is where the actual processing happens in the cerebrum: it's responsible for the higher brain functions like thinking and using language. Under the cerebral cortex, there is a layer of white matter, which connects the regions of the cerebrum with one another and the cerebrum itself with the rest of the body. It contains a special band of white matter that connects the two hemispheres, which is called the **CORPUS CALLOSUM**. The regions located under the white matter are divided into two groups: the basal nuclei, which help control and regulate the movement of muscles, and the limbic system, which plays a role in memory, emotions, and survival.

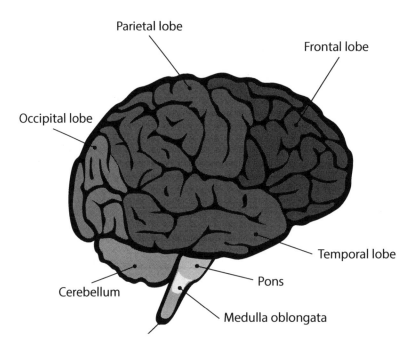

Figure 10.11. The brain

The **DIENCEPHALON** is a structure formed by the thalamus, hypothalamus, and the pineal gland. Made out of two gray matter masses, the **THALAMUS** is located around the third ventricle of the brain. Its role is to route the sensory signals to the correct parts of the cerebral cortex. Under the thalamus is the HYPOTHALAMUS, which plays a role in regulating hunger, thirst, blood pressure and body temperature changes, as well as heart rate and the production of hormones. The PINEAL GLAND is located beneath the hypothalamus (and is directly controlled by it) and produces the hormone melatonin, which plays a vital role in sleep.

The MESENCEPHALON is the topmost part of the brain stem. It's divided into two regions. The first is the TECTUM, which plays a role in reflex reactions to visual and auditory information. The second is the CEREBRAL PEDUNCLES, which connect the cerebrum and thalamus with the lower parts of the brain stem and the spinal cord. It also contains the SUBSTANTIA NIGRA, which is involved in muscle movement, reward seeking, and learning.

The RHOMBENCEPHALON consists of the brain stem and the cerebellum. The brain stem is further broken down into the medulla oblongata and the pons. The MEDULLA OBLONGATA connects the spinal cord with the pons. It's mostly made out of white matter, but it also contains gray matter that processes involuntary body functions like blood pressure, level of oxygen in the blood, and reflexes like sneezing, coughing, vomiting, and swallowing. The PONS is located between the medulla oblongata and the midbrain and in front of the cerebellum. It's in charge of transporting signals to and from the cerebellum and between the upper regions of the brain, the medulla, and the spinal cord.

The CEREBELLUM looks like a smaller version of the cerebrum—it has two spheres and is wrinkled. Its outer layer, called the CEREBELLAR CORTEX, consists of gray matter, while the inner part, called the ARBOR VITAE, consists of white matter that transports signals between the cerebellum and the rest of the body. The cerebellum's role is to control and coordinate complex muscle activities. It also helps us maintain posture and keep balance.

The Spinal Cord
The SPINAL CORD, located inside the vertebral cavity, is made out of both white and gray matter. It carries signals and processes some reflexes to stimuli. The spinal nerves stretch out from it.

Peripheral Nervous System (PNS)
The nerves that form the PNS are made of bundled axons whose role is to carry signals to and from the spinal cord and the brain. A single axon, covered with a layer of connective tissue called the ENDONEURIUM, bundles with other axons to form FASCICLES. These are covered with another sheath of connective tissue called the PERINEURIUM. Groups of fascicles wrapped together in another layer of connective tissue, the EPINEURIUM, form a whole nerve.

There are five types of peripheral nerves. The AFFERENT, EFFERENT, and MIXED nerves are formed out of the neurons that share the same name and perform the same roles. The SPINAL NERVES—thirty-one pairs in total—extend from the side of the spinal cord. They exit the spinal cord between the vertebrae, and they carry information to and from the spinal cord and the neck, the arms, the legs, and the trunk. They are grouped and named according to the region they originate from: eight pairs of cervical, twelve pairs of thoracic, five pairs of lumbar, five pairs of sacral, and one pair of coccygeal nerves. Lastly, the CRANIAL NERVES—twelve pairs in total—extend from the lower side of the brain. They are identified by their number, and they connect the brain with the sensory organs, head muscles, neck and shoulder muscles, the heart, and the gastrointestinal track.

The Sense Organs

The sense organs include the specialized sense organs, which are responsible for the specialized senses: hearing, sight, balance, smell, and taste. Sense organs also have sensory receptors for the general senses, which include touch, pain, and temperature. These senses are part of the PNS, and their role is to detect the stimuli and send the signal to the CNS when the detection occurs.

The Divisions of the Peripheral Nervous System

The PNS is divided into two parts based on our ability to exert conscious control. The part of the PNS we can consciously control is the SOMATIC NERVOUS SYSTEM (SNS), which stimulates the skeletal muscles. The AUTONOMIC NERVOUS SYSTEM (ANS) cannot be consciously controlled; it stimulates the visceral and cardiac muscle, as well as the glandular tissue.

The ANS itself is further divided into the sympathetic, parasympathetic, and enteric nervous systems. The SYMPATHETIC NERVOUS SYSTEM forms the fight or flight reaction to stimuli like emotion, danger, and exercise. It increases respiration and heart rate, decreases digestion, and releases stress hormones. The PARASYMPATHETIC NERVOUS SYSTEM is responsible for stimulating activities that occur when the body is at rest, including digestion and sexual arousal.

Lastly, the ENTERIC NERVOUS SYSTEM is responsible for the digestive system and its processes. This system works mostly independently from the CNS, although it can be regulated through the sympathetic and parasympathetic systems.

Examples

1. Which of the following forms the CNS with the brain?

   A) the peripheral nerves

   B) the sensory organs

   C) the spinal cord

   D) the cerebral cortex

2. The part of the neuron that is mainly responsible for transporting information from the cell is called the:

A) soma

B) axon

C) dendrites

D) sulci

3. The neurons that signal muscles to contract are called:

A) neuroglia

B) afferent neurons

C) interneurons

D) efferent neurons

4. Cerebrospinal fluid can be found in all the following except:

A) the arachnoid mater

B) the central canal

C) the ventricles

D) the subarachnoid space

5. The hypothalamus is located in the:

A) mesencephalon

B) rhombencephalon

C) prosencephalon

D) pineal gland

Answers: 1. C) 2. B) 3. D) 4. A) 5. C)

THE DIGESTIVE SYSTEM

The **DIGESTIVE SYSTEM** is a system of organs in the body that is responsible for the intake and processing of food and the removal of food waste products. The digestive system ensures that the body has the necessary nutrients and the energy it needs to function.

The digestive system includes the **GASTROINTESTINAL (GI) TRACT**, which is formed by the organs through which the food passes on its way through the body:

1. oral cavity
2. pharynx
3. esophagus
4. stomach
5. small intestines
6. large intestines

Throughout the digestive system there are also organs that have a role in processing food, even though food doesn't pass through them directly. These include the teeth, tongue, salivary glands, liver, gallbladder, and pancreas.

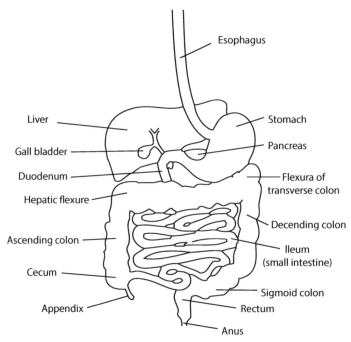

Figure 10.12. Digestive system

Questions about the order of the organs in the digestive tract are common on the GED.

The Mouth

The digestive system begins with the MOUTH. Also known as the oral cavity, the mouth contains other organs that play a role in digestion. The TEETH are small organs that cut and grind food. They are located on the edges of the mouth, are made out of dentin, which is a substance that resembles bone, and are covered by enamel. The teeth are very hard organs, and each of them has its own blood vessels and nerves, which are located in the matter that fills the tooth, called the pulp.

Also in the mouth is the TONGUE, which is a muscle located behind the teeth. The tongue contains the taste buds and moves food around the mouth as it's being processed by the teeth. It then moves food toward the pharynx when it's time to swallow. The SALIVARY GLANDS, located around the mouth, produce saliva. There are three pairs of salivary glands, and the saliva they produce lubricates and digests carbohydrates.

The Pharynx

The PHARYNX is a tube that enables the passage of food and air further into the body. This structure performs two functions. The pharynx needs the help of the epiglottis, which allows food to pass to the esophagus by covering the opening of the larynx, a structure that carries air into the lungs. When you need to breathe in, the esophagus is closed, so the air passes only into the larynx.

The Esophagus

The ESOPHAGUS begins at the pharynx and continues to carry food all the way to the stomach. The esophagus is a muscular tube, and the muscles in its wall help to push food down. During vomiting, it pushes food up.

The esophagus has two rings of muscle, called SPHINCTERS. These sphincters close at the top and the bottom ends of the esophagus when food is not passing through it. Heartburn occurs when the bottom sphincter cannot close entirely and allows the contents of the stomach to enter the esophagus.

The Stomach

The stomach is a round organ located on the left side of the body just beneath the diaphragm. It's divided into four different regions. The CARDIA connects the stomach to the esophagus, transitioning from the tubelike shape of the esophagus into the sack shape of the rest of the stomach. The cardia is also where the lower sphincter of the esophagus is located.

The BODY of the stomach is its largest part, and the FUNDUS is located above the body. The last part of the stomach is the PYLORUS, a funnel-shaped region located beneath the body of the stomach. It controls the passage of partially digested food farther down the GI tract through the PYLORIC SPHINCTER.

The stomach is made out of four layers of tissue. The innermost layer, the MUCOSA, contains a smooth muscle and the mucus membrane that secretes digestive enzymes and hydrochloric acid. The cells that secrete these products are located within the small pores called the GASTRIC PITS. The mucus membrane also secretes mucus to protect the stomach from its own digestive enzymes.

The SUBMUCOSA is located around the mucosa and is made of connective tissue; it contains nerves and blood vessels. The MUSCULARIS layer enables the movement of the stomach; it's made up of three layers of smooth muscle. This layer enables the movement of the stomach. The outermost layer of the stomach is the serosa. It secretes SEROUS FLUID, which keeps the stomach wet and reduces friction between the stomach and the surrounding organs.

The Small Intestine

The SMALL INTESTINE continues from the stomach and takes up most of the space in the abdomen. It's attached to the wall of the abdomen and measures around twenty-two feet long.

The small intestine can be divided into three parts. The DUODENUM is the part of the small intestine that receives the food and chemicals from the stomach. The JEJUNUM, which continues from the duodenum, is where most of the nutrients are absorbed

THE INTESTINAL TRACT
Dow **J**ones **I**ndustrial **C**limbing **A**verage **C**losing **S**tock **R**eport
- Duodenum
- Jejunum
- Ileum
- Cecum
- Appendix
- Colon
- Sigmoid colon
- Rectum

into the blood. Lastly, the ILEUM, which continues from the jejunum, is where the rest of the nutrients are absorbed.

Absorption in the small intestine is helped by the VILLI, which are small protrusions that increase the surface area available for absorption. The villi are made out of smaller microvilli.

The Liver and Gallbladder

The LIVER is not a part of the GI tract. However, it performs roles that are vital for digestion and life itself. The liver is located just beneath the diaphragm and is the largest organ in the body after the skin. It's triangular in shape and extends across the whole width of the abdomen.

The liver is divided into four lobes: the left lobe, the right lobe, the caudate lobe (which wraps around the inferior vena cava), and the quadrate lobe (which wraps around the gallbladder). The liver is connected to the peritoneum by the coronary, left, right, and falciform ligaments.

The liver is responsible for a number of functions, including detoxification of the blood, storage of nutrients, and production of components of blood plasma. Its role in digestion is to produce BILE, a fluid that aids in the digestion of fats. After its production, bile is carried through the bile ducts to the GALLBLADDER, a small, muscular, pear-shaped organ that stores and releases bile.

The Pancreas

The PANCREAS is another organ that is not part of the GI tract but which plays a role in digestion. It's located below and to the left of the stomach. The pancreas secretes both the enzymes that digest food and the hormones insulin and glucagon, which control blood sugar levels.

The pancreas is what is known as a HETEROCRINE GLAND, which means it contains both endocrine tissue, which produces insulin and glucagon that move directly into the bloodstream, and exocrine tissue, which produces digestive enzymes that pass into the small intestine. These enzymes include:

- pancreatic amylase, which breaks large polysaccharides into smaller sugars
- trypsin, chymotrypsin, and carboxypeptidase, which break down proteins into amino acid subunits
- pancreatic lipase, which breaks down large fat molecules into fatty acids and monoglycerides
- ribonuclease and deoxyribonuclease, which digest nucleic acids

The Large Intestine

The LARGE INTESTINE continues from the small intestine and loops around it. No digestion actually takes place in the large intestine. Rather, it absorbs water and some leftover vitamins. The large intestine carries waste (feces) to the RECTUM, where it's stored until it's expelled through the ANUS.

Examples

1. Food passes through all the following organs except:

    A) stomach

    B) large intestine

    C) esophagus

    D) liver

2. How many pair(s) of salivary glands are in the human body?

    A) 1

    B) 2

    C) 3

    D) 4

3. The esophagus performs all the following functions except:

    A) connecting the pharynx to the stomach

    B) preventing stomach acid from reaching the pharynx

    C) pushing food into the stomach

    D) moving food from the stomach to the small intestine

4. Which layer of the stomach contains blood vessels and nerves?

    A) the mucosa

    B) the submucosa

    C) the serosa

    D) the cardia

5. Bile is stored in the:

    A) liver

    B) duodenum

    C) gallbladder

    D) pancreas

Answers: 1. D) 2. C) 3. D) 4. B) 5. C)

CONTINUE

THE ENDOCRINE SYSTEM

The **ENDOCRINE SYSTEM** consists of many **GLANDS** that produce and secrete hormones, which send signals to molecules that are traveling through the bloodstream. **HORMONES** allow cells, tissues, and organs to communicate with each other, and they play a role in almost all bodily functions, including growth, sleeping, digestion, response to stress, and sexual functioning. The glands of the endocrine system are scattered throughout the body, and each has a specific role to play.

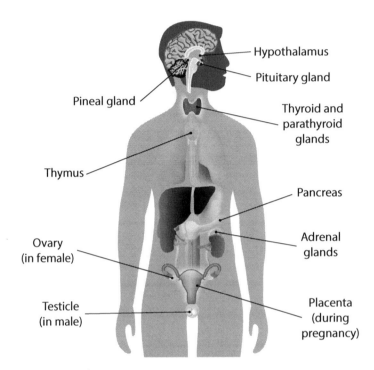

Figure 10.13. Endocrine system

- The **PITUITARY GLAND** hangs from the base of your brain and produces the hormone that controls growth and some aspects of sexual functioning (hormones: growth hormone, thyroid-stimulating hormone, oxytocin, follicle-stimulating hormone).

- The **HYPOTHALAMUS** is also located in the brain. Its main function is to control the pituitary gland, and many of the hormones it releases stimulate the pituitary gland to in turn release hormones itself (hormones: dopamine, thyrotropin-releasing hormone, growth-hormone-releasing hormone).

- The **PINEAL GLAND**, located in the brain, releases melatonin, a hormone that induces drowsiness and lowers body temperature (hormone: melatonin).

- The **THYROID GLAND** is found in the neck just below the Adam's apple. It controls protein production and the body's use of energy (hormones: T_3 and thyroxine).

The thyroid is regulated by the thyroid-stimulating hormone, which is released by the pituitary gland.

- The **PARATHYROID GLANDS** are located behind the thyroid. They produce parathyroid hormone, which regulates calcium and phosphate levels in the body (hormones: parathyroid hormone).

- The **PANCREAS,** discussed above, is located behind the stomach and releases hormones that regulate digestion and blood-sugar levels (hormones: insulin, glucagon, somatostatin).

- The **ADRENAL GLANDS** sit atop the kidneys. The adrenal glands have two regions that produce two sets of hormones: the adrenal cortex releases corticosteroids and androgens, while the adrenal medulla regulates the fight-or-flight response (hormones: cortisol, testosterone, adrenaline, noradrenaline, dopamine).

- The **TESTES** are glands found in males; they regulate maturation of sex organs and the development of secondary sex characteristics like muscle mass and growth of axillary hair (hormones: testosterone, estradiol).

- The **OVARIES** are glands found in females; they regulate the menstrual cycle, pregnancy, and secondary sex characteristics like enlargement of breasts and the widening of the hips (hormones: progesterone, estrogen).

Examples

1. Which gland(s) indirectly controls growth by acting on the pituitary?

   A) hypothalamus

   B) thyroid

   C) adrenal glands

   D) parathyroid glands

2. Which hormone is primarily responsible for the development of male secondary sexual characteristics?

   A) melatonin

   B) follicle-stimulating hormone

   C) estrogen

   D) testosterone

→

CONTINUE

3. A patient experiencing symptoms such as kidney stones and arthritis due to a calcium imbalance probably has a disorder of which gland?

   A) hypothalamus

   B) thyroid

   C) parathyroid

   D) adrenal glands

Answers: 1. A) 2. D) 3. C)

THE REPRODUCTIVE SYSTEM

Reproductive systems are the groups of organs that enable the successful reproduction of a species. In humans, fertilization is internal, with sperm being transferred from the male to the female during copulation.

The Male Reproductive System

The male reproductive system consists of the organs that produce and ejaculate SPERM, the male gamete. Sperm are produced in the TESTES, which are housed in the SCROTUM, which is located under the penis. During sexual arousal, the VAS DEFERENS carry sperm to the URETHRA, the tube which runs through the PENIS and carries semen (and urine) out of the body. Also emptying into the urethra is the PROSTATE GLAND, which produces a nutrient-filled fluid that protects sperm and makes up the majority of SEMEN. Before ejaculation, the COWPER'S GLAND produces a thin, alkaline fluid that flushes any remaining urine from the urethra and makes up a small portion of the semen.

The Female Reproductive System

Sexual reproduction in animals occurs in cycles that depend on the production of an OVULE, or egg, by the female of the species. In humans, the reproductive cycle occurs approximately once a month, when an egg is released from the female's ovaries.

The female reproductive organs, or gonads, are called OVARIES. Each ovary has a follicle that contains OOCYTES, or undeveloped eggs. The surrounding cells in the ovary help to protect and nourish the oocyte until it's needed. During the menstrual cycle, one or more oocytes will mature into an egg with help from the CORPUS LUTEUM, a mass of follicular tissue that provides nutrients to the egg and secretes estradiol and progesterone.

Once it has matured, the egg will be released into the FALLOPIAN TUBE, where fertilization will take place if sperm are present. The egg will then travel into the UTERUS. Unfertilized eggs are shed along with the uterine lining during MENSTRUATION. Fertilized eggs,

THE PATH OF SPERM
SEVEn UP
- Seminiferous tubes
- Epididymis
- Vas deferens
- Ejaculatory duct
- Urethra
- Penis

known as ZYGOTES, implant in the lining of the uterus, where they continue to develop.

Embryo Fertilization and Development

After fertilization, the cell will start to divide and, after four to five days, become a ball of cells known as a BLASTOCYST. The blastocyst is then implanted into the ENDOMETRIUM of the uterus. After the blastocyst has been implanted into the endometrium, the placenta develops. The PLACENTA is a temporary organ that attaches the embryo to the mother; it provides nutrients to the fetus, carries waste away from the fetus, protects the fetus from infection, and produces hormones that support pregnancy. The placenta develops from cells called the TROPHOBLAST, which come from the outer layer of the blastocyst.

In humans, the gestation period of the EMBRYO (also called the FETUS) is 266 days or roughly 8.8 months. The human development cycle in the womb is divided into three trimesters. In the first trimester, the organs responsible for the embryo's growth develop. This includes the placenta and umbilical cord. During this time, ORGANOGENESIS occurs, and the various stem cells from the blastocyst differentiate into the organs of the body. The organs are not fully developed at this point, but they do exist.

In the second trimester, the fetus experiences rapid growth, up to about twenty-five to thirty centimeters in length. At this point, it's usually apparent that the woman is pregnant, as the uterus grows and extends, and the woman's belly becomes slightly distended. In the third trimester, the fetus finishes developing. The baby exits the uterus through the CERVIX and leaves the body through the VAGINA.

Examples

1. All the following contribute material to semen except:

    A) the prostate

    B) Cowper's gland

    C) the penis

    D) the testes

2. Fertilization typically takes place in the:

    A) fallopian tubes

    B) ovaries

    C) uterus

    D) cervix

→

CONTINUE

3. Which of the following statements about the placenta is not true?

A) The placenta serves as part of the endocrine system because it releases hormones.

B) The placenta provides nutrients to the fetus.

C) The placenta develops from the outer layer of cells on the blastocyst.

D) The placenta is expelled during the menstrual cycle if fertilization does not take place.

Answers: 1. C) 2. A) 3. D)

11

CHEMISTRY

THE ATOM

The **ATOM** is the basic building block of all physical matter. It's composed of three subatomic particles: protons, electrons, and neutrons. A **PROTON** is a positively charged subatomic particle with a mass of approximately 1.007 atomic mass units. The number of protons in an atom determines which **ELEMENT** it is. For example, an atom with 1 proton is hydrogen, and an atom with 12 protons is carbon.

A **NEUTRON** is a noncharged subatomic particle with a mass of approximately 1.008 atomic mass units. The number of neutrons in an atom does not affect its chemical properties but will influence its rate of radioactivity. Both protons and neutrons are found in the center, or **NUCLEUS**, of the atom.

Lastly, an **ELECTRON** is a negatively charged subatomic particle with a mass of approximately 0.00055 atomic mass units. The number of electrons in an atom, in conjunction with the protons, determines the atom's charge. In addition, the number of electrons in the valence shell of an atom affects its reactivity. Electrons move in a cloud that surrounds the nucleus.

The modern concept of the atom, which provided the basis for all of chemistry, was first laid out in John Dalton's **ATOMIC THEORY**, which was developed in 1808. Atomic theory states that:

1. An element is composed of atoms, which are extremely small, indivisible particles. Although we now know that atoms are composed of smaller units such as protons, electrons, and neutrons, it's still recognized that atoms are the basic building block of matter.

2. Each individual element has a set of properties that are distinct and different from that of other elements.

3. Atoms cannot be created, destroyed, or transformed through physical changes. We now know that atoms can be created or destroyed, although this requires a massive amount of energy. Furthermore, radioactive elements can be transformed into other elements.

4. Compounds are defined by a specific ratio of atoms that are combined with one another, and the relative numbers and types of atoms are constant in any given compound.

Previous Models of the Atom

When the field of chemistry was young, people proposed many different models of the structure of an atom.

DALTON'S MODEL (EARLY 1800s)

Dalton was the first to propose some aspects of atomic theory, including atomic weights and a general shape. According to Dalton's model of the atom, each atom was a single, indivisible unit that was solid. Simply put, an atom was something like a very small marble, and a solid was something composed of many of these marbles.

Dalton's model was disproved in the early twentieth century when the proton and neutron were discovered by Ernest Rutherford. Rutherford found that a hydrogen atom could be extracted from a nitrogen atom by collision and that it had a positive charge. This showed that an atom was composed of smaller, positively charged pieces and was not a unified whole.

RUTHERFORD'S MODEL (1911)

Rutherford proposed that an atom was a core of heavier particles (protons and neutrons) surrounded by a layer of electrons. In this model, the electrons were evenly dispersed around the core of the atom.

In Rutherford's model, physics would predict that the evenly dispersed electrons would slowly lose energy while orbiting the nucleus. As a result, if Rutherford's model were true, all electrons would eventually collapse into the nucleus.

BOHR'S THEORY

To fix this problem with the model, Niels Bohr proposed that electrons can only orbit the nucleus in certain energy stages, or orbits, that are a set distance from the nucleus. The electrons orbiting closer to the nucleus have the highest energy, and shells have lower energy moving away from the nucleus. He further proposed that it's possible to change the energy state of electrons through the emission or addition of electromagnetic waves. The idea of electron shells was thus introduced by Bohr's theory, and Bohr's model is still used today (with some modifications).

Atomic Structure

The atom consists of a nucleus of protons and neutrons surrounded by a shell, or multiple shells, of electrons. The nucleus is very dense and contains the majority of mass in the atom. The actual size of the atom, due to the large electron shell, is much larger than the nucleus.

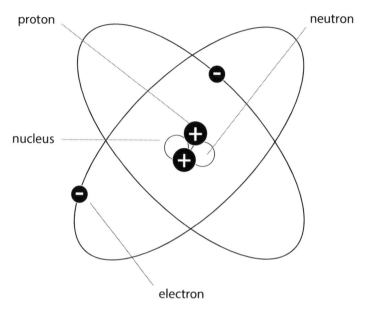

Figure 11.1. Atomic structure

Electrons surround the nucleus in clouds called **ORBITALS**; each orbital has a particular shape and holds a particular number of electrons. There are four orbital shapes: *s* orbitals hold 2 electrons, *p* orbitals hold 6 electrons, *d* orbitals hold 10 electrons, and *f* orbitals hold 14 electrons. The size and distance of the orbital from the nucleus is described by an integer value (1, 2, ...).

The location of an electron can be described with an integer number and orbital letter; for example the single electron in hydrogen is in orbital 1s. The number of electrons in each orbital is written as a superscript. For example, the two electrons in helium are described as $2s^2$. With some exceptions, electrons fill orbitals in a specific order (see Figure 11.2). This order can also be found using the periodic table (more on this later in the chapter).

→
CONTINUE

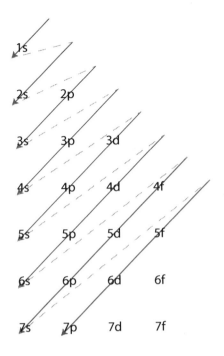

$$1s^22s^22p^63s^23p^64s^23d^{10}4p^65s^2\ldots$$

Figure 11.2. Electron orbitals

Valence Shell Reactivity

The reactivity of each individual atom is determined by the number of electrons in its electron shells, of which the most important is the outermost, or **VALENCE**, shell. Typically, the closer an atom is to reaching a full valence shell, the more reactive it is. Elements that have a single electron in a shell (such as sodium: last orbital $3s^1$) or need only a single electron to fill a shell (such as chlorine: last orbital $2p^5$) are the most reactive.

There are some elements that are not reactive at all. These are the noble gases, which possess a full valence shell. Thus, they have no free electrons with which to react. In chemistry, there are no common reactions that occur with a noble gas.

Examples

1. Which of these is the correct electron configuration for gold?

   A) $[Xe]\ 6s^2\ 5d^9$

   B) $[Xe]\ 5d^9\ 6s^2$

   C) $[Xe]\ 4f^{14}\ 5d^{10}\ 6s^1$

   D) $[Xe]\ 6s^2\ 5d^{10}\ 4f^{13}$

2. The electron configuration for phosphorus is:

A) $1s^2 2s^2 2p^6 3s^2 3p^3$

B) $1s^2 2s^2 2p^6 3s^2 3p^6$

C) $1s^2 2p^6 3s^2 3p^3$

D) $1s^2 2s^2 2p^2 3s^2 3p^3 4s^2 4p^3$

3. Which subatomic particles are found in the nucleus of an atom?

I.	protons
II.	electrons
III.	neutrons

A) I only

B) II only

C) I and III

D) I, II, and III

Answers: 1. C) 2. C) 3. C)

THE PERIODIC TABLE OF ELEMENTS

The **PERIODIC TABLE** is a table used to organize and characterize the various elements. The table was first proposed by Dimitri Mendeleev in 1869, and a similar organization system is still used today. In the table, each column is called a **GROUP** and each row is called a **PERIOD**. Elements in the same column have similar electron configurations and the same number of electrons in their valence shells.

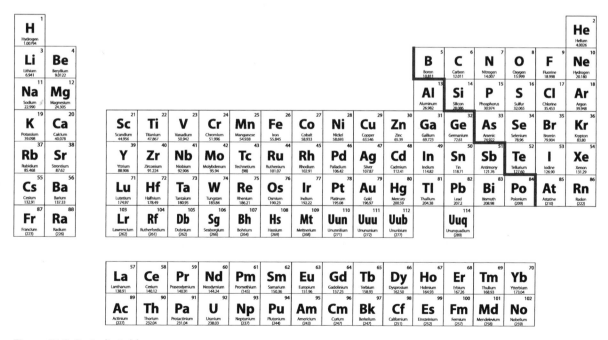

Figure 11.3. Periodic table

Reading the Periodic Table

Each cell in the table includes the symbol for the element, which is a letter or set of letters. For example, C for carbon and Fe for iron. The number at the top of each cell in the table is the ATOMIC NUMBER. This represents the number of protons in the element. The number below the element symbol is the ATOMIC MASS, which represents the total mass of the element (atomic mass – atomic number = # of neutrons).

Because atoms of the same element can have different numbers of neutrons, elements have no single standard atomic mass. Instead, the atomic mass is the weighted average of all commonly found species of the element. For this reason, it's almost never a whole number. For example, a small amount of carbon actually has an atomic mass of 13, possessing 7 neutrons instead of the usual 6, giving carbon an atomic mass of 12.011. Atoms of the same element with different numbers of neutrons are called ISOTOPES.

Trends in the Periodic Table

Some element properties can be predicted based on the placement of the element on the periodic table.

- Elements in groups 1 and 2 are the alkali and the alkali earth metals, which are very reactive.
- Elements in group 17 are the halogens, which are very reactive.
- Elements in group 18 are the noble gases, which are very unreactive.
- Elements along the "staircase" (marked in gray in the periodic table in Figure 11.3) consisting of boron, silicon, etc., are semimetallic. They have some properties of metals and some properties of nonmetals.
- The atomic radius of an element increases from the top left to the bottom right.
- ELECTRONEGATIVITY, which is a measure of how strongly an atom attracts electrons, increases roughly from lower left to the top right.
- IONIZATION ENERGY, which is a measure of how much energy is required to remove an electron from an atom, increases from lower left to top right.

Properties of Elements

Below are the important properties of various groups of elements.

GROUP 1 (THE ALKALI METALS)

The elements in group 1 are all silvery metals that are soft and can be easily crushed or cut. They all possess a single valence electron, which makes them very reactive. The presence of just a single valence electron means that there is a high likelihood of losing the electron,

Many elemental symbols are derived from the Latin names for elements. For example, gold's symbol is Au from its Latin name *Aurum*.

You don't need to memorize all of these properties, but be able to recognize the general similarities of a group's chemical properties.

resulting in a +1 cation. Because these metals are so reactive, they are not usually found in their pure form. Bonds that involve group 1 metals are always bonds that have high ionic character.

GROUP 2 (THE ALKALI EARTH METALS)

The elements in group 2 are also silvery metals that are soft. These metals contain two valence electrons, which fill the S-shell, so these elements are not as reactive as those in group 1. However, they still have a high tendency to lose these electrons and form a +2 cation. Normally, group 2 elements are found in this +2 oxidation state. Bonds that involve group 2 metals are almost always bonds that have high ionic character.

GROUPS 3 – 12 (THE TRANSITION METALS)

The elements from groups 3 to 12 are called the transition metals and are all capable of conducting electricity (some better than others). They are called transition metals in part due to their capability to possess multiple oxidation states. Because of the presence of the D-shell of electrons in these metals, they may have anywhere from a +1 to a +6 oxidation state, resulting in the formation of many different compounds and bonds. Transition metals are moderately reactive, malleable, and can conduct electricity due to the capability of gaining and losing many electrons in their outer electron shell.

GROUPS 13 AND 14 (SEMIMETALLIC)

The elements in groups 13 and 14 are semimetallic. They have moderate conductivity and are very soft. Elements in group 13 have three valence electrons, and elements in group 14 have four, allowing for five and four bonds respectively.

GROUP 15

This group is characterized by a shift from the top of this group (gases) to the bottom (semimetallic). This group has five valence electrons and can form three bonds. The semimetallic elements, such as arsenic and antimony, are relatively reactive.

GROUP 16

This group is also characterized by a shift from gases at the top of the group to semimetallic at the bottom. This group has six valence electrons and is quite reactive. The need to obtain only two more electrons to fill the valence shell means that these elements are electronegative and typically form an anion with a charge of –2. As a result, these elements are reactive and tend to bond with the alkali or alkali earth metals.

GROUP 17 (HALOGENS)

The halogens are all gases, and all contain seven electrons in their valence shell. They are extremely reactive, much like the alkali metals. Due to their reactivity and gaseous form at room temperature, they are often hazardous to humans. Inhaling chlorine or fluorine, for example, is usually deadly. The halogens will react to obtain a single additional electron to fill their valence shell and typically have a charge of –1.

Group 18 (The Noble Gases)

The noble gases already contain a full valence shell. Because their electron orbitals are already full, the noble gases are largely unreactive, except for a few rare exceptions. The heavier noble gases (xenon and radon) can sometimes react with other species under high temperature and pressure conditions. The noble gases have no net charge.

Examples

1. Which of the following is not true of the alkali metals?

   A) They are more likely to be oxidized than reduced.

   B) They typically form +1 monatomic cations.

   C) Large amounts of energy are required to remove their first electron.

   D) They are highly reactive.

2. Which of the following statements is not true regarding the halogens in the periodic table?

   A) All the halogens are extremely reactive.

   B) The halogen elements require 1 more electron to fill their valence shell.

   C) Halogen elements usually form ionic bonds with other elements.

   D) All the halogens are very electronegative, except for astatine and iodine.

3. Which of the following elements has the highest first ionization energy?

   A) sodium

   B) sulfur

   C) carbon

   D) argon

   Answers: 1. C) 2. D) 3. C)

CHEMICAL BONDING

Molecules and Compounds

Atoms can exist on their own or bond together. When two or more atoms are held together by chemical bonds, they form a **MOLECULE**. If the molecule contains more than one type of atom, it's a **COMPOUND**. Molecules and compounds form the smallest unit of a substance—for example, if water (H_2O) is broken down into hydrogen and oxygen atoms, it no longer has the unique properties of water. Molecules and compounds always have the same ratio of elements. Water, for example, always has two hydrogens for every one oxygen.

Intramolecular Forces

A chemical bond is a force that holds two atoms together. There are two primary types of bonds: ionic and covalent.

In an **IONIC BOND**, one atom has lost electrons to the other, which results in a positive charge on one atom and a negative charge on the other atom. The bond is then a result of the electrostatic interaction between these positive and negative charges. For example, in the compound sodium chloride, sodium has lost an electron to chlorine, resulting in a positive charge on sodium and a negative charge on chlorine.

In a **COVALENT BOND**, electrons are shared between two atoms; neither atom completely loses or gains an electron. This can be in the form of one pair of shared electrons (a single bond), two pairs (a double bond), or three pairs of electrons shared (triple bond). In diatomic oxygen gas, for example, the two oxygen molecules share two sets of electrons.

Covalent bonds are often depicted using Lewis diagrams, in which an electron is represented by a dot, and a shared pair of electrons is represented by a line.

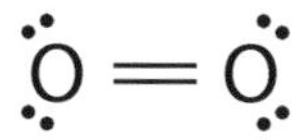

Figure 11.4. Lewis diagram of a covalent bond

Electrons within a covalent bond aren't always shared equally. More electronegative atoms, which exert a strong pull on the electrons, will hold onto the electrons longer than less electronegative atoms. For example, oxygen is more electronegative than hydrogen, so in H_2O (water), the oxygen atom has a slight negative charge, and the hydrogen atoms have a slight positive charge. This imbalance is called **POLARITY**, and the small charge a **DIPOLE**.

Note that there is a commonality between the two types of bonding. In both ionic and covalent bonding types, the bond results in each atom having a full valence shell of electrons. When bonding, atoms seek to find the most stable electron configuration. In the majority of cases, this means filling the valence shell of the atom through either the addition or the removal of electrons.

Intermolecular Forces

What causes water to stick together, forming a liquid at room temperature but a solid at lower temperatures? Why do we need more heat and energy to increase the temperature of water compared with other substances? The answer is INTERMOLECULAR FORCES: attractive or repulsive forces that occur between molecules. These are different from ionic and covalent bonds, which occur within a molecule.

There are two main types of intermolecular forces that you need to know for the test: dipole-dipole interactions and Van der Waals forces. In a DIPOLE-DIPOLE INTERACTION, the small charge on the atoms in a polar molecule interacts with the charge on other polar molecules. When a hydrogen is bonded to a very electronegative atom, the resulting interaction is called HYDROGEN BONDING. This force can be seen between the oxygen and hydrogen atoms in water and is responsible for many of water's distinctive properties. Hydrogen bonds are the strongest of the intermolecular forces.

VAN DER WAALS FORCES are the sum of small-force interactions between molecules that are a result of forces that **are not** covalent, ionic, or hydrogen bonding in nature. There are several distinct Van der Waals forces, but the most important is the LONDON DISPERSION FORCE, which arises from temporary dipoles created by the normal movement of electrons.

Chemical and Physical Properties

Substances, whether they are composed of individual atoms or molecules, all have unique properties that are grouped into two categories: physical and chemical. A change in a PHYSICAL PROPERTY does not result in a change in the chemical composition of a reactant but only the physical structure. For example, a change of state is a physical reaction. A change in a CHEMICAL PROPERTY is one in which the molecular structure or composition of the compound has been changed. Physical and chemical properties are often influenced by intra- and intermolecular forces. For example, substances with strong hydrogen bonds will have higher boiling points.

Examples

1. Which of these statements is not true of covalent bonds?

    A) They include two overlapping atomic orbitals.

    B) The net formal charge on the resulting compound must be zero.

    C) They allow bonded atoms to achieve electron configurations comparable with those of noble gases.

    D) They may include more than one pair of shared electrons.

2. Which of the following molecules does not have an ionic bond?

A) $FeCl_2$

B) H_3PO_4

C) KOH

D) C_2H_6

3. In organic biomolecules such as proteins and DNA, interactions between the constituent pieces of the chain contribute substantially to the molecule's secondary structure. While these bonds are fairly strong, they frequently break to permit the molecule to bend and flex. The described interactions are most likely caused by:

A) hydrogen bonding

B) ionic bonding

C) covalent bonding

D) Van der Waals forces

Answers: 1. C) 2. D) 3. C)

NAMING MOLECULES

A CHEMICAL FORMULA (sometimes called a molecular formula) describes the chemical composition of a compound or molecule using elemental symbols and integers to represent the number of each atom. There are two methods for writing a chemical formula. The first is the simplest and just states the ratio of elements in a compound. For example, the compound acetic acid has the formula $C_2H_4O_2$, which means that a single molecule of acetic acid has 2 carbon, 4 hydrogen, and 2 oxygen atoms.

However, this chemical formula does not describe the structure of the compound. For this, it's necessary to use FUNCTIONAL GROUP NOTATION. When you write a chemical formula using functional group notation, the letters are moved around in the formula to reflect the correct order of the elements in the compound. In functional group notation, acetic acid is written as CH_3COOH. From this formula, it's clear that the first carbon in the molecule is attached to three hydrogens, and then to the next carbon, which is attached to the O-O-H chain.

Molecules can also be described using their EMPIRICAL FORMULA, which is just the molecule's chemical formula reduced to its simplest ratio. The empirical formula for acetic acid is CH_2O.

Chemical Names: Ionic Compounds

Ionic compounds are formed from one or more CATIONS (with a positive charge) and one or more ANIONS (with a negative charge). The naming rules for ionic compounds are as follows:

1. The cation is written first, followed by the anion. The cation has no suffix added. The anion has a suffix of –ide in the majority of cases (such as sodium chloride).

2. The stoichiometry of the molecule, as indicated by the subscripts, must produce a molecule that has no net charge. For example, $NaCl_2^-$, sodium dichloride, is not a valid compound.

3. The compound should be an empirical formula, meaning it should have the lowest subscripts possible. For example Na_2Cl_2 is not correct.

4. A polyatomic anion such as SO_4^{2-} does not have parentheses unless there are multiples of the anion. For example, $Na_2(SO_4)$ is not correct. However, $Al_2(SO_4)_3$ is correct because there are three sulfate anions.

Chemical Names: Covalent Compounds

The naming of covalent compounds is similar to ionic naming. In the naming of covalent compounds, the following rules apply:

1. The first element is named, along with a prefix indicating the number of atoms of that element in the molecular formula.

2. The second element is named, along with an appropriate suffix.

3. The first element, if having a value of 1, does not use the prefix mono-.

CH_4 = carbon tetrahydride
CO_2 = carbon dioxide

Table 11.1. Naming prefixes

NUMBER	PREFIX
1	mono
2	di
3	tri
4	tetra
5	penta
6	hexa
7	hepta
8	octa
9	nona

Examples

1. Which of these is not a properly named chemical by ionic nomenclature?

   A) potassium acetate

   B) lithium hydroxide

   C) lead nitrate

   D) calcium sulfite

2. Which of the following is the correct formula for chromium (III) oxide?

A) Cr_3O

B) CrO_3

C) Cr_3O_2

D) Cr_2O_3

3. What is the correct name for Na_2SO_4?

A) disodium sulfite

B) disodium sulfur oxide

C) sodium sulfate

D) sodium (II) sulfate

Answers: 1. C) 2. D) 3. C)

STATES OF MATTER

A STATE is a description of the physical characteristics of a material. There are four states: solid, liquid, gas, and plasma.

- A SOLID is a dense phase characterized by close bonds between all molecules in the solid; they have a definite shape and volume.

- A LIQUID is a fluid phase characterized by loose bonds between molecules in the liquid; they have an indefinite shape but a definite volume.

- A GAS is a very disperse phase characterized by the lack of, or very weak bonds, between molecules; gases have both an indefinite shape and volume.

- The PLASMA phase occurs when a substance has been heated and pressurized past its critical point, resulting in a new phase that has liquid and gas properties.

A substance will change phase depending on the temperature and pressure. As temperature increases, the phase will progress from solid to liquid to gas. As pressure increases, the opposite is true, and the phase will progress from gas to liquid to solid.

These phase changes have specific names, as shown below. Note that reciprocal changes will involve the same amount of energy, but moving from a less to a more energetic state uses energy, while moving from a more to less energetic state will release energy.

- evaporation: liquid to gas (uses energy); occurs at boiling point

- condensation: gas to liquid (releases energy); occurs at boiling point

- melting: solid to liquid (uses energy); occurs at freezing point

- freezing: liquid to solid (releases energy); occurs at freezing point
- sublimation: solid to gas (uses energy)
- deposition: gas to solid (releases energy)

PHASE DIAGRAMS are used to show the relationships between phases, temperature, and pressure for a particular substance. In the phase diagram, there are two points that are interesting to note. At the TRIPLE POINT, all three phases exist together, and at the CRITICAL POINT, the substance enters the plasma phase.

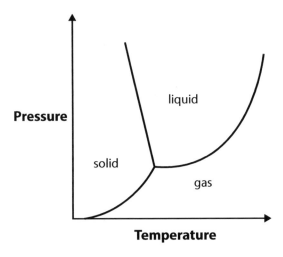

Figure 11.5. Phase diagram

Boiling Point and Freezing Point

The boiling point and freezing point of a molecule are related to its structure. There are three important factors that contribute to boiling and freezing points:

1. Strength of intermolecular forces: the greater the intermolecular force, the greater the boiling point of the substance will be.
2. Molecule size: as the molecule becomes larger, the boiling point of the molecule typically increases.
3. Molecule branching: as more branch points are present in the molecule, the molecule's boiling point will increase.

Let's look at an example. Methane has a molecular weight of 16 grams per mole, and water has a molecular weight of 18 grams per mole. Neither molecule is branched. As a result, factors 2 and 3 (as listed above) are not relevant. However, water has a boiling point of 100°C, while methane has a boiling point of –164°C.

This large difference is a result of intermolecular forces. Water is a highly polar molecule that has strong intermolecular forces. On the other hand, methane is an uncharged, nonpolar molecule with next to no intermolecular forces. Thus, the energy required to break the bonds between water molecules, and cause the phase change from liquid to vapor, is much greater than that for the methane molecule.

The Gas Laws

The interactions between each atom and molecule in a gas are extremely weak, and for this reason, gases have a low density compared with liquids and solids. However, due to their increased activity, the internal energy of a molecule in the gaseous phase is higher than that of a molecule in the liquid or solid phase.

Standard temperature and pressure (STP) is 0°C (298 K) and 1 atm (101.35 kPA).

When you discuss gases, it's important to differentiate between real gases and ideal gases. **REAL GASES** are what we experience in the real world. These gases are compressible, have intermolecular interactions, and may react. An **IDEAL GAS** is an idealized version of a gas that simplifies calculations in chemistry. An ideal gas is assumed to follow these rules:

- Each gas molecule occupies a very small volume (close to zero) compared with the overall volume of the container.
- All collisions between gas molecules are perfectly elastic.
- There are no attractive or repulsive forces acting on the gas molecules.
- The gas molecules are in constant motion and move completely randomly.

A gas under these conditions will follow a number of laws that describe the relationship between pressure (P), volume (V), temperature (T), moles (n), and a value called the ideal gas constant (R). The value of the ideal gas constant will change depending on the units used for the other variables.

- Ideal gas law: $PV = nRT$
- Boyle's law: $P_1 V_1 = P_2 V_2$
- Charles' Law: $\dfrac{V_1}{T_1} = \dfrac{V_2}{T_2}$
- Avogadro's Law: $\dfrac{V_1}{n_1} = \dfrac{V_2}{n_2}$

Table 11.2. The ideal gas constant

R VALUE	UNITS
8.314	J/(mol·K)
0.08205	(L·atm)/(mol·K)
1.987	cal/(mol·K)

CONTINUE

Examples

1. What is the correct term for the energy required for a solid to become a liquid?

   A) latent heat of vaporization

   B) latent heat of fusion

   C) latent heat of fission

   D) latent heat of condensation

2. Which of the following is not a state of matter?

   A) plasma

   B) liquid

   C) solid

   D) crystal

3. Which of the following is likely to have the highest number of molecules?

   A) 1 liter of water vapor

   B) 1 liter of water

   C) 0.5 liter of ice

   D) 0.5 liter of an ice-water mixture

4. Which of the following is not true of a liquid?

   A) A liquid fills the volume of the container holding it.

   B) A liquid is fluid and can change shape.

   C) A liquid is always warmer than a solid.

   D) Molecules in a liquid can have attractive interactions.

5. The freezing point of a compound is the same as the:

   A) boiling point of the compound

   B) melting point of the compound

   C) triple point of the compound

   D) critical point of the compound

6. When the pressure is increased on a sample of gas with a constant temperature, its volume:

   A) stays the same

   B) increases

   C) decreases

   D) oscillates

7. A scientist has 1 mole of a sample of gas at 274°C and 1 atm of pressure. How much volume will it occupy? ($R = 0.0821$ L·atm/K·mol)

A) 18.5 liters

B) 19.9 liters

C) 22.4 liters

D) 25.2 liters

Answers: 1. B) 2. D) 3. B) 4. A) 5. B) 6. C) 7. C)

ACIDS AND BASES

In general, an **ACID** can be defined as a substance that produces hydrogen ions (H^+) in solution, while a **BASE** produces hydroxide ions (OH^-). Acidic solutions, which include common liquids like orange juice and vinegar, share a set of distinct characteristics: they have a sour taste and react strongly with metals. Bases, such as bleach and detergents, will taste bitter and have a slippery texture.

There are a number of different technical definitions for acids and bases, including the Arrhenius, Bronsted-Lowry, and Lewis acid definitions.

- The **ARRHENIUS** definition: An acid is a substance that produces H+ hydrogen ions in aqueous solution. A base is a substance that produces hydroxide ions OH– in aqueous solution.

- The **BRONSTED-LOWRY** definition: An acid is anything that donates a proton H+, and a base is anything that accepts a proton H+.

- The **LEWIS** definition: An acid is anything able to accept a pair of electrons, and a base is anything that can donate a pair of electrons.

Measuring the Strength of Acids and Bases

The **pH** of a solution is a measure of the acidity or basicity of the solution. It's found by taking the negative log of the concentration of hydrogen ions, making pH an exponential scale. The pH scale runs from 0 to 14 with a low pH being more acidic and a high pH more basic. A pH of 7 is that of water with no dissolved ions and is considered neutral.

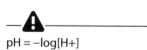

pH = –log[H+]

CONTINUE

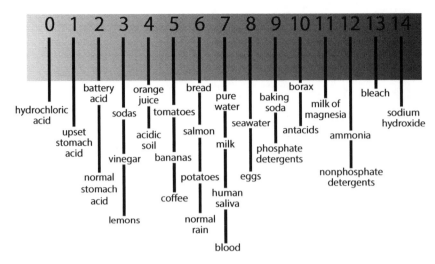

Figure 11.6. pH scale

Strong acids and bases will dissolve completely in solution, while weak acids and bases will only partially dissolve. Thus, strong acids and bases will have high or low pH values, respectively, and weak acids and bases will have pH values closer to 7.

Table 11.3. Strong and weak acids

STRONG ACIDS	WEAK ACIDS
Hydrobromic acid (HBr)	Acetic acid ($C_2H_4O_2$)
Hydrochloric acid (HCl)	Formic acid (HCOOH)
Sulfuric acid (H_2SO_4)	Butryic acid ($C_4H_8O_2$)

Acid Base Reactions

Acids and bases react with each other in solution to produce a salt and water, a process called NEUTRALIZATION. As a result of this reaction, if an equal amount of strong acid is mixed with an equal amount of strong base, the pH will remain at 7. For example, mixing hydrochloric acid and sodium hydroxide yields sodium chloride (a salt) and water, as shown below:

$$HCl(aq) + Na(OH)(aq) \rightarrow H_2O + NaCl(aq)$$

Examples

1. One of the characteristic properties of an acid is that it increases the concentration of:

   A) hydrogen ions

   B) hydroxyl ions

   C) hydroxide ions

   D) oxide ions

2. A solution with a pH of 12 is:

A) very acidic

B) neutral

C) very basic

D) slightly acidic

3. Proper blood pH level for humans is:

A) 7.0

B) 7.2

C) 7.6

D) 7.4

Answers: 1. A) 2. C) 3. D)

SOLUTIONS

In chemistry, the term **MIXTURE** describes a set of two or more substances that have been mixed together but are not chemically joined. In a **HOMOGENOUS** mixture, the substances are evenly distributed; in a **HETEROGENEOUS** mixture, the substances are not evenly distributed.

A **SOLUTION** is a specific type of homogenous mixture in which all substances share the same basic properties and generally act as a single substance. In a solution, a **SOLUTE** is dissolved in a **SOLVENT**. For example, in salt water, salt is the solute and water is the solvent. The opposite process, in which a compound comes out of the solution, is called **PRECIPITATION.**

The **CONCENTRATION** of a solution—the amount of solute versus the amount of solvent—can be measured in a number of ways. Usually it's given as a ratio of solute to solvent in the relevant units. Some of these include:

- weight per volume (e.g., grams per liter)
- volume per volume (e.g., milliliter per liter)
- weight per weight (e.g., milligrams per gram)
- moles per volume (e.g., moles per liter)—also called **MOLARITY**
- moles per weight (e.g., moles per kilogram)—also called **MOLALITY**

Solubility

Solubility is a measure of how much solute will dissolve into a solvent. When a solution contains the maximum amount of solute possible, it's called a **SATURATED SOLUTION**. A solution with less solute is **UNSATURATED**, and a solution with more solute than can normally be dissolved in that solvent is **SUPERSATURATED**.

Are the following mixtures homogenous or heterogeneous?
- lemonade
- concrete
- air
- trail mix
- salt water

There are many factors that can affect the solubility of a compound, including temperature and pressure. Another factor affecting solubility is the COMMON ION EFFECT, which occurs in solutions with two compounds that share a common ion. When the two compounds are mixed into a solvent, the presence of the common ion reduces the solubility of each compound. For example, NaCl and $MgCl_2$ share the common ion of chlorine. When they are mixed in a solution, the maximum saturation of the chlorine ion in water will be reached before the saturation of either sodium or magnesium is reached. This causes a reduction in the overall solubility.

Examples

1. In a carbonated soda, carbon dioxide is dissolved in water. In this solution, water is the

   A) common ion

   B) solvent

   C) solute

   D) precipitant

2. How much ethanol should be added to 2.5 L of water to produce a solution with a molarity of 5 M?

   A) 2 mol

   B) 2.5 mol

   C) 7.5 mol

   D) 12.5 mol

Answers: 1. B) 2. D)

REACTIONS

In a CHEMICAL REACTION, one set of chemical substances, called the REACTANTS, is transformed into another set of chemical substances, called the PRODUCTS. This transformation is described in a chemical equation with the reactants on the left and products on the right. In the equation below, methane (CH_4) reacts with oxygen (O_2) to produce carbon dioxide (CO_2) and water (H_2O).

$$CH_4 + 2O_2 \rightarrow CO_2 + 2H_2O$$

When a reaction runs to COMPLETION, all the reactants have been used up in the reaction. If one reactant limits the use of the other reactants (i.e., if one reactant is used up before the others), it's called the LIMITING REACTANT. The YIELD is the amount of product produced by the reaction.

Balancing Equations

The integer values placed before the chemical symbols are the COEFFICIENTS that describe how many molecules of that substance are involved in the reaction. These values are important because in a chemical reaction, there is a conservation of mass. The inputs, or reactant mass, must equal the outputs, or products. For example, the reaction shown on the previous page includes one carbon, four hydrogen, and four oxygen on either side of the arrow.

To BALANCE AN EQUATION, you'll need to add the coefficients necessary to match the atoms of each element on both sides. In the reaction below, the numbers of bromine (Br) and nitrate ions (NO_3^-) do not match up:

$$CaBr_2 + NaNO_3 \rightarrow Ca(NO_3)_2 + NaBr$$

To balance the equation, start by adding a coefficient of 2 to the products to balance the bromine:

$$CaBr_2 + NaNO_3 \rightarrow Ca(NO_3)_2 + 2NaBr$$

There are now 2 sodium ions on the right, so another 2 need to be added on the left to balance it:

$$CaBr_2 + 2NaNO_3 \rightarrow Ca(NO_3)_2 + 2NaBr$$

Notice that adding this 2 also balances the nitrate ions, so the equation is now complete.

Types of Reactions

There are five main types of chemical reactions.

- In a SYNTHESIS reaction, two or more reactants will form a single product. $A + B \rightarrow C$

- In a DECOMPOSITION reaction, a single reactant will decompose into two products. Decomposition reactions typically require an input of energy. $A \rightarrow B + C$

- In a SINGLE DISPLACEMENT reaction, one reactant will dissociate, and its complement ion will react with another species in solution. $AB + C \rightarrow A + BC$

- In a DOUBLE DISPLACEMENT reaction, two reactants will dissociate and exchange complement ions. $AB + CD \rightarrow AC + BD$

- In a COMBUSTION reaction, a fuel (alkane or carbohydrate is typical) will react with oxygen to form carbon dioxide and water. $C_xH_yO_z + O_2 \rightarrow CO_2 + H_2O$

Oxidation and Reduction

An oxidation and reduction reaction (often called a redox reaction) is one in which there is an exchange of electrons. The species that loses electrons is OXIDIZED, and the species that gains electrons is REDUCED. The species that loses electrons is also called the REDUCING AGENT, and the species that gains electrons the OXIDIZING AGENT.

The movement of electrons in a redox reaction is analyzed by assigning each atom in the reaction an OXIDATION NUMBER (or state) that corresponds roughly to that atom's charge. (The actual meaning

OIL RIG
Oxidation
Involves
Loss
Reduction
Involves
Gain

of the oxidation number is much more complicated.) Once all the atoms in a reaction have been assigned an oxidation number, it's possible to see which elements have gained electrons and which elements have lost electrons. The basic rules for assigning oxidation numbers are given in the table below.

Table 11.4. Assigning oxidation numbers

SPECIES	EXAMPLE	OXIDATION NUMBER
Elements in their free state and naturally occurring diatomic elements	$Zn(s)$, O_2	0
Monoatomic ions	Cl^-	−1
Oxygen in compounds	H_2O	−2
Hydrogen in compounds	HCl	+1
Alkali metals in a compound	Na	+1
Alkaline earth metals in a compound	Mg	+2

RULES		
The oxidation numbers on the atoms in a neutral compound sum to zero.	NaOH	Na: +1; O: −2; H: +1 $1 + -2 + 1 = 0$
The oxidation numbers of the atoms in an ion sum to the charge on that ion.	SO_3^{-2}	S: +4; O: −2 $4 + (-2)(3) = -2$

Reaction Stoichiometry

STOICHIOMETRY is the use of the relative amounts of reagents and products in a reaction to find quantities of those reagents and products. Stoichiometry can be used to find a number of variables, including the quantities of products and reagents involved in a reaction, and to identity the limiting reagent (the reagent that gets used up first).

An important unit to know when doing stoichiometry is the MOLE, which is defined as the amount of a substance that contains 6.02×10^{23} particles (either individual atoms or molecules). On the periodic table, the atomic mass of an element is also the number of grams per mole of that element; these values can be used in stoichiometry to convert between moles and grams.

For example, in the single displacement reaction shown below, 1 mole of magnesium chloride is needed for every 2 moles of sodium to complete the reaction. This reaction creates 1 mole of magnesium and 2 moles of sodium chloride.

$$MgCl_2 + 2Na \rightarrow Mg + 2NaCl$$

So, if 50 grams of sodium are used in the reaction, stoichiometry can be used to find the number of grams of magnesium that are produced:

$$\frac{50 \text{ g Na}}{1} \times \frac{1 \text{ mol Na}}{23 \text{ g Na}} \times \frac{1 \text{ mol Mg}}{2 \text{ mol Na}} \times \frac{24.3 \text{ g Mg}}{1 \text{ mol Mg}} = 26.4 \text{ g Mg}$$

Examples

1. In a furnace, natural gas (methane) is burned to produce heat to keep a house warm. What sort of reaction is this?

   A) acid base reaction

   B) combustion reaction

   C) single displacement reaction

   D) synthesis reaction

2. If 4 moles of methane are used in the reaction below, how many moles of water will be produced?

   $CH_4 + 2O_2 \rightarrow CO_2 + 2H_2O$

   A) 2

   B) 8

   C) 12

   D) 16

3. Which of the following is a substance or compound that is entering into a reaction?

   A) mole

   B) reactant

   C) product

   D) yield

4. Sulfur trioxide (SO_3) is produced when sulfur is burned. Which of the following is the correct general reaction for this process?

   A) sulfur + nitrogen $\rightarrow$ sulfur trioxide

   B) sulfur + oxygen $\rightarrow$ sulfur dioxide

   C) sulfur dioxide + oxygen $\rightarrow$ sulfur trioxide

   D) sulfur + oxygen $\rightarrow$ sulfur trioxide

5. In a balanced equation,

   A) the mass of the reactants equals the mass of the products.

   B) the number of moles of reactants equals the number of moles of the products.

   C) the size of each molecule in the reaction remains the same.

   D) the number of moles of each element in the reaction remains the same.

6. Balance the following equation:

A) $2KClO_3 \rightarrow KCl + 3O_2$

B) $KClO_3 \rightarrow KCl + 3O_2$

C) $2KClO_3 \rightarrow 2KCl + 3O_2$

D) $6KClO_3 \rightarrow 6KCl + 3O_2$

Answers: 1. B) 2. B) 3. B) 4. D) 5. D) 6. C)

CHEMICAL EQUILIBRIUM

CHEMICAL EQUILIBRIUM is a state reached in reversible reactions in which the rate of forward reaction equals the rate of reverse reaction. Once equilibrium has been reached, it will appear as though the reaction has stopped because there is no noticeable change in the creation of products. However, this isn't true: at chemical equilibrium, reactions are still occurring, just at an equal rate.

Le Chatelier's Principle

LE CHATELIER'S PRINCIPLE states that a chemical reaction at equilibrium will respond to changes in concentration, pressure, volume, or temperature by shifting to reestablish equilibrium. This new equilibrium will favor either the reactants or the products relative to the original equilibrium.

An increase in the concentration of a reactant or product will shift the equilibrium to the other side (e.g., adding a reactant will result in the production of more products to offset the addition). Decreasing the concentration of a reactant or product will shift the reaction toward that side of the reaction (e.g., removing a reactant will result in the production of more reactants and a corresponding decrease in the concentration of the products).

In a reaction involving gases, changes in pressure and volume can shift the equilibrium; the direction of the shift will depend on the number of moles of reactants and products. Decreasing the pressure (or increasing the volume) will result in a shift toward the side of the equation with more moles. Increasing the pressure (or decreasing the volume) will result in a shift toward the side of the equation with fewer moles.

Shifts in chemical equilibriums due to changes in temperature are determined by whether the equation is endothermic (uses energy) or exothermic (gives off energy). Increasing the temperature will favor the products in endothermic reactions and the reactants in exothermic reactions. The opposite is true when decreasing the temperature of a system.

Examples

1. According to Le Chatelier's principle, if hydrochloric acid (HCl) is removed from the reaction below, what will happen?

$BaCl_2$ (aq) + H_2SO_4 (aq) → $BaSO_4$ (s) + 2HCl (aq)

A) The reaction will shift to the left, and more reactants will be formed.

B) The reaction will shift to the right, and more products will be formed.

C) The reaction will not be able to reestablish equilibrium.

D) The reaction will stop.

2. Which of the following statements about chemical equilibrium is true?

A) Chemical equilibrium cannot be reestablished if the concentration of reactants is changed.

B) In chemical equilibrium, all the reactants have been turned into products.

C) Chemical equilibriums cannot be reached by reversible reactions.

D) In chemical equilibrium, forward and reverse reactions are occurring at the same rate.

Answers: 1. B) 2. D)

CHEMICAL KINETICS

Collision Theory

COLLISION THEORY refers to the idea that a chemical reaction cannot occur until two molecules that may react collide with one another. In a solid, although molecules are all touching one another, there is not much movement. As a result, chemical reactions in solid phase have a low reaction rate, or none at all. A solid usually only reacts when its surface comes into contact with a liquid or gas.

In liquids or gases, molecules are able to move freely, which allows greater interaction and an increased chance that two capable molecules will react. For this reason, the majority of chemical reactions occur in the liquid phase or the gas phase. However, even if two molecules collide that could react, most of the time, they do not. For a reaction to take place, the reaction must have a minimum amount of energy, a quantity known as the reaction's ACTIVATION ENERGY.

Reaction Rates

Different reactions will occur at different rates. This REACTION RATE is determined by a number of factors, including the concentration of reactants, particle surface area, and temperature. Generally, increasing any of these variables will increase the reaction rate by providing more opportunities for particles to collide.

- Increasing the concentration of reactants introduces more particles to the system, meaning they are more likely to collide.
- Increasing particle surface area makes it more likely particles will come in contact with each other.
- Increasing the temperature increases the velocity of the particles, making them more likely to collide.

Catalysts

There are some substances, called CATALYSTS, that are able to reduce the activation energy of a reaction, which subsequently will increase the reaction rate. A chemical catalyst is commonly a metal or other elemental compound with many electrons in their valence shell; they assist in the stabilization of reaction intermediates. Common chemical catalysts include platinum, palladium, nickel, or cobalt.

A biological catalyst is known as an ENZYME. Common enzymes include cellulase, amylase, or DNA polymerase. Biological catalysts typically function by bringing two reactants close together. Many enzymes also have active sites in their protein chains that function similarly to a chemical catalyst and assist in stabilizing reaction intermediates.

There are two types of catalysts subdivided by their phase: homogenous and heterogeneous. A HOMOGENOUS CATALYST is in the same phase as the reactants. Most enzymes are homogenous and are soluble in the same phase as the reactants.

A HETEROGENEOUS CATALYST is not in the same phase as the reactants. An example of a heterogeneous catalyst is the platinum found in the catalytic converter in the exhaust stream of cars. The catalyst is in the solid phase, and the reactants are in the gas phase.

Examples

1. A reaction with a high-activation energy will:
   A) require energy to begin
   B) require a catalyst to begin
   C) produce energy
   D) produce enzymes

2. A company is trying to make ammonia from the reaction of nitrogen (N_2) and hydrogen (H_2), but the reaction is progressing very slowly. Which of the following would be effective in increasing the reaction rate?

A) increasing the temperature

B) increasing the pressure

C) adding a catalyst

D) all the above

Answers: 1. A) 2. D)

LAWS OF THERMODYNAMICS

THERMODYNAMICS is the study of energy in a system and its relationship to chemical reactions. The use of thermodynamics can help explain the rate at which a reaction will occur and whether a reaction will occur at all. There are three basic laws of thermodynamics:

The **FIRST LAW OF THERMODYNAMICS** states that the internal energy of a system (U) is equal to the heat in the system (Q) minus the work performed by the system (W): $U = Q - W$. This law also confirms the conservation of energy (that energy can neither be created nor destroyed).

This law is probably the most important for chemistry; it helps explain energy shifts in a reaction. For example, if the internal energy of reactants is greater than the internal energy of the products, energy must be released during the course of the reaction, in the form of either heat or work.

The **SECOND LAW OF THERMODYNAMICS** states that the entropy of a system increases with time and with action. In layman's terms, this law states that any action results in an increase of entropy, a property that describes disorder. The **THIRD LAW OF THERMODYNAMICS** states that the entropy of a substance approaches zero as the temperature approaches absolute zero (0 Kelvin).

Endothermic and Exothermic Reactions

There are three types of reactions: endothermic, exothermic, and isothermic. An **ENDOTHERMIC** reaction requires heat to proceed, while an **EXOTHERMIC** reaction releases heat during the course of the reaction. An **ISOTHERMIC** reaction has no net input or output of energy.

$\longrightarrow$
CONTINUE

Examples

1. In chemistry class, a student mixes two unknown chemicals in a beaker. He notices that the beaker becomes hot to the touch. What type of reaction must be taking place in the beaker?

   A) exothermic

   B) endothermic

   C) combustion

   D) single replacement

2. Which of these processes is exothermic?

   A) freezing water

   B) baking a cake

   C) melting iron

   D) breaking up a gaseous diatom

   Answers: 1. A) 2. A)

NUCLEAR CHEMISTRY AND RADIOACTIVITY

The nuclei of some elements are unstable and will emit radioactive particles or energy in order to stabilize; together these emissions of particles and energy are called **RADIOACTIVE DECAY** or **RADIATION**. The three types of radiation that will be covered on the test are alpha, beta, and gamma radiation.

ALPHA PARTICLES consist of two protons and two neutrons (i.e., a helium nucleus). They are written as $_0^2 He$. In beta decay, high-energy electrons or positrons are emitted from the nucleus. **BETA PARTICLES** are written as $_{-1}^0 \beta$ (for electrons) and $_{+1}^0 \beta$ (for positrons). Lastly, **GAMMA RADIATION** is a high-frequency (and thus high-energy) electromagnetic radiation written as $_0^0 \gamma$. All three types of radiation can cause serious health issues ranging from nausea to cancer; both alpha and beta particles are relatively large and thus can be stopped by simple protective barriers. Gamma radiation, however, can travel through most substances, including concrete; lead is usually needed to provide protection from gamma rays.

Half-Life

The time it takes for half a sample of a radioactive substance to decay is called the substance's **HALF-LIFE** ($t_{\frac{1}{2}}$). A sample of lead-210 has a half-life of 22.2 years, meaning a 100 gram sample of lead-210 would be reduced to 50 grams after 22.2 years, 25 grams after 44.4 years, 12.5 grams after 66.6 years, and so on.

Examples

1. Uranium 233 has a half-life of about 70 years. If an area is contaminated with this compound, how long will it take to reach less than 5 percent of its original concentration? Round to the nearest number.

    A) 3 half-lives

    B) 4 half-lives

    C) 5 half-lives

    D) 6 half-lives

2. In the nuclear reaction shown below, what is the missing product?

    $^{11}_{5}B \rightarrow$ product $+ ^{4}_{2}He$

    A) $^{9}_{5}B$

    B) $^{7}_{5}Li$

    C) $^{7}_{3}Li$

    D) $^{9}_{3}B$

    Answers: 1. C) 2. C)

12

PHYSICS

P hysics is the science of matter and energy and the interaction between the two. Physics is grouped into fields such as acoustics (the study of sound), optics (the study of light), mechanics (the study of motion), and electromagnetism (the study of electric and magnetic fields).

MECHANICS

Motion

$$d = \tfrac{1}{2}at^2 + v_i t \ (d = vt \text{ when } a = 0)$$

$$v_f = v_i + at$$

$$v_f^2 = v_i^2 + 2ad$$

m = mass
d = displacement
v = velocity
a = acceleration
t = time

Newtonian mechanics is the study of masses in motion using five main variables. **MASS** (m), as discussed above, is the amount of matter in an object; it's measured in kilograms (kg). **DISPLACEMENT** (d) is a measure of how far an object has moved from its starting point, usually given in meters (m). **VELOCITY** is the distance covered by an object over a given period of **TIME**, usually given in meters per second (m/s). Finally, the change in velocity over time is called **ACCELERATION** (a) and is measured in meters per second squared (m/s^2).

Velocity and displacement are both **VECTORS,** meaning they have a magnitude (e.g., 4 m/s) and a direction (e.g., 45°). **SCALARS,** on the other hand, have only a magnitude. **DISTANCE** is a scalar: it describes how far something has traveled. So, if you run 1000 meters around a track and end up back where you started, your displacement is 0 meters, but the distance you covered was 1000 meters. **SPEED** is also a scalar; it's the distance traveled over the time the trip took.

The motion of objects with uniform acceleration is described by a set of equations that define the relationships between distance, velocity, time, and acceleration. These equations can be used to solve for any of these five variables. When the object is moving in a single dimension, problems can be solved using the following steps:

1. Identify the variables given in the problem and the variable to be solved for.
2. Choose the equation that includes the variables from Step 1.
3. Plug the values from the problem into the equation and solve.

When the object is moving in two dimensions, it's necessary to separate the variables into their horizontal and vertical components because only variables in a single dimension can be used within the same equation. Often, it's necessary to solve for a variable in one dimension and use that value to solve for a variable in the second dimension.

Examples

1. How far will a car moving with a constant velocity of 40 mi/hr travel in 15 minutes?

   A) 2.7 miles

   B) 10 miles

   C) 40 miles

   D) 600 miles

2. A ball is dropped from a building with a height of 20 m. If there is no air resistance, how long will it take the ball to reach the ground ($g = 9.8$ m/s^2)?

   A) 2 s

   B) 4 s

   C) 5 s

   D) 10 s

   Answers: 1. B) 2. A)

Momentum

$$p = mv$$

$$J = \Delta P$$

p = momentum
J = impulse

$$m_1 v_{1_i} + m_2 v_{2_i} = m_1 v_{1_f} + m_2 v_{2_f} \text{ (elastic collision)}$$

$$m_1 v_{1_i} + m_2 v_{2_i} = (m_1 + m_2) v_f \text{ (inelastic collision)}$$

Multiplying an object's mass by its velocity gives a quantity called MOMENTUM (p), which is measured in kilogram meters per second ((kg·m)/s). Momentum is always conserved, meaning when objects collide, the sum of their momentums before the collision will be the same as the sum after (although their kinetic energy may not remain the same). Because momentum is derived from velocity, it's a vector. The change in momentum is called IMPULSE (*J*); it's measured in Newton seconds (N·s).

Examples

1. What is the momentum of an object of 1.5 kg mass moving with a velocity of magnitude 10 m/s?

   A) 1.5 (kg·m)/s

   B) 15 (kg·m)/s

   C) 150 (kg·m)/s

   D) 1500 (kg·m)/s

2. Two objects are traveling in the same direction at different speeds. Object 1 moves at 5 m/s and has a mass of 1 kg. Object 2 moves at 2 m/s and has a mass of 0.5 kg. If object 1 collides with object 2 and they stick together, what will be the final velocity of the two objects?

   A) 2.5 m/s

   B) 3 m/s

   C) 4 m/s

   D) 7 m/s

   Answers: 1. B) 2. C)

FORCES

$$G = 6.67408 \times 10^{-11} \text{ m}^3 \text{ kg}^{-1} \text{ s}^{-2}$$

$$g = 9.8 \text{ m/s}^2$$

$$F_g = mg \text{ (for falling objects)}$$

$$F_g = \frac{Gm_1 m_2}{r_2} \text{ (for the gravitational force between two masses)}$$

$$F = ma$$

$$F_f = \mu_k F_N$$

Obviously, objects need a reason to get moving: they don't just start accelerating on their own. The "push" that starts or stops an object's motion is called a FORCE (*F*) and is measured in Newtons (N). Examples of forces include GRAVITY (created by the mass of objects), FRICTION (created by the movement of two surfaces in contact with each other), TENSION (created by hanging a mass from a string or chain), and ELECTRICAL FORCE (created by charged particles). A force that creates circular motion is called a CENTRIPETAL FORCE.

Note that all of these forces are vectors with a magnitude and direction. Gravity, for example, always points down toward the

Gravitational force is proportional to the masses of two objects and the distance between the center of mass of the two objects, not the distance between the surfaces.

earth, and friction always points in the opposite direction of the object's motion. On a FREE BODY DIAGRAM, forces are drawn as vectors, and vectors in the horizontal and vertical directions can be added to find the total force.

Newton's three laws of motion describe how these forces work to create motion:

> **LAW #1**: An object at rest will remain at rest, and an object in motion will continue with the same speed and direction unless acted on by a force. This law is often called "the law of inertia."

> **LAW #2**: Acceleration is produced when a force acts on a mass. The greater the mass of the object being accelerated, the greater the amount of force needed to accelerate the object.

> **LAW #3**: Every action requires an equal and opposite reaction. This means that for every force, there is a reacting force both equal in size and opposite in direction. In other words, whenever an object pushes another object, it gets pushed back in the opposite direction with equal force.

Examples

1. An object is being acted on by only 2 forces as shown below. If the magnitudes of F1 and F2 are equal, which of the following statements must be true?

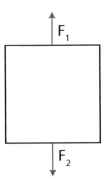

A) The velocity of the object must be zero.

B) The velocity of the object must be constant.

C) The velocity of the object must be increasing.

D) The velocity of the object must be decreasing.

2. An object is pulled across a rough surface with a force of 20 N. If the object moves with a constant velocity and the surface has a coefficient of kinetic friction equal to 0.2, what is the magnitude of the normal force acting on the object?

A) 4 N

B) 10 N

C) 20 N

D) 100 N

Answers: 1. B) 2. D)

CIRCULAR AND ROTATIONAL MOTION

Rotational Motion

$$\theta = \frac{1}{2}\alpha t^2 + \omega_i t$$

$$\omega_f = \omega_i + \alpha t$$

$$\omega_f^2 = \omega_i^2 + 2\alpha\theta$$

θ = angular displacement
ω = angular speed
a = angular acceleration

In addition to moving in a straight line, objects can also rotate. This ROTATIONAL MOTION is described using a similar set of variables and equations to those used for linear motion. However, the variables have been converted to represent rotational motion, as shown in the table below.

Table 12.1. Rotational motion

LINEAR VARIABLE	ROTATIONAL VARIABLE
displacement (*d*)	angular displacement (θ)
velocity (*v*)	angular speed (ω)
acceleration (*a*)	angular acceleration (*a*)

Example

The motor of an engine is rotating about its axis with an angular velocity of 100 rev/minute. After being switched off, it comes to rest in 15 s. If the angular deceleration is constant, how many revolutions does the engine make before it comes to rest?

A) 10.5 rev

B) 11.5 rev

C) 12.5 rev

D) 13.5 rev

Answer: C)

CONTINUE

Torque

$$\tau = rF\sin(\theta)$$

TORQUE is a form of work that is applied in a circular motion; it's measured in newton meters (N·m). A wrench, for example, employs torque to apply force to turning a bolt. The specific definition of torque is a force that is applied over a distance and an angle to generate circular motion (as seen below). The amount of torque depends on the radius of the arm (r), the force applied (F), and the angle of the force (θ).

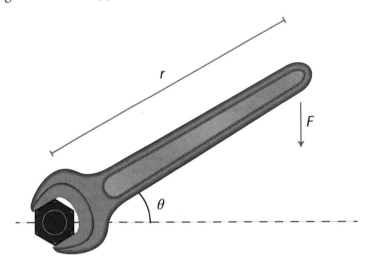

Figure 12.1. Torque

Example

A force of magnitude 10 N is applied at point A to cause a bar to rotate around point B, as shown below. What is the torque produced by the force?

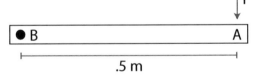

.5 m

A) – 20 N·m

B) – 5 N·m

C) 5 N·m

D) 20 N·m

Answer: B)

Circular Motion

$$a = \frac{v^2}{r}$$

$$F = ma_c = m \times \frac{v^2}{r}$$

CIRCULAR MOTION is the movement of an object around a central point. **CENTRIPETAL ACCELERATION**, which points toward the center of the circle, changes the direction of the object's velocity and keeps the object on a circular path. The force that creates centripetal acceleration can be tension (e.g., swing a weight on a string), friction(e.g., car tires on a turn), or other forces.

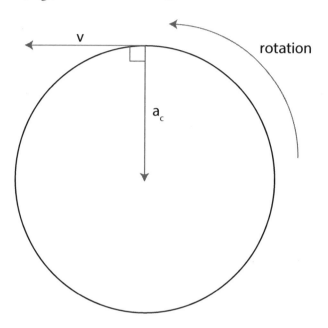

Figure 12.2. Circular motion

Example

An object of mass *m* undergoes uniform circular motion with a speed *v* at a distance *r* from the center of the circle. Which of the following will result in an increase in the centripetal force?

A) a decrease in *r* while maintaining the same speed

B) an increase in *r* while maintaining the same speed

C) a decrease in the speed of the mass by a factor of 4 and a decrease in *r* by a factor of 2

D) an increase in the speed of the mass by a factor of 2 and an increase in *r* by a factor of 4

Answer: A)

CONTINUE

ENERGY, WORK, AND POWER

Energy

$$KE = \frac{1}{2}mv^2$$

$$PE_g = mgh$$

In simple terms, energy is the capacity to do work; in other words, it's a measurement of how much force a system could apply. Energy is measured in Joules (J), which are J = kg · m²/s². There are two main categories of energy. The energy stored within an object due to its relative position is its **POTENTIAL ENERGY**: that object has the potential to do work. Potential energy can be created in a number of ways, including raising an object off the ground or compressing a spring. **KINETIC ENERGY** is present when an object is in motion. The sum of an object's kinetic and potential energies is called its **MECHANICAL ENERGY**.

Energy can be neither created nor destroyed; it can only be converted from one form to another. For example when a rock is lifted some distance from the ground, it has **GRAVITATIONAL POTENTIAL ENERGY**; when it's released, it begins to move toward the earth, and that potential energy becomes kinetic energy. A pendulum is another example: at the height of its swing, the pendulum will have potential energy but no kinetic energy; at the bottom of its swing, it has kinetic energy but no more potential energy.

⚠
Generally, kinetic energy is the energy of an object in motion, and potential energy is the energy of an object at rest.

Examples

1. The mass of a rider and his cycle combined is 90 kg. What is the increase in kinetic energy if a 90 kg bike increases its speed from 6 km/h to 12 km/h?

    A) 300 J

    B) 350 J

    C) 375 J

    D) 400 J

2. A skier starts from rest at the top of a hill. If the height of the hill is 20 m, what is the speed of the skier at the bottom of the hill? (Assume no air resistance or friction.)

    A) 4 m/s

    B) 20 m/s

    C) 200 m/s

    D) 400 m/s

    Answers: 1. C) 2. B)

Work

$$W = Fd$$

$$P = \frac{W}{t}$$

WORK is defined in physics as a force exerted over a distance; work is also measured in Joules (J). Work has to take place over a distance: if an object is acted upon by a force, but does not move, then no work has been performed. For example, if someone pushes against a wall with 50 N of force, she has not performed any work. However, if she lifted a baseball off the ground, then she performed work.

Work is a scalar quantity and cannot be expressed in terms of a vector. However, the force applied to do work is a vector quantity, and thus the net force used to perform work can change depending on the angle at which it's applied.

POWER is force applied over time; it's measured in Watts.

Examples

1. A child pushes a truck across the floor at a velocity of 1 m/s for 5 m using 1 N of force. How much work did the child do?

   A) 0.25 J

   B) 5 J

   C) 2.5 J

   D) 25 J

2. In the same scenario described above, the child pushes the truck for 5 s. How much power did the child deliver to the truck?

   A) 0.05 W

   B) 0.25 W

   C) 0.5 W

   D) 1 W

   Answers: 1. B) 2. D)

THERMODYNAMICS

TEMPERATURE is a measure of the average kinetic energy of the atoms or molecules of a substance. Substances with a higher temperature have more kinetic energy, meaning their molecules are moving at a higher velocity. Lowering the temperature of the substance will slow the speed of the molecules. The SI unit for temperature is Celsius, but it also measured in Fahrenheit and Kelvin.

HEAT is the transfer of energy between substances; it's measured in Joules. When the air warms a block of ice, or a soda gets cold in the fridge, that transfer of energy is heat. Heat always moves from warmer substances to colder ones. Heat can be transferred

q = heat

Fahrenheit and Celsius are reference scales, while Kelvin is an absolute scale.

in several different ways. One is **CONDUCTION**, which occurs when heat is transferred between neighboring molecules; conduction is what makes a person's hand cold when she holds ice. During **CONVECTION**, heat is transferred away from an object by the movement of gases or fluids, for example when warm air rises from a radiator.

Heat is not an intrinsic property. It would not be correct to say that an object contains 100 Joules of heat. It would be correct to say that an object has transmitted 100 Joules of heat.

Heat Capacity

$$q = mc\Delta T$$

The **HEAT CAPACITY** of an object is best defined as its resistance to temperature change. A material with a higher heat capacity will have a lower change in temperature when exposed to a greater amount of heat. For example, water has one of the highest heat capacities of 4.18 J/(g·K), meaning 4.18 Joules are needed to increase the temperature of one gram of water by one degree Kelvin. On the other hand, most metals have low heat capacities. Copper has a heat capacity of just 0.39 J/(g·K). This means that if copper and water are exposed to the same amount of heat, copper will heat up more than 10 times faster than water will.

Example

If 27.53 J of heat are needed to increase the temperature of a 15 g mass by 7.3 K, what is the mass's heat capacity?

A) 0.251 J/(g·K)

B) 1.835 J/(g·K)

C) 3.977 J/(g·K)

D) 13.398 J/(g·K)

Answer: A)

FLUID MECHANICS

Pressure

$$P = \rho g h$$

P = pressure
ρ = density

PRESSURE is the force applied over a specific area; it's measured in Pascal's, atmospheres, or bars. When an object is submersed in a fluid, the weight of the fluid will exert pressure on that object. The magnitude of the pressure depends on the acceleration due to gravity (g), the depth of the object (h), and the fluid's density.

Fluid pressure is affected by depth, not by shape.

The **DENSITY** (ρ) of a material is defined as its mass per unit volume. For example, water has a density of 1 gram per cubic centimeter, or 1 gram per milliliter. The **SPECIFIC DENSITY** or specific gravity of a material is defined as its density when compared with water. In this case, water has a set value of 1. Gold has a specific gravity of 19.3, which means that it's 19.3 times denser than water.

Example

Objects A, B, C, and D are submersed in water as shown below. Which of the following statements is true?

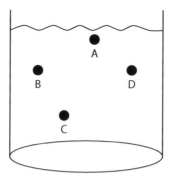

A) The pressure at B is less than the pressure at A.

B) The pressure at A is equal to the pressure at C.

C) The pressure at B and D is equal.

D) The pressure at points A, B, C, and D is equal.

Answer: C)

Buoyancy

BUOYANCY is the ability of an object to float in a fluid that has a greater density than the object. For example, wood might float in water, but a steel marble will not, due to the much higher density of the steel marble compared with the wood.

The buoyant force of an object is a principle first determined by Archimedes, who stated, "The strength of the buoyant force is equal to the weight of the fluid displaced by the object." Thus, the magnitude of the upward buoyant force on a floating object can be found by calculating the volume of displaced fluid.

Example

When a block is completely submerged in a vessel filled to the top with liquid, the amount of liquid that overflows the vessel—

A) has equal weight to that of the block.

B) has equal volume to that of the block.

C) has the same relative density as that of the block.

D) has the same mass as that of the block.

Answer: B)

$\longrightarrow$
CONTINUE

Fluid Flow

$$A_1 v_1 = A_2 v_2$$

$$P_1 + \rho g h_1 + \frac{1}{2}\rho v_1^2 = P_2 + \rho g h_2 + \frac{1}{2}\rho v_2^2$$

When fluid is flowing through a pipe, the area of the pipe and the fluid's velocity have an inverse relationship. Thus, if a pipe gradually becomes thinner, then the water flowing through it will become faster. Based on this understanding, the **Bernoulli Equation** establishes the flow rate of a fluid through a pipe depending on the energy of a fluid flowing through a pipe, the height of the pipe, and the corresponding pressure.

Example

A fluid whose density remains constant is flowing through a tube with radius r_1. It then moves into a section of the tube with a radius r_2. If $r_2 > r_1$, what effect will the increase in radius have?

A) decrease the speed of the fluid

B) increase the speed of the fluid

C) increase the volume of fluid that flows past a given point

D) decrease the volume of fluid that flows past a given point

Answer: A)

WAVES

Types of Waves

A **wave** is a periodic motion that carries energy through space or matter. There are two main types of waves: mechanical and electromagnetic. **Mechanical waves** travel through a physical medium; ripples in a pond and sound waves traveling through the air are both examples of mechanical waves. **Electromagnetic waves** do not require a medium to travel because they consist of oscillating magnetic and electric fields. These waves are classified on the **electromagnetic spectrum** and include visible light, x-rays, and radio waves.

Waves can also be classified by how the particles in the wave vibrate. **Longitudinal waves** cause particles to vibrate parallel to the movement of the wave; **transverse waves** cause particles to vibrate perpendicular to the movement of the wave.

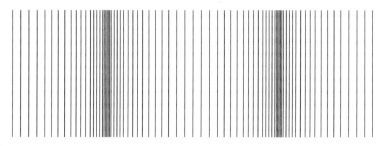

longitudinal wave

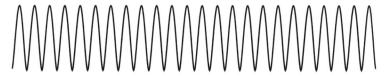

transverse wave

Figure 12.3. Types of waves

Example

Which of the following requires a medium to travel?

A) visible light

B) microwaves

C) radio waves

D) sound waves

Answer: D)

Characteristics of Waves

$$v = \lambda f = \frac{\lambda}{T}$$

$$T = \frac{1}{f}$$

The four major characteristics of waves are wavelength, amplitude, period, and frequency. The **WAVELENGTH** (λ) is the distance from the peak of one wave to the next (or from the trough of one wave to the next). The **AMPLITUDE** (A) of a wave is the distance from the top of the wave to the bottom. Both wavelength and amplitude are measured in meters (the SI unit for distance).

The **PERIOD** (T) of a wave is the time it takes the wave to complete one oscillation; it's usually measured in seconds. The **FREQUENCY** (f) of a wave is the number of oscillations that occur per second; it's measured in Hertz (Hz). The period and frequency of a wave are inverses of each other: the shorter the period of a wave, the higher its frequency.

Example

A wave with a speed of 10 m/s is traveling on a string at a frequency of 20 oscillations per second. What is the wave's wavelength?

A) 0.2 m

B) 0.5 m

C) 2 m

D) 200 m

Answer: B)

Properties of Waves

Waves of all kinds exhibit particular behaviors. Waves can interact to create either CONSTRUCTIVE INTERFERENCE, where the resulting wave is bigger than either original wave, or DESTRUCTIVE INTERFERENCE, which creates a wave that is smaller than either original wave. Waves will also bend when passing through a slit, a process called DIFFRACTION. Waves will also REFRACT, or bend, when they pass from one medium into another.

Example

What is the maximum possible amplitude of the wave created by the interference of a wave with an amplitude of 0.5 m and a wave with an amplitude of 2 m?

A) 0 m

B) 0.5 m

C) 2.5 m

D) 5 m

Answer: C)

Sound

I = intensity

$I_0 = 1 \times 10^{-12}$ W/m² (smallest intensity that can be heard by the human ear)

$$DB = 10\log\left(\frac{I}{I_0}\right)$$

SOUND is composed of waves that are usually produced by the vibration of an object, such as the strings of an instrument or the human vocal cords. The vibrations cause the air to vibrate as well, which creates a pressure variation in the air, creating a longitudinal wave. When humans hear a sound, it's the detection of the pressure variation by our ear drums. The speed of a sound wave depends on the medium that it's moving through. In air, sound has a speed of about 340 meters per second or 761 miles per hour.

Sound waves travel much faster in water than in air.

Humans can typically detect sound waves between 20 Hz to 20,000 Hz. Sound waves with a lower frequency have a "lower" pitch to human ears, and sound waves with a high frequency have a "high" pitch to human ears.

Sound INTENSITY (*I*) is the sound power over a specific area; it's measured in W/m² or decibels (DB). Intensity represents the amount of energy carried by the sound wave; the louder the sound (and larger the amplitude), the greater the intensity. However, sound wave energy is inversely proportional to the distance from which it's heard. Thus, as you move away from a sound source, the intensity of the sound decreases exponentially.

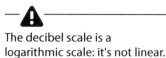

The decibel scale is a logarithmic scale: it's not linear.

Example

Sound waves will move fastest through which medium?

A) water

B) air

C) a vacuum

D) wood

Answer: D)

PERIODIC MOTION

An oscillation is a **PERIODIC MOTION** that occurs at a specific frequency. Examples of objects that oscillate include pendulum clocks, springs, and the strings in musical instruments.

Springs

$$F = -kx$$

A **SPRING** is a coil of metal or other ductile material that, when compressed or stretched, will return to its original shape if not held by a force. The force required to stretch or compress a spring is related to the distance the spring will be displaced and its spring constant (*k*). The greater the spring constant, the stiffer the spring. The springs that make up the suspension of a car, for example, have very high spring constants, in the range of 3000 – 5000 Newtons per meter, whereas the spring that is used in a ballpoint pen might have a spring constant value of 2 – 3 Newtons per meter.

x = displacement
k = spring constant

Example

What is the magnitude of the force required to compress a spring 35 cm if the spring has a spring constant of 55 Newtons per meter?

A) 6.74 N

B) 19.25 N

C) 674 N

D) 1925 N

Answer: B)

L = length of pendulum

The mass of the pendulum does not have a significant effect on its period of the swing, as long as there is no air resistance.

Pendulums

$$f = \frac{1}{2\pi}\left(\frac{\sqrt{g}}{L}\right)$$

A **PENDULUM** is a mass hanging on a string that is swinging back and forth. In a pendulum, as the mass reaches its lowest point, the velocity is the greatest. As it reaches its height on either side, the stored potential energy is the highest, but at its peak, the velocity is exactly equal to zero. The frequency of a pendulum is dependent on two things: the gravitational force and the length of the rope.

Examples

Which of the following would increase the frequency of a pendulum?

A) moving the pendulum to a planet with a higher acceleration due to gravity

B) making the length of the pendulum longer

C) adding more mass to the end of the pendulum

D) increasing the angle of the initial release point

Answer: A)

LIGHT

LIGHT is a form of electromagnetic radiation that makes up a small spectrum of all the electromagnetic waves. Visible light is the wavelength range of 400 to 800 nanometers and is one of the few types of radiation that is able to penetrate the Earth's atmosphere.

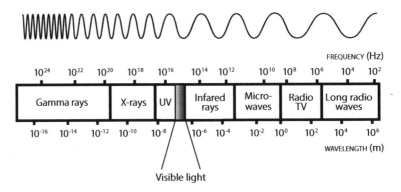

Figure 12.4. Electromagnetic spectrum

Properties of Light

$$n_1 \sin\theta_1 = n_2 \sin\theta_2$$

$$n = \frac{c}{v_s}$$

Light, which is an electromagnetic wave, has a number of special properties because it acts as both a particle and a wave—a phenomenon called the **WAVE-PARTICLE DUALITY OF LIGHT**. Light will reflect off some materials: the **INCIDENT RAY** will bounce off a surface, and the incident angle will be equal to the angle of reflection. Light will also bend when it passes from one media to another in a process called REFRACTION. The angle of refraction can be found using Snell's law and the material's index of refraction (*n*).

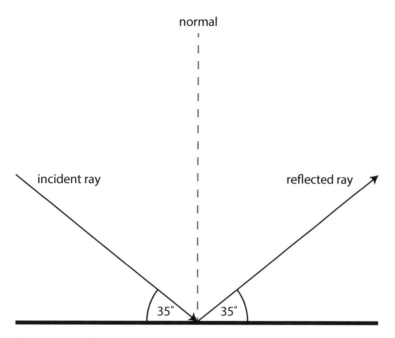

Figure 12.5. Reflection

Light waves can experience both interference and diffraction like any other wave. Because light is made up of discrete packets of energy (called quanta), light also sometimes acts as a particle. For example, when light strikes a metal surface, the packets of energy can eject electrons from atoms in a process called the PHOTOELECTRIC EFFECT.

Example

A ray of light is directed at a reflective surface as shown below.

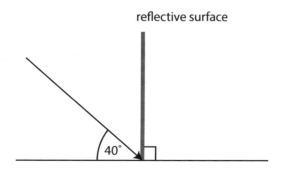

CONTINUE

What angle does the reflected ray make with respect to the normal?

A) 0°

B) 40°

C) 50°

D) 90°

Answer: B)

ELECTRICITY

Electric Charge

$$k = 9 \times 10^9 \text{ N} \times \text{m}_2/\text{C}_2$$

$$F = k\frac{q_1 q_2}{r^2}$$

An electric charge is generated due to the difference in CHARGE (q) potential between protons, which have a +1 charge, and electrons, which have a –1 charge. The charges on a proton or electron are elementary, meaning that they cannot be further subdivided into smaller units. The charge is measured in coulombs (C). A single electron has a charge of -1.6×10^{-19} C. One proton has the exact same amount of charge but of the opposite sign. Electricity is generated by the flow of electrons through a conducting coil, such as copper or steel.

Charged particles are naturally attracted to or repulsed from each other based on their charge. An electron will repel another electron, and a proton will repel another proton. An electron and proton will be attracted to one another. COULOMB'S LAW is used to predict the strength of the attractive or repulsive force between two particles. A positive value of force indicates that the particles are being repelled from one another.

Example

Two particles are separated by a distance of 0.5 m. If one particle has a charge of 1 μC and the other particle has a charge of −2 μC, what is the magnitude of the force between the particles ($k = 9 \times 10^9$ Nm²/C²)?

A) 9×10^{-3} N

B) 7.2×10^{-2} N

C) 7.2×10^{10} N

D) 9×10^9 N

Answer: B)

Electric Fields

$$\Delta V = Ed$$

$E = \frac{F}{q}$

Charged particles create an **ELECTRIC FIELD** (E) in which they will exert an electric force on other charged particles. The strength of an electric field is measured in newtons per coulomb and is proportional to the charge of the particle experiencing the force (i.e., a particle with a higher charge will experience a larger force, and vice versa).

Moving a particle through an electric field will change the potential electrical energy of that particle in an amount proportional to the displacement and force of the electric field. The difference in potential electrical energy between two points is known as **VOLTAGE** (V), which is measured in volts.

Example

A particle is placed in a uniform electric field of magnitude 1×10^4 N/C. If the particle experiences a force of 0.1 N, what is the magnitude of the charge on the particle?

A) 0.1 μC

B) 1 μC

C) 10 μC

D) 100 μC

Answer: C)

Circuits

$$V = IR$$

$$P = IV = \frac{V^2}{R}$$

I = current
R = resistance
P = power

In an electric **CIRCUIT**, a closed loop is formed that is connected to the positive and negative ends of a voltage source. The voltage source provides the charge potential that drives electrons through the circuit to create electricity. The movement of electrons is called **CURRENT**, which is measured in Amps (A).

Current in a circuit can be thought of as analogous to water in a pipe.

A **RESISTOR** is an electrical component that provides resistance to the flow of current through an electric circuit. A resistor is usually composed of a series of materials that are not conducive to electron flow. The units of resistance are Ω. According to Ohm's law, current and resistance are inversely related, and both are proportional to voltage.

Resistors in a circuit can be wired in series or in parallel. In a **SERIES** circuit, the current can only follow one path, while in a **PARALLEL** circuit, the current can follow multiple pathways.

Resistors in series are additive. Resistors in parallel have a lower total resistance than any individual resistor.

CONTINUE

Table 12.2. Series and parallel circuits

	SERIES	PARALLEL
Current	$I_1 = I_2 = I_3 = ... = I_n$	$I_t = I_1 + I_2 + ... + I_n$
Voltage	$V_t = V_1 + V_2 + ... + V_n$	$V_1 = V_2 = V_3 = ... = V_n$
Resistance	$R_t = R_1 + R_2 + ... + R_n$	$\frac{1}{R_t} = \frac{1}{R_1} + \frac{1}{R_2} + ... + \frac{1}{R_n}$

Examples

1. What is the current running through a 2 Ω resister in a circuit with a 10 V battery?

   A) 2 A

   B) 5 A

   C) 20 A

   D) 50 A

2. If a circuit wired in series includes five 10 Ω resisters, what is the total resistance of the circuit?

   A) 2 Ω

   B) 10 Ω

   C) 50 Ω

   D) 500 Ω

Answers: 1. B) 2. C)

MAGNETISM

MAGNETIC FIELDS can be produced by moving electric charges or can be the result of the alignment of subatomic particles in a substance. The SI unit for magnetism is the Tesla, named after the Russian inventor Nikola Tesla. Electricity and magnetism are closely related: moving particles (like electricity) will create magnetic fields. Similarly, magnetic fields will exert a force on moving charged particles, and a moving magnetic field will create an electric current.

All magnets have a north and a south pole. As with charges, like poles repel each other and opposite poles attract each other; the magnitude of this force is directly proportional to the strength of the magnets and inversely proportional to their distance. Magnetic field lines always flow from north to south.

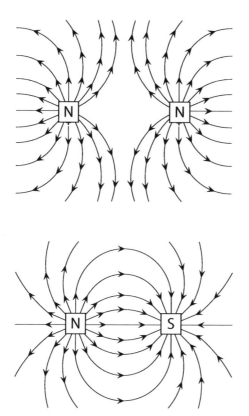

Figure 12.6. Magnetic field lines

Example

The north poles of two magnets are held near each other. At which distance will the magnets experience the most force?

    A) 0.1 m

    B) 1 m

    C) 10 m

    D) 100 m

    Answer: A)

13

EARTH AND SPACE SCIENCE

ASTRONOMY

Astronomy is the study of celestial objects and everything that occurs outside the Earth's atmosphere. This includes everything from planets and stars to, at times, the nature of the universe itself.

The GED will not heavily test astronomical concepts, but it will be helpful to know basic terminology:

- A **PLANET** is an astronomical object that is large enough to have its own gravity but not large enough to undergo thermonuclear fusion. It's also large enough to have cleared the local area of other celestial objects smaller than it.

- A **STAR** is a luminous plasma ball that is being held together by nothing but its own gravity. The Sun is a star, as are the vast majority of lights seen in the night sky.

- A **SOLAR SYSTEM** is a star and all the objects that are orbiting that star. The objects do not necessarily have to be planets.

- A **GALAXY** is a system of stars, interstellar gas, dust, dark matter, and stellar remnants that are bound together by an immense gravity field.

- The **SUN** is the star found at the center of our solar system. It's also the primary source of energy for the planets that orbit it (including the Earth).

- **HELIOCENTRIC** is a term that describes a system that has a sun as its center (such as our solar system).

- A **ROTATION** is the circular movement of a given object around a single point (usually the center of the object).

- **REVOLUTION** might be considered another term for orbit, astronomically speaking. This term is used when one object moves around another one.

- An **ELLIPTICAL PATH** (or elliptical orbit) is a type of orbit around an object that is roughly egg shaped, rather than being perfectly spherical.

The Planets

Our solar system includes eight planets that follow elliptical orbits around the sun. The immense gravitational field of the sun holds the planets in orbit, and the output of electromagnetic radiation from the sun is what provides the energy from which life on Earth is derived.

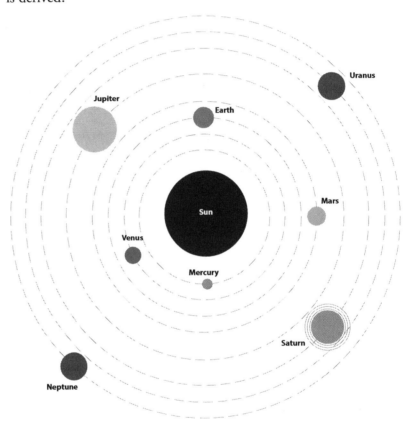

Figure 13.1. Solar system

MERCURY is the planet closest to the sun; it's not much larger than the Earth's moon. On the day side, the temperatures reach around 840°F, while on the night side, temperatures can drop to very far below freezing. There is nearly no atmosphere on Mercury and thus nothing to protect it from impacts of meteors.

VENUS is the second planet from the sun. It's even hotter than Mercury, and the atmosphere is toxic due to a greenhouse effect (which also traps heat). The pressure on the surface of the planet is immense. Venus has a very slow rotation around its axis and spins in the opposite direction from most of the planets of the solar system. Venus is one of the brightest objects in the sky (other than the moon and the sun).

EARTH is the third planet from the sun. This is a water-dominant planet, with around two-thirds of the surface covered by water, and is the only known planet that has life on it. The atmosphere consists primarily of nitrogen and oxygen. The movement of the Earth is responsible for many familiar characteristcs:

- The Earth rotates along its axis while moving counter-clockwise around the sun.
- A day is the time it takes the Earth to make one rotation around its axis, which tilts at an angle of 23.5 degrees.
- A year is the time it takes the Earth to make one revolution around the sun.
- The cycle of night and day is created by the Earth's rotation on its axis.
- The seasons are created by the movement of the Earth around the sun combined with the tilt of the Earth's axis, which determines the amount of sunlight that reaches the Earth's surface.

MARS is the fourth planet from the sun and is a cold and dry planet. The dust that makes up the surface of the planet is a form of iron oxide, which is also what gives the planet its red color. The topography of Mars is very similar to that of Earth, and ice has been found in some locations on Mars. Additionally, though the atmosphere is currently too thin for water to exist on the surface in liquid form, it's theorized that water was abundant on the planet in the past.

JUPITER is the largest planet in the solar system and the fifth planet from the sun. The planet itself is primarily gaseous, being composed of hydrogen and helium (along with other gases in smaller amounts). The Great Red Spot is an enormous storm that has been ongoing on the planet for hundreds of years. The planet has dozens of moons and a very strong magnetic field.

The sixth planet from the sun, **SATURN**, is known for the rings that orbit it. The planet is primarily gaseous, being composed of helium and hydrogen. The planet has multiple moons.

URANUS is the seventh planet from the sun. The equator of Uranus is at a right angle to the orbit of the planet, so it appears to be on its side. This planet is about the same size as Neptune. Uranus has faint rings, multiple moons, methane, and a bluish-green tint.

The eighth planet from the sun, **NEPTUNE**, is characterized by its cold temperature and its very strong winds. Neptune is about seventeen times the size of Earth. The planet was originally discovered when scientists theorized that the irregular orbit of

Uranus was the result of a gravitational pull from an undiscovered planet.

In recent years, **Pluto**, formerly the ninth planet from the sun, has been reclassified from a true planet to a dwarf planet. Pluto is smaller than the Earth's moon, and it has an orbit near the outer edge of the local solar system. Its orbit around the sun takes around 248 Earth years. The planet itself is rocky and extremely cold. Its atmosphere is extremely thin.

The Sun

Made of hot plasma, our sun, like other stars, is essentially a gigantic reactor where nuclear reactions occur naturally. Around one million Earths could fit into the sun, which accounts for 99.8 percent of the mass in the entire solar system. Astronomers consider our sun to be a type G, main sequence star, which means that it's a fairly typical star. While it's no giant star, it's actually estimated to be brighter than about 85 percent of the stars in our galaxy, since most of the stars in existence are red dwarfs.

Located in the "suburbs" of the **Milky Way galaxy**, about two-thirds of the way out from the center, the sun came into being 4.6 billion years ago. Most scientists think that our sun, as well as the rest of our solar system, formed from a large cloud of rotating dust and gas. Due to gravity this cloud collapsed into a rotating disk, and most of the material was drawn into the center. This material grew increasingly hot and dense until nuclear fusion was initiated, and our sun was officially born.

Our sun is considered a Population I star, which means that it's relatively young and rich in elements that are heavier than helium. Elements heavier than helium (He) all the way up the Periodic Table to iron (Fe) are produced through the process of nuclear fusion, which happens inside stars. Elements heavier than iron are produced during supernova explosions, which occur when very massive stars die. It's thought that the birth of our solar system was triggered by shock waves from one or more such supernovae, due to the presence of elements like gold and uranium, which are higher on the Periodic Table than iron.

Though the sun often appears from afar as a uniform object, it's not. First, temperatures across the sun are not consistent. The sun's exterior burns at about 10,000° Fahrenheit, but its core—where nuclear reactions take place—can climb up to 27 million degrees Fahrenheit. Second, the sun's "body" doesn't rotate uniformly, either. Due to convective motion and the **Coriolis effect**, the star rotates faster at its equator than its poles. Finally, though it's an almost perfect sphere, the sun actually doesn't have a definite boundary—though for practical purposes, the edge of the photosphere (the sun's apparent visible surface) is considered its boundary.

Although it's largely composed of hydrogen (74.9 percent in its PHOTOSPHERE—the outer shell of the sun that radiates light) and helium (23.8 percent), heavier elements like oxygen, carbon, iron, and neon make up less than 1 percent each of the photosphere. The composition of the inner sun is more variable, as it has changed from possessing more hydrogen to possessing more helium via nuclear fusion, which converts hydrogen into helium.

The sun has multiple regions: its CORE, where the thermal energy that heats the sun (and then escapes out into space in the form of sunlight or kinetic energy) is produced; the RADIATIVE ZONE, which extends from the core to 70 percent of the sun's surface and scatters light coming from the sun's core; the TACHOLINE, which separates the radiative and convective zones and may cause the sun's magnetic field; and the CONVECTIVE ZONE, which features convection cells of gas to carry the sun's heat outward to the photosphere, where it escapes into space.

However, as is evident during total solar eclipses, the sun actually has one more layer—an atmosphere. Counterintuitively, the sun's atmosphere is actually hotter than the photosphere. The atmosphere has several parts: the CHROMOSPHERE, where temperature increases with altitude; a thin transition region, the CORONA, where solar winds are produced; and the HELIOSPHERE, which is a magnetic bubble extending beyond the orbit of Pluto to the edge of our solar system.

The sun has a magnetic field that can vary greatly and be very strong in some spots, though on average it's about twice as strong as Earth's. The sun's nonuniform magnetic field is largely a by-product of its nonuniform rotation, and these distortions are the main causes behind some of the most interesting phenomena associated with the sun: SUNSPOTS (temporary areas of reduced surface temperature), SOLAR FLARES (the most violent eruptions), and CORONAL MASS EJECTIONS (where billions of tons of matter spew out into space).

EARTH SCIENCES

The earth sciences include all the sciences that study the Earth. These disciplines look at topics as varied as the structure of the Earth's crust, the movement of Earth's oceans, and the causes of Earth's weather.

Geology

Geology is the study of the solid components of the Earth. The Earth is not a uniform mass: it has many different layers and a disparate topography. Among the layers of the Earth are the crust, the asthenosphere, the mantle, and the core. The thinnest of those layers is the CRUST, which is also the outermost layer (and the layer that humanity calls home). The crust is not uniform and, in fact, has a unique topology. Valleys, mountains, plains, and basins are all variations in the height and thickness of the crust. Together with the topmost layer of the mantle (the most solid part of the mantle), the core forms the LITHOSPHERE.

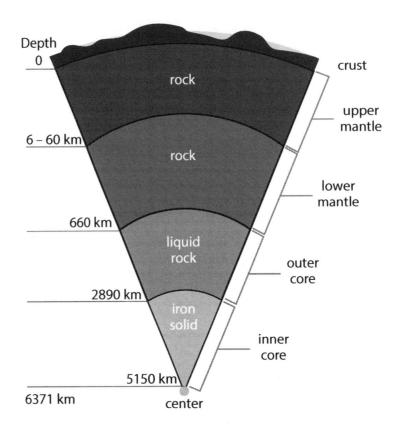

Figure 13.2. Layers of the Earth

The crust is composed of TECTONIC PLATES, which move over the asthenosphere. This movement is what explains many natural phenomena, including volcanoes, the creation and destruction of mountains, changes in the sea floor, and earthquakes. The crust is usually only stable for a small time frame, geologically speaking, as these events are constantly occurring across the Earth's surface.

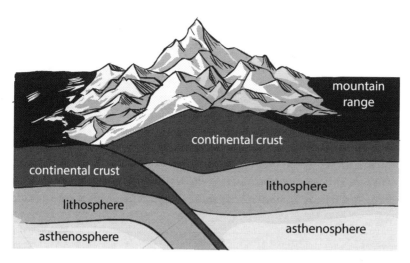

Figure 13.3. The Earth's crust

Rocks on the Earth are also changing. Generally, rocks are made up of a combination of different inorganic crystalline substances known as MINERALS. Each type of mineral will have a specific chemical makeup and will have properties that are unique to them. Here are some of the most common minerals:

- Bauxite is a type of rock composed primarily of aluminum oxides that have been hydrated.
- Quartz is the most abundant mineral in the crust of the Earth. This is the most common and simplest form of all silicates. It's an oxide of silicon.
- Talc is a common and soft mineral that can be scratched with a fingernail.
- Pyrite is a mineral composed of iron and sulfur. Pyrite is commonly known as "fool's gold" because of its resemblance to actual gold.
- Graphite is a form of carbon. You may recognize this as being used in pencils and some other commercial applications.

Also included in this list would be all the types of precious stones: emerald, ruby, opal, diamond, sapphire, etc.

There are three main types of rocks: igneous, sedimentary, and metamorphic. IGNEOUS ROCKS have been formed through the melting and cooling of minerals within the mantle beneath the surface of the Earth. These can surface, initially, as lava. Some common examples of igneous rocks are granite, basalt, and solid volcanic lava.

SEDIMENTARY ROCKS are formed from the accumulation of sediment, often at the bottom of bodies of water, which is then compressed to form rocks. This sediment can derive from biological detritus, weathering of rocks, or the chemical breakdown of minerals.

METAMORPHIC ROCKS are rocks that have gone through a transformation. When rock is put under immense heat and pressure, both physical and chemical changes can occur within it. Some of the examples of this type of rock include slate, gneiss, and marble.

Rocks are subject to several destructive forces. WEATHERING is the process of rocks and soil breaking down through contact with the atmosphere and waters of the Earth. This occurs without movement. EROSION is the process of rocks and soil breaking down and being moved and deposited somewhere else through nature processes such as the flowing of water, wind, and storms.

DEPOSITION is a process through which soil and rocks are added to a mass through transport as a result of erosion and a loss of kinetic energy. Deposition would be rocks breaking off of a mountain because of a hard storm and then "depositing" them down at the bottom of the mountain when they no longer have enough kinetic energy to move.

Oceanography

The HYDROSPHERE is the term that is used for the collective water of the Earth. This includes everything from oceans to lakes, ponds, and rivers. On the Earth, the hydrosphere is about 70 percent of the surface. This water contains minerals and salts that have been dissolved, and the vast majority of the water is held in four ocean basins. Seas, porous rocks, ice caps, lakes, and rivers contain the rest of the water on Earth. From smallest to largest, the oceans are the Arctic Ocean, the Indian Ocean, the Atlantic Ocean, and the Pacific Ocean.

The OCEANS play a large role in maintaining the environment of the Earth. Oceans are able to absorb and release heat; thus, they help to regulate both the climate and the weather. Because of the tilt and rotation of the Earth, sunlight strikes the Earth's surface unevenly. Oceans trap this heat and distribute it around the planet. This uneven heating also helps create ocean currents.

Oceanography itself is a pretty broad topic and is a term used to describe the study of the ocean as well as oceanic ecosystems, currents, fluid dynamics, plate tectonics, and marine organisms. One of the current major areas of study in oceanography is the ACIDIFICATION of the ocean, which is a term used to describe the decreasing pH of the ocean due to carbon dioxide emissions.

Meteorology

The ATMOSPHERE is a term for the layer of gases that surround planets (or any large body with a significant amount of mass) and that are being held in place by the gravity of those planets. The atmosphere of the Earth has multiple layers that reflect, refract, and absorb the light energy being emitted from the sun. These processes cause the movement of energy that creates the weather and climate of the Earth. The study of the atmosphere, weather, and climate is called **METEOROLOGY**.

The atmosphere of the Earth consists of many elements, but it's primarily composed of nitrogen (78 percent) and oxygen (21 percent). About 1 percent of the atmosphere is made up of other gases, such as carbon dioxide, ozone, and argon.

There are multiple layers of the atmosphere, all of which are separated from each other by pauses (which have the largest variation in characteristics): exosphere, thermosphere, mesosphere, stratosphere, and troposphere.

The **EXOSPHERE** is the most distant part of the atmosphere. This is where satellites are orbiting the planet and where molecules have the potential to escape into space itself. The very bottom of the exosphere is known as the thermopause. The thermopause is about 375 miles above the surface of the Earth. The outermost boundary of the exosphere is about 6200 miles above the surface of the Earth.

The **THERMOSPHERE** is the next layer when coming toward Earth from space. This layer is between 53 and 375 miles above the surface of the Earth and is known colloquially as the upper atmosphere. The gases in this layer are very thin, but they become denser the closer you get to the Earth. That energy is what leads to high temperatures: the top of this layer is around –184° Fahrenheit, while the bottom is around 3600° Fahrenheit.

Between thirty-one and fifty-three miles above the surface of the Earth lies a denser layer of atmosphere and gases called the **MESO-SPHERE**. The temperatures in this layer are around 5° Fahrenheit. Gases here are usually thick enough to stop most small meteors that enter the atmosphere of the Earth, causing them to burn up. This layer, along with the stratosphere, is collectively known as the middle atmosphere. The boundary between the two layers is called the stratopause.

The **STRATOSPHERE** is from eight to thirty-one miles above the surface of the Earth. About 19 percent of the gases in the atmosphere are contained in the stratosphere, which has a very low water content. The temperature of this layer increases with the height; the heat is a by-product of the creation of ozone in this layer. This is the layer that absorbs much of the energy coming in from the sun (particularly ultraviolet radiation and x-ray radiation). The barrier between this layer and the troposphere is the tropopause.

The **TROPOSPHERE** is the lowest layer. This is where weather takes place. It goes from the surface of the Earth to between four and twelve miles above the surface. (The exact height of this layer varies.)

The density of gas in the troposphere decreases with the height, and the air becomes thinner (which is why mountaintops have thin air).

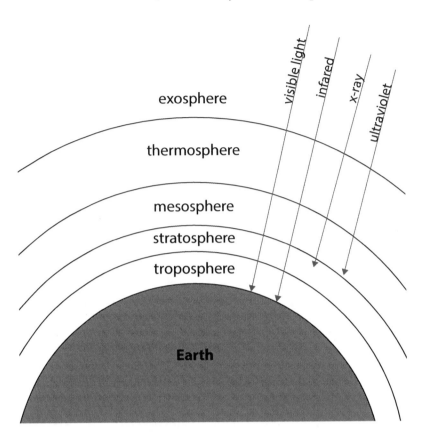

Figure 13.4. Earth's atmosphere

The layer that humans live in is known as the troposphere, which is also the layer in which weather takes place. **WEATHER** is a temporary (e.g., day to day) atmospheric condition such as rain, snow, or heat waves. Note that this is different from **CLIMATE**, which is the condition in a particular area over a long period of time. (Think about how the northwestern United States is generally cold and rainy, or how the Southwest is hot and dry.)

Some of the variables that are governed by weather conditions include the weight of the air (barometric pressure), air temperature, humidity, air velocity, clouds, and the levels of precipitation. Instruments are commonly used to help determine the relative levels of all of these variables. Below are some common weather measurement instruments:

- A **THERMOMETER** is a tool that is used to measure the temperature of the air, usually using either mercury or alcohol.
- A **BAROMETER** is used to measure the pressure of the air. If the pressure is going up, calm weather is coming. If the pressure if going down, expect rain.
- A **PSYCHROMETER** is a device used to measure relative humidity through the use of evaporation.

- An **ANEMOMETER** is an instrument that measures wind speed using a series of cups that catch the wind and then turn a dial.

- A **RAIN GAUGE** is used to determine how much rain has fallen in a given period of time.

- **WIND VANES** are used to help determine the direction of the wind.

- A **HYGROMETER** is an instrument that is used to help measure the humidity of the air.

- **WEATHER MAPS** show the atmospheric conditions over geographical areas.

- A **COMPASS** is an instrument that is used primarily for navigation and can be used to determine directions.

- **WEATHER BALLOONS** are commonly used to help measure the conditions of weather in the upper atmosphere.

Most meteorologists will utilize readings from a weather map and a number of these tools to determine what air masses are moving around in the troposphere. Air masses are defined as sections of air that have a uniform content of moisture and temperature. The way that these air masses move and interact with each other determine the weather and, thus, are what most meteorologists use when determining changes in the weather.

Examples

1. Fill in the blanks: Nuclear fusion is the _____ of atomic nuclei, and it happens in _____, while nuclear fission is the _____ of atomic nuclei, and it happens in _____.

   A) splitting, stars, combining, nuclear power plants

   B) combining, stars, splitting, nuclear power plants

   C) splitting, nuclear power plants, combining, stars

   D) combining, nuclear power plants, splitting, stars

2. Which of the following statements is true?

   A) The sun's rate of rotation is consistent throughout its surface, but its temperature is not.

   B) The sun's temperature is consistent throughout its surface, but its rate of rotation is not.

   C) Both the sun's temperature and rate of rotation are consistent throughout its surface.

   D) Neither the sun's temperature nor rate of rotation is consistent throughout its surface.

CONTINUE

3. The Earth's crust and upper mantle form the

    A) outer core

    B) inner core

    C) lithosphere

    D) asthenosphere

4. The layer of the atmosphere that absorbs most of the sun's ultraviolet radiation is the

    A) exosphere

    B) thermosphere

    C) stratosphere

    D) troposphere

Answers: 1. B) 2. D) 3. C) 4. C)

PART IV: SOCIAL STUDIES

14

UNITED STATES HISTORY

PRE-COLONIAL NORTH AMERICA

North American Societies

Prior to European colonization, diverse Native American societies controlled the continent; they would later come into economic and diplomatic contact, and military conflict, with European colonizers and United States forces and settlers.

Major civilizations that would continue to play an important role in North American history included the **IROQUOIS** and **ALGONQUIN** in the Northeast; the Iroquois in particular were known for innovative agricultural and architectural techniques. Both of those tribes would be important allies of the French and English, respectively, in conflict in that part of the continent; the young United States would also come into conflict with the Iroquois Confederacy in early western expansion. In the South, major tribes included the **CHICKASAW** and **CHOCTAW**, which also formed alliances with the British and French and fought proxy wars on their behalf. These settled, agricultural tribes, along with the **CHEROKEE**, **CREEK**, and **SEMINOLE**, would fall victim to Andrew Jackson and the Indian Removal Act as the United States consolidated its control of the continent. Farther west, the **SIOUX**, **CHEYANNE**, **APACHE**, **COMANCHE**, and **ARAPAHO**, migratory tribes who traditionally inhabited the Great Plains and Rocky Mountain areas, would later come into conflict with American settlers as westward expansion continued. These tribes were known for their military and equestrian skill. Ultimately, through both violent conflict and political means, Native American civilizations lost control of most of their territories and were forced onto reservations by the United States. Negotiations continue today over rights to land and opportunities and reparations for past injustices.

Figure 14.1. Mississippi Mounds

Examples

1. List some major Native American civilizations in North America.

   Major tribes in North America included the Iroquois, Algonquin, Cherokee, Creek, Chickasaw, Kickapoo, Miami, Shawnee, Sioux, Cheyanne, Comanche, Arapaho, Apache, and many others.

2. What consequences did these civilizations face as a result of European colonization of North America and the expansion of the United States?

   These tribes and many others participated in diplomatic, economic, social, political and military interactions with European and United States powers in North America. The Iroquois and Algonquin, as well as the Chickasaw and Choctaw, would form alliances with the British and French and fight proxy wars on the continent. Various tribes would become important trading partners. The Cherokee, Creek, and other Southeastern tribes would eventually be driven from their lands by the Indian Removal Act, even going so far as the United States Supreme Court to challenge this atrocity, ultimately unsuccessfully. Plains tribes came into military conflict for decades with the United States with westward expansion as a result of manifest destiny. The Bureau of Indian Affairs and movement of Native Americans onto reservations and into assimilationist boarding schools would damage traditional relationships. In the twentieth century, Native American activism would continue with the American Indian Movement (AIM) in the 1960s. Social and economic problems on reservations and strained relationships with the United States government continue today.

COLONIES, REVOLUTION, AND THE EARLY UNITED STATES

Colonial North America

The Americas were quickly colonized by Europeans after Christopher Columbus first laid claim to them for the Spanish, and the British, French, and Spanish all held territories in North America throughout the sixteenth, seventeenth, eighteenth, and nineteenth centuries. The British ultimately controlled most of the Atlantic coast and some territories inland—what became known as the **THIRTEEN COLONIES**—while France controlled most of what is today Quebec, the Midwest, and the Mississippi River Valley region. Spain's holdings extended through Mexico into Texas, the Southwest, and eventually California, reaching as far north into what are today parts of Montana and Wyoming, in addition to Florida. The Northeast and Upper Midwest was rich in game and beaver pelts, and the areas on the mid-Atlantic coast were agriculturally fertile. They also contained important commercial centers like New York, Boston and Philadelphia where North American products went to port.

Meanwhile, Europeans also migrated to the Southern colonies of Virginia and the Carolinas to invest in and profit from the considerable natural agricultural resources of **COTTON** and **TOBACCO**. To harvest these labor-intensive crops, the North American colonies joined other parts of the Americas in the slave trade as part of the **ATLANTIC WORLD**, taking part in the **TRIANGULAR TRADE** between the Americas, Africa, and Europe, where slaves were exchanged in the Americas for raw materials shipped to Europe to be processed into goods for the benefit of the colonial powers and exchanged for slaves in Africa. In this way, North America was also part of the **COLUMBIAN EXCHANGE** (see chapter fifteen, *World History,* for further details).

Revolution

The Colonies were populated not only by those seeking economic profit but also by those in search of religious freedom and more political autonomy. The famous pilgrims, Puritan dissidents known as **SEPARATISTS** who disagreed with policies of the Church of England, arrived in the seventeenth century seeking autonomy and established a precedent for government by consent of the governed framed in the **MAYFLOWER COMPACT**. The **MARYLAND TOLERATION ACT** was the first colonial act to guarantee religious freedom (to Christians). Revolutionary ideas from Europe like John Locke's notion of **REPUBLICANISM** fueled colonial discontent with the Crown, which was enforcing increasingly restrictive acts limiting colonial trade for the benefit of Britain, to the detriment of colonists' profit.

After the Seven Years' war in Europe and conflict on North American soil between France and England in the FRENCH AND INDIAN WAR, Britain needed cash. By the mid-eighteenth century, King George III was abandoning the British policy of SALUTARY NEGLECT and enforced heavy taxes and restrictive acts on the colonies to generate income for the Crown and punish disobedience. These included the Stamp Act, the Quartering Act, the Tea Act, the Intolerable Acts, and others. Ultimately, the colonies rebelled; the SECOND CONTINENTAL CONGRESS, led by figures like Thomas Jefferson, John Adams, and Benjamin Franklin, issued the DECLARATION OF INDEPENDENCE in 1776. It also adopted the ARTICLES OF CONFEDERATION providing for a weak central government. George Washington led the Continental Army to victory, and the American Revolution ended with United States independence in 1783.

Figure 14.2. Join or die

Aftermath

Joy in the victory over Great Britain was short lived. It soon became clear that the Articles of Confederation were not strong enough to keep the nation united. Shay's Rebellion of indebted farmers who rose up to prevent courts from seizing property quickly showed the need for a stronger federal government if the United States was to remain one country. A CONSTITUTIONAL CONVENTION was organized to write a stronger Constitution as the foundations of a stronger federal government, favored by the FEDERALISTS, who were led by John Adams. Despite the separation of powers provided for in the Constitution, ANTI-FEDERALISTS called for more limitations on the power of the federal government. The first ten amendments to the Constitution, or the BILL OF RIGHTS, a list of guarantees of American freedoms, were a concession to the anti-Federalists, led by Thomas Jefferson; they would later become the DEMOCRATIC-RE-

PUBLICAN PARTY (eventually, the Democratic Party). In addition, in what became known as the GREAT COMPROMISE, the states decided upon a bicameral legislature to most fairly represent the large and small states at the federal level. (See chapter 17, *Civics and Government*, for more information.)

Federalists and Anti-Federalists

The early United States was dominated by questions over the limits of federal power. John Adams, a Federalist, was the second president, but perceived federal and presidential overreach in the form of an expanded federal government and the Alien and Sedition Act led to the election of Thomas Jefferson, a Democratic-Republican, to the presidency in 1801. Jefferson shrank the federal government. Economic policies favored small farmers and landowners, in contrast to Federalist policies, which supported big business. However, Jefferson also oversaw the LOUISIANA PURCHASE, which nearly doubled the size of the United States. This troubled some Democratic-Republicans, who saw this as federal overreach, but the Louisiana Purchase would be a major step forward in westward expansion.

Figure 14.3. Louisiana Purchase

Monroe Doctrine, Manifest Destiny, and Jacksonian Democracy

British provocation at sea and in the Northwest led to the WAR OF 1812, when the United States declared war. Despite a British alliance with the Shawnee leader TECUMSEH, who had organized the NORTHWEST CONFEDERACY of tribes including the Shawnee, Lenape, Miami, Kickapoo, and others who sought independent territory at the Northwest of the United States (today, the region including Indiana), the U.S. prevailed. At the war's end, the United States had successfully defended itself as a country and reaffirmed its independence. The **ERA OF GOOD FEELINGS** began with the presidency of James Monroe as a strong sense of national identity and patriotism pervaded in the country. During this period, religious revival became popular, and people turned from Puritanism and predestination to Baptist and Methodist faiths, among others, following revolutionary preachers and movements. This period was called the **SECOND GREAT AWAKENING**.

With the Louisiana Purchase, the country had almost doubled in size. In the nineteenth century, the idea of **MANIFEST DESTINY**, or the sense that it was the fate of the United States to expand westward and settle the continent, pervaded. The **MONROE DOCTRINE**, James Monroe's policy that the Western Hemisphere was "closed" to any further European colonization or exploration, asserted U.S. hegemony in the region. With continental expansion came conflict with Native Americans. President Andrew Jackson enforced the **INDIAN REMOVAL ACT**, forcing Cherokee, Creek, Chickasaw, Choctaw, and others from their lands in the Southeast on the infamous **TRAIL OF TEARS** to make way for white settlers. Violent conflicts would continue on the Frontier farther west between the U.S. and the Apache, Comanche, Sioux, Arapaho, Cheyanne, and other tribes throughout the nineteenth century.

During Jackson's presidency, the **TWO-PARTY SYSTEM** also emerged. As a Democrat, Jackson supported states' rights, small government, and policies in favor of rural landowners and small farmers. With the dissolution of the Federalists after the War of 1812, the opposition was the Whig Party, previously a Democratic-Republican splinter group. The Whigs supported big business and urbanization. Jackson's popularity with the "common man," white, male farmers and workers who felt he identified with them, and the fact that owning property was no longer a requirement to vote gave him the advantage and a two-term presidency.

Examples

1. Why did the Crown abandon the policy of salutary neglect? What were the consequences for the Colonies and for the Crown?

    Following the Seven Years' War in Europe, known in North America as the French and Indian War, Britain needed income, and so King George III raised taxes on the Colonies, which had enjoyed great autonomy under the policy of salutary neglect. When faced with colonial resentment and resistance through events like the Boston Tea Party, the Crown imposed a series of restrictive measures like the Intolerable Acts, which heightened tensions, eventually leading to revolution.

2. What was the immediate impact of the Louisiana Purchase? What were some of the long-term consequences?

Despite Jefferson's status as a Democratic-Republican favoring limited federal power, many felt that his purchase of the Louisiana Territory was an example of federal overreach. However, the Louisiana Purchase more than doubled the size of the United States, setting the stage for westward expansion—the precedent for manifest destiny. Furthermore, President Monroe's Monroe Doctrine asserted United States hegemony in the Americas, intending to close the hemisphere to further European colonization. Purchasing this enormous territory from a major European power, coupled with U.S. successes in the War of 1812, illustrated the potency and sovereignty of the United States on the North American continent at the international level.

CIVIL WAR

Causes

The Civil War was rooted in nearly a century of conflict over slavery, states' rights, and the reach of the federal government. In 1820, the **MISSOURI COMPROMISE (COMPROMISE OF 1820)** admitted

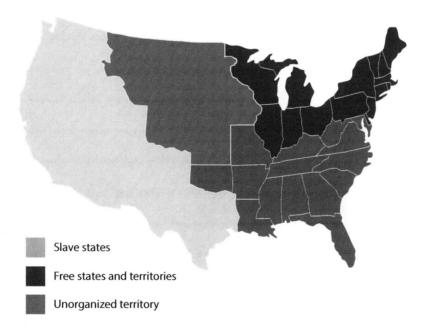

Slave states

Free states and territories

Unorganized territory

Figure 14.4. Missouri Compromise

Missouri as a slave state and Maine as a free state; it also banned slavery north of the 36th parallel (basically, north of Missouri). Later, the **COMPROMISE OF 1850** admitted California as a free state and Utah and New Mexico with slavery to be decided by **POPULAR SOVEREIGNTY**, or by the residents. It also reaffirmed the **FUGITIVE SLAVE ACT**, which allowed slave owners to pursue escaped slaves to free states and recapture them. Shortly thereafter, the **KANSAS-NE-BRASKA ACT OF 1854** allowed those two territories to decide slavery by popular sovereignty as well, effectively repealing the Missouri Compromise. The **NEW REPUBLICAN PARTY** was formed in opposition to this; later, one of its members, Abraham Lincoln, would be elected to the presidency. Finally, the Supreme Court's **DRED SCOTT DECISION** in 1856 reaffirmed the Fugitive Slave Act and decreed that African Americans were not entitled to U.S. citizenship. The **LINCOLN-DOUGLAS DEBATES**, between the presidential candidates, Republican **ABRAHAM LINCOLN** and Democrat **STEPHEN DOUGLAS**, showed the deep divides in the nation over slavery and states' rights; Lincoln spoke out against slavery, while Douglas supported the right of states to decide its legality on their own.

In 1860, Lincoln was elected to the presidency. Given his outspoken stance against slavery, South Carolina seceded immediately thereafter, followed by Mississippi, Alabama, Florida, Louisiana, Georgia, and Texas. They formed the Confederate States of America, or the **CONFEDERACY**, on February 1, 1861.

North versus South

Shortly after the South's secession, Confederate forces attacked Union troops in Sumter, South Carolina; the **BATTLE OF FORT SUMTER** (April 12–14, 1861) kicked off the Civil War. As a result, Virginia, Tennessee, North Carolina, and Arkansas seceded and joined the Confederacy. West Virginia was formed when the western part of Virginia refused to join the Confederacy.

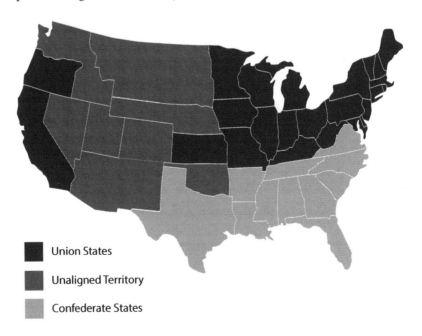

Union States

Unaligned Territory

Confederate States

Figure 14.5. The Union and Confederacy

Both sides believed the conflict would be short lived; however, after the **FIRST BATTLE OF BULL RUN** (July 16, 1861, in Manassas,

VA), when the Union failed to route the Confederacy, it became clear that the war would not end quickly. Realizing how difficult it would be to defeat the Confederacy, the Union developed the **ANACONDA PLAN**, a plan to "squeeze" the Confederacy, including a naval blockade and taking control of the Mississippi River. Since the South depended on international trade in cotton for much of its income, a naval blockade would have serious economic ramifications for the Confederacy. However, the **SECOND BATTLE OF BULL RUN** (August 28–30, 1862) was a tactical Confederate victory, led by **GENERAL ROBERT E. LEE** and **STONEWALL JACKSON**. The Union army remained intact, but the loss was a heavy blow to Union morale.

The **BATTLE OF ANTIETAM** (September 17, 1862, Sharpsburg and Antietam Creek, MD) was the first battle to be fought on Union soil. Union General **GEORGE B. MCCLELLAN** halted General Lee's invasion of Maryland but failed to defeat Confederate forces. Undaunted, on January 1, 1863, President Lincoln decreed the end of slavery in the rebel states with the **EMANCIPATION PROCLAMATION**. The **BATTLE OF GETTYSBURG** (July 1–3, 1863, Gettysburg, PA) was a major Union victory, led by General George Meade. It was the bloodiest battle in American history up to this point; the Confederate army would not recover.

President Lincoln later delivered the Gettysburg Address onsite, in which he framed the Civil War as a battle for human rights and equality.

Meanwhile, following the **SIEGE OF VICKSBURG, MISSISSIPPI** (May 18 – July 4, 1863), Union forces led by **GENERAL ULYSSES S. GRANT** gained control over the Mississippi River, completing the Anaconda Plan. The Siege and **BATTLE OF ATLANTA**, Georgia (July 22 – September 2, 1864) was the final major battle of the Civil War; following the Union victory led by **GENERAL WILLIAM T. SHERMAN**, the Union proceeded into the South, and the Confederacy fell. One of the final conflicts of the war, the Battle of **APPOMMATOX COURT HOUSE** resulted in the Confederate surrender at Appommatox, Virginia, on April 9, 1865, where General Lee surrendered to General Grant and the war ended.

Aftermath and Reconstruction

Despite the strong leadership and vast territory of the Confederacy, a larger population, stronger industrial capacity (including weapons-making capacity), the naval blockade of Southern trade, and superior leadership resulted in Union victory. Yet bitterness over Northern victory persisted, and President Lincoln was assassinated by Confederate sympathizers on April 15, 1865. Post-war **RECONSTRUCTION** would continue without his leadership.

Before his death, Lincoln had crafted the **TEN PERCENT PLAN**: if ten percent of a Southern state's population swore allegiance to the Union, that state would be readmitted into the Union. In 1866, Congress passed the **CIVIL RIGHTS ACT**, granting citizenship to African Americans and guaranteeing African American men the same rights as white men (later reaffirmed by the FOURTEENTH AMENDMENT). Conflict over how harshly to treat the South persisted in Congress between Republicans and Democrats, and in 1867 a Republican-led Congress passed the RECONSTRUCTION ACTS, placing former Confederate states under the control of the U.S. Army. Former Confederate states also had to ratify the THIRTEENTH AMENDMENT, which had abolished slavery in 1865, the Fourteenth Amendment, and the FIFTEENTH AMENDMENT, which granted African American men the right to vote in 1870. Resentment over the Reconstruction Acts never truly subsided, and military control of the South finally ended with the COMPROMISE OF 1877, which resolved the disputed presidential election of 1876 and removed troops from the South.

Examples

1. What were some reasons for the Civil War? List three events or pieces of legislation, and explain their importance.

    Important legislation included the Compromise of 1820, which halted the expansion of slavery to the west; in contrast, over the course of the nineteenth century, the Compromise of 1850, the Kansas-Nebraska Act, and the Dred Scott Decision weakened the Missouri Compromise and eventually repealed it altogether. The Lincoln-Douglas Debates not only reflected divisions over slavery in the U.S. at the time but also arguably contributed to growing tensions. A student could also argue that more straightforward events like Southern Secession itself or the attack on Fort Sumter started the war, but knowledge of the political events of the nineteenth century would make for a stronger answer.

2. What were the 13th, 14th and 15th Amendments?

    The 13th Amendment abolished slavery; the 14th Amendment defined citizenship, affirming that African Americans had rights as American citizens; and the 15th Amendment guaranteed the right to vote to African American men (no women of any race would have the right to vote until the twentieth century).

INDUSTRIALIZATION

The Gilded Age and the Second Industrial Revolution

Following the war, the INDUSTRIAL REVOLUTION, which had begun with textile production in Great Britain fueled in great part by supplies of Southern cotton, accelerated in the United States. The GILDED AGE saw an era of rapidly growing income inequality, justified by theories like SOCIAL DARWINISM and the GOSPEL OF WEALTH, which argued that the wealthy had been made rich by God and were socially more deserving of it. Much of this wealth was generated by heavy industry in what became known as the

Despite ratifying the amendments, Southern states instituted the Black Codes to continue oppression of freedmen, or freed African Americans, who faced ongoing violence.

The cotton gin, invented by Eli Whitney, sped up labor-intensive cotton production exponentially and increased profits for Southern planters.

SECOND INDUSTRIAL REVOLUTION (the first being textile-driven and originating in Europe). Westward expansion required railroads; railroads required steel, and industrial production required oil: all these commodities spurred the rise of powerful companies like John D. Rockefeller's Standard Oil and Andrew Carnegie's U.S. Steel. The creation of MONOPOLIES and TRUSTS helped industrial leaders consolidate their control over industries thanks to HORIZONTAL and VERTICAL INTEGRATION of industries.

While the free markets and trade of the CAPITALIST economy spurred national economic and industrial growth, the WORKING CLASS, composed largely of poor European and Chinese IMMIGRANTS working in factories and building infrastructure, suffered from dangerous working conditions and other abuses. Furthermore, NATIVE AMERICANS were harmed and lost land as westward expansion continued with little to no regulations on land use—white farmers also suffered. Government corruption led only to weak restrictive legislation like the INTERSTATE COMMERCE ACT of 1887, which was to regulate the railroad industry, and the SHERMAN ANTI-TRUST ACT (1890), which was intended to break up monopolies and trust to allow for a fairer marketplace; however, these measures would remain largely toothless until President Theodore Roosevelt's "trust-busting" administration in 1901.

Populism and the Progressive Era

The PEOPLE'S (POPULIST) PARTY formed in response to corruption and industrialization injurious to farmers (later, it would also support reform in favor of the working class and oppressed groups like women and children). Farmers were suffering from crushing debt in the face of westward expansion, which destroyed their lands; they were also competing (and losing) against industrialized and mechanized farming. Groups like the NATIONAL GRANGE advocated for farmers. Meanwhile, despite legislative measures after the Civil War, African American farmers suffered in the south as SHARECROPPERS and TENANT FARMERS, with limited control over land and heavy debts. The COLORED FARMERS' ALLIANCE formed to support them. SEGREGATION, or JIM CROW laws, remained in place in much of the South, reaffirmed by the Supreme Court case *PLESSY V. FERGUSON.* The National Association for the Advancement of Colored People, or the NAACP, was formed to advocate for African Americans nationwide and still works today.

At the same time, the LABOR MOVEMENT emerged to support mistreated industrial workers in urban areas. SAMUEL GOMPERS led the AMERICAN FEDERATION OF LABORERS (AFL), using STRIKES and COLLECTIVE BARGAINING to gain protections for the unskilled workers who had come to cities seeking industrial jobs. With the rise of the MIDDLE CLASS, women took a more active role in advocating for the poor and for themselves. Leaders like ELIZABETH

CADY STANTON and SUSAN B. ANTHONY and the NATIONAL AMERICAN WOMAN SUFFRAGE ASSOCIATION fought for women's right to vote, won in 1919 with the NINETEENTH AMENDMENT. Women were also active in the temperance movement. Organizations like the Woman's Christian Temperance Union advocated for the prohibition of alcohol, which was finally achieved with the Eighteenth Amendment, although it was later repealed with the Twenty-First. Finally, women activists also aligned with labor and the emerging PROGRESSIVE MOVEMENT to advocate for the poor. At the same time, Native Americans continued to suffer with westward expansion: policies pursued by the BUREAU OF INDIAN AFFAIRS like the establishment of RESERVATIONS and ASSIMILATION broke down tribal social bonds. The death of the Lakota Sioux CHIEF SITTING BULL in the 1890 Massacre at Wounded Knee marked the end of serious Native American resistance to westward expansion, following ongoing conflict since the Indian Wars and SIOUX WAR in the mid-nineteenth century.

With the Progressive Theodore Roosevelt's ascension to the presidency in 1901 following President McKinley's assassination, the Progressive Era reached its apex. The "TRUST-BUSTER" Roosevelt enforced the Sherman Anti-Trust Act and prosecuted the NORTHERN SECURITIES railroad monopoly under the Interstate Commerce Act, breaking up trusts and creating a fairer market. He led government involvement in negotiations between unions and industrial powers, developing the "SQUARE DEAL" for fairer treatment of workers. The Progressive Era also saw a series of acts to protect workers, health, farmers, and children under Presidents Roosevelt and Taft.

Roosevelt continued overseas expansion following McKinley's SPANISH-AMERICAN WAR (1898 – 1901), in which the U.S. gained control over Spanish territory in the Caribbean, Asia, and the South Pacific. The ROOSEVELT COROLLARY to the Monroe Doctrine, which promised U.S. intervention in Latin America in case of European intervention there, essentially gave the U.S. total dominance over Latin America. This NEW IMPERIALISM expanded U.S. markets and increased U.S. presence and prestige on the global stage.

🔒

During this period, the U.S. annexed Hawaii, Guam, and Puerto Rico and took over the Panama Canal; made Cuba a U.S. protectorate; and annexed the Philippines, which would fight an ongoing guerrilla war for independence.

Examples

1. Why was the Second Industrial Revolution important?
   The Second Industrial Revolution accelerated American westward expansion by providing the technology to move west. It also accelerated urbanization by creating jobs for unskilled workers in urban areas, attracting immigrants, and growing cities. This provided more opportunities for the middle class to grow and resulted in movements like the Progressives, who sought fairer treatment for workers and women, among others.

2. What did Roosevelt do about the Sherman Anti-Trust Act and why?

Roosevelt enforced the Sherman Anti-Trust Act by prosecuting trusts and breaking up monopolies, notably the powerful Northern Securities railroad monopoly. This made a fairer marketplace, giving companies more opportunities in markets previously dominated by one company or industrial group, and put a stop to government corruption.

ARMED CONFLICT AND GLOBAL ECONOMIC DEPRESSION

World War I and U.S. Foreign Policy

During the Progressive Era in the U.S., Europe was becoming increasingly unstable. With the Spanish-American War, debate had arisen within the U.S. between INTERVENTIONISM and ISOLATIONISM, that is whether the U.S. should intervene in international matters or not. This debate became more pronounced with the outbreak of WORLD WAR I in Europe. Inflammatory events like German SUBMARINE WARFARE (*U-boats*) in the Atlantic Ocean, the sinking of the *LUSITANIA*, which resulted in many American civilian deaths, the embarrassing ZIMMERMAN TELEGRAM (in which Germany promised to help Mexico in an attack on the U.S.), and growing American NATIONALISM, or pride in and identification with one's country, triggered U.S. intervention in the war. On December 7, 1917, the U.S. declared war. With victory in 1918, the U.S. had proven itself a superior military and industrial power. Interventionist PRESIDENT WOODROW WILSON played an important role in negotiating the peace; his FOURTEEN POINTS laid out an idealistic international vision, including an international security organization. However, European powers negotiated and won the harsh TREATY OF VERSAILLES, which placed the blame for the war entirely on Germany and demanded crippling REPARATIONS from it, one contributing factor to WORLD WAR II later in the twentieth century. The LEAGUE OF NATIONS, a collective security organization, was formed, but a divided U.S. Congress refused to ratify the treaty, so the U.S. did not join it. Divisions between interventionists and isolationists continued with the NEUTRALITY ACTS of the 1930s in the face of conflict in Asia and ongoing tensions in Europe.

Great Depression

Following WWI, the U.S. experienced an era of consumerism and corruption. The government sponsored LAISSEZ-FAIRE policies and supported MANUFACTURING, flooding markets with cheap consumer goods. Union membership suffered; so did farmers, due to falling crop prices. While mass production helped the emerging middle class afford more consumer goods and improve their living standards, many families resorted to CREDIT to fuel consumer spending. These

Speculation, or margin-buying, meant that speculators borrowed money to buy stock, selling it as soon as its price rose. However, since the price of stocks fluctuated, when buyers lost confidence in the market and began selling their shares, the value of stocks fell. Borrowers could not repay their loans; as a result, banks failed.

risky consumer loans, **OVER SPECULATION** on crops and the value of farmland, and weak banking protections helped bring about the **GREAT DEPRESSION**, commonly dated from October 29, 1929, or *BLACK TUESDAY*, when the market collapsed. Americans faced unemployment and poverty.

Figure 14.6. A soup kitchen during the Great Depression

At the same time, a major drought occurred in the Great Plains. What would the impact have been on ordinary Americans?

Following weak responses by the Hoover administration, **FRANKLIN DELANO ROOSEVELT** was elected to the presidency in 1932. FDR offered the U.S. a *NEW DEAL*: a plan to bring the country out of the Depression. In the *FIRST HUNDRED DAYS* of FDR's administration, a series of emergency acts were passed for the immediate repair of the banking system, notably the establishment of the FDIC to insure customer deposits in the wake of bank failures; later in FDR's administration, more legislation was passed focusing on long-term relief for the poor and broader economic reform. Programs included the Works Progress Administration, Social Security, the Tennessee Valley Authority, and others. These acts provided jobs; support for small businesses, farmers, retirees, and organized labor; and rural development programs, among others. Due to the heavy use of acronyms to refer to these programs, they were referred to as an **ALPHABET SOUP** of programs.

International Affairs and World War II
The entire world suffered from the Great Depression, and Europe became increasingly unstable. With the rise of the radical Nazi Party in Germany, the Nazi leader Adolf Hitler led German takeovers of several European countries and became a threat to U.S. allies, bombing Britain. To ally with and support Great Britain without

technically declaring war on Germany, the U.S. enacted the **ATLANTIC CHARTER** and the **LEND-LEASE ACT**, supplying Britain with military aid. However, after the Japanese attack on **PEARL HARBOR** on December 7, 1941, the U.S. entered the war, effectively ending it four years later with the bombing of **HIROSHIMA** and **NAGASAKI** in Japan, the only times that **NUCLEAR WEAPONS** have been used in conflict.

In the wake of WWII, the **UNITED NATIONS** was formed, modeled after the failed League of Nations. Unlike the League, however, it included a **SECURITY COUNCIL** composed of major world powers, with the power to militarily intervene for peacekeeping purposes in unstable global situations. With most of Europe destroyed, the victorious U.S. and the Soviet Union emerged as the two global **SUPERPOWERS**. The U.S.-led **MARSHALL PLAN** began a program to rebuild Europe, but the U.S.S.R. consolidated its presence and power in eastern European countries, forcing them to reject the Marshall Plan. This division would destroy the alliance between the Soviets and the West, leading to the **COLD WAR** between the two superpowers and the emergence of a **BIPOLAR WORLD**.

Examples

1. How did the U.S. recover from the Great Depression?
   FDR's New Deal put in place a series of immediate relief programs to repair the banking system, including the FDIC, which insured customer deposits in banks. Later, the government established an "alphabet soup" of programs to generate jobs for unemployed Americans, also building national infrastructure, supporting farmers, the elderly, and workers, and promoting rural development.

2. Why was the United Nations important?
   The U.N. was a way to prevent major world conflict like WWI or WWII from erupting again by providing not only a forum for international diplomacy but also a mechanism for international security. The U.N. Security Council strengthened this international body modeled after the League of Nations by enabling major world powers—members of the Security Council—to intervene militarily in unstable situations to prevent further conflict, as per Article VII of the U.N. Charter.

POSTWAR AND CONTEMPORARY UNITED STATES

1950s: Cold War at home and abroad

With the collapse of the relationship between the U.S.S.R. and the U.S., distrust and even fear of **COMMUNISM** grew. Accusations of communist sympathies against public figures ran rampant during the **MCCARTHY ERA** in the 1950s, reflecting domestic fears. President

Harry S. Truman's **TRUMAN DOCTRINE** stated that the U.S. would support any country threatened by authoritarianism (communism), leading to the **KOREAN WAR** (1950 – 1953), a conflict between the U.S. and Soviet-backed North Korean forces, which ended in a stalemate. The policy of **CONTAINMENT**, to contain Soviet (communist) expansion, defined U.S. foreign policy; according to the **DOMINO THEORY**, once one country fell to communism, others would quickly follow. Other incidents included the **BAY OF PIGS** invasion in Cuba (1961), a failed effort to topple the communist government of Fidel Castro, and the **CUBAN MISSILE CRISIS** (1962), when Soviet missiles were discovered in Cuba and military crisis was narrowly averted, both under the administration of the popular **PRESIDENT JOHN F. KENNEDY**.

Meanwhile, in Southeast Asia, communist forces in North Vietnam were gaining power. Congress never formally declared war in Vietnam but gave the president authority to intervene militarily there through the **GULF OF TONKIN RESOLUTION** (1964). However, this protracted conflict—the **VIETNAM WAR**—also led to widespread domestic social unrest, which only increased with U.S. deaths there, especially after the Vietnamese-led **TET OFFENSIVE** (1968). The U.S. ultimately withdrew from Vietnam, and the North Vietnamese forces, or **VIET CONG**, led by **HO CHI MINH**, took over the country.

Social Change, Liberalism, and the Vietnam War (1960s)

During the 1960s, the U.S. experienced social and political change, starting with the election of the young and charismatic John F. Kennedy in 1960. Following JFK's assassination in 1963, **PRESIDENT LYNDON B. JOHNSON**'s administration saw the passage of **LIBERAL** legislation in support of the poor and of civil rights. The **CIVIL RIGHTS MOVEMENT**, led by activists like the **REV. DR. MARTIN LUTHER KING, JR.** and **MALCOLM X**, fought for African American rights in the South, including the abolition of segregation, and also for better living standards for Blacks in northern cities, to which many African Americans had moved in the **GREAT MIGRATION**.

Civil disobedience included sit-ins to protest segregation in public places, like lunch counters at department stores in the South. Coupled with boycotts of these establishments, many of them changed their policies of segregation.

The Supreme Court case ***BROWN V. BOARD OF EDUCATION*** found segregation unconstitutional in 1954. Believing in **CIVIL DISOBEDIENCE**, Dr. King led peaceful protests and boycotts to protest segregation, including marches from Selma to Montgomery, Alabama, to protest unfair voting restrictions on African Americans. In 1964, Congress passed the **CIVIL RIGHTS ACT**, which outlawed discrimination, ending segregation; in 1965, Congress passed the **VOTING RIGHTS ACT**, which forbade restrictions impeding the ability of African Americans to vote.

The Civil Rights Movement also included **FEMINIST** activists who fought for fairer treatment of women in the workplace and for women's reproductive rights; the landmark case of ***ROE V. WADE*** struck down federal restrictions on abortion. Latino and American

Figure 14.7. March on Washington, 1963

Indian activists also advocated for the civil rights of their communities. Another element of LBJ's liberal agenda was the **WAR ON POVERTY**, with a vision of a **GREAT SOCIETY**, passing reform legislation like Medicare and Head Start.

The Rise of Conservatives and the Changing World Stage (1970s and 1980s)

During the administration of the conservative President Richard Nixon, the conflict in Vietnam ended, and a diplomatic relationship with China began. However, the **WATERGATE** scandal, in which the administration was found to have engaged in corrupt practices to reelect the president, resulted in his resignation and destroyed many Americans' faith in their government. During the 1970s, the economy suffered due to U.S. involvement in the Middle East; U.S. support for Israel in the Six-Day and Yom Kippur Wars caused **OPEC**, the Organization of Petroleum Exporting Countries, led by Saudi Arabia and other allies of Arab foes of Israel, to boycott the U.S. in 1973; as a result, oil prices skyrocketed. In the 1979

Iranian Revolution and the resulting HOSTAGE CRISIS, when the U.S. Embassy in Teheran was taken over by anti-American activists, the economy suffered from another oil shock.

These international threats and perceived weak leadership on the part of the Democrat **PRESIDENT JIMMY CARTER** resulted in the presidency of the Republican **RONALD REAGAN**, who championed domestic tax cuts and aggressive foreign policy against the Soviet Union. Investment in military technology—the ARMS RACE with the Soviet Union—helped bring about the end of the Cold War with the 1991 fall of the U.S.S.R. and later, a new era of globalization.

OPEC Countries

Algeria	Kuwait	United Arab
Ecuador	Libya	Emirates
Indonesia	Nigeria	Venezuela
Iran	Quatar	
Iraq	Saudi Arabia	

Figure 14.8. OPEC countries

The End of the Cold War and Globalization

With Iraq's invasion of Kuwait in 1990, more conflict over oil in the Middle East broke out, and the U.S. intervention—the **GULF WAR**, or **OPERATION DESERT STORM** (1991)—cemented its status as the world's sole superpower. With the election of **PRESIDENT BILL CLINTON** in 1992, the U.S. took an active role in international diplomacy, helping broker peace deals in the former Yugoslavia, Northern Ireland, and the Middle East. The Clinton administration also formed FREE-TRADE AGREEMENTS like **NAFTA**, which removed trade restrictions between countries. Even though political culture remained torn between liberal and conservatives, with a strong congressional conservative movement throughout the 1990s, society became increasingly liberal: technology like the INTERNET emerged, minority groups like the LGBT community engaged in more advocacy, and environmental issues gained more visibility.

NAFTA countries

Non-NAFTA countries

Figure 14.9. NAFTA countries

The Twenty-First Century

The terrorist attacks by **AL QAEDA** on the U.S. on **SEPTEMBER 11, 2001** led to an aggressive military and foreign policy under the administration of President **GEORGE W. BUSH**. Following the attacks, the U.S. struck suspected al Qaeda bases in Afghanistan, beginning the **AFGHANISTAN WAR**, which lasted until 2013 and during which time the U.S. occupied the country. Suspected terrorist fighters there were held in a prison in **GUANTANAMO BAY**, Cuba, which was controversial because it did not initially offer any protections generally given to prisoners of war. In 2003, the U.S. attacked **IRAQ**, under the Bush policy of **PREEMPTION**: believing that Iraq held **WEAPONS OF MASS DESTRUCTION**, in what later turned out to be a false presumption, the U.S. should preempt an attack by hitting that country first. Congress passed the USA PATRIOT Act to respond to fears of more terrorist attacks on U.S. soil; this legislation gave the federal government unprecedented—and, some argued, unconstitutional—powers of surveillance over the American public.

Despite the tense climate, social liberalization continued in the U.S. Following the Bush administration, during which tax cuts and heavy reliance on credit helped push the country into the **GREAT RECESSION**, the first African American president, **BARACK OBAMA**, was elected in 2008. Under his presidency, the U.S. stopped the recession, ended its occupations of Iraq and Afghanistan, passed the Affordable Care Act, which reformed the healthcare system, and gained the legal right to same-sex marriage.

CONTINUE

Examples

1. Why were the Civil Rights and Voting Rights Acts necessary?

    Despite the 14th and 15th Amendments, African Americans in the South still lived under the oppressive Jim Crow laws, and throughout the country, there were limited or no restrictions on hiring, wage, housing, and other practices: housing could be denied to applicants because of their race, and African Americans and other people of color could be paid less than whites or denied a job. (Women are still paid less than men in many cases today.) In the wake of *Brown v. Board of Education*, which declared segregation unconstitutional, the Civil Rights Act solidified the rights of African Americans and other people of color to the same treatment as whites in society. Furthermore, in many parts of the South, practices like poll taxes prevented African Americans, who were more likely to be unable to afford to pay them, from exercising their right to vote. The Voting Rights Act prevented such practices, ensuring that all Americans were able to get to the polls.

2. Compare containment with the fight against terrorism.

    The foreign policy of Containment, the fear of the spread of communism, led to two wars—in Korea and Vietnam—and numerous proxy conflicts. Likewise, the fight against terrorism led to the war in Afghanistan to fight al Qaeda and later, according to preemption, to the attack on and war in Iraq.

15

WORLD HISTORY

EARLY CIVILIZATIONS AND THE GREAT EMPIRES

Middle East and Asia

The earliest humans were hunter-gatherers until the development of agriculture in about 11,000 B.C.E. The earliest world **CIVILIZATIONS**, or settled communities, stretched from the **NILE VALLEY** of Egypt through **MESOPOTAMIA**, the territory around the **TIGRIS** and **EUPHRATES** Rivers in the the Middle East: the **FERTILE CRESCENT**. These important civilizations included the ancient **EGYPTIANS**, known for their pyramids, art, and pictorial writing (**HIEROGLYPHS**), the **SUMERIANS**, who developed irrigation and **CUNEIFORM**, the earliest written language, and the **BABYLONIANS**, whose Code of Hammurabi was an early form of rule of law.

Meanwhile, early civilizations also developed farther east: the **INDUS VALLEY CIVILIZATIONS** flourished in the Indus and Ganges river basins, where **BUDDHISM** developed, likely around 300 B.C.E. In **CHINA**, the **SHANG** dynasty, the first known dynasty, ruled the **HUANG HE** or **YELLOW RIVER** area around the second millennium B.C.E. and developed the earliest known Chinese writing, which helped unite Chinese-speaking people throughout the region. Later, the **ZHOU** dynasty, which succeeded the Shang and expanded Chinese civilization to the **CHIANG JIANG** or **YANGTZE RIVER** region, developed the concept of the **MANDATE OF HEAVEN**, where the emperor had a divine mandate to rule. Following the **WARRING STATES PERIOD** (c. 475 – 221 B.C.E.), the **QIN** dynasty emerged, unifying Chinese civilizations under the first Emperor.

Settled communities needed the reliable sources of food and fresh water a temperate climate could provide. Surpluses of food allowed for cultural development, not just survival.

Shared customs like the use of silkworms, jade, chopsticks, and the practice of Confucianism also indicate early Chinese unity.

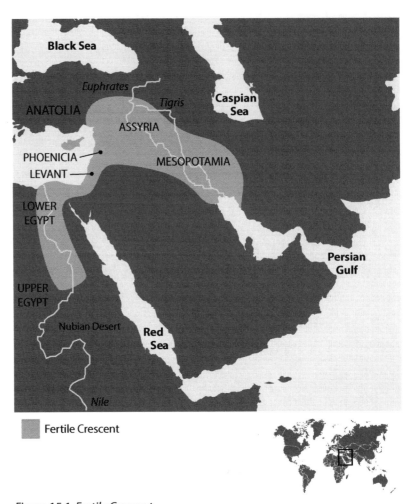

Figure 15.1. Fertile Crescent

Persia, Greece, and Rome

The **PERSIAN** emperor **CYRUS**, founder of the **ACHAEMENID EMPIRE**, conquered the Babylonians in the sixth century B.C.E. His son **DARIUS** extended Persian rule from the Indus Valley to Egypt and north to **ANATOLIA** by about 400 B.C.E., where the Persians encountered the ancient **GREEKS**. Known for its fundamental impact on Western civilization to this day, Greek or **HELLENIC CIVILIZATION** included political, philosophical, and mathematical thought; art and architecture; and poetry and theater.

Greece was composed of **CITY-STATES** like **ATHENS**, the first known **DEMOCRACY**, and the military state **SPARTA**. Historically these city-states had been in conflict: in fact, Athens and Sparta were at odds during the **PELOPONNESIAN WAR** in the fifth century B.C.E. However, following that conflict, Greeks came to the aid of Ionian Greeks under Persian rule; in Anatolia, the Persian king **XERXES** led two campaigns against Greek forces. The Greeks held the Persians at bay and became a unified state following the war; during this period, the **GOLDEN AGE** of Greek civilization, much of the art, architecture, and philosophy known today were developed. In the fourth century B.C.E., Philip II of Macedonia had taken

How is Greek philosophy and its focus on reason important in modern culture?

over most of Greece; his son **ALEXANDER THE GREAT** would go on to spread Greek civilization throughout Eastern Europe and much of Western and Central Asia.

Meanwhile, the ancient Romans began consolidating their power throughout the Italian peninsula; the Romans developed a **REPUBLIC**, electing lawmakers (Senators) to the **SENATE**. Rome was heavily influenced by the Greeks, borrowing styles of architecture, art, and even religion. The Romans developed highly advanced infrastructure, including roads, some still in use today. Rome conquered areas around the Mediterranean with its powerful military. However, the Senate, composed of wealthy **PATRICIANS**, became increasingly corrupt, disregarding the needs of regular Romans or **PLEBEIANS**. The Roman military leader **JULIUS CAESAR** forced the corrupt Senate to give him control, and Rome transitioned from a republic to an empire. Under his successor, his nephew **AUGUSTUS CAESAR**, Rome reached the height of its power, and the Mediterranean region enjoyed a period of stability known as the *PAX ROMANA.*

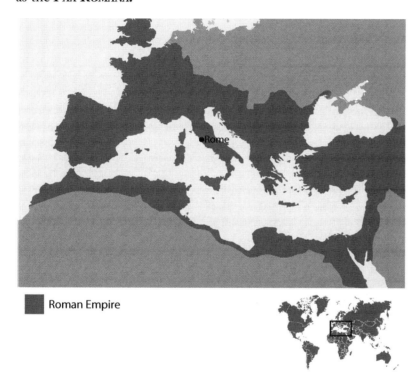

Roman Empire

Figure 15.2. Pax Romana

By 300 C.E., Rome was in decline and divided. The Western Roman Empire gradually fell into disarray, while the Eastern Roman Empire, with its capital at Constantinople, became the **BYZANTINE EMPIRE**. Emperor **JUSTINIAN** reconquered parts of North Africa, Egypt, and Greece, established rule of law, and reinvigorated trade with China. In 1054, the now-widespread Christian religion became divided in the **GREAT SCHISM** between the Roman Catholic Church and the Eastern Greek Orthodox Church.

Examples

1. What were the contributions of early Middle Eastern civilizations?

   Early Middle Eastern civilizations developed agriculture in the Fertile Crescent and the Nile Valley. The Sumerians introduced the first form of written language, cuneiform. The Babylonians developed codified law, the Code of Hammurabi. Mesopotamian and Egyptian civilizations developed art and architecture, notably the ancient Egyptians, who created pyramids and art that are admired to this day.

2. How did Julius Caesar rise to and retain power?

   Julius Caesar took advantage of his popularity as a successful military leader, having conquered Gaul for the Roman Empire. Roman plebeians were dissatisfied with the corrupt, wealthy patricians of the Senate. The Senate's corruption and weakness, Caesar's popularity with the plebeians, support of the military following his service and popularity, and strong leadership enabled Julius Caesar to take control.

WORLD RELIGIONS

Judaism

Judaism was the first **MONOTHEISTIC** religion; its adherents believe in only *one* god. It's believed that God came to the Hebrew Abraham and that the Hebrews—the Jews—were to be God's *chosen people* to serve as an example to the world. Later, **MOSES** would lead the Jews out of slavery in Egypt, and God gave him **TEN COMMANDMENTS** or laws, the basis of what would become Judeo-Christian and Islamic moral codes. Notably, these moral codes applied to all people, including slaves. In addition to confirming the singular nature of God, the Ten Commandments laid out social rules for an organized society under that one god: to refrain from theft and murder and to honor one's parents, among others. Judaism's holy texts are the **TORAH** and the **TALMUD** (religious and civil law). There are different branches of Judaism with varying teachings, including Orthodox, Conservative, and Reform Judaism, among others.

Christianity

In Roman Palestine, the Jewish carpenter **JESUS** taught that he was the son of the singular, Jewish God. Christians believe that Jesus came to suffer and die for the sins of mankind so that all mankind may be forgiven for sin. He gained many followers for his teaching; ultimately, he was crucified. Christians believe that Jesus rose from the dead three days later (the **RESURRECTION**) and ascended to heaven. Christians believe that Jesus was miraculously born from a virgin mother (the **VIRGIN MARY**) and believe in the **HOLY TRINITY**, that God is made up of the Father, the Son, and the Holy Spirit, all parts of one God. The **CATHOLIC CHURCH** is led by the Pope and descended from the early western Church that followed the **SCHISM OF 1054,** when theological disagreement divided the Church into the western Catholic Church and **EASTERN ORTHODOX** Christianity. Later in Western Europe, the **PROTESTANT REFORMATION** gave rise to other forms of Protestant, or non-Catholic, Christianity.

Islam

Islam is rooted in the Arabian Peninsula. Muslims believe that the angel Gabriel spoke to the **PROPHET MUHAMMAD,** transmitting the literal word of **ALLAH** (God), which was later written down as the **QUR'AN.** Muhammad is considered by Muslims to be the final prophet of the god of the Jews and Christians, and Islam shares similar moral teachings. Islam recognizes leaders like Abraham, Moses, and Jesus, but unlike Christianity, views Jesus as a prophet, not as the son of God. The Prophet Muhammad was a religious, military, and political leader; in conquering the Arabian Peninsula and other parts of the Middle East, he protected the **PEOPLE OF THE BOOK,** or Jews and Christians. After his death, discord among his followers resulted in the **SUNNI-SHI'A SCHISM** over his succession and some teachings; to this day, deep divisions remain between many Sunnis and Shi'ites. Like Judaism, Islam also has a book of legal teachings called the **HADITH.**

Hinduism

Major tenets of Hindu belief include **REINCARNATION,** or that the universe and its beings undergo endless cycles of rebirth and **KARMA,** or that one creates one's own destiny. The soul is reincarnated until it has resolved all karmas, at which point it attains **MOKSHA,** or liberation from the cycle. Hindus believe in multiple divine beings. Religion is based on the **VEDIC SCRIPTURES;** other important texts include the **UPANISHADS,** the **MAHABHARATA,** and the **BHAGAVAD GITA.** Hinduism is the primary religion in India and is intertwined with the **caste system**, the hierarchical societal structure.

Buddhism

In Buddhism, the Prince **SIDDHARTHA GAUTAMA** is said to have renounced worldly goods and lived as an ascetic in what is today northern India, seeking **ENLIGHTENMENT** around the third century B.C.E. Buddhism teaches that desire—the ego, or self—is the root of suffering and that giving up or **TRANSCENDING** material obsessions will lead to freedom, or **NIRVANA**—enlightenment. While Buddhism originated in India, it's practiced throughout Asia and the world. The main Buddhist schools of theology are the **MAHAYANA,** which is prevalent in northern and eastern Asia (Korea, parts of China, Mongolia), and **THERAVADA,** dominant in Southeast Asia and Indian Ocean regions. **VAJRAYANA** Buddhism is central to Tibetan Buddhism.

Confucianism

Confucianism teaches obedience and adherence to tradition to maintain a harmonious society. Ideally, practicing integrity and respecting wisdom would ensure that authority would be used for beneficial purposes. Confucius himself was a Chinese scholar in the sixth century B.C.E.; his philosophy would go on to inform Chinese culture for centuries.

Examples

1. Explain Monotheism. What are the major monotheistic religions and who are their main figures?

   Monotheism is the belief in one god. Judaism, Christianity, and Islam are the major monotheistic religions. Judaism, the oldest monotheistic religion upon which the others are based, is traced back to the Hebrew leader Abraham, to whom God appeared; God told him that He was the one true god and that the Jews were a chosen people to serve as a moral example to the world. Later, Jesus taught that he was the Son of God and that he had come to die for the forgiveness of the sins of humankind; Christians believe that he was resurrected after his death and is part of the Holy Trinity of God the Father, God the Son, and God the Holy Spirit. In Islam, the Prophet Muhammad is the primary figure. Muslims believe that the angel Gabriel transmitted the word of Allah to Muhammad in what later became the Qur'an and that Muhammad was the final Prophet of the God of the Jews and Christians.

2. Compare Hinduism and Buddhism.

   In Hinduism, the soul is reincarnated to resolve karmas in each lifetime, destinies brought on by one's behavior that must be resolved. The soul is finally released from this cycle and attains moksha, a state of freedom. In Buddhism, the ego is the root of suffering; rather than reincarnation, the renouncement of desire is the path to freedom: enlightenment, or nirvana.

FEUDALISM THROUGH THE ERA OF EXPANSION

The Middle Ages in Europe

A weakening Rome had agreements with different European clans like the **ANGLO-SAXONS**, the **FRANKS**, the **VISIGOTHS**, the **HUNS** and the **SLAVS**, among others, to protect its western and northern borders; eventually, these groups rebelled against the government, and what was left of the Roman Empire in the west finally fell. Meanwhile, the Byzantine Empire remained a strong civilization and a place of learning. Later, missionaries traveled north to Russia, spreading Greek Orthodox Christianity and literacy. In 988 C.E., the Russian Grand Prince of Kiev, **VLADIMIR I**, converted to Greek Orthodox (Byzantine) Christianity and ordered his subjects to do

These groups and others from Central Asia were able to defeat the Romans in the north and settle in Europe, thanks to their equestrian skills, superior wheels, and iron technology.

so as well. In Western Europe however, the last Roman emperor was killed in **476 C.E.**, and the **MIDDLE AGES** began.

The Middle Ages were characterized by decentralized, local governance, or **FEUDALISM**, a hierarchy where land and protection were offered in exchange for loyalty. **PEASANTS** lived and worked on the territory, or **FIEF**, in a small, self-sustaining area called a **MANOR**, under the protection of a hierarchy of **LORDS** who were **VASSALS** of a **KING** or of the Catholic Church. Lords hired **KNIGHTS** to defend their land, but many knights also became landowners themselves. Peasants were **SERFS**, or not entirely free; they could not own land but did not fight for the lords. The **CATHOLIC CHURCH** grew in power, and the **POPE** became not only a religious leader but also a military and political one. In what is considered the reemergence of centralized power in Europe, parts of Western and Central Europe were organized under **CHARLEMAGNE**, who was crowned emperor by the Pope in **800 C.E.** of the **CAROLINGIAN EMPIRE**. In **962 C.E.**, **OTTO I** became emperor of the **HOLY ROMAN EMPIRE** in Central Europe, a confederation of small states that remained an important European power until its dissolution in **1806**.

There were limits on sovereign power, however; in 1215, English barons forced King John to sign the Magna Carta, which protected their property and rights from the king and was the basis for today's parliamentary system in that country.

The Islamic World

Meanwhile, in the wake of the decline of the Byzantine Empire, **ARAB-ISLAMIC EMPIRES** characterized by brisk commerce, advancements in technology and learning, and urban development in Damascus and Baghdad arose in the Middle East. Following the development of Islam in the Arabian Peninsula under **MUHAMMAD** and his death in **632 C.E.**, his followers went on to conquer land beyond Arabia north into the weakening Byzantine empire; winning

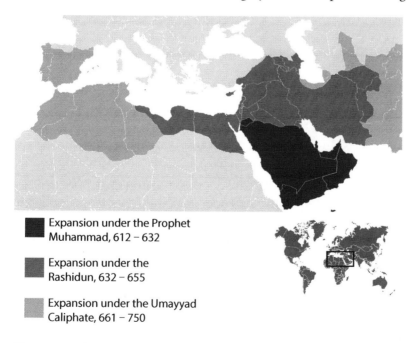

Figure 15.3. Islamic expansion

over dissatisfied minorities in the modern-day Levant and eastern Turkey, the **Umayyad Caliphate** (empire) formed.

Conflict over Muslim leadership after Muhammad's death led to the **Sunni-Shi'a Schism**. Muhammad's cousin and son-in-law **Ali**, his wife **Fatima**, and their followers fled to modern-day Iraq, where **Shi'ite Islam** emerged. The Shi'ites believed that Ali was the rightful heir to Muhammad's early Islamic empire, while the followers of the Meccan elites who expelled them became known as **Sunnis**.

Ongoing conflict among Arab elites resulted in the **Abbasid Caliphate** in 750 C.E., based in Baghdad. Under the Abbasids, political thought, science, literature, exploration, and rule of law flourished. International commerce was vigorous along the **Silk Road**, trading routes that stretched from the Arab-controlled Eastern Mediterranean to **Tang Dynasty** China, where science and learning also blossomed.

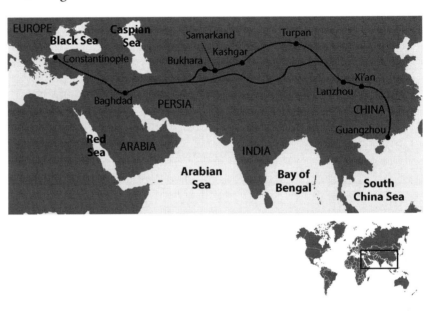

Figure 15.4. Silk Road

The diverse Arab-Islamic and Ottoman empires would control lands for centuries from the Iberian Peninsula in Europe through North Africa into Persia.

Toward the eleventh century, the Abbasid Caliphate dissolved, breaking up into territories ruled by the **Mongols** in Central Asia, the **Fatimids** and later the **Mamluks** in Egypt, the **Seljuks** in Persia, and the **Ottoman Turks**, who developed in Anatolia and later came to rule most of the Middle East, the Balkans, and North Africa under the **Ottoman Empire** until the end of World War I.

Islam also spread along trans-Saharan trade routes into West Africa and the Sahel. Brisk trade between the gold-rich **Kingdom of Ghana** and Muslim traders based in Morocco brought Islam to the region around the eleventh century. The Islamic **Mali Empire** (1235 – 1500), based farther south in Timbuktu, eventually extended beyond the original Ghanaian boundaries all the way to the West African coast and controlled the valuable gold and salt trades. It became a center of learning and commerce. At the empire's peak, the ruler **Mansa Musa** made a pilgrimage to Mecca in 1324. However, by 1500, the **Songhai Empire** had overcome Mali and eventually dominated the Niger River area.

Crusades

Loss of Byzantine territory to the Islamic empires meant loss of Christian lands in the Levant—including Jerusalem and Bethlehem—to Muslims. In **1095 C.E.**, the Byzantine Emperor asked **Pope Urban II** for help to defend what little was left of the Byzantine Empire (Constantinople). With Muslim incursions into Spain and France, anti-Muslim sentiment was strong in Europe, and Christians there were easily inspired to fight them in the Levant, or **Holy Land**; the Pope offered lords and knights the chance to keep lands and bounty they won from conquered Muslims (and Jews) in this **Crusade**. He also offered Crusaders **indulgences**—forgiveness for sins committed in war and *guarantees* they would enter heaven. While the ongoing Crusades never resulted in permanent European control over the Holy Land, they did open up trade routes between Europe and the Middle East, stretching all the way along the Silk Road to China. This increasing interdependence led to the European Renaissance.

Renaissance and Reformation

Cultural exchange between Europeans and Muslims exposed Europeans, who could now afford them thanks to international trade, to improved education and goods. However, the **Bubonic (Black) Plague** spread to Europe as a result of global exchange, killing off a third of its population from 1347 – 1351. The plague had a worldwide impact: empires fell in its wake. The Mongol empire in Central Asia collapsed, including the Mongol-led **Yuan dynasty** in China, leading to instability in Asia and the rise of the **Ming dynasty**, which saw the construction of the **Forbidden City**. Meanwhile, **Ivan the Great** defeated the Mongols in **Russia**, gaining control of Moscow; a century later, **Ivan the Terrible** expanded Russia even farther. The Ottomans were able to conquer much of the Middle East and North Africa, creating the **Ottoman Empire**. The Ottomans made their capital at Constantinople, and the remaining Christian Byzantines fled to Italy, bringing Greek, Middle Eastern, and Asian learning with them and enriching the emerging European Renaissance.

The **Renaissance**, or *rebirth*, included the revival of ancient Greek and Roman learning, art, and architecture. This also inspired new art in Europe like painting, sculpture, literature, and poetry; major figures included Leonardo da Vinci, Michelangelo, Botticelli, and Donatello. Meanwhile, scholars like Galileo, Isaac Newton, and Copernicus made discoveries in what became known as the

The Scientific Revolution changed European thinking. What was the impact of using reason and scientific methodology rather than religion to understand the world?

SCIENTIFIC REVOLUTION, rooted in the scientific knowledge of the Islamic empires. With the invention of the PRINTING PRESS, people had more access to information beyond what their leaders told them. This ENLIGHTENMENT would be the basis for reinvigorated European culture and political thought that would drive its development for the next several centuries. However, Russia would not experience these cultural changes until the eighteenth century, when PETER THE GREAT and CATHERINE THE GREAT copied modern European culture, modernized the military, and updated technology, including building the new capital city of ST. PETERSBURG, a cultural center.

With these cultural changes, the power of the Catholic Church was threatened; new scientific discoveries and secular Renaissance thought were at odds with teachings of the Church. The Catholic monk MARTIN LUTHER wrote a letter of protest to the Pope in 1517 known as the NINETY-FIVE THESES, outlining ways he believed the Church should reform; his ideas gained support, especially among rulers who wanted more power from the Church. Protestant thinkers like Luther and JOHN CALVIN spoke against the INFALLIBILITY of the Pope (its teaching that the Pope was without fault) and the selling of indulgences, or guarantees of entry into heaven. The English KING HENRY VIII developed the Protestant CHURCH OF ENGLAND, further consolidating his own power, famously allowing divorce.

The division between Protestants and Catholics split Europe, and a series of wars ensued between Protestant and Catholic rulers from 1524 – 1628 (the Hundred Years' War), ending in the TREATY OF WESTPHALIA, based on the concept of sovereign states and noninterference, marking a transition into modern international relations when politics and religion would no longer be inexorably intertwined. Over the next several centuries, the Church and religious empires like the Ottomans would eventually lose control over ethnic groups and their lands, giving way to smaller NATION-STATES.

Colonization of the Western Hemisphere

Interest in exploration grew in Europe during the Renaissance period. Technological advancements made complex navigation and long-term sea voyages possible, and economic growth resulting from international trade drove interest in market expansion. Global interdependence got a big push from Spain when King Ferdinand and Queen Isabella agreed to sponsor CHRISTOPHER COLUMBUS' exploratory voyage in 1492 to find a sea route to Asia to speed up commercial trade there. Instead, he stumbled upon the Western Hemisphere, which was unknown to Europeans, Asians, and Africans to this point.

Columbus landed in the Caribbean; he and later explorers would claim the Caribbean islands and eventually Central and South

America for Spain and Portugal. However, those areas were already populated by major civilizations like the Aztecs, Incas, and Mayas. The **Aztecs** in modern-day Mexico and Guatemala were ruled by a king, with an independent priestly class and a hierarchical social structure. Known as fierce warriors, they were based in what is today Mexico City. The agricultural **Incas** in the Andean region engaged in collective farming, developing terraced agriculture on the mountainous terrain. The Incan king was also considered to be a god, but conquered tribes were allowed to keep their rulers as long as they did not rebel against him. However, these long-standing civilizations were quickly wiped out when the Spanish *CONQUISTADORES* arrived.

Spain took over the silver- and gold-rich Mesoamerican and Andean territories and the Caribbean islands where sugar became an important cash crop. Thus **MERCANTILISM** developed, whereby the colonizing or *MOTHER COUNTRY* took raw materials from the territories they controlled for the colonizers' own benefit. Sometimes this involved manufacturing goods and then selling them back to those colonized lands at an inflated price. The **ENCOMIENDA** system granted European landowners the "right" to hold lands in the Americas and demand labor and tribute from the local inhabitants. Spreading Christianity was another important reason for European expansion. Local civilizations and resources were exploited and destroyed.

The **COLUMBIAN EXCHANGE** enabled mercantilism to flourish. Conflict and illness brought by the Europeans—**SMALLPOX**—decimated the Native Americans, and the Europeans were left without labor to mine the silver and gold or to work the land. **AFRICAN SLAVERY** was the solution. Slavery was an ancient institution in many societies worldwide; however, with the Columbian Exchange, slavery came to be practiced on a mass scale the likes of which the world had never seen. Throughout Africa and especially on the West African coast, Europeans traded for slaves with some African kingdoms and also raided villages, kidnapping people. Captured Africans were taken in horrific conditions to the Americas; those who survived were forced to work in mining or agriculture for the benefit of expanding European imperial powers. The Columbian Exchange described the **TRIANGULAR TRADE** across the Atlantic: slaves went from Africa to the Americas, where they were exchanged for sugar and raw materials; these materials were traded in Europe for manufactured goods, which were then exchanged in Africa for slaves, and so on.

Enslaved Africans suffered greatly, forced to endure ocean voyages crammed on dirty ships, only to arrive in the Americas to a life of slavery in mines or on plantations. However, throughout this period, Africans did resist both on ships and later, in the Americas; **MAROON COMMUNITIES** of escaped slaves formed throughout the Western Hemisphere, the **UNDERGROUND RAILROAD**

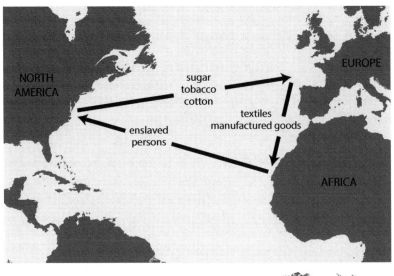

Figure 15.5. Triangular trade

in the nineteenth-century United States helped slaves escape the South, and **TOUSSAINT L'OUVERTURE** led a successful slave rebellion in Haiti, winning independence from the French for that country in 1791.

Examples

1. What was destructive about the encomienda system?

   The encomienda system granted colonists the right to own land and demand tribute and labor from the local inhabitants. This destroyed local societies and perpetuated systems of oppression and slavery. It also perpetuated mercantilism; as raw materials were harvested from the lands in the colonies, they benefitted the mother country, not the colony.

2. Describe the Columbian Exchange.

   The Columbian Exchange describes the economic and social system of the Atlantic World during the colonization of the Americas. Slaves were exported from Africa to provide agricultural and mining labor in the Americas, harvesting raw materials. These resources were sent to Europe, which would use them or transform them into manufactured goods to sell for profit in the colonies or in Africa. This system of triangular trade—mercantilism—benefitted the mother country.

ARMED CONFLICTS

New Europe and the Age of Revolutions

While Spain and Portugal consolidated their hold over territories in the Americas, conflict between Protestants and Catholics continued until the Peace of Westphalia (see above). Post-Reformation conflict also rocked Great Britain; while King Henry VIII had founded the Protestant Church of England, rulers since had been divided and at odds over Anglicanism and Catholicism. Likewise, Enlightenment ideals of democracy and republicanism were at odds with the ABSOLUTE MONARCHY. The ENGLISH CIVIL WAR (1642 – 1651) established Protestantism as the dominant religion in Britain; the GLORIOUS REVOLUTION (1688) solidified the idea that a monarch cannot be in power without Parliament's consent. Informed by thinkers like JOHN LOCKE, who believed in REPUBLICANISM, or consent of the governed to their government, the AGE OF REVOLUTIONS would begin, including the AMERICAN REVOLUTION in 1776, heavily influenced by Locke, and later the FRENCH REVOLUTION (1789).

The French Revolution was the precursor to the end of monarchy in most of Europe. KING LOUIS XIV, the *Sun King* (1643 – 1715), had consolidated the monarchy in France, taking true political and military power from the nobility. The ESTATES-GENERAL, a weak representative assembly, reflected French society: the clergy, nobility, and the THIRD ESTATE—the BOURGEOISIE, or middle class, and the poor peasants. The burden of taxation fell greatly on the peasantry. Meanwhile, French Enlightenment thinkers like JEAN-JACQUES ROUSSEAU, MONTESQUIEU, and VOLTAIRE criticized absolute monarchy and the repression of freedom of speech and thought; in 1789, the French Revolution broke out.

Following a period of instability, in 1804, NAPOLEON BONAPARTE emerged as emperor of France and proceeded to conquer much of Europe. By 1815, other European powers had managed to halt his expansion; at the CONGRESS OF VIENNA in 1815, European powers, including the unified PRUSSIA (which had emerged from the states of the Holy Roman Empire), the AUSTRO-HUNGARIAN EMPIRE, RUSSIA, BRITAIN, and FRANCE, agreed on a BALANCE OF POWER in Europe. The Congress of Vienna was the first real international peace conference and set the precedent for European political organization.

Finally, Latin American countries joined Haiti and the United States in revolution against colonial European powers. Inspired by the American and French Revolutions, SIMÓN BOLIVAR led or influenced independence movements in VENEZUELA, COLOMBIA (including what is today PANAMA), ECUADOR, PERU, and BOLIVIA in the early part of the nineteenth century.

After King Charles I's execution by Parliamentary forces in 1649 and Oliver Cromwell's military dictatorship, Charles II became king in 1660. Upon his death, his Catholic son James took over; however Parliament rebelled again and placed James' Protestant daughter Mary and her husband, William, in power. The 1689 English Bill of Rights established constitutional monarchy, in the spirit of the Magna Carta.

European Division

The nineteenth century was a period of change and conflict, and the roots of the major twentieth century conflicts—world war and decolonization—are found in it. Following the Congress of Vienna, **PRUSSIA** dominated the German-speaking states that once composed the Holy Roman Empire. **OTTO VON BISMARCK** led German unification; fueled by **NATIONALISM** and the **NATION-STATE**, or the idea that individuals with shared experience (including ethnicity, language, religion, and cultural practices) should be unified under one government. Prussia, later **GERMANY**, became powerful militarily, surrounded by other military powers like France; the **OTTOMAN EMPIRE,** which had gained control over the Balkans, the Middle East, and North Africa under **SULEIMAN THE MAGNIFICENT (1520 – 1566)** and held the land until the nineteenth century; the **AUSTRO-HUNGARIAN EMPIRE**, controlled by the powerful **HAPSBURGS**; and the powerful **RUSSIAN EMPIRE**, which not only controlled Russia and northern Asia, but also had proven itself an important European military power by defeating Napoleon. Nationalism also led to **ITALIAN UNIFICATION**.

In the model of European diplomacy following the Congress of Vienna, Russia, Germany, and Austria-Hungary formed the **THREE EMPERORS' LEAGUE (1873)**, where if one country went to war, the others would remain neutral, and the powers would consult each other on matters of war. Later, the **TRIPLE ALLIANCE (1882)**, a political and military alliance, formed between Austria-Hungary, Germany, and Italy. In response, Russia, Great Britain, and France formed the **TRIPLE ENTENTE (1907)**.

Germany was not the only country to benefit from nationalism. Russia took advantage of nationalism in the form of **PAN-SLAVISM**, in which it encouraged Slavic ethnic groups throughout Eastern and Southeastern Europe to embrace their Slavic heritage and turn toward Russia for support—in particular, the **SERBIANS**. Serbian nationalism contributed toward the **BALKAN CRISES** of the late nineteenth century, which resulted in Ottoman loss of the Balkans to Austria-Hungary; despite Austria-Hungary's political control over Serbia, Russia and Serbia maintained strong ties, and Serbian nationalism eventually triggered the chain of events leading to the **FIRST WORLD WAR**.

Imperialism

Meanwhile, Great Britain, despite losing its colonies in North America after the American Revolution, was becoming an important world power thanks to **IMPERIALISM**. In the nineteenth century, Britain became the strongest naval power in the world and expanded its empire, notably under **QUEEN VICTORIA**, in the search for new markets for its manufactured goods to support its industrial economy. The concept of the *WHITE MAN'S BURDEN*, wherein white

Europeans were "obligated" to bring their "superior" culture to other civilizations around the globe, also drove imperialist adventure. Britain established the **Raj** in **India**, taking over the Subcontinent.

To gain access to closed Chinese markets, Britain forced China to buy Indian opium; the **Opium Wars** ended with the **Treaty of Nanking (1842)**. As a consequence, China lost great power to Britain and later, other European countries, which gained **spheres of influence**, or areas of China they effectively controlled, and **extraterritoriality**, or privileges in which their citizens were not subject to Chinese law. The unsuccessful **Boxer Rebellion** in 1900 was one example of resistance against Western presence in and exploitation of China.

Britain also joined other European powers in what became known as the *Scramble for Africa*; the industrial economies of Europe would profit from the natural resources abundant in that continent, and the white man's burden continued to fuel colonization. At the **1884 Berlin Conference**, control over Africa was divided among European powers (Africans were not consulted in

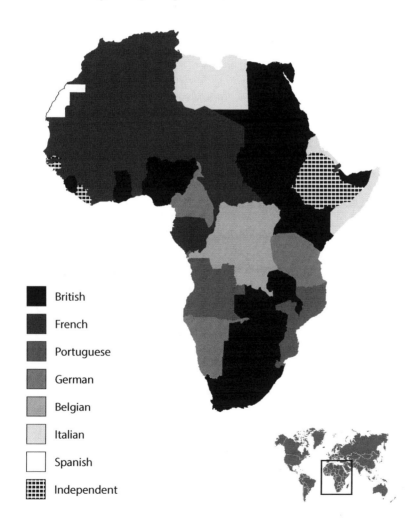

British

French

Portuguese

German

Belgian

Italian

Spanish

Independent

Figure 15.6. African colonies

Britain also controlled the vast territories of Canada, Australia, and New Zealand, which are still associated with the Crown as part of the Commonwealth today.

this process). Following the **Boer War (1899 – 1902)** between Afrikaaners of Dutch origin and the English, Britain gained control of South Africa, and whites would rule the country until the end of **Apartheid** in the early 1990s. Britain also controlled much of East Africa, including Kenya. France controlled West Africa and eventually North Africa, especially Algeria, Mali, Niger, Chad, Cameroon, and what has become the Republic of the Congo. Tiny Belgium gained control over the Congo, the enormous, resource-rich territory in the Congo River basin.

However, not all non-European countries fell to European imperialism. During the **Meiji Restoration** in Japan in 1868, the Emperor Meiji promoted modernization of technology, especially the military. Japan proved itself a world power when it defeated Russia in the Russo-Japanese War in 1905, and would play a central role in twentieth-century conflict.

Industrial Revolution, Economics, and Society

Throughout this entire period, raw goods from the Americas fueled European economic growth and development, leading to the **Industrial Revolution** in the nineteenth century. This economic revolution began with textile production, fueled by American **cotton**, in Britain. The first factories were in Manchester, where **urbanization** began as poor people from rural areas flocked to cities in search of higher-paying unskilled jobs in factories. Early industrial technology sped up the harvesting and transport of crops and their conversion to textiles. This accelerated manufacturing was based on **capitalism**, the *laissez-faire* (or **free market**) theory developed by **Adam Smith**, who believed that an *invisible hand* should guide the marketplace—that government should stay out of the economy no matter what. The German philosophers **Karl Marx** and **Fredrich Engels**, in response to the abusive conditions suffered by industrial workers, developed **socialism**, the philosophy that workers, or the **proletariat**, should own the means of production and reap the profits, rather than the **bourgeoisie**, who had no interest in the rights of the workers at the expense of profit. Socialism would later help Russia become a major world power.

Marx and Engels encouraged international revolution by the proletariat through their publication *The Communist Manifesto*.

Russia's loss to Japan in 1905 was just another example of its difference from other European powers. While technically a European country, Russia had been slow to industrialize, due in part to its size and terrain. A largely agrarian country at the turn of the century, **serfdom** had only been abolished in 1861; most Russians were still poor, rural farmers, and industrial activities in cities did not compare with those in London, Paris, or Manchester. Russia also continued to have an absolute monarchy, unlike many European powers whose governments had shifted during the Age of Revolution. A protest in 1905 ended in a bloody massacre of civilians by the Tsar's troops—**Bloody Sunday**, as the event came to be called, was the precursor to the revolution that would take place in 1916.

Examples

1. **What was the Age of Revolution?**

   Thinkers like John Locke and Jean-Jacques Rousseau, who believed in the consent of the governed to their government and freedom of thought and speech, influenced revolutions against absolute monarchy and oppressive political systems in England, North America, France, and Latin America, including the successful slave rebellion in Haiti.

2. **List some important European alliances in the nineteenth century.**

   The Three Emperor's Alliance between Russia, Germany, and Austria-Hungary was an early alliance in which the powers would consult each other on military matters, but not necessarily go to war to support each other. The later Triple Alliance between Germany, Austria-Hungary, and Italy was a stronger military and political alliance. Finding this a threat, France, Britain, and Russia formed the Triple Entente in response. These alliances were precursors to the alliances that would set off WWI.

3. **What were reasons for imperialism?**

   Economic benefits, the white man's burden, and feelings of nationalism inspired imperialism. The Industrial Revolution called for new markets for European-made manufactured products; raw materials for production were harvested from the colonies, and the manufactured products were sold there, bringing income to the imperial power (mercantilism). The white man's burden, or the feeling that Europeans needed to force the adoption of their values on other cultures, also brought imperialism popular support throughout Europe. Finally, nationalism among European powers resulted in the scramble for Africa, in which the imperial powers competed to gain the most land in that continent and, in general, worldwide.

TWENTIETH CENTURY

World War I

Meanwhile, growing nationalism in Europe culminated with the assassination of the Austro-Hungarian Archduke **FRANZ FERDINAND** by the Serbian nationalist **GAVRILO PRINCIP** on June 28, 1914 in Sarajevo. In protest of continuing Austro-Hungarian control over Slavic Serbia, Princip's action kicked off the **SYSTEM OF ALLIANCES** that had been in place between European powers. Immediately, Austria-Hungary invaded Serbia, and Russia came to Serbia's aid. As an ally of Austria-Hungary as part of the Triple Alliance, Germany declared war on Russia. Germany had been emphasizing military growth since its consolidation under Bismarck; now, under **Kaiser Wilhelm II**, who sought expanded territories in Europe and overseas for Germany (including the potential of overseas British and French colonies), Germany was a militarized state. With the **Schlieffen Plan**, Germany had planned to fight a war on two fronts against both Russia and France. However, Russia's unexpectedly rapid mobilization stretched the German army too thin on the Eastern Front, where it became bogged down in **trench warfare** on the Western Front against the British and later the Americans.

🔒

The first international war to use industrialized weaponry, WWI was called "the Great War" because battle on such a scale had never before been seen.

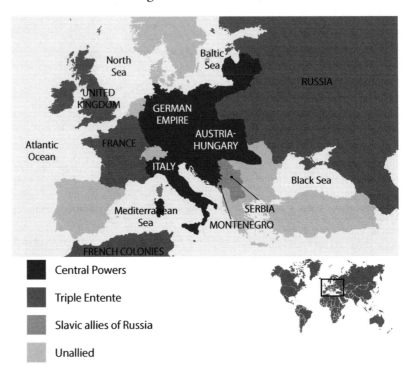

Figure 15.7. WWI alliances

Germany lost the war and was punished with the **Treaty of Versailles,** which held it accountable for the entirety of the war, bringing economic hardship on the country by forcing it to pay **reparations**. The Treaty also created the **League of Nations**, an international organization designed to prevent future outbreaks of international war; however, it was largely toothless, especially because the powerful United States did not join.

Russian Revolution

During WWI, enormous Russian losses helped dissatisfaction with the rule of the **Tsar Nicolas II** coalesce into a revolutionary movement, resulting in the overthrow of his family, the Romanovs, in 1917. Communist revolutionaries led by **Vladimir Lenin** and **Leon Trotsky** took control of Russia, extracted it from the war, and turned it into a communist country—the Soviet Union. Lenin's Bolshevik movement believed in socialism (that the means of production should be owned by the people) but also in the dictatorship of the proletariat, or that the country should not be democratic—

that is, in COMMUNISM. JOSEF STALIN, part of Lenin's movement, took power in the 1920s and implemented forced labor, collective farms, and rapid industrialization programs called Five Year Plans. The U.S.S.R. quickly became an industrial power at the expense of millions of Russians, Ukrainians, and other groups who lost their lives in purges, forced labor camps, and famine.

Japanese Expansion

In Asia, Japan continued to gain power, invading MANCHURIA in 1931 and controlling other parts of China and KOREA throughout the 1930s. Civil war in China between communists led by MAO ZEDONG and nationalists led by CHIANG KAI-SHEK was interrupted by the SINO-JAPANESE WAR in 1937, when Japan tried to extend its imperial reach deeper into China, resulting in atrocities like the RAPE OF NANKING (1927 – 1928). When Japan joined the AXIS powers of Germany and Italy, this war would be subsumed under the Second World War, ending in 1945. Mao Zedong would later go on to win power in China, and it became a communist country in 1949.

Nazi Germany and World War II

Meanwhile, Germany suffered under the provisions of the Treaty of Versailles. Reparations and worldwide economic depression resulted in inflation, impoverishing Germans under the WEIMAR REPUBLIC. Economic ruin and bitterness at Germany's treatment after the war in comparison with the other members of the Triple Alliance helped trigger the rise of the extremist NATIONAL SOCIALIST PARTY, or NAZI PARTY, led by ADOLF HITLER, in the 1930s. Hitler was a FASCIST, believing in a free market but a dictatorial government with a strong military. He sought to restore Germany's power and expand its reach by annexing Austria and the SUDETENLAND (part of what is today the Czech Republic); in an effort to maintain stability in Europe and avoid another war, European powers granted this to Hitler in a policy called APPEASEMENT. However, appeasement failed when Hitler invaded Poland in 1939, commonly understood as the beginning of the SECOND WORLD WAR.

War exploded in Europe in 1939 as Hitler gained control of more land than any European power since Napoleon. The ALLIES—Britain, France, and the Soviet Union—struggled against the AXIS powers (Germany, Italy, and Japan); however, when Japan attacked the United States in 1941, the war changed as the U.S. joined Allied efforts. WWII and the period immediately preceding it saw horrific violations of human rights in Europe and Asia, including the atrocities committed during the Japanese invasions of China, Korea, and Southeast Asia, and the horrific German-organized mass murder, or HOLOCAUST, of Jews and other groups like Roma and homosexuals. The war finally ended with the U.S. atomic bombings of Hiroshima and Nagasaki in 1945, ending years of firebombing civilians in Germany and Japan, devastating ground and naval warfare throughout Europe, Asia, the South Pacific, and Africa, and the deaths of millions of soldiers and civilians all around the world.

The extreme horrors of WWII helped develop the concept of GENOCIDE, or the effort to extinguish an entire group of people because of their ethnicity, and the idea of HUMAN RIGHTS. The UNITED NATIONS was formed, based on the League of Nations, as a body to champion human rights and uphold international security; its SECURITY COUNCIL was made up of permanent member states that could intervene militarily in the interests of international stability. Allied forces took the lead in rebuilding efforts: the U.S. occupied areas in East Asia and Germany, while the Soviet Union remained in Eastern Europe. The Allies had planned to rebuild Europe according to the MARSHALL PLAN; however, Stalin broke his promise made at the 1945 YALTA CONFERENCE to adhere to that plan and allow Eastern European countries to hold free elections. Instead, the U.S.S.R. occupied these countries, and they came under communist control. The COLD WAR had begun.

The Cold War

With Stalin's betrayal of the Allies' agreement, in the words of the British Prime Minister WINSTON CHURCHILL, an *IRON CURTAIN* had come down across Europe, dividing east from west. Consequently, Western states organized the North Atlantic Treaty Organization, or **NATO**, an agreement wherein an attack on one was an attack on all; this treaty provided for COLLECTIVE SECURITY in the face of Soviet expansionist threat. In response, the Soviet Union created the WARSAW PACT, a similar organization consisting of Eastern European communist countries. NUCLEAR WEAPONS, especially the development of the extremely powerful HYDROGEN BOMB, raised the stakes of the conflict. The concept of MUTUALLY-ASSURED DESTRUCTION, or the understanding that a nuclear strike by one country would result in a response by the other, ultimately destroying the entire world, may have prevented the outbreak of active violence.

Meanwhile, the former colonies of the fallen European colonial powers had won or were in the process of gaining their independence. One role of the United Nations was to help manage the DECOLONIZATION process. Already, the leader MOHANDAS GANDHI had led a peaceful independence movement in INDIA against the British, winning Indian independence in 1949. His assassination by Hindu radicals led to conflict between HINDUS and MUSLIMS in the SUBCONTINENT, resulting in PARTITION, the bloody division of India: Hindus fled into what is today India, while Muslims fled to EAST PAKISTAN (now BANGLADESH) and WEST PAKISTAN. Instability is ongoing on the Subcontinent.

Bloody conflict in Africa like the ALGERIAN WAR against France (1954 – 1962), the MAU MAU REBELLION against the British in

Germany itself was divided into West Germany and communist East Germany; the city of Berlin was divided by the Berlin Wall into West Berlin and communist East Berlin.

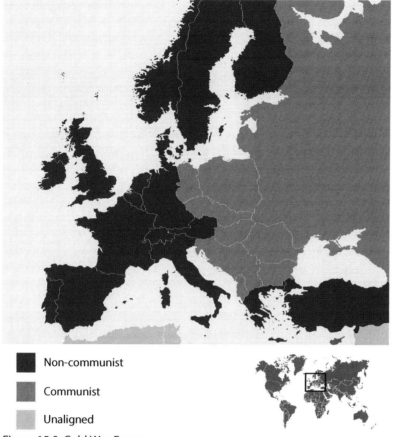

Non-communist

Communist

Unaligned

Figure 15.8. Cold War Europe

Kenya in the 1950s, and violent movements against Belgium in the **Congo** ultimately resulted in African independence for many countries in the 1950s, 1960s, and 1970s; likewise, so did strong leadership by African nationalist leaders and thinkers like **Jomo Kenyatta, Julius Nyerere,** and **Kwame Nkrumah.** The apartheid regime in South Africa, where segregation between races was legal and people of color lived in oppressive conditions, was not lifted until the 1990s; **Nelson Mandela** led the country in a peaceful transition process.

In the Middle East, following the fall of the Ottoman Empire after WWI, European powers had taken over much of the area; these ***protectorates*** became independent states with arbitrary borders drawn and rulers installed by the Europeans. The creation of the state of **Israel** was especially contentious: in the 1917 **Balfour Declaration**, the British had promised the **Zionist** movement of European Jews that they would be given a homeland in the British-controlled protectorate of Palestine; however, the U.S. assured the Arabs in 1945 that a Jewish state would not be founded there. Israel emerged from diplomatic confusion, chaos, and tragedy after the murder of millions of Jews in Europe, and violence on the ground in Palestine carried out by both Jews and Arabs. This legacy of conflict lasts to this day in the Middle East.

The **NON-ALIGNED MOVEMENT** arose in response to the Cold War. Instead of the bipolar world of the Cold War (one democratic, led by the U.S., the other communist, led by the U.S.S.R.), the Non-Aligned Movement sought an alternative: the **THIRD WORLD**. Non-Aligned or Third World countries wanted to avoid succumbing to the influence of either of the superpowers, and many found a forum in the United Nations in which to strengthen their international profiles. However, throughout the Cold War, **PROXY WARS** between the U.S. and the U.S.S.R. were fought around the world. Examples include the **KOREAN WAR**, the **VIETNAM WAR**, the **ANGOLAN CIVIL WAR**, the **MOZAMBICAN CIVIL WAR**, and the **NICARAGUAN REVOLUTION**. In the **SOVIET WAR IN AFGHANISTAN** (1979 – 1989), when the U.S. supported *MUJAHIDEEN* fighters against an invading Soviet force, the U.S.S.R. was eventually defeated, preceding its collapse.

Post-Cold War World

In 1991, the Soviet Union fell when Soviet Premier **MIKHAIL GORBACHEV**, who had implemented reforms like *GLASNOST* and *PERESTROIKA* (or *openness* and *transparency*), was overthrown in a coup; a democratic movement took over, and the communist government fell permanently. The war in Afghanistan and military overspending in an effort to keep up with American military spending weakened the U.S.S.R. to the point of collapse, and the Cold War ended. For a period, the U.S. was the sole world superpower. Steps toward European unification had begun as early as the 1950s; in 1991, the **EUROPEAN UNION**, as it's known today, was formed in 1993 after the Maastricht Treaty was signed, and it grew to twenty-eight countries as of 2015. European Union countries remain independent, but they cooperate in international affairs, justice, security and foreign policy, environmental matters, and economic policy. Many also share a common currency, the **EURO**.

In this era of **GLOBALIZATION**, international markets became increasingly open through free-trade agreements like **NAFTA** (the North American Free Trade Agreement) and **MERCOSUR** (the South American free-trade zone) and associations like the **WORLD TRADE ORGANIZATION**. Technological advances like the **INTERNET** made international communication faster, easier, and cheaper. However, in the early twenty-first century, the U.S. launched two major land wars in **AFGHANISTAN** and **IRAQ** following terrorist attacks on New York City and Washington, D.C. on **SEPTEMBER 11, 2001**.

🔒

While many Middle Eastern countries remain under dictatorial regimes, reform movements began in the 2011 "Arab Spring" in Tunisia, Egypt, Bahrain, and Syria. Conflict continues in Syria, Iraq, Israel and the Palestinian Territories, and elsewhere.

Examples

1. How did the Cold War erupt between the former allies the U.S. and the Soviet Union?

   At Yalta, the Allies had planned for the post-war world, particularly the rebuilding of Europe. The Allies agreed to the Marshall Plan and that European countries would be able to have free elections. Once Germany was defeated, the U.S. and U.S.S.R. occupied certain parts of Europe. Stalin reneged on his promise to allow free elections in the countries occupied by the Soviets, and the "iron curtain" fell across Europe, starting the Cold War between communist countries led by the U.S.S.R. and the democratic capitalist countries led by the U.S.

2. What was a proxy war and why was it important?

Proxy wars are wars where countries fight each other through third parties. For example, the U.S. fought a proxy war against the Soviet Union in Afghanistan: the U.S. did not fight the U.S.S.R. directly, but did support the fighters the Soviets were trying to defeat with weapons and other assistance. In this way, a country does not risk direct conflict but can still attack and weaken its enemy, as was the case for the Soviets in Afghanistan.

16

ECONOMIC THEORY

MICROECONOMICS

Basics

Economics is the exchange of goods and services. To receive a good or service, you must exchange, or **TRADE**, something in return: that is the **COST** of your item—the price you pay.

SCARCITY describes the fundamental economic problem when resources are limited in the face of unlimited want for them. Due to scarcity, people cannot have everything they want and must prioritize their choices to maximize the utility from available resources. Scarcity provides the basis for choice and opportunity cost.

The concept of **CHOICE** is based on a person selecting the best out of several possible alternatives. Economics assumes that people are rational and choose that which provides them with the highest utility. Utility is the subjective feeling of satisfaction; it encompasses monetary value, emotional satisfaction, social well-being, and others. Numerous factors can affect choice, including personal preference, associations, habits, ethnic heritage, tradition, values, social pressure, emotional comfort, availability, convenience, financial motives, social standing/image, medical conditions, and nutrition.

Making a choice means giving up the potential utility gained from the other choices. In microeconomic theory, the **OPPORTUNITY COST** refers to the "lost" utility from the option that the person did not choose. Economics assumes that a rational person will choose the best option (i.e., that which provides the greatest utility), and opportunity cost can be considered the cost incurred by not choosing the alternative. Opportunity cost is not limited to monetary value, and encompasses utility from forgone output, lost time, pleasure, and social standing, among others. This concept describes the fundamental relationship between scarcity and choice.

To purchase or just obtain anything, a consumer conducts a cost-benefit analysis, weighing the cost against the benefits. This is simply determining whether it's worth the money, time, or any other variable to purchase an item or carry out an action.

Supply and Demand

Microeconomics uses supply and demand as the economic model of determining prices in the market. The model posits that in a competitive market, the price of one good will reach **EQUILIBRIUM** at a point where the quantity consumers demand at current prices will equal the quantity producers supply at current prices This results in an economic equilibrium of price and quantity.

DEMAND refers to the utility for a good or service available on the market and subject to a budget constraint. Demand is a buyer's willingness to buy a particular commodity at a particular time, or the relationship between price and quantity demanded. **SUPPLY** is the quantity of a good that sellers (producers) are able and willing to sell to buyers (consumers) at a given price, all other factors held constant. The market is in equilibrium when the quantity of goods supplied by sellers is equal to the quantity of goods demanded by buyers. Graphically, market equilibrium is the point where the supply curve intersects with the demand curve. The **EQUILIBRIUM PRICE** is the price at which the goods are sold by the sellers (and bought by the buyers).

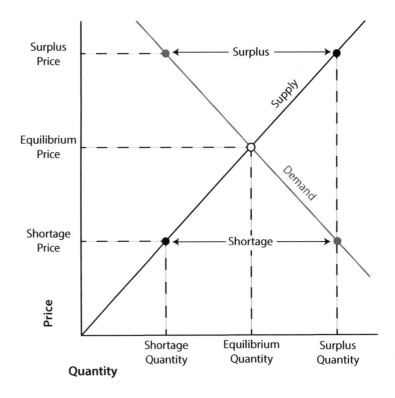

Figure 16.1. Equilibrium price

According to the **LAW OF SUPPLY**, as the price of a good increases, the manufacturers of that good will make more of it available in an effort to maximize their profit by selling as much as possible. However, according to the **LAW OF DEMAND**, as the price of a good increases, consumer demand for that good will decrease. The higher the price of the good, the higher the opportunity cost for the consumer—the more the consumer has to lose by purchasing the good. The equilibrium price of a good is the price at which the quantity supplied equals the quantity demanded, so this is the price at which goods are ultimately sold. In cases of EXCESS DEMAND, some consumers will be unable to get the good they seek and so will offer a higher price for it; the price for the good will go up reflecting this SHORTAGE or SCARCITY. In contrast, EXCESS SUPPLY means that sellers have too much extra stock of their good because of limited demand, and so they will lower the price to entice buyers to purchase it, CLEARING the market of this SURPLUS.

Examples

1. After Halloween, candy was on sale at the supermarket for half price. Explain why, using the terminology discussed above.

   After Halloween, demand for candy goes down because the holiday is over; people are no longer preparing for trick-or-treaters, so they are not buying as much candy as they were before. Therefore, stores have a surplus of candy, which they hope to sell to uninterested shoppers by lowering the price.

2. The international price of widgets has skyrocketed. How should American widget makers respond?

   To sell as many widgets as possible, American widget makers should immediately increase their production. That way, according to the law of supply, they would maximize their profit by selling many widgets at a high price for as long as they can—at least until demand starts dropping according to the law of demand.

Utility and Elasticity

UTILITY is a measure of customer satisfaction with a product. MARGINAL UTILITY indicates how much additional consumption of a good will bring satisfaction to the consumer, helping businesses predict how much of their product they can expect to sell. However, according to SCARCITY, consumers have unlimited wants but limited resources to satisfy them; they must determine how to allocate their resources most efficiently (stay on a budget). PRICE ELASTICITY of demand, another determinant of consumer behavior, indicates how flexible the demand for a product is: as the price of cigarettes goes up, for example, some smokers may quit smoking, while others may continue regardless. Consumers will purchase some products no matter what the price; these goods are PERFECTLY INELASTIC, as there are no substitutes for them. Examples could include types of medication. On the other hand, goods with plenty of substitutes are PERFECTLY ELASTIC.

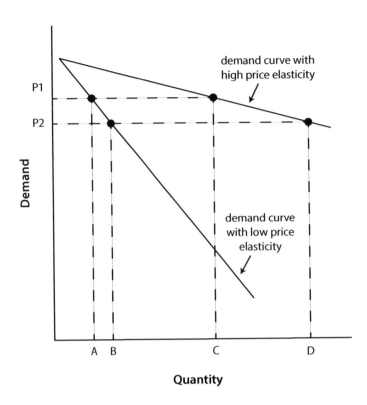

Figure 16.2. Price elasticity

PRICE CEILINGS are the highest price a customer is willing to pay; **PRICE FLOORS** are the lowest price a company will offer for its product. A variety of other factors influence microeconomic decision making, like access to **CREDIT** and **BRAND LOYALTY**, or the extent to which a customer prefers a particular company.

🔒

Maintaining a balanced budget is important in any household: generating income greater than or equal to a household's expenses will avoid debt.

Examples

1. Draw a supply curve. Draw a demand curve.

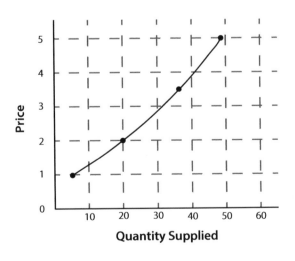

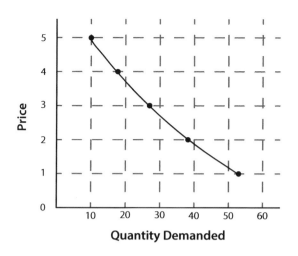

2. What are some inelastic goods? What are some elastic goods?

   Inelastic goods include necessities like water, electricity, perhaps an inexpensive car, and household basics like soap, food, and clothing. There will always be demand for these things. Elastic goods are things you can go without: luxury items like expensive clothing, high-end cars, alcohol, cigarettes, and other nonessential goods. Depending on the price of these products, demand may increase or decrease.

MACROECONOMICS

MACROECONOMICS refers to the **AGGREGATE** economy—the big picture. It studies unemployment, national economic growth, gross domestic product (GDP), inflation, and other national and international issues. **AGGREGATE SUPPLY AND DEMAND** refer to the total amount of the supply or demand for all goods and services in the economy at a given time. Most countries experience **EXPANSION** and

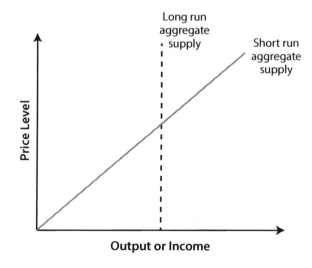

Figure 16.3. Aggregate supply

CONTRACTION in BUSINESS CYCLES. The economy expands in periods of high INFLATION and low unemployment as industries grow, then contracts in periods of UNEMPLOYMENT and slow growth—periods of RECESSION or even DEPRESSION. Ideally, during economic upswings of high employment and inflation, wages keep up with price increases, as demand for goods and services increases across the board.

Wages are the money workers earn; when they stay stagnant or fall, spending goes down and the economy weakens.

Examples

1. Explain aggregate supply and demand.

   Aggregate supply and aggregate demand are the sum of all supply and demand in an economy. They cover the supply and demand for all goods and services in an economy at a certain time.

2. What is a business cycle?

   A business cycle is a period of time in which an economy changes: it expands and contracts. When an economy expands, it experiences high levels of employment, business growth, and inflation. When it contracts, it experiences unemployment and slow or stagnant growth—recession or depression.

The Government's Role in the Economy

In the kind of purely *LAISSEZ-FAIRE* or FREE MARKET economy espoused by the philosopher ADAM SMITH, an INVISIBLE HAND would guide the workings of the market and the government would have no economic role. However, this can result in MONOPOLIES and other unfair trade practices, and the market may come to be dominated by a few. The U.S. has a MIXED ECONOMY, in which the government steps in to correct the market in periods of expansion and contraction through FISCAL AND MONETARY POLICIES, an approach championed by the economist JOHN MAYNARD KEYNES. The FEDERAL RESERVE banks and the FDIC help protect the banking system and consumers. Other laws and regulations prevent monopolies through ANTI-TRUST ACTS, price-fixing, false advertising, and ensuring product safety. The government also has a role in managing external factors that impact the market (for example, a storm that wipes out a farmer's crops, leaving him unable to sell them). The government protects the poor, needy, and unemployed through PUBLIC ASSISTANCE programs. On the other hand, in a COMMAND ECONOMY, the entire economy—what is produced and how much—is planned out by the central government.

Taxation is part of a mixed economy. Income tax is a portion of income paid to the federal government (and, in some cases, city and state governments). Sales tax is a tax on a sale of an item or service. Taxes fund government services.

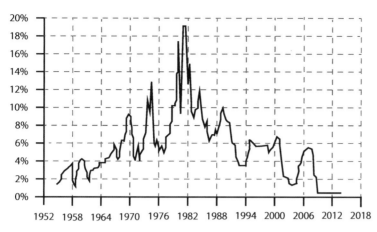

Figure 16.4. Federal funds rate

Examples

1. Why would a monopoly be a problem for business owners and consumers?

   A monopoly prevents business competition, because only one business controls the market for a given good. Moreover, consumers do not have a choice of products and so are forced to buy the product from that one company, meaning the company can charge whatever it wants.

2. Discuss why public assistance programs are important, especially in business cycles.

   Due to the nature of business cycles, it's a given that countries will suffer from periods of unemployment. In that case, the government can ensure that people do not suffer when they are unable to find work by providing assistance in food, housing, and other needs working people would usually be able to fulfill on their own.

Global Markets

GLOBALIZATION connects people all over the world with each other through migration, war, technology, communications, trade, and cultural exchange. Today, it's mostly associated with international trade. IMPORTS are the goods a country might purchase and bring in from another country; EXPORTS are the goods a country sells to another. International currencies affect trade; if an importer's national currency increases in value relative to the currency of the country from which she imports, she will benefit by being able to buy more product at the same cost to her. A country's BALANCE OF TRADE is the ratio of its imports to its exports. According to the LAW OF COMPARATIVE ADVANTAGE, a country might prioritize production of a good for which it has the lowest opportunity cost in order to export it, rather than produce what it needs domestically and remain SELF-SUFFICIENT. TARIFFS are taxes placed on imports,

Another way countries can influence international relations is through embargoes, when they refuse to trade with another country altogether.

usually due to PROTECTIONISM; if a country wishes to protect a domestic industry in the production of a certain good, placing high tariffs on imports of that good from another country will force consumers to purchase the domestically produced good, according to the law of demand. However in recent years, FREE-TRADE AGREEMENTS, or FTAs, have multiplied throughout the world, breaking down TRADE BARRIERS to facilitate trade between countries.

Examples

1. Define the law of comparative advantage.

    In comparative advantage, a country produces mostly or only one product for which it has the lowest opportunity cost, perhaps due to an abundance of particular resources or other reasons. For example, many countries in the Persian Gulf primarily produce oil, selling it internationally.

2. How could FTAs be harmful to domestic industries?

    If one country has a comparative advantage in the production of a particular good, then producers of that good in another country will suffer, as their markets may become saturated with cheaper alternatives of that good; according to the laws of supply and demand, they will lose customers unless they drop their prices.

17

CIVICS AND GOVERNMENT

POLITICAL THOUGHT AND ACTION

The framers of the Constitution were inspired by **ENLIGHTENMENT** thought, including philosophers like **JOHN LOCKE**, whose *Second Treatise* posited that people had **NATURAL RIGHTS** (the basis of the American rights to life, liberty, and the pursuit of happiness) and **JEAN-JACQUES ROUSSEAU**, who believed in the rule of law and that democracy was essential to safeguard the rights of the individual. Other influences included **MONTESQUIEU**, whose influential work *The Spirit of the Laws* articulated the separation of powers between legislative, executive, and judicial branches of government. **THOMAS HOBBES** established individual rights and equality, as well as the social contract in *Leviathan*. The theory of the **SOCIAL CONTRACT** posited that people would retain their rights but must consent to a government that would work to ensure their rights and protect them—**CONSENT OF THE GOVERNED** to relinquish their rights of self-defense to a protective government. The **MAYFLOWER COMPACT** of 1620 was the first example of consent by the governed to a government, following the escape of the persecuted Pilgrims from England.

In 1776, the Thirteen Colonies issued the **DECLARATION OF INDE-PENDENCE** from England, becoming the United States of America. Based on Locke's philosophy of natural rights, the document stated Americans' belief in the equality of all men (women and those of non-European descent would not enjoy those rights until later). It also listed grievances with the British relating to abuses of Americans' rights and lack of representation of their interests in British government. Setting the stage for **REPUBLICAN** government, or **REPRESENTATIVE DEMOCRACY** based on the social contract wherein the people democratically elect leaders to represent their interests, the Declaration of Independence became an important document

U.S. government is also rooted in the Magna Carta, which asserted equality for all—including the ruler—under the law.

in the Age of Revolution in the nineteenth century, and the basis for American political and cultural values.

Today, citizens' interests may be represented by political parties and interest groups. The major political parties are the **Democratic Party**, which leans liberal, and the more conservative **Republican Party**. The conservative base tends to be older, whiter, and Evangelical Protestant voters with traditional values who advocate for a smaller government and a society that is less influenced by laws and regulations. Liberals tend to be more racially diverse, less politically motivated by religious concerns, and more likely to show an interest in social welfare programs, such as health care reform under the Affordable Care Act.

Interest groups are dedicated to a particular cause or goal. Individuals within the group may share a common cause, background, or traits. An interest group can be organized around race, religion, a goal, or cause. While interest groups may work for the election of a candidate, they do not put forth candidates or actively participate in the electoral process. Both Political Action Committees (**PACs**) and 527 groups exist to provide funding for political parties and politicians. These are fundraising organizations. PACs allow groups to fund elections and political campaigns outside of traditional campaign finance restrictions. For instance, corporations and labor unions are not allowed to directly donate to

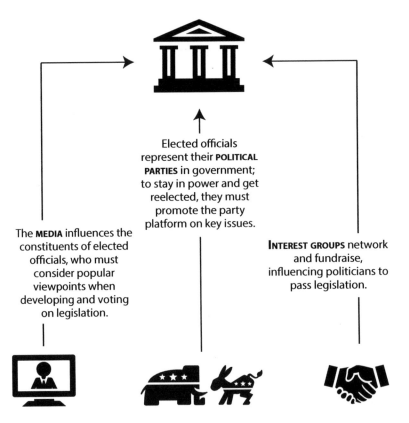

The **MEDIA** influences the constituents of elected officials, who must consider popular viewpoints when developing and voting on legislation.

Elected officials represent their **POLITICAL PARTIES** in government; to stay in power and get reelected, they must promote the party platform on key issues.

INTEREST GROUPS network and fundraise, influencing politicians to pass legislation.

Figure 17.1. Political influence

campaigns, but PACs may donate to political parties and candidates. These donations are limited by federal law to relatively small amounts overall; however, groups may create multiple PACs.

Examples

1. **What did John Locke and Thomas Hobbes believe? How do their visions exist today?**

   John Locke believed in the natural rights of humans and in the social contract between the government and the people, in which the people would willingly give up some of these rights in exchange for government protection. For example, today in the U.S., we have police departments and permit them to temporarily detain people who may be breaking the law and posing a threat to the safety of others.

2. **Why was the Mayflower Compact important?**

   The Mayflower Compact was the first example of consent by the governed in the early Americas, an example of the social contract in action.

THE CONSTITUTION

Federalism and States' Rights

Following the American Revolution, dissent within the United States persisted over the degree to which the federal government should hold power. **FEDERALISTS** believed in a strong federal government; **ANTI-FEDERALISTS** believed that **STATES' RIGHTS** should be paramount. The 1781 **ARTICLES OF CONFEDERATION** created a weak central government; however, instability in the late eighteenth century made it clear that a stronger government was needed, leading to the **CONSTITUTIONAL CONVENTION** where the **CONSTITUTION** and **BILL OF RIGHTS** (the first ten amendments to the Constitution) were created. The document was finally ratified by all states in 1789.

The Constitution and the Bill of Rights

The U.S. Constitution is a single document **CODIFYING** the foundational laws of the country. It provides for a **FEDERAL GOVERNMENT** but one that is based on **POPULAR SOVEREIGNTY**, **SEPARATION OF POWERS**, **LIMITED GOVERNMENT**, and **CHECKS AND BALANCES** in order to protect from federal overreach. Popular sovereignty, in the tradition of John Locke, meant that government can only exist with the consent of the governed. One important example of protection of that consent in the Constitution is **HABEAS CORPUS**, according to which the government cannot detain a person indefinitely without charges. The three articles of the Constitution laid out a framework for a limited federal government, including a separation of powers between the **LEGISLATIVE** (Article I), **EXECUTIVE** (Article II), and **JUDICIAL** (Article III) **BRANCHES**. Each of these branches has the

Other checks and balances in American political culture include the press, which keeps citizens informed of government activities, the citizens themselves, who have the power to vote legislators in and out of office, political parties, which limit each other and civil associations that represent citizens' interests.

ability to check, or limit, the powers of the others. Powers held by more than one branch of government are called CONCURRENT powers.

The first ten amendments to the Constitution are known as the BILL OF RIGHTS. A concession to the anti-Federalists who feared that the Constitution still provided for too strong a federal government, the Bill of Rights clarifies and guarantees specific rights of Americans. Some examples include: the FIRST AMENDMENT, which safeguards freedom of speech, religion, and the right to assembly; the controversial SECOND AMENDMENT, which guarantees the right to bear arms (sometimes interpreted to mean with restrictions); the FOURTH AMENDMENT, protecting Americans from unreasonable search and seizure; the FIFTH AMENDMENT, protecting one from double jeopardy or testifying against oneself in a court of law; the SIXTH AMENDMENT, guaranteeing the right to a speedy and public trial; the EIGHTH AMENDMENT, protecting against cruel and unusual punishment; and the TENTH AMENDMENT, stipulating that any powers not specifically articulated in the Constitution or prohibited by the states are left to the states or to the people themselves.

The Constitution can also be further amended. Important amendments throughout history have included the THIRTEENTH AMENDMENT, prohibiting slavery; the FOURTEENTH AMENDMENT, which defined citizenship, granting it to former slaves; the FIFTEENTH AMENDMENT, guaranteeing African-American men the right to vote; the NINETEENTH AMENDMENT, which gave women the right to vote; the EIGHTEENTH and TWENTIETH AMENDMENTS, which prohibited the sale of alcohol and then overturned Prohibition, respectively; and the TWENTY-FOURTH AMENDMENT, which forbade a poll tax, which had been used to deny African Americans the right to vote.

Examples

1. How does the Constitution protect from federal overreach? Provide details.

   The Constitution's three articles created three branches of government: the legislative, the executive, and the judicial. This separation of powers provides for a system of checks and balances, which lets each branch limit the powers of the others, helping prevent federal overreach. Moreover, the Bill of Rights specifically stipulates certain rights that Americans are always entitled to, and the Tenth Amendment ensures that anything not specified should be determined by the state or the people themselves.

2. Why was the Bill of Rights important to the anti-Federalists?

   The Bill of Rights made it clear that there are certain specific rights to which Americans are entitled. More detailed and specific than the Constitution, the Bill of Rights guarantees Americans the rights to free speech, protection from abuses of power like cruel punishment or secret trials, and more. Ensuring that certain rights were specifically mentioned in the Constitution would help protect them from any movements by the federal government to eliminate them.

THE FEDERAL GOVERNMENT

Legislative Branch

In early American history, disagreement over the nature of the federal government persisted between the very different states. The **VIRGINIA PLAN** proposed a federal legislature based on state population size—a boon for that large state. The **NEW JERSEY PLAN**, in contrast, proposed a federal legislature made up of equal representation from each state, benefitting the smaller states. The resulting **GREAT COMPROMISE** created a **BICAMERAL LEGISLATURE**, with a **HOUSE OF REPRESENTATIVES** whose size was based on state population. To determine population, states arrived at the **THREE-FIFTHS COMPROMISE**, which counted slaves as three-fifths of a person, even though they could not vote and did not have the same rights as other Americans. The **SENATE** would be composed of two representatives, or **SENATORS**, from each state, regardless of its size. Today there are 435 members of the House and one-hundred senators (two for every state).

The **LEGISLATIVE BRANCH** of government, or **CONGRESS**, is responsible for creating laws. Elected directly by the people, representatives write legislation, or laws. These ideas are proposed in the form of **BILLS**, which require a congressional sponsor. American citizens can also write bills but need their representative to sponsor them. The bill goes to the relevant congressional **COMMITTEE** for study and debate; if released, it's voted on by the House. If it passes the vote (by **SIMPLE MAJORITY**), it then moves on to the Senate, where it once again goes to committee, and if it passes, goes to the Senate for a vote, passing again by majority. Once the bill is voted on and approved by the House and Senate, it goes to a final **CONFERENCE COMMITTEE** of both House and Senate members to iron out any differences over the bill. Finally, it moves to the president, who can sign it into law or **VETO** it within ten days. However, Congress has the power to **OVERRIDE** a presidential veto, which requires a **TWO-THIRDS VOTE** in both the House and the Senate. This is one part of the **SYSTEM OF CHECKS AND BALANCES**. Congress also has the power to declare **WAR**; however, in the twentieth and twenty-first centuries, it has voted to authorize the president to decide whether to take military action in several conflicts.

CONTINUE

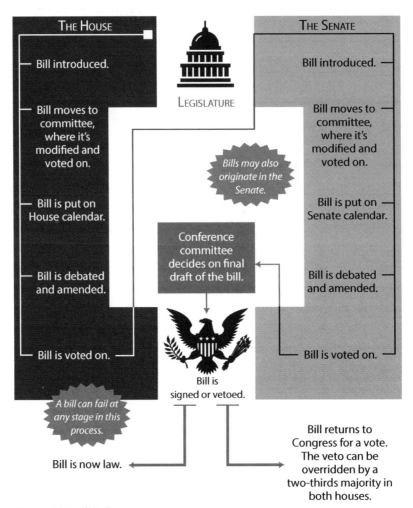

Figure 17.2. Bill to law

Executive Branch

Like the members of Congress, the **PRESIDENT** is elected by the people; however, this process occurs through the **ELECTORAL COLLEGE**. In voting for president, the voters are actually voting for their candidate's group of electors. The electors correspond to a state's members in its congressional delegation; counting the District of Columbia, there are a total of 538. A candidate needs 270 electors to win the presidency.

The executive branch is responsible for government administration and enforcing the law. The president is the **HEAD OF STATE** and the **COMMANDER-IN-CHIEF** of the armed forces. He or she chooses a **CABINET** and the heads of federal agencies to implement and enforce the laws created by Congress. Presidential powers include: the power to **SIGN TREATIES** (although they must be ratified by the Senate); to approve or veto legislation; to issue **EXECUTIVE ORDERS**; and to offer **PARDONS** for federal crimes. The **VICE PRESIDENT** also acts as the president of the Senate but can only vote in case of a tie. Next in line of succession should the president be killed or incapacitated, the vice president can also have an important advisory role to the president and take on a role in policy.

The heads of fifteen executive departments compose the **CABINET**. These departments manage the day-to-day operations of the federal government. They are the Department of Agriculture; the Department of Commerce; the Department of Defense; the Department of Education; the Department of Energy; the Department of Health and Human Services; the Department of Homeland Security; the Department of Housing and Urban Development; the Department of the Interior; the Department of Justice; the Department of Labor; the Department of State; the Department of Transportation; the Department of the Treasury; and the Department of Veterans Affairs. These departments control federal agencies as diverse as the Food and Drug Administration, the FBI, the Fair Housing Administration, and the Armed Services.

Judiciary

The role of the **JUDICIARY** is to interpret the law created by the legislative branch and enforced by the executive branch. In this way, it acts as part of the system of checks and balances on the power of the government, limiting the power of the other branches. Unlike the other two branches, members of the judicial branch, including the **SUPREME COURT** and other federal courts, are appointed by the president and confirmed by the Senate, not directly elected by the

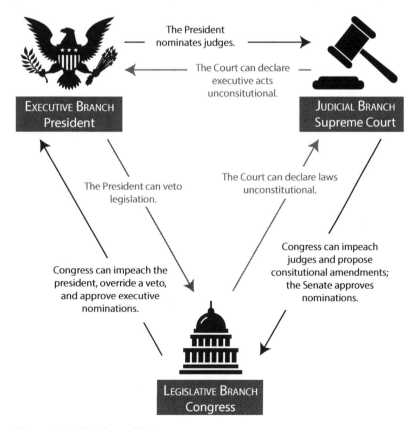

Figure 17.3. Checks and balances

people. Some important Supreme Court cases included ***MARBURY v. MADISON***, which established JUDICIAL REVIEW, giving the Supreme Court the ability to declare acts of Congress unconstitutional; ***McCULLOCH v. MARYLAND***, strengthening federalism by giving Congress more authority to take action not explicitly stated in the Constitution; ***GIBBONS v. OGDEN***, where the Court ruled that Congress had the sole right to regulate interstate commerce; ***SCOTT v. SANFORD***, which ruled that African Americans, whether enslaved or free, did not have rights as American citizens; ***PLESSY v. FERGUSON***, which upheld segregation; ***BROWN v. BOARD OF EDUCATION***, which struck down segregation; and ***ROE v. WADE***, which struck down federal restrictions on abortion.

Examples

1. Explain the Bill of Rights.

   The Bill of Rights consists of the first ten amendments of the Constitution. While the Constitution provides for a system of checks and balances between the three branches of government in an effort to safeguard democracy, the Bill of Rights ensures specific rights enjoyed by Americans like freedom of speech.

2. Provide some examples of the system of checks and balances.

   The president can veto bills passed by Congress, but Congress can override a presidential veto. Congress can pass laws that the president can approve, but the Supreme Court can strike them down.

18

GEOGRAPHY

PHYSICAL SYSTEMS

Maps

MAPS are two-dimensional representations of the world or portions thereof. Map-making is called **CARTOGRAPHY**. Maps provide information about both absolute and relative location and may also provide information about landscape features. Two-dimensional maps, by the nature of a flat representation, distort space. Three-dimensional representations, or globes, are more accurate reflections of the earth. **PHYSICAL MAPS** represent features of the natural landscape. **POLITICAL MAPS** represent human-created places and regions, such as cities and countries. **THEMATIC MAPS** display data that correlates with places; for instance, a thematic map might color-code countries to represent their population density. Thematic maps represent information in several different ways:

- **ISOLINE MAPS**: These are topographic maps, providing information about elevation and landscape.
- **CARTOGRAMS**: Cartograms are a type of map with specific, population-related distortion.
- **CHOROPLETH MAPS**: These maps provide information about a specific variable and how that variable is measured in given areas.
- **DOT MAPS**: Dot maps use dots to provide information about density and numbers, from population to other factors.

Maps are also affected by their **SCALE**, **RESOLUTION**, and **DISTORTION**. A globe, for instance, has little distortion and items are portrayed to scale; however, the resolution is rather low. You cannot see smaller features on the landscape on a globe (because they usually aren't that large!). On the other hand, if you're looking at a reference map of your own community, the resolution is typically quite high. Distortion refers to the changes in shape that occur when a curved surface is portrayed in two-dimensions, as you would see on a paper map of the world or a specific part of the world. The type of projection used will determine the distortion in a two-dimensional map.

- The **ROBINSON PROJECTION** is the most commonly used today. This projection slightly distorts all features to avoid significantly distorting any one feature and is considered a compromise projection.
- The **GALL-PETERS PROJECTION** preserves size accurately but distorts shape significantly.
- The **MERCATOR PROJECTION** depicts the shape of land masses with a high degree of accuracy but sacrifices accurate portrayal of size and area.
- **EQUIDISTANT PROJECTIONS** distort both size and shape but accurately portray the distances between land masses.

Maps that depict larger areas, including a significant part of the world or the entire world, will experience more distortion than large-scale maps displaying a smaller area. Given this distortion, maps may be more or less accurate depending upon how the map is made, the size and scale of the map, and the projection used for the map.

You'll need to employ this understanding of mapmaking and projection to fully understand all elements of human geography, including studies of population, agriculture, and urban development.

Regions of the World

The seven continents are **NORTH AMERICA, SOUTH AMERICA, EUROPE, ASIA, AFRICA, OCEANIA (AUSTRALIA)**, and **ANTARCTICA**. However, shared regional landscapes and cultural and historical experiences make this regional division more accurate: **NORTH AMERICA, LATIN AMERICA, SUB-SAHARAN AFRICA, NORTH AFRICA, EUROPE, SIBERIA, CENTRAL ASIA, SOUTHWEST ASIA, SOUTH ASIA (THE SUBCONTINENT), EAST ASIA, SOUTHEAST ASIA**, and **OCEANIA**. Keep these regions in mind as you prepare for the GED. The globe is divided into four hemispheres: the Northern and Southern Hemispheres are divided by the **EQUATOR**, while the Eastern and Western Hemispheres are divided by the **PRIME MERIDIAN**. The Earth is mapped out by coordinate systems called **LATITUDE** and **LONGITUDE**

On the following page, you can see the various regions of Africa, as defined by the United Nations. While these definitions are related to relative and absolute location, in many cases, there are also aspects of shared physical traits and cultural traits creating these regions and the borders between these various regions of Africa.

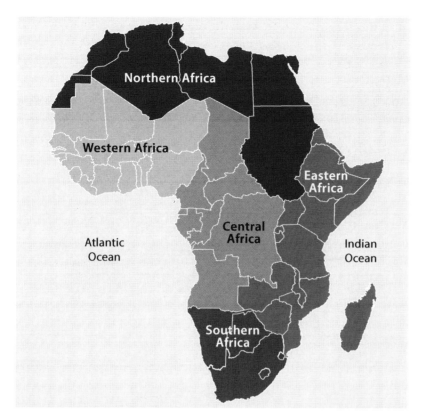

Figure 18.1. Regions of Africa

The map of Asia below includes Central, Southern, Eastern and Southeastern Asia, as well as Northern and Western Asia. In this map, "Northern Asia" represents the Russian Federation and many of the former territories of the Soviet Union, which still share many physical and cultural traits.

Figure 18.2. Regions of Asia

Latin America (shown below), including all of South America, Central America, the Caribbean, and the southernmost portion of North America, is connected by shared language, shared history, and other aspects of culture.

Figure 18.3. Regions of South America

The various regions of Europe are perceptual regions and may not follow national boundaries. For example, the Baltic states are more politically aligned with Central rather than Eastern Europe.

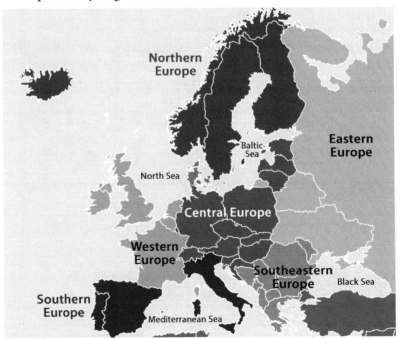

Figure 18.4. Regions of Europe

North America may also be divided into a number of different regions. While North America includes only a few countries, it's still divided into a number of regions by culture and landscape.

Figure 18.5. Regions of North America

Landforms

An **ISLAND** is a body of land surrounded entirely by water; an island can be as small as the island of Manhattan in New York City or as large as the country of Australia. However, an **ATOLL** is a small reef that encloses a **LAGOON**, or isolated circular body of salt water in an ocean. An **ARCHIPELAGO** is a chain of islands. Examples include Japan and Indonesia. On the other hand, a **PENINSULA** is a body of land that is surrounded by water on three sides but remains connected to a larger landmass; examples include the Arabian Peninsula, the Balkans, the Horn of Africa, Italy, the Indian Sub-continent, and the Indochina Peninsula, composing many of the countries of Southeast Asia. An **ISTHMUS** is a strip of land connecting two larger bodies of land, like the Isthmus of Panama. A mountain is a landform that extends to a peak. Major mountain chains of the world include the Andes, the Rockies, the Alps, the Urals, the Caucasus, the Himalayas, and the Atlas. In contrast, a **PLATEAU** is an elevated mass of land that remains at the top; much of India is on the Deccan Plateau, and the highest plateau in the world is the Tibetan Plateau. **MAGMA**, or molten rock underneath the surface of the earth, may reach the surface in a VOLCANO, becoming LAVA. All these formations are based in the LITHOSPHERE, or the Earth's crust and outer shell; PLATE TECTONICS determine the shape and nature of these formations.

Climate and Water

METEOROLOGISTS study the CLIMATE of an area, its typical weather pattern over an extended period of time. For example, much of the United States experiences a four-season cycle, or TEMPERATE climate, while Central Africa, Southeast Asia, and parts of Central and South America (located between the Tropic of Cancer and the Tropic of Capricorn) have TROPICAL climates, characterized by high HUMIDITY. Climates can determine the nature of land: a DESERT is an area where there is little PRECIPITATION, or rain, resulting in limited vegetation and infertile land. In the HYDROLOGIC CYCLE, water circulates between the land, the ATMOSPHERE, and the HYDROSPHERE, or bodies of water on the Earth. Storms like HURRICANES, found in the tropical west Atlantic Ocean and the Caribbean Sea, TYPHOONS, in the western Pacific, and CYCLONES in the Indian Ocean are all major storms with winds that reach speeds of at least seventy-four miles per hour.

Bodies of water have been essential for human development, and settled agricultural societies leading to major civilizations developed on the ALLUVIAL PLAINS in the fertile lands of RIVER VALLEYS. Important world rivers include: the Tigris, Euphrates, Irrawaddy, Ganges, Nile, Niger, Huang He (Yellow), Chiang Jiang (Yangtze), Mississippi, Danube, and the Volga. An OCEAN is an enormous body of saltwater; world oceans include the ATLANTIC, PACIFIC, INDIAN, and ARCTIC oceans. SEAS are bodies of salt water but are smaller than oceans; examples include the CARIBBEAN SEA and the MEDITERRANEAN SEA. A GULF is a large bay or partially enclosed body of water extending from the ocean or a sea, like the Gulf of Mexico or the Persian Gulf. Weather in these areas tends to be milder than on the ocean. A STRAIT is a narrow passage between two landmasses from one body of water to another, like the Straits of Hormuz and the Straits of Malacca. DELTAS are nutrient-rich areas where rivers empty into the sea; the Mississippi and Nile Deltas are rich in plant and animal life. ESTUARIES are coastal areas where salt and fresh water mix.

Examples

1. What are the major regions of the world?

   North America, Latin America, Europe, North Asia, East Asia, South Asia, Central Asia, Southeast Asia, Oceania, North Africa, Sub-Saharan Africa. They are divided as such because these regions share similar cultures and historical ties. They may also share regional features that affect their societies and histories (for example, the Sahara Desert in North Africa).

The climate of an area also determines its ecosystem, or the relationship between the climate, the land, and the organisms that live in the area. Human activity often causes change in ecosystems.

How are temperate climates conducive to the development of human civilization?

These straits are strategically important for trade, as they allow ships to pass from one body of water into another to access ports and resource-rich regions. Thus, they give the countries that control them a strategic advantage in international trade and affairs.

2. Why are rivers important? Name three important rivers and discuss their regions.

Rivers allow the development of human civilization because they create river valleys, where alluvial plains or fertile land is found. Agricultural development led to settled civilizations in river valleys around the world like the Nile Valley, the Fertile Crescent in Mesopotamia, the Indus Valley, and the Huang He and Chiang Jiang regions. Later important cultural centers and countries developed around rivers like the Irrawaddy, the Danube, and the Mississippi.

HUMAN SYSTEMS

Modern Agriculture

Despite the industrial revolution, agriculture remains the dominant human occupation.

Developed or modern farming, sometimes called AGRIBUSINESS, is distinguished from subsistence and intermediate farming by high rates of MECHANIZATION. As a result, fewer people are involved in farming than in the past, small family farms have been replaced by large, industrial farms, food production continues to increase, and there is increased reliance on chemical fertilizers and insecticides. The transition from small-scale agriculture to commercial agriculture altered how we grow and eat our food. COMMERCIAL AGRICULTURE, common in developed regions of the world, required not only new farming technology, but also transportation technology. Farming companies needed to transport goods much longer distances over time without spoilage. Technology like food processing has made a significant difference. Fresh foods can also be transported with refrigeration. Commercial agriculture also extends beyond the developed world and into countries that are less economically developed. In these nations, commercial agriculture commonly takes the form of PLANTATION AGRICULTURE. Plantation agriculture developed during the colonial period and continues, with massive farms producing goods like sugar, coffee, and cocoa. Plantations require significant human labor, including slave labor before slavery was abolished. This is CASH-CROP PRODUCTION, designed for long-distance export; these crops are not used to feed the country's population.

However, modern farming techniques have done more than just enrich large companies. They have also alleviated hunger in the developing world. The GREEN REVOLUTION was an effort in the 1950s and 1960s to introduce new crops and farming techniques to developing nations for the purpose of increasing output and resisting crop failures. While famines still exist around the world, they are less often the result of natural issues and more often the result of political ones. The rise of crops that are genetically modified to increase yields, resist pests, or develop other favorable traits is part of the so-called Third Agricultural Revolution, in which a range of advanced technologies are being employed to boost production. While modern technology has made farming more efficient, reduced hunger, and improved the yield of food crops, there are a number of controversies surrounding some or many aspects of modern farming. These include the environmental effects of large-scale farming, the safety of genetic modification, and trade practices, among others.

Demography and Migration

DEMOGRAPHY is the study of population; demographers keep track of statistics like birth rates and also look at where and how people live, studying changes over time. Historically, most humans lived in rural areas.

Demographics includes a range of subjects that can influence population, including food supply, agricultural policies, life expectancy, and the movements of populations. The human population began on a very small scale, with a number of relatively isolated human groups. Groups remained relatively small until the end of the Ice Age and progressive developments associated with the Neolithic era. With this in mind, the study of population demographics begins in earnest with the population growth associated with increased stability, settlement, and improved food supplies.

In broad terms, populations are most dense in areas that support food production. These are typically midrange latitudes. Less fertile regions, including deserts, high altitudes, and tundra, support significantly smaller populations. These regions typically experience colder and hotter temperatures, less rainfall, and often have a shorter or nonexistent growing season for plant foods. Population density is measured in two different ways. First, population density may be measured quite directly, with the total number of people per square kilometer or square mile. This is arithmetic density. You can also consider population density in terms of farmland or arable land, counting the total number of people per square mile or kilometer of farmland. This is physiological density. Population is often portrayed in population pyramids, which show information about gender, age, and proportions of the population.

Approximately one-quarter of the world population is found in East Asia. The majority of people in these regions are farmers, working in agricultural fields; however, industry is also growing in this region of the world. While some rural areas have low-population density, the population density is quite high in this region, even outside of urban areas. South Asia is the second-most populous region of the world. In East Asia, populations are largely located in coastal region, with substantial numbers along major rivers. Similar trends are found in South Asia.

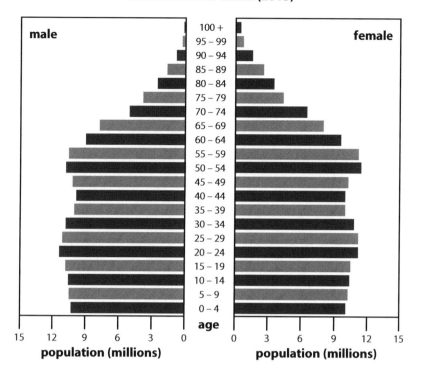

Figure 18.6. Population pyramid

While East Asia and South Asia remain predominantly agricultural, Europe is the third-most populous region and is primarily urban, rather than agricultural. Urban areas in Europe are typically consolidated near coal-mining regions. North America has a number of large cities, but much of the region is relatively sparsely populated, unlike Europe. The highest population concentrations in North America are along the eastern coast of the United States and Canada.

Population growth rates have varied over time. A fertility rate of 2.1 to 2.5 children per woman is considered a replacement rate, creating a stable population without either an increase or a decrease. In many parts of the world, birth rates have dropped in the latter part of the twentieth century through today. Improved access to family planning services, including contraception, have impacted birth rates significantly, as has a tendency to marry later and an overall increase in women's status in society. In China, a one-child policy dramatically reduced population growth but brought a number of new social concerns. In less economically developed parts of the world, including much of Africa, birth rates continue to increase.

Birth rate is not the only factor impacting population. Death rates can also have a significant impact on population. In areas with good access to health care, life expectancies are significantly longer. Infant and child mortality also affects overall population rates in substantial ways. Average life expectancy numbers, in particular, can be altered by high infant and child mortality. Demographics is also concerned with the dependency rate. This is the total percentage of the population under fifteen years of age or over sixty-four years of age, typically relying upon others to provide their support.

Theories of population change are critical to your understanding of human populations. These include:

- The Demographic Transition
- Epidemiological Theories of World Health
- Malthusian Theory of Population

The Demographic Transition is based upon Western Europe's industrial revolution and the changes that went along with it. The Demographic Transition is marked by four stages, with a clear shift in the mortality rate, moving from higher to lower. A comparable shift occurs in birth rates, with birth rates moving from higher to lower. This results, in the second stage, in an overall increase in population as the death rate decreases while the birth rate remains stable. Originally developed by Warren Thompson, this theory was improved by Frank Notestein. There are a few weaknesses to this theory. Today, some European countries are experiencing a falling population, as the birth rate is less than the death rate. Additionally, the Demographic Transition assumes industrialization will occur. In some cases, particularly in less economically developed nations in Africa, there are questions as to whether these countries will ever experience this transition.

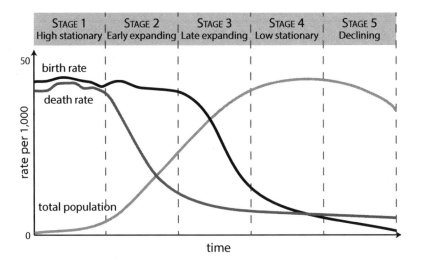

Figure 18.7. Demographic transition model

Epidemiology, or the study of patterns of disease, also has an impact on population. In less economically developed countries, infectious diseases, including those spread by contaminated water, are common. In more developed countries, illnesses associated with old age and infirmity are more common, since life spans are longer. This analysis can also be broken into distinct stages.

1. In the transition from a hunting-gathering society to a settled society with domesticated agriculture, infectious disease appeared and became a significant factor in population demographics. Close proximity to others and animals increased the risk of disease. This stage continues until economic development allows for the control of infectious disease.

2. In the next stage, chronic, degenerative illnesses become a significant factor. Infectious diseases are less common; however, life spans are still not terribly long as medical care is not fully available or developed.

3. Generative and human-created illnesses occur in this stage. These include cancer of various types, cardiovascular disease, and Type II diabetes. These illnesses are uncommon in the developing world.

4. Delayed degenerative illnesses require a significant extension of life span and occur in very old age. These illnesses require access to medical care and may be the result of medical interventions extending life.

5. In stage 5, infectious diseases reemerge even in developed nations. These may be bacterial, viral, or parasitic in nature.

Thomas Malthus is one of the best-known and earliest scholars of population. In 1798, Malthus postulated that population would always exceed food supply. He believed that population grew exponentially, while food supply grew arithmetically. Thus, as food supply increased, population would increase even more. Changes in agricultural production following World War II dramatically altered the ability to produce adequate amounts of food. While some scholars, called Neo-Malthusians, continue to support the Malthusian theory, evidence has shown that food supply continues to increase at a higher rate than population, reducing the risk of a Malthusian Catastrophe. Neo-Malthusians do remain concerned with overpopulation, particularly with regard to the carrying capacity of a given region. The carrying capacity may be defined as the total ability of a given area to support the population, in terms of food supply and production.

Restrictive policies discourage a high birth rate. These may include moderate measures, like financial incentives for smaller families and improved access to contraception, or may be more extreme, like China's one-child policy. In China, under a communist regime, many couples were limited to a single child. A second child was only allowed in specific situations. Families who violated the policy were punished and forced abortion and sterilization were used. Today, China is beginning to relax these policies as a result of population issues, including significantly fewer young women than men. Some countries have fluctuated between expansionist and restrictive policies, depending upon political and religious conditions within the country.

MIGRATION refers to human movement, particularly long-term or permanent movement from place to place. Other types of migration are associated with seasonal work or a nomadic lifestyle, for instance, following herds of animals from place to place. **EMIGRATION** is leaving a country, while **IMMIGRATION** is entering a country. Migration can dramatically impact population. For instance, during the nineteenth century, the population of the United States increased massively as individuals emigrated from other countries.

Migration rate per
1,000 people in 2011

< −10

−9.9 to −5

−4.9 to −0.1

0 to 5

5.1 to 10

> 10.1

Figure 18.8. Migration

Migration is impacted by various factors, referred to as push-pull factors. Push factors encourage individuals to leave the country, while pull factors make another country more appealing. Examples of **PUSH FACTORS** include:

- Economic conditions, including recession or depression, lack of job opportunities, and low pay
- Environmental conditions, like drought or natural disasters
- Political situations, including war or the threat of war
- Cultural issues, like religious intolerance

These are all negative factors or qualities about a home country or country of origin. Individuals typically choose to leave their country of origin to seek out a better life, improved financial stability, and increased personal freedom. **PULL FACTORS** make another country more appealing. Examples of pull factors might include:

- Better economic opportunities, including job opportunities, higher salaries, or more ability to get and keep work
- Improved political conditions, a stable, democratic government, and peaceful nation
- Cultural or religious factors, including tolerance, but also an established immigrant community
- Favorable environmental conditions, including climate and fertile land

While the push-pull factors are often key reasons for immigration, immigrants often share a number of characteristics. Immigration is more likely when the distance is relatively short, and young, single individuals are more likely to immigrate than families. Immigration is most successful when there is an established social support system, ranging from family already in the new region to a religious or cultural community. Migration is most often rural to urban and may occur in stages. Immigrants are most likely to perceive their immigration experience accurately when the move is shorter, rather than longer.

Immigration can have a substantial impact on population. For instance, the United States in the nineteenth century grew in population largely because of the immense influx of immigrants. These immigrants hoped for improved financial opportunities, religious tolerance, and to avoid oppressive governments. Prior to 1840, some 90 percent of immigrants to the United States were British; however, this changed over time.

Migration may also occur within a single nation. The westward expansion of the United States is an excellent example of this internal migration, as is the Great Migration, the movement of African-Americans north to avoid Jim Crow laws and rampant racism in the southern U.S. These migrations may be individual and spread out over time or can occur in relatively large numbers in a short time, like the wagon trains that moved families west in the nineteenth century. Individuals typically move within a single country for the same reasons as people immigrate to another nation, seeking a better life, improved job opportunities, or increased personal freedom.

Countries control immigration with laws and regulations. These typically limit the number of immigrants allowed into the country, as well as setting limits on the number of immigrants from various countries. Many countries have regulations and rules regarding the educational and income background of immigrants. For instance, it's easier for someone with a college degree to immigrate into another country than for someone without education. This has, at times, led to a "brain drain," as large numbers of educated people leave countries looking for a better life. Some countries may offer preferential treatment to individuals who have particular and appealing job skills, and most countries offer preference to family members of residents or citizens.

In times of violence or persecution, individuals may leave their homes with little and with no preparation. These individuals, called REFUGEES, typically have no legal standing and often leave without even the most basic legal paperwork. They may leave their home country to avoid the violence of war, or because they fear persecution on the basis of race, religion, nationality, social group, or political opinions. Many flee their homes on foot in an attempt to avoid danger, but they may also travel by bicycle, car, boat, or even public transit. During times of civil war, refugee camps are often established outside the war zone or across a national border. Refugee camps are commonly run by international organizations, other nations, or charitable groups and provide shelter, health care, and food to those fleeing a war zone. In some countries, an individual with refugee status may have preferential status with regard to immigration. In many cases, refugees are unable to return to their home or may have no home to return to, requiring assistance in eventually resettling in another country. Today, there are significant refugee crises in a number of areas, including parts of Africa and the Middle East; however, there are still ongoing refugee crises in locations around the world. People may also be displaced within their own countries due to violent conflict and face similar circumstances, but without the legal protections granted refugees. These are INTERNALLY DISPLACED PERSONS, or IDPs.

As people, products, customs, and ideas that arise in one place move to other areas, CULTURAL DIFFUSION happens. RELOCATION DIFFUSION occurs when people physically move and take their belongings and cultural practices with them. The process of tortilla-making has diffused into California with the relocation of people from Mexico. EXPANSION DIFFUSION is the diffusion of traits or practices such that new people participate in those practices and traits. When non-Mexican families adopt the culinary practices of their Mexican neighbors, the consumption of foods such as tortillas and tacos expands. There are three patterns of expansion diffusion. CONTAGIOUS DIFFUSION takes place when traits move between adjacent places; often, traits will expand in a circle, with the original location in the middle. HIERARCHICAL DIFFUSION takes place when a trait leaps over territory and expands in a pattern that follows an existing hierarchy; typically, this takes place among cities, with traits diffusing from large cities to smaller cities. Fashion typically diffuses this way, with new trends starting in places like New York and Los

Angeles and eventually making their way to smaller cities. Finally, STIMULUS DIFFUSION entails the creation of a new trait that is adapted from a trait that has diffused. For instance, the creation of vegetarian burgers at McDonald's restaurants in India is a response to the initial diffusion of McDonald's, combined with Indian social norms against eating beef.

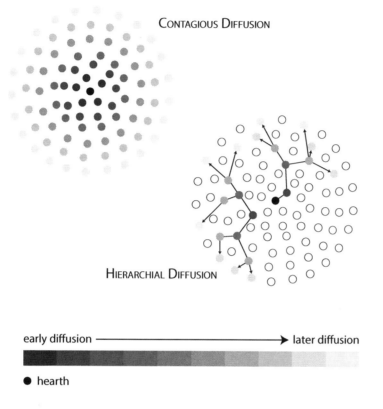

Figure 18.9. Contagious and hierarchial diffusion

Population is impacted by birth rates, death rates, life expectancy, and migration. The population of a country may drop due to famine, higher death rates, or mass emigration, while population may increase as infant mortality drops, life expectancies increase, and disease is better managed. Increased immigration also results in a higher population. Individuals migrate in search of improved living conditions, with the exception of forced migrations and refugees. Forced migrants move under threat of immediate violence, while refugees flee for their lives, avoiding civil war or persecution.

Culture, Ethnicity, and Race

Culture is a term that encompasses the beliefs, manners, products, traditions, arts, and relationships—the shared experiences—that characterize a group and that distinguish groups from each other. A CULTURAL TRAIT is any example of a practice or product that is characteristic of a given culture, like a recipe, song, or ritual. When sets of traits are consistent throughout a group of people, that group may be considered a culture. Together, these elements combine to create the identities we connect to places. Often, culture is linked to ethnicity. **ETHNICITY** relates to a particular ethnic group, which is defined by shared traits, including customs and traditions, religion, language, and sometimes race (see below). Ethnicities can encompass many of these traits, but individuals may differ racially, geographically, and culturally. Ethnicity may sometimes also be linked to political organization. Ethnicities are linked to a particular place, either legally or through custom and practice. Culture may be linked to ethnicity but is, like political boundaries, not always linked to it. Ethnicity is a designation that relies on a complex combination of cultural traits; RACE—superficial biological differences that differentiate groups of humans—may be one of those traits, but race is not synonymous with ethnicity.

Race as a concept has been thoroughly debunked from a biological standpoint, but its social implications are vast. Historically, race was defined on the basis of physical features, including skin tone, facial features, and hair type. Racial discrimination has impacted countries around the world; however, the strongest impact has arguably been on the African continent. Slavery, of course, depleted the population of Africa, causing significant human and cultural loss. White colonists from Britain and elsewhere established colonies throughout Africa, particularly in the nineteenth century, leading to a loss of traditional leadership and significant and lasting political challenges.

Colonialism also significantly impacted, depleted, or destroyed the aboriginal populations of the Americas, Australia, and New Zealand, as well as parts of Asia and Southeast Asia. Colonialism depended on racism; to colonize a nation, the colonial power had to believe in its racial "superiority." This ranged from viewing the native populations of the Americas as subhuman, to taking on an imperial status and believing that bringing European people and culture to a region would improve things, because the people needed that assistance, given their "weaknesses." Even with the abandonment of legalized policies of segregation in many countries (like the Jim Crow laws in the U.S. and South African apartheid), economic and social factors ensure that de facto segregation persists in places like the U.S. South and urban areas in many regions throughout the world.

States, Nations, and Nation-States

STATES are independent political entities, with territory, sovereignty, and centralized governments. *State* is a synonym for a country or for what is colloquially, but incorrectly, referred to as a nation. The use of *state* in the United States is also misleading and arguably incorrect. In the U.S., the fifty "states" each have individual state governments but are not independent political entities. From the global perspective, the United States is a single state, and the fifty states are sub-state entities, on the order of provinces. A nation, meanwhile, refers to a group of people—not to a territory or abstract entity—that constitutes, or wants to create, an independent state. Many of the states of Europe reflect nations; for example, Denmark primarily consists of the Danish people, while Hungary is the center and home of much of the Hungarian population and culture of the world. A state that roughly corresponds to a nation is known as a NATION-STATE.

Independent states have a number of rights and responsibilities. They tax citizens, but they also provide services to citizens, like maintaining roads, providing a justice system, and making laws. States raise armies and may require military service of their citizens. States can only exist if the people believe in the existence of the state and share a national identity. State governments may vary but are typically federal or unitary. In a federal system, individual territories have significant rights; the United States is a federal system (see chapter seventeen, *Civics and Government*, for more details). In a unitary system, those rights are only granted by the state governing body.

Economic Development

ECONOMIC DEVELOPMENT is a catchall term that encompasses a range of elements related to the prosperity, wealth, and quality of life in a given place. A more subtle measure than mere wealth—which is typically expressed as gross domestic product—development measures aspects of health, education, modernization and other factors that describe the way that people live. Typically, development is discussed on a country-by-country basis, though the development of cities, regions, and sub-state entities can be measured too. There is no single definition of development. It's a subjective notion, and economists have extensive debates over how to quantify it. The most widely accepted measure of development is the Human Development Index devised by the United Nations.

The terms *MORE DEVELOPED COUNTRIES* and *LESS DEVELOPED COUNTRIES* have replaced the less-used *FIRST WORLD* and *THIRD WORLD* designations that came about during the Cold War. Today, countries are considered in comparison with one another using the broader, "more or less developed" terminology. Development encompasses a continuum: there is no limit to a country's potential development, and countries are always developing further (and, in some cases, becoming less developed).

GROSS NATIONAL PRODUCT, commonly written as **GNP**, is the total of all goods and services produced by corporations or citizens of a country in a given year. The GNP includes goods and services produced by a given nation outside its borders. The GROSS DOMESTIC PRODUCT (**GDP**) is similar and may also be used as a measure of economic development; it measures only those goods and services produced or generated within the country, including that which may be generated by individuals or companies from elsewhere working in the country in question.

The per capita GDP is divided by the total population. A small nation with a lower overall GDP might still have a much higher per capita GDP. The following map illustrates the per capita GDP of various countries around the world.

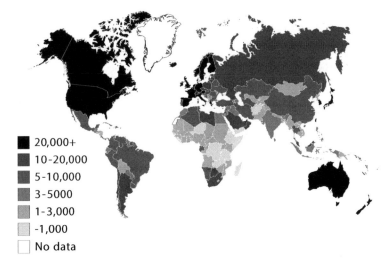

Figure 18.20. Per capita GDP

The map above illustrates the significant differences in per capita GDP around the world. You can see the countries in darker hues have the highest per capita GDP. Those colored in lighter hues have the lowest per capita GDP. Even at a glance the distribution is relatively unsurprising. Below, you can see a graphic showing the growth rate of per capita GNP over the thirty-year period between 1980 and 2010. Darker hues represent higher growth, and lighter hues represent lower growth.

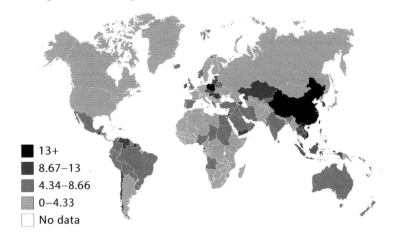

Figure 18.21. Per capita GNP

Here, it's clear that some regions have experienced substantial growth, like China, while others have experienced very little or no change in GDP over this period. The majority of countries, including the United States and Russian Federation, show low to moderate growth.

POPULATION GROWTH is another marker of economic development; however, lower population growth is correlated with higher economic development. More economically developed nations show a fertility rate of fewer than three children per woman, while less economically developed nations show a much higher fertility rate. A decrease in fertility rates is often accompanied by improved economic growth, better living conditions, and a higher quality of life for citizens of a less developed state.

Economic development is also reflected in the **OCCUPATIONAL STRUCTURE OF THE LABOR FORCE** in a country. There are three main categories to consider:

1. **PRIMARY ACTIVITIES** take resources from the earth. These include farming of all sorts, mining, and other activities. While these activities go on in all countries, in a less developed country, the majority of the population is employed in primary activities.

2. **SECONDARY ACTIVITIES** are manufacturing. For instance, lumber harvested by individuals involved in a primary activity might be made into paper by people working in a paper plant. Secondary activities deal with tangible goods and processes that add value to those primary goods.

3. **TERTIARY ACTIVITIES** are services, ranging from relatively low-paying jobs like food service and domestic help to high-paying jobs like banking, medicine, and law. These activities are based on the worker's knowledge—be it of the human body or of a line of clothing—and do not produce material goods.

The more developed a nation, the more workers are employed in tertiary activities. In a less developed country, the majority is employed in primary activities. In a developing country, secondary activities will become more important. For instance, in the United States, the vast majority of adults are, in some way, employed in tertiary fields.

Typically, as per capita income increases, **CONSUMPTION** of fuel, food, or any other good rises. For instance, a subsistence rice farmer uses little in daily life. On the other hand, an urban professional uses significantly more resources of all kinds: food, fuel, electricity, clothing, buildings, etc.

ONE-WAY CONSUMPTION is often measured by looking at CO^2 emissions (also called greenhouse gas emissions). Up to the end of the twentieth century, there was typically a proportional relationship between energy consumption and development. However, recently some of the most developed countries have reduced their per capita energy consumption. These countries have pursued deliberate policies to reduce their greenhouse gas emissions, and they are also wealthy enough to purchase efficient technologies, such as hybrid cars. Energy consumption is therefore an example of an economic activity that seems to indicate prosperity but that, increasingly, lowers a country's quality of life.

INFRASTRUCTURE is a broad term for the physical, often public, structures that a society needs to function. Schools, roads, railways, airports, and hospitals are all part of infrastructure. Extensive infrastructure is a sign of a more developed country. Less developed countries are less likely to have even basic infrastructure, including roads, access to utilities, and sanitation facilities. Without access to appropriate sanitation, including clean water and toilet facilities, disease runs rampant. Railways and roads allow both people and goods to move quickly and efficiently from place to place. Airports facilitate global trade, and telecommunications facilitates business at every level, from small stores to multinational corporations. In some areas, infrastructure is only established in parts of the country, leaving others lacking key services.

SOCIAL CONDITIONS are important indicators of economic development. These include:

- Less developed countries experience a higher rate of INFANT MORTALITY. Various factors contribute to this, including a lack of prenatal care, a lack of access to pediatric health care, including vaccinations, inadequate food, and a lack of clean water.

- LIFE EXPECTANCY is lower in less developed countries. High infant mortality lowers life expectancy, as does a lack of health care and a high rate of deaths in child birth.

- High rates of LITERACY are expected in more developed countries, where all children have access to education. In less developed countries, many children do not have access to schools and may not have the opportunity to learn to read. Improved education is consistently linked to economic growth and development.

- HEALTH CARE is key to reduced infant mortality and increased life expectancy. In many less developed countries, access to health care is highly limited, with many people having no access to medical assistance at all.

- CALORIC INTAKE directly relates to personal income and access to resources. Individuals in more developed nations are more likely to have an acceptable or high caloric intake than those in less developed countries.

The United Nations devised the Human Development Index to combine factors and create an easily understood rating of the development of different countries into different tiers. The Human Development Index includes the following criteria:

- Life expectancy
- Education, including adult literacy and enrollment in primary, secondary, and tertiary education
- Real GNP per capita

Each of these is a relatively measurable statistic that is meant to stand in for larger development criteria. Life expectancy is a measure of health; education is a measure of social conditions and equity; and GNP per capita is a measure of quality of life.

It's important to have a general sense of development in different regions and of the geographical distribution of development. Most notably, development diffuses contagiously. Adjacent countries—with the notable exception of the U.S. and Mexico and some borders in Eastern Europe—tend to have similar development levels.

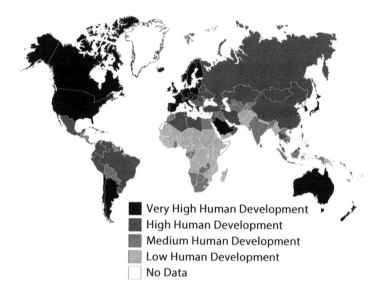

Figure 18.22. Human development index

The biggest shortcoming of the UN HDI, as well as most other measures of development, is that it considers only the FORMAL ECONOMY. In many less developed countries, both money and goods frequently change hands outside the formal economy. These transactions are not recorded or taxed, but occur at small markets and elsewhere. These measures also do not consider any form of illegal economy, for instance, the drug trade, which may impact the economic development of the state.

GENDER INEQUALITY is an important indicator of development. While women contribute economically around the world, often their contribution goes unrecognized, and they lack control over their own economic destiny. Therefore, the extent to which women's rights are protected in a given country often correlates with development.

Early marriage deprives girls and young women of educational opportunities and the chance to work and support themselves; early motherhood does the same. Furthermore, early and multiple pregnancies pose health risks to girls and young women, especially in areas with limited infrastructure and health services. Gender preferences and inequalities have led to unsustainable population growth in several countries, due to gender-selective abortion and infanticide or killing of female infants in countries like India and China. While this practice is illegal, it remains widespread in many areas. In many countries, women still require a dowry to marry, and daughters are considered less desirable than sons. Laws prohibiting dowries and infanticide are poorly enforced. In China, the one-child policy enforced for many years has led to the widespread abortion or abandonment of females. Dowry deaths, or murders when women's dowries are not paid, still exist in India, while in many Muslim regions, "honor killings" take women's lives if they are deemed to have morally dishonored their male relatives, such as through acts like premarital sex.

Industrialization

For much of modern history, development has been synonymous with **INDUSTRIALIZATION**, the process of using labor, energy, and raw materials to produce goods and services with more complexity and value than their raw materials alone. Industrialization began with the Industrial Revolution in the eighteenth and nineteenth centuries with textile factories in Europe. Previously, most goods had been made by hand, in small workshops or cottage industries. What little machinery existed was simple and typically human- or animal-powered. The Industrial Revolution was made possible by the wealth flowing into Europe, and England in particular, from its colonies; the political, geographical, and natural resources of England (the country was politically stable, somewhat isolated geographically and rich in resources, like coal and iron); and willingness to invest time, energy, and resources into new inventions and innovations.

The Industrial Revolution created the iron industry, leading to the steam engine, trains, and steam-powered ships. It moved people from the countryside to the cities and changed the way they lived their lives. Consumer goods became more accessible and affordable, and travel and movement became easier. The industrial revolution diffused throughout the world as new technology spread. Significant mining and manufacturing centers rose up in North America and Europe by the middle of the nineteenth century. Industrialization later moved into Eastern Europe and Russia.

Production methodologies have changed over time to increase efficiency and improve the quality of goods produced. In the early twentieth century, Henry Ford invented mass production with the assembly line. Modern industrial practices have shifted and moved to increased specialization. Today, new industrial centers and centers of manufacturing are growing, especially in South and Southeast Asia and Latin America.

Urbanization

URBANIZATION, or URBAN DEVELOPMENT, is the process of building up a city and of a society's evolution from rural to urban. For much of history, humans lived in small communities. With the introduction of agriculture, communities grew to form villages and eventually towns and cities. One of the factors distinguishing the village from the city is food production. In a village, nearly all residents are involved in food production. In a city, relatively few are involved in food production, and most food is brought into the city from the surrounding countryside. Cities are typically political, commercial, cultural, and religious centers. People are typically drawn to cities by the promise of better economic opportunities. AGGLOMERATION is the great asset of cities. Physical proximity allows for complex, sophisticated economic relationships whereby individuals and firms constantly interact with each other, ideally for mutual benefit and widespread prosperity.

Until the twentieth century, the world had only a handful of cities that would be considered large by today's standards. In the twentieth century, urbanization progressed rapidly as more people moved from smaller communities to larger ones. Rates of urbanization differ between countries. Today, cities dominate the cultural landscape. As of the early 2000s, fully half the world's population lived in cities, with more arriving literally every day. Many scholars view the city, rather than the nation-state, as the primary unit of economic activity. URBAN SYSTEMS describe the relationship—typically the economic relationship—among cities.

At any given scale, be it that of a state or even a sub-state region, the relative populations of cities fall into one of two patterns: URBAN HIERARCHY, in which city populations follow the rank-size rule (with the second-largest city one-half as big as the largest, the third-largest one-third as big, and so forth) or URBAN PRIMACY, in which the largest, or PRIMATE CITY is more than twice as large (and often many times larger than) the next largest city. Generally, urban hierarchies apply to more developed countries and urban primacy to less developed countries.

Urbanization in the twentieth and twenty-first centuries has been dominated by SUBURBANIZATION. Mass migration to cities in the nineteenth century led to overcrowding and dysfunction. The availability of the automobile gave residents the opportunity to escape the city and, in the United States, pursue the "American dream" of a single-family home. Suburbs are independent towns that are primarily residential and linked, physically and functionally, to CENTER CITIES. By the end of the twentieth century, a plurality of Americans lived in suburbs. However, suburbanization has led to URBAN SPRAWL: geographic isolation, lack of diversity, long commutes, high costs, and environmental degradation. (In many cases, it was also inspired by racism, as white residents became uncomfortable with increasing numbers of minority residents.)

Meanwhile, center cities tended to decay, partly for lack of tax revenue and the economic stimulation that would have accompanied middle class families. Many center cities wound up with large proportions of poor, minority residents who clustered in decayed neighborhoods with high crime rates, poor schools, and few job opportunities. In some cases, ETHNIC ENCLAVES of immigrants remained relatively intact and prosperous.

In the early years of the twenty-first century, the process of suburbanization has ebbed, and center cities have regained some prominence. Some Americans are preferring high-density living (as many Europeans always have), and cities have reinvested in urban amenities like public transit and, famously, stadiums and arenas. Real estate developers have rehabilitated and added to old, high-density buildings, and residents often trade personal automobiles for walking, biking, and public transit. This trend is collectively known as SMART GROWTH. City dwellers may use less gasoline and even pay less to heat and cool their homes; as a result, they often have smaller CARBON FOOTPRINTS than their suburban counterparts do. And the compact nature of cities provides easy access to services, government, cultural institutions, recreational opportunities, and abundant and diverse employment opportunities.

The process of repopulating center cities is often associated with GENTRIFICATION, which occurs when a formerly poor neighborhood becomes so prosperous that long-term, low-income residents may be no longer be able to afford it. At its most strained, urban life is still marked by segregation; residents in the poorest inner city neighborhoods struggle with poverty, violence, and lack of access to decent housing, grocery stores, medical facilities, and other necessities.

Urbanization in the developing world looks dramatically different than it does in the developed world. Typically, primate cities are the only places that offer job opportunities, so rural migrants flock to them by the thousands. Cities like Mumbai, Lagos, and Shanghai have grown into megacities of over 15 million each because of this pattern.

In the least developed countries, this influx creates significant problems. Roads, sewage, and power systems are strained. Informal economies develop, as people work illegally. Often, the sought-after jobs pay very little, as there is an oversupply of willing employees. In the physical environment, these cities develop vast INFORMAL SETTLEMENTS, known as shantytowns, favelas, or simply slums. These are places where homes have been built without government permission and where city services, including law enforcement, are essentially absent.

The ECONOMIC DEVELOPMENT of a country generally refers to the use of its resources to power industrial development. One measure of economic development is a country's GROSS DOMESTIC PRODUCT, or **GDP**, which is the value of goods and services in a given time period (usually a year) produced within that country. Today, there is increased focus on SUSTAINABLE DEVELOPMENT, in which resource exploitation does not outpace resource renewal. Development also increasingly refers to developing the quality of life of the people of a country—improving health, infrastructure, and education. Today, less developed countries (**LDCs**) are urbanizing at a high rate, as wealthy and middle-income countries have done in the past. LDCs are characterized by a lower GDP, low literacy rates, high birth rates, high infant mortality rates, poor water quality, poor sanitation, limited infrastructure, limited rights for women, and lower life expectancies, among others. Many of these challenges are rooted in histories of conflict, natural disaster, economic mismanagement, and loss of natural resources and land to European imperialism.

Examples

1. Define urbanization.

   Urbanization is the movement of people from rural to urban areas, usually in search of industrial jobs; people settle in the cities and the cities grow as a result.

2. Why are some countries LDCs? What are the features of a typical LDC?

   LDCs may regularly suffer from natural disaster, be or have recently been mired in conflict, or have a history of exploitation and colonization, having lost resources—both material and human—to imperial powers. LDCs are at a further disadvantage, suffering from long-term consequences like poor education, low literacy rates, and poor water quality and sanitation. These trigger high rates of illness and infant mortality. Despite the lower life expectancies of their inhabitants, most LDCs have a very high birth rate, a contributing factor to restrictions on the rights of women in many countries, who usually have less access to education and work as a result.

BEHAVIORAL SCIENCES

EARLY PSYCHOLOGY

Nineteenth-century scholars and scientists of psychology were among the first to consider the causes of mental illness, to develop an interest in the origins of thoughts and feelings, and to question the relationship between thoughts and behavior. Meanwhile, new movements arose advocating for the rights of those with mental illness. Activists like Dorothea Dix lobbied for the creation of asylums, or mental institutions, to provide care for individuals suffering from mental illness or developmental difficulties. Though psychology was a relatively new field of study, its inquiries into the nature of human thought and behavior held widespread appeal.

Structuralism and Functionalism

In 1879, Wilhelm Wundt established the first psychology laboratory, in Germany. He asked individuals to record responses to and observations about specific stimuli, and he used this data to study cognitive structures, or the basic principles of thought. From these early observations, Wundt developed the theory of STRUCTURALISM. Structuralists believed that psychologists could study subjective experience by analyzing its component parts, or that all thoughts could be reduced to their most basic elements. For example, according to structuralists, a subject's experience of a meal could be defined in terms of his or her experiences of the tastes, textures, and appearance.

By 1890, the study of psychology had advanced enough to lead to the first textbook, *The Principles of Psychology*, by William James. Unlike Wundt, James theorized that the mind was an ever-developing flow of ideas and experiences (STREAM OF CONSCIOUSNESS). Thus, FUNCTIONALISTS are concerned not with determining the cognitive structures that compose thoughts, but with understanding how the mind as a whole functions and evolves in response to daily life to drive our thoughts and decisions. Despite their differences, structuralism and functionalism are both considered introspective theories, as they concern themselves with the inner workings of the individual mind. While these specific theories serve no therapeutic application today, they represent a significant early step in the field of psychology: contemporary psychologists still employ introspection as an important tool, and new fields (like educational and organizational psychology) have emerged from the tradition of studying the human response to environmental factors.

Behaviorism

Behaviorism arose in opposition to the introspective tendencies of the structuralists and functionalists. John Watson, the researcher responsible for popularizing behavioralism, argued that introspection was unreliable and that the science of psychology should only study what can be outwardly observed.

Early behaviorists such as Ivan Pavlov and B.F. Skinner practiced what is today sometimes known as RADICAL BEHAVIORISM because it rejected any inquiry into the thoughts that accompany human behaviors. Though it's considered extreme by today's standards, this early form of behaviorism led to some of psychology's most significant findings, such as those that arose from research into classical and operant conditioning.

Behaviorism remained the primary psychological theory from around 1920 until the 1960s. However, its influence has never completely disappeared. Today, behaviorism continues to influence the work of psychologists, many of whom subscribe to the theories of cognitive behaviorism. COGNITIVE BEHAVIORISM is a field in which practitioners question not only the behaviors themselves but also the thoughts, or cognitions, that underlie and accompany behaviors.

Gestalt Psychology

Like behaviorists, GESTALT PSYCHOLOGISTS rejected structuralist theories, though they did so for a different reason: Gestalt psychologists argued that experiences and perceptions could not be understood by studying their component parts in a vacuum. German psychologist Max Wertheimer, who first introduced Gestalt theory to the world of psychology, posited that thoughts and behavior were system-like, in that the experience of the whole was greater than the combined experiences of the individual parts. In the example of structuralism mentioned earlier, an individual's experience of a meal would be understood by evaluating his or her experiences of its tastes, textures, and appearance; Gestalt psychologists, on the other hand, would argue that the individual's overall perception of the meal is an experience that exists beyond these components.

Psychoanalytic Psychology

The field of PSYCHOANALYTIC PSYCHOLOGY was founded by Sigmund Freud and remained the most widely practiced form of psychotherapy throughout the first part of the twentieth century. In his early writing, Freud theorized that awareness is divided into three distinct parts: the conscious, or what the individual thinks about at any given moment; the preconscious, or that which the individual is aware of but not thinking about; and the unconscious, those things of which the individual is not actively aware. Of particular interest to Freud was the unconscious mind, as he believed that the repressed thoughts, feelings, and experiences contained in it could impact, even determine, our daily actions. Further, he argued that our repressed thoughts and feelings were shaped by conflicts, especially those experienced in childhood. (Consequently, parents, particularly mothers, were commonly considered to be to blame for challenges occurring in adulthood.) Thus, to overcome mental illness and psychological distress, Freud argued that one only had to reveal his or her unconscious mind and cope directly with the repressed material therein. To assist his patients in accomplishing this goal, Freud created PSYCHOANALYSIS and the closely related dream analysis, interview techniques that were intended to allow the psychoanalyst to probe the patient's unconscious mind.

While Freud's theories are much less favored today, psychoanalytic psychology remains a relevant part of our popular culture and continues to influence the evolution of modern psychodynamic theory.

Humanistic Psychology

HUMANISTIC PSYCHOLOGY is a field that emphasizes the subjective experience and unique potential of each individual. Unlike earlier theories, which posited that thoughts and behaviors were the results of forces outside our control, humanist theory emphasized free will, the ability of each individual to make purposeful decisions about how to think and behave.

Humanistic psychology introduced many concepts that are still important in modern psychological practices. For example, the humanists were the first to introduce the concept of SELF-ACTUALIZATION, the process of developing oneself (mentally, physically, emotionally, and spiritually) to the fullest potential. Though humanistic psychology has, until recently, taken a largely unscientific approach to the study of human experiences, its modern practitioners employ the same scientific approaches as other practitioners in their work.

Other perspectives

The COGNITIVE PERSPECTIVE is concerned primarily with thought, positing that thoughts, rather than external stimuli or biological factors, function as the basis for most behaviors. According to cognitive psychologists, personal interpretations and ingrained thought processes are responsible for determining most of our actions; behavioral change, therefore, must result from a change in thinking.

The sociocultural perspective holds that behavior is the result of social conditioning and expectations. Cultural norms for behavior are especially important in this perspective, as the guidelines that define abnormal behavior vary widely by culture. As a result, practitioners of these theories argue that cultural upbringing must always be taken into account when evaluating an individual's mental well-being.

The **EVOLUTIONARY PERSPECTIVE** suggests that thought and behavior are the result of evolutionary processes over a long period. Because evolution should theoretically lead to behaviors that provide an advantage for the species, behavior is looked at through the lenses of natural selection.

Examples

1. Define Gestalt psychology and its main proponents.

   Gestalt psychology posited that human experience was greater than the combination of singular events; that experiences did not exist in a vacuum but were rather explained in a systematic context. Max Wertheimer introduced the theories of Gestalt psychology, which built upon structuralism.

2. Define psychoanalytic psychology and its main proponents.

   Sigmund Freud developed psychoanalytic psychology and psychoanalysis. Freud believed that the unconscious mind contained repressed thoughts, feelings, and experiences that determined an individual's behavior, and that these experiences and actions were shaped by conflicts, especially those experienced in childhood.

RESEARCH METHODS

RESEARCH METHODS are scientific means of gathering and processing information. Before conducting any research, a psychologist must consider what form his or her research will take (research design) and how he or she will collect and analyze the results (data collection and analysis).

Research Design

In psychology, as in all empirical sciences, the scientific method is at the center of all good research. The **SCIENTIFIC METHOD** is an organized, multistep process that relies upon observable data to produce results.

In its simplest form, the scientific method is composed of four steps:

Step 1: Observe a phenomenon or group of phenomena.

Step 2: Form a hypothesis to explain the phenomenon.

Step 3: Test the hypothesis and collect data.

Step 4: Analyze data and draw conclusions.

In considering how they will complete the third step, researchers might explore a number of research design options: they may choose to conduct an experiment, an observational study, a correlational study, a survey, or a case study. Each of these research plans has unique applications and limitations, and a psychologist must understand these complexities to design a research model that will produce valid, reliable results.

Experiments

EXPERIMENTS are the most controlled, and therefore the most sound, research methods because they allow the researcher to determine almost definitively that a cause-and-effect relationship does or does not exist between two variables.

Generally, experimental designs consist of three variables, changeable conditions that have the potential to affect the outcome of the experiment. The INDEPENDENT VARIABLE is the condition that the researcher manipulates to study its effects; it's the cause in the cause-effect relationship being studied. The DEPENDENT VARIABLE is the condition that changes as a result of the independent variable; it's the effect in the cause-effect relationship being studied. EXTRANEOUS VARIABLES are other factors that may affect the outcome of the experiment; the researcher attempts to minimize the effects of these extraneous variables to increase the credibility of his or her results.

Experimental research requires participants, or individuals to be studied. The process used in choosing participants of a sample group is called SAMPLING. For the research results to be credible, samples must be both random and representative of the larger population or of a specific group being studied (in both size and demographic construction).

Examples

1. What is a hypothesis?

   A hypothesis is a testable idea or explanation for an observed phenomenon or phenomena. It's tested as part of the scientific method.

2. What is sampling? Why is it important?

   Sampling is the process of choosing participants of a sample group for an experiment to test a hypothesis. Sampling must be representative of a larger population in order for an experiment to be broadly reflective of the population or group being studied in order for an experiment to be valid.

SOCIAL PSYCHOLOGY

Individuals are shaped by their relationships with other people. However, until recent decades, psychology was studied primarily in the context of the individual experience. **SOCIAL PSYCHOLOGISTS** study how people interact with each other and influence each other's thoughts, attitudes, and behaviors.

Social Cognition

One of the key components of social psychology is the study of **SOCIAL COGNITION**, the way individuals interpret and understand social events in their lives. Individuals use the information they gain through interaction with their social world to understand and make predictions about themselves and others.

ATTRIBUTION THEORY concerns the tendency of the individual to make predictions about others based on observations and inferences. **PERSONAL ATTRIBUTION** attributes the cause of a behavior to the person performing it. **SITUATIONAL ATTRIBUTION**, on the other hand, attributes the cause of behavior to external factors. According to research by Harold Kelley, people make attributions based on three factors: **CONSENSUS**, determining whether the behavior can be contributed to controllable or uncontrollable factors; **CONSISTENCY**, determining whether the behavior is reflective of a pattern of behavior over time; and **DISTINCTIVENESS**, comparing the behavior with behaviors in other, similar situations.

Attitudes, Persuasion, and Cognitive Dissonance

ATTITUDES, a key focus of social psychologists, can be defined as stable opinions that affect an individual's feelings, thoughts, and behaviors toward specific issues and groups. Attitudes are evaluative, generally categorized as positive or negative, and shaped by varying factors. People acquire some attitudes through interactions and experiences with other people. **DIRECT CONTACT** shapes our attitudes by putting us in direct relationship with the issue; for example, you may have a strong opinion about gun rights because you are a hunter, so the issue directly impacts your life. **CHANCE CONDITIONING** occurs when exposure to a particular issue or group is limited, but our experiences have nevertheless shaped our opinions; for example, if you have only gone to two dentists in your life and they were both insensitive, you may have a negative attitude toward dentists. **INTERACTION AND GROUP MEMBERSHIP** both affect our attitudes by exposing us to the attitudes of others rather than exposing us to the issue itself. Finally, our upbringing likely affects our attitudes, as parental attitudes and beliefs are transmitted during child rearing.

Other, more subtle, factors may shape our attitudes as well. The **EXPOSURE EFFECT** states that a person will respond more positively toward something simply because she is exposed to it more. Advertising relies, in part, upon this effect to encourage us to buy specific consumer goods. A consumer might, for instance, be more likely to buy name-brand cereal because he has seen commercials and other advertisements for that brand of cereal. According to the **FALSE-CONSENSUS EFFECT**, we are also more likely to overestimate how common our own beliefs are, which makes it more difficult for us to change our ideas. Interestingly, just as our attitudes can be influenced by environment, our environment can be influenced or affected by our attitudes. A **SELF-FULFILLING PROPHECY** occurs when our attitudes or predictions about a particular group end up causing members of that group to behave in a way that makes the predictions come true. For example, in Robert Rosenthal and Lenore Jacobsen's 1968 study, students whose teacher perceived them as intelligent received more support and encouragement and, consequently, ended up performing better than those students whose teacher perceived them to be less intelligent.

PERSUASION is one significant factor that shapes our attitudes every day, in particular through advertising. The first form of persuasion is relatively direct. In this type of advertising, we are encouraged to believe in the positive qualities of a given product; for instance, advertising for a particular product might highlight the fact that the cereal can reduce cholesterol. The peripheral route, on the other hand, is less direct. For instance, that same ad for cereal might feature attractive, healthy people living in a beautiful home, or living an active lifestyle. You might buy the cereal because you connect it to your subconscious desire for these traits, rather than because you want the health benefits or believe the product will taste good. Advertising may vary depending upon the intended audience. Research suggests that more educated audiences are less likely to be susceptible to advertising, unless it's fact based. Fear-based advertising can also, in some cases, be effective, but must be handled with extreme care to avoid creating negative product associations.

COGNITIVE DISSONANCE refers to situations when individuals do not act in accordance with their stated attitudes. According to **COGNITIVE DISSONANCE THEORY**, developed by Leon Festinger in the 1950s, humans generally want their behaviors to agree with their attitudes. As a result, behaviors may be responsible for shaping attitudes: a number of experiments have shown that people will change their attitudes to better align them with behaviors that have already occurred. The effect of cognitive dissonance, the change in attitude, increases when there is less external motivation for the change, forcing the individual to rectify the discrepancies on his or her own accord. With greater external motivation, individuals did not experience dissonance because they can point to a clear, uncontrollable reason for their behavior. For example, if an individual believes that cigarette smoking is an unhealthy habit but heavily smokes, he might first attempt to quit smoking; however, if he is unable to quit, he may then change his attitude—either by changing the cognition (*the research is not compelling enough*) or by adding a new cognition (*it may be unhealthy, but it helps me relax*).

Social Influence

SOCIAL INFLUENCE is our tendency to change our behaviors in response to other people's words or actions. Sometimes, the influence of others can change our behaviors in a positive way: for example, we often perform better on simple tasks (like running) in the presence of others than we do on the same tasks when we are alone, a tendency called SOCIAL FACILITATION. On the other hand, social influence can sometimes affect our behaviors negatively; one phenomenon, called SOCIAL LOAFING, occurs when an individual in a group stops exerting effort because she knows she will still be able to take partial credit for the work of the group.

Other forms of social influence include conformity, compliance, obedience, and group dynamics. CONFORMITY is the tendency to go along with the opinions or desires of others in a group, despite a lack of pressure to do so. This type of social influence is unintentional on the part of the group and probably stems from the conforming individual's perception that he or she will not be accepted for his or her own beliefs. COMPLIANCE occurs when an individual changes his or her behaviors in response to a direct request by an individual who is not in a position of authority. There are a few factors that might influence the likelihood of an individual to comply: the FOOT-IN-THE-DOOR EFFECT suggests that once you have agreed to a small request, you are more likely to agree to a larger request; the DOOR-IN-THE-FACE STRATEGY suggests that once you have refused a larger request, you are more likely to agree to a small one; NORMS-OF-RECIPROCITY are social norms that encourage individuals to return a favor so that if you are given something, you are more likely to look favorably on a store, business, or person and do something nice in return.

OBEDIENCE occurs when an individual behaves according to direct orders from an authority figure. Stanley Milgram's obedience studies found that, when told to shock volunteers (who were actually actors who were not being shocked at all) for incorrect responses, most of the study's subjects were willing to do so. However, obedience dropped when the study participants were in closer contact with the subject being shocked. Finally, when the behavior was challenged by the researcher's asking the participants to increase the voltage to dangerous level, many of the participants refused to continue. Still, this study showed that, to a certain extent, participants were willing to hurt others on the instruction of a leader.

GROUP DYNAMICS can also influence our thoughts and behaviors. Most individuals belong to many different groups, including family groups, groups of friends, and professional groups, and group dynamics vary drastically from group to group. Different groups have different norms of thought, attitude, and behavior. For example, in some groups, social roles may be quite strictly defined (mother, father, child), while in others, social roles are more fluid (coworkers might also be friends). An interesting illustration of the power of social roles can be found in Phillip Zimbardo's prison experiment. Zimbardo, studying a group of college students, assigned some of his participants to be prisoners and others to be guards. With no restraints in place and simply because of their contextual authority, the "guards" began to act abusively toward the prisoners, while the prisoners became fearful and submissive. The experiment, which was intended to last two weeks, had to be halted after six days.

Group dynamics can influence individual thoughts and behaviors in various ways, including through group polarization, groupthink, and deindividuation. GROUP POLARIZATION occurs when a group makes a more extreme decision than any individual in the group would; this phenomenon is probably at least partially to blame for the partisan polarization that has occurred in America's contemporary political world. GROUPTHINK occurs when members of a group conform to the group's ideas at the expense of individual, critical thinking in order to receive acceptance; DEINDIVIDUATION occurs when individuals in a group lose or sacrifice their own sense of identity and subscribe entirely to the group's opinions. ANONYMITY, a related concept, makes group participants feel protected and may cause them to act, as part of the group, in ways they would not act individually; sometimes these choices even cross personal ethical lines and result in a loss of self-restraint.

Stereotypes, Prejudice, and Discrimination

Attitudes play a key role in stereotyping, prejudice, and discrimination. Expectations about groups of people that result from ingrained attitudes are called STEREOTYPES. Stereotypes can be positive or negative, but both can be damaging to those being stereotyped. PREJUDICE is an undeserved negative attitude toward a group, typically as the result of stereotyping. Because explicit prejudice is no longer acceptable by today's societal standards, prejudice is often SYMBOLIC, meaning it's expressed indirectly through the expression of other attitudes. As a result, prejudice can be hard to detect, even by those who hold prejudicial attitudes themselves. IMPLICIT PREJUDICE is present when an individual holds unconscious, unrecognized prejudicial attitudes. To combat this type of prejudice, there have arisen a number of IMPLICIT ASSOCIATION TESTS, which are designed to give the participant insight into his or her own implicit, unconscious prejudices.

DISCRIMINATION moves beyond prejudicial attitudes and concerns behavior and actions; often discrimination refers to the systematic unequal treatment of people because of their inclusion in a certain group. For example, if a manager avoids hiring someone on the basis of race or age, he or she would be guilty of discrimination. Like prejudice, discrimination is less explicit today than it was in America's history; still, less explicit forms of discrimination (like racial profiling) occur every day.

On the whole, people believe their own groups, or IN-GROUPS, are more diverse than members of other groups. This tendency, referred to as IN-GROUP BIAS, is at the root of most stereotyping, prejudicial, and discriminatory behaviors. For example, a person in Group A will likely believe that members of Group B all share the same negative qualities but will not generalize in the same way about the qualities of his or her own group. However, in-group bias and other prejudicial thoughts and behaviors can sometimes be curbed; to return to the above example, the individual in Group A may dispel his prejudices against the members of Group B by interacting with them in social settings or working with them in pursuit of shared goals.

> Stereotypes, prejudice, and discrimination are common topics of discourse in our modern-day society. Practice making connections by considering how these three behaviors contribute to social unrest.

Examples

1. Explain social psychology. Why is it important?

    Social psychology is the study of how people's relationships and interactions with each other shape their behaviors and influence each other's attitudes and experiences. Social psychology evolved from traditional psychological thought, which focused primarily on an individual's sole experience divorced from his or her interactions in a group setting and relationships with others.

2. How can groupthink lead to deindividuation? What are the consequences?

    Groupthink, or when an individual abandons critical thinking in order to conform to the values of the group, can lead to deindividuation, when an individual completely loses his or her own identity and values, subsuming to those of the group. Due to group polarization, in which a group tends to adopt more extreme values than people would individually, social groups may become more extreme and social conflict more intense.

PART V: TEST YOUR KNOWLEDGE

20

MATHEMATICS PRACTICE TEST

Work the problem and choose the correct answer.

1. Find an equivalent expression:
   $2\frac{y}{x} + \frac{1}{x}(3y)$

   A) $\frac{y}{x}$

   B) $\frac{5y}{x^2}$

   C) $\frac{5y}{6x}$

   D) $\frac{5y}{x}$

2. What is the solution to the equation?
   $2(b + 4.8) = 11b - 1.2$

   A) $b = 0.6$

   B) $b = 1.2$

   C) $b = 4.5$

   D) $b = 5.4$

3. A data set contains n points with a mean of μ. If a new data point with the value x is included in the data set, which of the following expressions is equal to the new mean?

   A) $\frac{\mu + x}{n}$

   B) $\frac{\mu n + x}{n + 1}$

   C) $\frac{\mu n + x}{n}$

   D) $\frac{(\mu + x)n}{n + 1}$

4. Sequential terms in an arithmetic series are found by adding a constant to the previous value in the sequence. Find the 10th term in the following arithmetic sequence if the constant being added is -12: 20, 8, -4, -16...

   Write in the answer: _____

5. Find the slope of a line parallel to the line given by the equation $3y - 1 = 2x$.

   A) $-1\frac{1}{2}$

   B) $\frac{1}{3}$

   C) $\frac{2}{3}$

   D) $1\frac{1}{2}$

6. If a spherical water balloon is filled with 113 milliliters of water, what is the approximate radius of the balloon?

   A) 3.0 centimeters

   B) 3.3 centimeters

   C) 3.6 centimeters

   D) 4.0 centimeters

7. Melissa is ordering fencing to enclose a square area of 5625 square feet. How many feet of fencing does she need?

   Write in the answer: _____

8. Evaluate the expression $\frac{x^2 - 2y}{y}$ when $x = 20$ and $y = \frac{x}{2}$.

   A) 0

   B) 19

   C) 36

   D) 38

9. In July, gas prices increased by 15%. In August, they decreased by 10%. What is the total percent change since June?

   A) 5% increase

   B) 3.5% decrease

   C) 3.5% increase

   D) 1.5% increase

10. Solve for x: $16x^2 + 8x + 2 = 0$.

    A) $x = -4, 4$

    B) $x = -\frac{1}{4}$

    C) $x = -\frac{1}{4}, \frac{1}{4}$

    D) $x = 1, 4$

11. A circular swimming pool has a circumference of 49 feet. What is the diameter of the pool?

    A) 7.8 feet

    B) 12.3 feet

    C) 15.6 feet

    D) 17.8 feet

12. If a cube with sides 4 centimeters in length weighs 16 grams, what is its density in grams per cubic centimeter? (Note: density $= \frac{mass}{volume}$.)

    Write in the answer: _____

13. There are 3 red, 4 blue, and 6 black marbles in a bag. When Carlos reaches into the bag and selects a marble without looking, what are the chances he will select a black marble?

    A) 0.23

    B) 0.31

    C) 0.46

    D) 0.86

14. Consider the chart for cumulative snowfall during a blizzard shown below. During which period of time was the rate of snowfall the fastest?

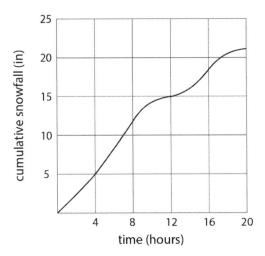

    A) 0 to 4 hours

    B) 8 to 12 hours

    C) 12 to 16 hours

    D) 12 to 20 hours

15. A cylindrical canister is 9 inches high and has a diameter of 5 inches. What is the maximum volume this canister can hold?

    A) 45 inches²

    B) 141 inches²

    C) 176.6 inches²

    D) 706.9 inches²

16. Jesse rides her bike 2 miles south and 8 miles east. She then takes the shortest possible route back home. What was the total distance she traveled?

    A) 7.75 miles

    B) 8.25 miles

    C) 17.75 miles

    D) 18.25 miles

17. Evaluate the function:

    $f(x) = \frac{4x}{(x - 1)}$

    What is $f(5)$?

    Write in the answer: _____

18. If x is the proportion of men who play an instrument, y is the proportion of women who play an instrument, and z is the total number of men, which of the following is true?

   A) $\frac{z}{x}$ = number of men who play an instrument

   B) $(1 - z)x$ = number of men who do not play an instrument

   C) $(1 - x)z$ = number of men who do not play an instrument

   D) $(1 - y)z$ = number of women who do not play an instrument

19. On an airplane, there are 2 window seats, 2 aisle seats, and 1 middle seat per row (each row sits 3 people on one side of the aisle and 2 people on the opposite side). Two friends have requested to be seated in the same row. What is the probability that both friends will be assigned to aisle seats?

   A) 2.0%

   B) 4.1%

   C) 4.8%

   D) 10%

20. James is building an octagonal gazebo with equal sides in his backyard. If one side is 5.5 feet wide, what is the perimeter of the entire gazebo?

   A) 22 feet

   B) 30.25 feet

   C) 44 feet

   D) 242 feet

21. A sporting goods store is offering an additional 30% off all clearance items. Angie purchases a pair of running shoes on clearance for $65.00. If the shoes originally cost $85.00, what was her total discount?

   A) 22.9%

   B) 39.2%

   C) 46.5%

   D) 53.5%

22. The table below shows the number of hours worked by employees during the week. What is the median number of hours worked per week by the employees?

EMPLOYEE	HOURS WORKED PER WEEK
Suzanne	42
Joe	38
Mark	25
Ellen	50
Jill	45
Rob	46
Nicole	17
Deb	41

   A) 38

   B) 41

   C) 41.5

   D) 42

23. A restaurant employs servers, hosts, and managers in a ratio of 9:2:1. If there are 36 total employees, how many hosts are there?

   A) 3

   B) 4

   C) 6

   D) 8

24. Consider this polynomial expression:

   $(3x^3 + 4x) + (-2x - 5y) + y$

   What is the sum of the polynomials?

   A) $3x^3 + 2x + y$

   B) $11x - 4y$

   C) $3x^3 + 2x - 4y$

   D) $29x - 4y$

25. What is the solution to the equation?
   $8(x + 5) = -3x - 48$

   A) $x = -8$

   B) $x = 0.625$

   C) $x = 8$

   D) $x = 12.8$

26. If m represents a car's average mileage in miles per gallon, p represents the price of gas in dollars per gallon, and d represents a distance in miles, which of the following algebraic equations represents the cost (c) of gas per mile?

A) $c = \dfrac{dp}{m}$

B) $c = \dfrac{p}{m}$

C) $c = \dfrac{mp}{d}$

D) $c = \dfrac{m}{p}$

27. If $f(x) = 0.5^x + 1$, evaluate $f(-2)$.

A) 0.75

B) 2

C) 4

D) 5

28. Which names the function for the following arithmetic series?

$11, 7, 3, -1\ldots$

A) $f(x) = 11 + 4(x - 1)$

B) $f(x) = 11(4)^{(x-1)}$

C) $f(x) = 15 - 4x$

D) $f(x) = 11 - 4x$

29. A cleaning company charges $25 per hour per room. Added to this charge is a 7% sales tax. If t represents the number of hours and r represents the number of rooms, which of the following algebraic equations represents the total cost c of cleaning?

A) $c = 25.07(t)(r)$

B) $c = 32.00(t)(r)$

C) $c = 26.75(t)(r)$

D) $c = \dfrac{26.75(t)}{r}$

30. A 650 square foot apartment in Boston costs $1800 per month to rent. What is the monthly rent in dollars per square foot?

Write in the answer: _____

31. Let $f(x) = 2x + 1$. If $g(x)$ is obtained by reflecting $f(x)$ across the y-axis and translating it 4 units in the positive y direction, what is $g(x)$?

A) $g(x) = 3 - 2x$

B) $g(x) = 5 - 2x$

C) $g(x) = 2x + 5$

D) $g(x) = 8x + 1$

32. The perimeter of an isosceles triangle is 25 centimeters. If the legs are twice as long as the base, what is the length of the base in centimeters?

Write in the answer: _____

33. If $f(x) = 2x - 3$, what is $f^{-1}(x)$?

A) $f^{-1} = \dfrac{x - 3}{2}$

B) $f^{-1} = \dfrac{x}{2} - 3$

C) $f^{-1} = -2x + 3$

D) $f^{-1} = -\dfrac{x}{2} - 3$

34. The standard deviation of a data set is found by first finding the set's mean. Next, subtract the mean from each value in the set, and square the result. Finally, take the average of each squared difference, and take the square root of the result.

The table below shows the number of snow days per school year. What is the standard deviation of the data set?

YEAR	NUMBER OF SNOW DAYS
2007–2008	3
2008–2009	0
2009–2010	3
2010–2011	4
2011–2012	5
2012–2013	6
2013–2014	3
2014–2015	4

A) 0.89

B) 1.66

C) 2.75

D) 4.69

35. A bag contains twice as many red marbles as blue marbles, and the number of blue marbles is 88% of the number of green marbles. If g represents the number of green marbles, which of the following expressions represents the total number of marbles in the bag?

A) $2.32g$

B) $2.64g$

C) $3.64g$

D) $3.88g$

36. A car rental company charges a daily fee of $48 plus 25% of the daily fee for every hour the car is late. If you rent a car for 2 days and bring it back 2 hours late, what will be the total charge?

A) $72

B) $108

C) $120

D) $144

37. The annual profits of Company A for 2000 – 2005 are shown in the graph below. How much did Company A's profit increase from 2003 to 2004?

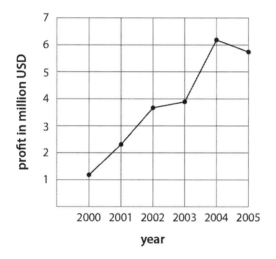

A) $2.3 million

B) $3.2 million

C) $3.9 million

D) $5.0 million

38. Find an equivalent expression:
$9x^2 + 42xy + 49y^2$

A) $(3x - 7y)^2$

B) $(3x + 7y)^2$

C) $(3x + 7)(x + y)$

D) $(3x + 7y)(3x - 7)$

39. Find the missing value for the function shown in the table below.

X	Y
-2	5
-1	2
0	1
1	2
2	5
3	?

Write in the answer: _____

40. If ∡C measures 112°, find ∡F.

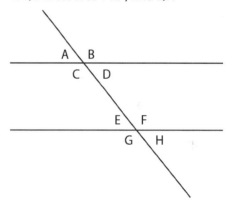

A) 22°

B) 68°

C) 112°

D) 158°

41. Jane earns $15 per hour babysitting. If she starts out with $275 in her bank account, which of the following equations represents how many hours she will have to babysit for her account to reach $400?

A) $275 = 400 + 15h$

B) $400 = 15h$

C) $400 = \frac{15}{h} + 275$

D) $400 = 275 + 15h$

42. A square is drawn on a coordinate plane. If 2 of the corners are located at points $(-6, 14)$ and $(8, 14)$, what is the area of the square?

Write in the answer: _____

43. The slope of a straight line is -3 and its y-intercept is -2. Find the line's x-intercept.

A) $x = -3$

B) $x = -2$

C) $x = -\frac{2}{3}$

D) $x = 1\frac{1}{2}$

44. The county is instituting a new license plate system. The new plates will have 6 digits: the first digit will be 1, 2, or 3, and the next 5 digits can be any number from 0 to 9. How many possible unique combinations does this new system offer?

A) 53

B) 1×10^6

C) 3×10^5

D) 3×10^6

45. The relationship between x and y in the table below can best be described as:

x	y
-2	-2
-1	1
0	4
1	7
2	10
3	13

Write in the answer: _____

46. A pizza has a diameter of 10 inches. If you cut a slice with a central angle of 40 degrees, how many inches of crust does that slice include?

A) 3.3 inches

B) 3.5 inches

C) 7.0 inches

D) 31.4 inches

21

REASONING THROUGH LANGUAGE ARTS PRACTICE TEST

Read the text carefully, and then answer the following questions.

Excerpt from *Treasure Island*

BY ROBERT LOUIS STEVENSON

In this excerpt, the narrator tells about an old sailor staying at his family's inn.

He had taken me aside one day and promised me a silver fourpenny on the first of every month if I would only keep my "weather-eye open for a seafaring man with one leg" and let him know the moment he appeared. Often enough when the first of the month came round and I applied to him for my wage, he would only blow through his nose at me and stare me down, but before the week was out he was sure to think better of it, bring me my fourpenny piece, and repeat his orders to look out for "the seafaring man with one leg."

How that personage haunted my dreams, I need scarcely tell you. On stormy nights, when the wind shook the four corners of the house and the surf roared along the cove and up the cliffs, I would see him in a thousand forms, and with a thousand diabolical expressions. Now the leg would be cut off at the knee, now at the hip; now he was a monstrous kind of a creature who had never had but the one leg, and that in the middle of his body. To see him leap and run and pursue me over hedge and ditch was the worst of nightmares. And altogether I paid pretty dear for my monthly fourpenny piece, in the shape of these abominable fancies.

But though I was so terrified by the idea of the seafaring man with one leg, I was far less afraid of the captain himself than anybody else who knew him. There were nights when he took a deal more rum and water than his head would carry; and then he would sometimes sit and sing his wicked, old, wild sea-songs, minding nobody; but sometimes he would call for glasses round and force all the trembling company to listen to his stories or bear a chorus to his singing. Often I have heard the house shaking with "Yo-ho-ho, and a bottle of rum," all the neighbors joining in for dear life, with the fear of death upon them, and each singing louder than the other to avoid remark. For in these fits he was the most overriding companion ever known; he would slap his hand on the table for silence all round; he would fly up in a passion of anger at a question, or sometimes because none was put, and so he judged the company was not following his story. Nor would he allow anyone to leave the inn till he had drunk himself sleepy and reeled off to bed.

His stories were what frightened people worst of all. Dreadful stories they were—about hanging, and walking the plank, and storms at sea, and the Dry Tortugas, and wild deeds and places on the Spanish Main. By his own account he must have lived his life among some of the wickedest men that God ever allowed upon the sea, and the language in which he told these stories shocked our plain country people almost as much as the crimes that he described. My father was always saying the inn would be ruined, for people would soon cease coming there to be tyrannized over and put down, and sent shivering to their beds; but I really believe his presence did us good. People were frightened at the time, but on looking back they rather liked it; it was a fine excitement in a quiet country life, and there was even a party of the younger men who pretended to admire him, calling him a "true sea-dog" and a "real old salt" and such like names, and saying there was the sort of man that made England terrible at sea.

In one way, indeed, he bade fair to ruin us, for he kept on staying week after week, and at last month after month, so that all the money had been long exhausted, and still my father never plucked up the heart to insist on having more. If ever he mentioned it, the captain blew through his nose so loudly that you might say he roared, and stared my poor father out of the room. I have seen him wringing his hands after such a rebuff, and I am sure the annoyance and the terror he lived in must have greatly hastened his early and unhappy death.

1. In this excerpt, the narrator says, *And altogether I paid pretty dear for my monthly fourpenny piece, in the shape of these abominable fancies.* The author most likely included this sentence to

   A) explain that the narrator worked very hard.

   B) show that the narrator's fears of the sailor were almost not worth the money he earned for looking out for him.

   C) clarify that these visions were just the nightmares of a little boy.

   D) show that the sailor was actually a sea monster.

2. In this excerpt, the narrator describes the sailor's stories by saying, *Dreadful stories they were—about hanging, and walking the plank, and storms at sea, and the Dry Tortugas, and wild deeds and places on the Spanish Main.* What does this statement reveal?

   A) The sailor captivated the audience.

   B) The old man's ramblings were boring to listeners.

   C) The narrator dreamed of living an exciting life at sea.

   D) The sailor was a liar.

3. What definition best matches the use of the word *diabolical* in the second paragraph?

   A) angry

   B) judgmental

   C) stoic

   D) fearsome

4. The narrator says that *If ever he mentioned it, the captain blew through his nose so loudly that you might say he roared, and stared my poor father out of the room.* What does the author's phrasing *blew through his nose* show about the sailor's demeanor?

   A) He's sickly.

   B) He's easily surprised.

   C) He's pretentious.

   D) He's bad-tempered.

5. Which sentence from the text best emphasizes the enduring impact the sailor had on the people at the inn?

   A) *To see him leap and run and pursue me over hedge and ditch was the worst of nightmares.*

   B) *But though I was so terrified by the idea of the seafaring man with one leg, I was far less afraid of the captain himself than anybody else who knew him.*

   C) *His stories were what frightened people worst of all.*

   D) *People were frightened at the time, but on looking back they rather liked it; it was a fine excitement in a quiet country life…*

6. What definition best matches the use of the word *tyrannical* in the fourth paragraph?

   A) bullied

   B) cajoled

   C) frightened

   D) robbed

7. Which definition best matches the use of the word *terrible* in the fourth paragraph?

    A) formidable

    B) wicked

    C) criminal

    D) poor sailors

8. What statement best describes the inn when the sailor was there?

    A) People spent a lot of money.

    B) The sailor always talked to everyone and made them sing with him.

    C) The atmosphere was unpredictable.

    D) People started going to other inns because the inappropriate nature of the sailor's stories made them uncomfortable.

9. By using the phrase *they rather liked it* in the fourth paragraph, the author most likely means

    A) that the patrons of the inn enjoyed singing.

    B) that the sailor and others appreciated the rum available for sale at the inn.

    C) that the sailor provided entertainment at the inn, which would otherwise be boring.

    D) that the narrator and his friends liked the stories the captain told.

10. Write a summary of this excerpt from *Treasure Island*.

Renting your first apartment can be an exhilarating undertaking, but it is also a nerve-wracking experience. (1) There are several issues to consider, like whether to have a roommate, what kind of neighborhood to live in, or whether access to parking or public transportation is important. (2) However, budget is usually at the top of the list. (3)

    You should keep in mind that upon signing a lease, landlords will require a deposit in addition to the first month's rent. (4) Some landlords even require first and last month's rent in addition to the deposit at the time of signing, so be prepared to fork over a lot of money, depending on where you live, because that requirement can vary by state, city, even from building to building. (5) But budget extends beyond just the costs at lease-signing. (6) You might run across your dream apartment, but only be able to afford it if it is in a dangerous neighborhood. (7) In that case, you may need to sacrifice that dream (or at least put it off for a few years) for safety, and find a place to live in a safer area even if that place is smaller than you wanted. (8)

11. Which sentence should be inserted before sentence 4 (to begin the second paragraph) for the best transition between the two paragraphs?

    A) Be prepared to spend a considerable amount of money even to sign a lease in the first place.

    B) Landlords have varying expectations.

    C) Some landlords are more flexible than others, and you can usually count on them to be understanding in case you cannot afford the apartment you want right away.

    D) You don't always have to sign a lease to rent a place to live, but you might have to.

12. What would be the best sentence to add after sentence 1?

    A) It can be fun to search for housing, but dealing with landlords, brokers, and rules about leasing can be stressful.

    B) Getting a roommate, budgeting, and talking to landlords—these are serious considerations.

    C) You might even want to consider getting a real estate agent.

    D) However, for some people, the stress can be part of the fun!

13. What sentence would best begin a new paragraph after the second paragraph?

A) Speaking of neighborhood (excluding budget), choosing an area to live in depends on things like where you work or go to school, what activities you enjoy, and whether you own a car or use public transportation.

B) It doesn't really matter where you live as long as it's safe and affordable—especially in your first apartment; it's better to be safe than sorry.

C) Choosing where to live depends on budget, but it can also depend on where you work or attend school, whether you own a car or require public transportation, and what kinds of activities you enjoy.

D) Even if you can afford to live in an area that you like, it makes more sense to spend as little as possible on your first apartment and save as much money as you can; you can always live somewhere nicer when you are older.

Read the draft of the following essay and complete the task that follows.

A student is writing an argumentative essay for a website about the cultural significance of boy bands.

Some people are surprised to learn that the phenomenon of "boy bands" is nothing new. One Direction is only the latest iteration in a long line of distinguished performers, whose musical roots stretch back to the barbershop quartets of the early twentieth century. Far from being a silly fad, boy bands represent an important trend in American culture stretching back over a century.

Beginning in the 1900s, barbershop quartets kicked off over one hundred years of harmony. Impromptu gatherings of singing young men in barbershops gave way to organized groups of singers like the Mills Brothers. Later, the Ink Spots made it big as doo-wop music became popular in the 1950s. By the 1960s, major international bands like the Beatles, the Temptations, the Monkees, the Jackson Five, and the Beach Boys became huge stars in their own right. The music and style of these performers is the bedrock on which today's boy band music is based.

However, the term "boy band" was not used until the 1980s, when arguably the greatest boy band of all, New Edition, burst on the scene. A model for the bands that would follow, New Edition ushered in a new era of bands beginning with New Kids on the Block, the rock and roll answer to New Edition's R&B boy band style, Boyz II Men, and later the 1990s legends the Backstreet Boys and 'N SYNC. This crop of musicians boasted some of America's greatest stars like Donnie Wahlberg, Justin Timberlake, and Bobby Brown. At the turn of the century, a lull in the music made it seem like it was going out of style, but boy bands resurfaced with the Jonas Brothers and then One Direction.

14. This essay is missing a conclusion. Write a conclusion that follows from the argument.

15. Move the sentences from the left into the appropriate boxes on the right so that each claim is appropriately supported and the paragraph is coherent.

A) Lincoln and Douglas had met around the country in a series of debates reflective of the national mood.

In 1860, the United States was in a state of turmoil.

B) Lincoln was vehemently against slavery; Douglas, while not a supporter of slavery, spoke in favor of states' rights, which included deciding whether slavery ought to be legal in a state or not.

Drop Area 1

C) Following decades of debate over the extension of slavery westward, the country was divided over the practice.

Major legislation had placed restrictions on slavery in the West and then lifted them.

This division played a key role in the presidential election of 1860, which pitted Abraham Lincoln against Stephen Douglas.

Drop Area 2

Drop Area 3

The 1860 presidential election saw Lincoln elected to the highest office in the land, with Southern Secession and the Civil War soon to follow.

Passage One: Excerpt from *Tradition and the Individual Talent*

BY T.S. ELIOT

No poet, no artist of any art, has his complete meaning alone. His significance, his appreciation is the appreciation of his relation to the dead poets and artists. You cannot value him alone; you must set him, for contrast and comparison, among the dead. I mean this as a principle of aesthetic, not merely historical, criticism. The necessity that he shall conform, that he shall cohere, is not one-sided; what happens when a new work of art is created is something that happens simultaneously to all the works of art which preceded it. The existing monuments form an ideal order among themselves, which is modified by the introduction of the new (the really new) work of art among them. The existing order is complete before the new work arrives; for order to persist after the supervention of novelty, the whole existing order must be, if ever so slightly, altered; and so the relations, proportions, values of each work of art toward the whole are readjusted; and this is conformity between the old and the new. Whoever has approved this idea of order, of the form of European, of English literature, will not find it preposterous that the past should be altered by the present as much as the present is directed by the past. And the poet who is aware of this will be aware of great difficulties and responsibilities.

Passage Two: Excerpt from *Art*

BY CLIVE BELL

To criticize a work of art historically is to play the science-besotted fool. No more disastrous theory ever issued from the brain of a charlatan than that of evolution in art. Giotto[1] did not creep, a grub, that Titian[2] might flaunt, a butterfly. To think of a man's art as leading on to the art of someone else is to misunderstand it. To praise or abuse or be interested in a work of art because it leads or does not lead to another work of art is to treat it as though it were not a work of art. The connection of one work of art with another may have everything to do with history: it has nothing to do with appreciation. So soon as we begin to consider a work as anything else than an end in itself we leave the world of art. Though the development of painting from Giotto to Titian may be interesting historically, it cannot affect the value of any particular picture: aesthetically, it is of no consequence whatever. Every work of art must be judged on its own merits.

For questions 16 – 20, place each sentence within the appropriate author's box.

T.S. ELIOT	CLIVE BELL
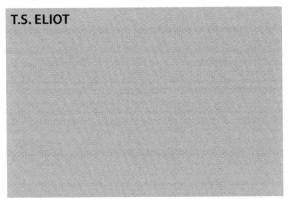	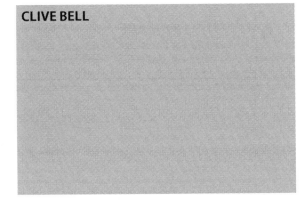

16. To understand a novel written in the twentieth century, it is necessary to have some knowledge of nineteenth-century literature.

17. A painting should be judged on its own merits, not on its relationship to previous works of art.

---

[1] Giotto was an Italian painter during the Middle Ages.

[2] Titian was an Italian painter during the Renaissance.

18. Art critics should evaluate whether works of art are consequential and worth appreciating.

19. A new piece of art influences how historical works of art are evaluated.

20. Art cannot be seen as a systematic process of growth stretching across centuries.

21. The author of Passage One would be most likely to support

    A) an artist who imitated the great works of the past.

    B) an art critic who relied solely on evaluating the aesthetics of new art.

    C) a historian who studied the aesthetic evolution of art.

    D) an artist who shouldered the burden of creating something new, while affecting the old, in the world of art.

Who doesn't love a good cat meme? (1) It turns out that cats are more popular around the world than anyone had realized; with the proliferation of YouTube and social media, cats have taken the internet by storm. (2) From Grumpy Cat to Waffles, from the United States to Japan, cats appear in funny pictures, hilarious videos, and have even gone on to make their owners millions of dollars. (3)

    Until recently, it had been believed that dogs were the most popular pet in the United States, with cats lagging behind in second place. (4) Dogs, "man's best friend," can be trained to do certain tricks and tasks, can be fun workout companions who play Frisbee and fetch with their owners, and can even help protect property. (5) While cats may have their uses in pest control, they are often reluctant to work on command, and very few are willing to submit to the humiliation of a collar and leash for a walk outside. (6) Still, it turns out that their funny antics and remarkable athletic prowess, even indoors, make for good TV.

    (7) And so the Internet is filled with cats large and small, lean and fat, wearing pieces of bread, making playthings out of boxes, jumping to amazing heights, and just looking hilariously grumpy. (8) Cats of internet fame now appear at conventions and festivals around the world, and people wait in line for hours just for a glimpse of their favorite feline celebrity. (9)

22. Which sentence best completes the first paragraph to create a good transition between two paragraphs?

    A) But cats have not always been in the spotlight; in fact, they had been relegated to a secondary position in the known hierarchy of pet popularity in popular culture.

    B) Indeed, cats are taking the world by storm.

    C) Cats are by far the most popular pet in the world, and cat ownership continues to rise.

    D) Thanks to the Internet, cat marketability is becoming a field requiring true expertise, and there are even entrepreneurs who specialize in representing felines and their owners in public relations.

23. What would be a good title for this essay, keeping in mind both the topic and the tone?

    A) The Rise and Fall of Famous Felines: From Grumpy Cat to Smushy Face

    B) Canine versus Feline: the Battle Continues, from the Internet to the Convention Center

    C) Felines Online! Pet Popularity, Feline Fame, and the Internet Age

    D) Cats for Cash: is Feline Fame Really Catsploitation?

24. Which revision more concisely revises sentences (6) and (7)?

   A) no change

   B) Cats are useful for pest control, but they are often reluctant to work on command; moreover, very few are willing to submit to the humiliation of a collar and leash for a walk outside. (6) But it turns out that cats are more interesting—and funnier—than anyone realized, and their antics make for good TV. (7)

   C) On the other hand, cats have their uses in pest control, they are often reluctant to work on command, and very few are willing to submit to the humiliation of a collar and leash for a walk outside. (6) However, it turns out that their funny antics and remarkable athletic prowess, even indoors, make for good TV. (7)

   D) Cats are funnier and more interesting than dogs, but are only good for pest control—they won't go for walks on leashes or learn commands.

25. What would be the best sentence to follow sentence 9, keeping with the theme of the entire paragraph?

   A) We mourn internet sensations like Chairman Meow who have passed on, and laud newcomers like Smushy Face who have risen to the challenge of feline fame.

   B) Some of the cat owners have become quite media savvy, and their cats now grace everything from coffee mugs to key chains to t-shirts; while waiting in line, fans are often enticed to buy these trinkets, but this irritates some fans.

   C) Some dog owners are getting in on the act too, filming their dogs doing funny things and putting them on YouTube, but they don't get nearly as many hits as the cats do... at least not yet.

   D) Some commentators believe that the cat owners are exploiting their cats, who no doubt would prefer to be at home napping in the sun or chasing mice.

Influenza, or the flu, has historically been one of the most common and deadliest human sicknesses. While many people who contract this virus will recover, others will not. Over the past 150 years, tens of millions of people have died from the flu, and millions more have been left with lingering complications including secondary infections.

Although it's a common disease, the flu is actually not highly infectious; that is, it is relatively difficult to contract. The virus can only be transmitted when individuals come into direct contact with the bodily fluids of people infected with it, often when they are exposed to expelled aerosol particles resulting from coughing and sneezing. Since these particles only travel short distances and the virus will die within a few hours on hard surfaces, it can be contained with simple health measures like hand washing and face masks.

However, the spread of this disease can only be contained when people are aware that such measures must be taken. One of the reasons the flu has historically been so deadly is the window of time between a person's infection and the development of symptoms. Viral shedding—when the body releases a virus that has been successfully reproducing in it—takes place two days after infection, while symptoms do not usually develop until the third day. Thus, infected individuals may unknowingly infect others for least twenty-four hours before developing symptoms themselves.

26. Why isn't the flu considered to be highly infectious?

   A) Many people who get the flu will recover and have no lasting complications, so only a small number of people who become infected will die.

   B) The process of viral shedding takes two days, so infected individuals have enough time to implement simple health measures that stop the spread of the disease.

   C. The flu virus cannot travel far or live for long periods of time outside the human body, so its spread can easily be contained.

   D. Twenty-four hours is a relatively short period of time for the virus to spread throughout a population.

27. What can the reader conclude from the passage above?

   A) Preemptively implementing health measures like hand washing and face masks could help stop the spread of the flu virus.

   B) Doctors are not sure how the flu virus is transmitted, so they are unsure how to stop it from spreading.

   C) The flu is dangerous because it is both deadly and highly infectious.

   D) Individuals stop being infectious three days after they are infected.

The bacteria, fungi, insects, plants, and animals that live together in a habitat have evolved to share a pool of limited resources. They've competed for water, minerals, nutrients, sunlight, and space, sometimes for thousands or even millions of years. As these communities have evolved, the species in them have developed complex, long-term interspecies interactions known as symbiotic relationships.

Ecologists characterize these interactions based on whether each party benefits. In mutualism both individuals benefit, while in synnecrosis both organisms are harmed. A relationship in which one individual benefits and the other is harmed is known as parasitism. Examples of these relationships can easily be found in any ecosystem. Pollination, for example, is mutualistic—pollinators get nutrients from the flower, and the plant is able to reproduce—while tapeworms, which steal nutrients from their host, are parasitic.

There's yet another class of symbiosis that is controversial among scientists. Commensalism has long been defined as a relationship in which one species benefits while the other is unaffected. But is it possible for two species to interact and for one to remain completely unaffected? Often, relationships described as commensal include one species that feeds on another species' leftovers; remoras, for instance, will attach themselves to sharks and eat the food particles the sharks discard. It might seem like the shark gets nothing from the relationship, but a closer look will show that sharks in fact benefit from remoras, which clean the sharks' skin and remove parasites. In fact, many scientists claim that relationships currently described as commensal are just mutualistic or parasitic in ways that haven't been discovered yet.

28. Why is commensalism controversial among scientists?

   A) Many scientists believe that an interspecies interaction where one species is unaffected does not exist.

   B) Some scientists believe that relationships where one species feeds on the leftovers of another should be classified as parasitism.

   C) Because remoras and sharks have a mutualistic relationship, no interactions should be classified as commensalism.

   D) Only relationships among animal species should be classified as commensalism.

CONTINUE

29. Which of the following best defines the word *controversial* as it is used in the third paragraph?

    A) objectionable

    B) debatable

    C) confusing

    D) upsetting

It could be said that the great battle between the North and South we call the Civil War was a battle for individual identity. The states of the South had their own culture, one based on farming, independence, and the rights of both man and state to determine their own paths. Similarly, the North had forged its own identity as a center of centralized commerce and manufacturing. This clash of lifestyles was bound to create tension, and this tension was bound to lead to war. But people who try to sell you this narrative are wrong. The Civil War was a not a battle of cultural identities—it was a battle over slavery. All other explanations for the war are a either a direct consequence of the South's desire for wealth at the expense of her fellow man, or a fanciful invention to cover up this sad portion of our nation's history. And it cannot be denied that this time in our past was very sad indeed.

30. Which of the following indicates how the author would likely state his or her position on the Civil War?

    A) The Civil War was the result of cultural differences between the North and South.

    B) The Civil War was caused by the South's reliance on slave labor.

    C) The North's use of commerce and manufacturing allowed it to win the war.

    D) The South's belief in the rights of man and state cost it the war.

Whenever Vi entered that old house, it felt like she was coming home. Even though she hadn't lived there in almost twenty years, the memories of the years she had spent there felt as fresh as the newly fallen snow that blanketed the yard. When she walked through the living room she didn't see the rickety old chairs and peeling paint—she saw the many evenings she'd enjoyed there with her mom, dad, and kid sister. To her, the old dining room didn't smell like dust and moldy table linens; it smelled like home-cooked meals. They may have had their share of troubles in that house, but it had been her family's house—a place they called their own.

Vi's sister, on the other hand, worried about the more practical matters. That dust and mold had been accumulating in the house ever since their mother moved out, and it didn't seem like their father planned to do anything about it. She hired cleaners, plumbers, and painters, but her father just sent them away.

31. Select the three words from the list below that describe Vi.

    nostalgic

    practical

    forgetful

    loving

    emotional

32. Which sentence best concludes the following paragraph?

Many people think that the U.S. president is elected directly by the people, but that is not exactly the case. Each candidate has a group of electors; these electors are members of the Electoral College. When Americans vote at the polls for the president, they are actually voting for their candidate's group of electors, who then technically vote in the president.

   A) So even though the people do ultimately choose the president, it is not in a direct election.

   B) The Electoral College is really confusing.

   C) Some Americans, however, believe that the Electoral College should be abolished.

   D). Clearly, most people do not understand the presidential election.

33. They left for the party, but Rebecca had to return home because _____ forgot her purse.

Which of the following correctly completes the sentence?

   A) he

   B) they

   C) we

   D) she

34. Which of the following sentences is grammatically correct?

   A) You can have either the cake nor the cookie.

   B) You can't have neither the cake or the cookie.

   C) You can have either the cake or the cookie.

   D) You can having either the cake or the cookie.

35. Which of the following sentences is correct?

   A) The head zookeeper, who has been with the zoo for over twenty years, have agreed to set up a new enclosure for the elephants.

   B) Of all the elephants owned by the zoo, only some has been approved to move to the new enclosure.

   C) The rest of the elephants has been given to a well-respected rescue organization.

   D) The rescue organization, which takes in animals from zoos across the country, has agreed not to sell the elephants to another zoo.

36. Which of the following sentences is punctuated correctly?

   A) Make a study plan to learn the parts of the respiratory system, the muscles, and the heart.

   B) Make a study plan to learn the: parts of the respiratory system, the muscles, and the heart.

   C) Make a study plan to learn the parts of the respiratory system the muscles and the heart.

   D) Make a study plan to learn the parts: of the respiratory system, the muscles, and the heart.

CONTINUE

For questions 34 – 44, choose the option that correctly completes the sentence.

Anyone who has been given a nickname knows that these informal labels can sometimes be difficult to shake. In the 1980s, one group of young actors earned a group nickname—the Brat Pack—that would follow them for decades. While some members of the Brat Pack still went on to have successful (37)_____ struggled to make their own names stand out against the backdrop of the group.

The members of the Brat Pack earned their fame by appearing together in a series of films made for teen and young adult audiences. (38)_____ these movies (39)_____ made in the early 1980s, the Brat Pack label did not appear until 1985, when New York magazine writer David Blum wrote an article about his experience socializing with some of the group's members. The article (40)_____ these young actors as immature, unprofessional, and spoiled, and though Blum's experience with them was limited to one night with just three individuals, his label quickly caught on and tarnished the reputations of many of the other young actors who worked alongside the three. Many of these individuals struggled professionally as a result of the negative label, and most of them denied being a part of any such group.

Today, despite the initial repercussions of the unfortunate nickname, the Brat Pack label is still in use, largely because of the (41) _____relevance and significance of the Brat Pack films. Most of these films are coming-of-age stories, in which one or more of the characters gains experience or learns an important lesson about adult life. For example, the famous film *The Breakfast Club* features five main characters, (42) _____ are all from different social circles at one high school, learn to look past labels and appearances, and find that they have more in common than they ever imagined.

Because of the talent and the relatability of the Brat Pack members, (43) _____.
(44)_____

37. A) careers; others

    B) careers, others

    C) careers, but others

    D) careers. Others

38. A) Though the first of

    B) The first of

    C) Because the first of

    D) Consequently, the first of

39. A) were

    B) was

    C) is

    D) are

40. A) is portraying

    B) would portray

    C) was portraying

    D) portrayed

41. A) ongoing and perpetual

    B) perpetually ongoing

    C) never-ending, perpetual

    D) ongoing

42. A) whom

    B) who

    C) which

    D) and

43. A) these characters and their stories continue to appeal to young people and influence popular culture in the new millennium.

    B) these movies were hugely successful in appealing to all age groups.

    C) these movies drew in enormous box office profits.

    D) these movies propelled a few of their stars into hugely successful careers.

44.

A) Thus, the Brat Pack nickname has been freed of its negative connotations by the actors who once despised and wore the label.

B) Thus, the Brat Pack label that was worn by the actors has been freed of the negative connotations it had, making it less despised.

C) Thus, the label that was once despised by the actors, the Brat Pack, has been altogether freed of its negative connotations.

D) Thus, the Brat Pack nickname, which was once so despised by the actors who wore the label, has been altogether freed of its negative connotations.

For questions 45 – 47, place the events in proper chronological order according to the passage.

Popcorn is often associated with fun and festivities, both in and out of the home. We eat it in theaters, smothering it in butter, and at home, fresh from the microwave. But popcorn isn't just for fun—it's also a multimillion-dollar industry with a long and fascinating history.

While popcorn might seem like a modern invention, its history actually dates back thousands of years, making it one of the oldest snack foods enjoyed around the world. Popping is believed by food historians to be one of the earliest uses of cultivated corn. In 1948, Herbert Dick and Earle Smith discovered old popcorn dating back 4,000 years in the New Mexico Bat Cave. For the Aztecs who called the caves home, popcorn (or *momochitl*) played an important role in society, both as a food staple and in ceremonies. The Aztecs cooked popcorn by heating sand in a fire; when it was heated, kernels were added and would pop when exposed to the heat of the sand.

The American love affair with popcorn began in 1912, when it was first sold in theaters. The popcorn industry flourished during the Great Depression by advertising popcorn as a wholesome and economical food. Selling for five to ten cents a bag, it was a luxury that the downtrodden could afford. With the introduction of mobile popcorn machines at the World's Columbian Exposition, popcorn moved from the theater into fairs and parks. Popcorn continued to rule the snack food kingdom until the rise in popularity of home televisions during the 1950s.

The popcorn industry quickly reacted to its decline in sales by introducing pre-popped and un-popped popcorn for home consumption. However, it wasn't until microwave popcorn became commercially available in 1981 that at-home popcorn consumption began to grow exponentially. With the wide availability of microwaves in the United States, popcorn also began popping up in offices and hotel rooms. The home still remains the most popular popcorn eating spot, though: today, seventy percent of the sixteen billion quarts of popcorn consumed annually in the United States is eaten at home.

45. Microwave popcorn become commercially available. (1, 2, 3)

46. Home televisions become popular. (1, 2, 3)

47. Popcorn is first sold in theatres. (1, 2, 3)

Analytical Writing Question: "Analyze an Issue" #1

Do you agree or disagree with the following statement? Explain why or why not and address examples that could be supportive or detrimental to your position.

Almost every industry in the world depends on oil and gas extraction, so it is vital that companies be allowed to use whatever methods necessary to continue supplying the world with this resource—even practices like fracking that pollute sensitive ecosystems.

→

CONTINUE

Analytical Writing Question: "Analyze an Argument" #2

In your response, explain whether you agree or disagree with this argument. Propose a solution to the dilemma raised by this situation.

Powerful and often unexpected disruptive weather patterns and storms in recent years around the world like Hurricane Sandy on the United States North Atlantic coast, Typhoon Haiyan in the Philippines, and Cyclone Pam in Vanuatu have caused extreme destruction in these places. Furthermore, rapid population growth and urban development to accommodate it in areas vulnerable to storms and flooding, from the United States Gulf Coast and New York and New Jersey to Southeast Asia and the Indian Subcontinent, is putting millions at risk. It is true that these growing centers of population are the economic engines of the local and global economies; furthermore, they accommodate the workforces that drive the economic growth of these industrial powers. However, development must be curtailed in the interest of public safety. Rapid population growth has not permitted adequate urban planning, and the proliferation of slums means that more lives will be lost in the case of storms or floods. If slowing urban growth means limiting economic growth, so be it: the risks of flooding from unpredictable and violent climate patterns are too great.

22

SCIENCE PRACTICE TEST

Read the text carefully, and choose the correct answer.

1. The most common isotope of oxygen has a weight of 16 AMU. Heavy oxygen is a stable oxygen isotope with a weight of 18 AMU. The presence of heavy oxygen in a molecule can be tracked using a mass spectrometer.

   A scientist provides a growing sunflower plant with CO_2 that has been made with heavy oxygen. He then tracks the movement of the oxygen molecules through the photosynthetic pathway.

   After the carbon dioxide has been metabolized, where will the heavy oxygen be found?

   A) in water secreted by the plant

   B) in glucose created by the plant

   C) in pyruvate created by the plant

   D) in oxygen released by the plant

2. Which of the following cellular processes does not use ATP?

   A) facilitated diffusion

   B) DNA replication

   C) active transport through the cell membrane

   D) movement of the mot complex in a flagellum

3. Hemophilia is a hereditary genetic disorder that prevents blood from clotting correctly. The allele for hemophilia is recessive and carried on the X chromosome.

   A couple has two sons, one who has hemophilia and one who does not. What can be said about the genotype of the couple?

   A) The mother is an asymptomatic carrier of the disorder.

   B) The father is an asymptomatic carrier of the disorder.

   C) The mother does not carry the gene for the disorder.

   D) The father does not carry the gene for the disorder.

4. Which of the following would most likely decrease the efficiency of the C3 pathway but not of the C4 pathway?

   A) an increase in available sunlight

   B) an increase in atmospheric oxygen

   C) an increase in temperature

   D) an increase in available water

5. Over a period of several hundred years, a glacier melts and is transformed into a lake populated by many species of birds, algae, and other aquatic organisms. Later, the lake slowly dries up and becomes a valley, where grasses and shrubs predominantly grow.

This passage describes which of the following ecological processes?

A) convergence

B) succession

C) adaption

D) evolution

6. The chart depicts a graph of a patient's antibody count during the course of two infections by the same pathogen. The *x*-axis shows the number of days that have passed, and the *y*-axis shows the patient's antibody count in millimolars.

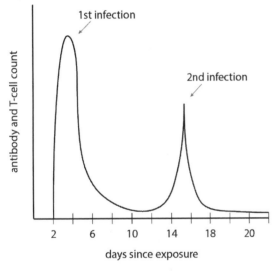

What is the most probable explanation for the shorter duration of the immune response during the second infection?

A) The patient started an antibiotic regimen on day 16.

B) The patient was vaccinated against the infection on day 16.

C) The patient's adaptive immune system was able to more efficiently fight the second infection.

D) The patient's innate immune system had been strengthened by the first infection.

7. Photosynthetic organisms use a variety of pathways to create glucose (a process known as carbon fixation). The most common of these pathways is C3 carbon fixation, so-called for the three-carbon glucose precursor it produces. Plants that use the C3 pathway thrive in environments with moderate temperatures and a consistent water supply. However, the pathway is inefficient in hot, dry conditions. In these environments, C3 plants must close their stomata to avoid water loss, which decreases the concentration of CO_2 in cells. This decrease will in turn increase the rate of photorespiration, a wasteful process in which O_2 replaces CO_2 in reactions with the RUBISCO enzyme.

Plants that use the C4 pathway have found a way around this inefficiency. This pathway—which is named for its four-carbon glucose precursor—decreases the rate of photorespiration, allowing plants to fix carbon more efficiently in hot, dry climates. However, this process requires more energy than the C3 pathway, so the C4 pathway is only more useful under specific conditions.

Which of the following is a distinguishing feature separating the C3 from the C4 pathway?

A) The C4 pathway is more commonly used than the C3 pathway.

B) The C3 pathway produces a three-carbon glucose precursor, while the C4 pathway produces a four-carbon glucose precursor.

C) The C4 pathway is able to operate in extreme cold temperatures, but the C3 pathway cannot.

D) The C4 pathway is more efficient than the C3 pathway because it increases the amount of photorespiration that occurs.

8. A scientist discovers a new species of snail that lives in the ocean. He tested the ability of this species to handle heat by measuring its growth rate as he increased the temperature of the water. He also tested two different concentrations of salt to determine which type of marine environment the snail would be best suited for.

    In the experiment described previously, what is the dependent variable?

    A) salt concentration

    B) temperature

    C) growth rate

    D) number of snails

9. A student proposes the idea that the modern-day sparrow is a descent of the genus Archaeopteryx, an ancient bird. Which of the following findings would best support this hypothesis?

    A) Archaeopteryx and sparrows had the same diet.

    B) Archaeopteryx and sparrows lived in the same region.

    C) Archaeopteryx and sparrows were both able to fly.

    D) Archaeopteryx and sparrows have homologous bone structures.

10. A strand of DNA isolated by a scientist has the following sequence: 3'–ATGGTGCTTAGT – 5'. If an mRNA transcript of this strand were made, what would its sequence be?

    A) 5' – TACCACGAATCA – 3'

    B) 5' – UTCCTCGUUTCA – 3'

    C) 5' – UACCAGAAUCA – 3'

    D) 5' – GTCAAGTACCA – 3'

11. A particular species of ladybug feeds exclusively on red flowers. During this process, the ladybugs pollinate the flowers and also mate. Over time, a mutation appears in the plant population that results in yellow flowers. Some of the ladybugs start to pollinate and mate on the yellow flowers. Eventually, the ladybugs that feed on red flowers and those that feed on yellow flowers can no longer mate with one another. What is the most likely explanation for this occurrence?

    A) allopatric speciation driven by geographic isolation

    B) sympatric speciation driven by behavioral isolation

    C) allopatric speciation driven by natural selection

    D) sympatric speciation driven by habitat differentiation

12. In a certain species of rose, color is determined by a single allele. The dominant allele, R, produces red flowers, and the recessive allele, r, produces white flowers. A scientist crosses a red rose with another red rose to produce the F1 generation of offspring. He then randomly selects two of the F1 generation and crosses them, resulting in the F2 generation. All the F1 generation had red flowers. The F2 generation consisted of 75 percent red roses and 25 percent white roses.

    What were the genotypes of the two roses in the parent generation?

    A) RR and rr

    B) Rr and Rr

    C) RR and Rr

    D) There is not enough information to determine the genotype.

CONTINUE

13. A scientist believes that a particular species of algae, *S. sponferus,* is able to grow even when living deep underwater. However, he hypothesizes that this species may grow more slowly than algae in other environments due to the lack of sunlight at this depth. Which of the following findings would not support the scientist's hypothesis?

A) Many other species of algae are able to live at depths of 1000 meters under the surface of the water.

B) Laboratory experiments show that *S. sponferus* grows equally well under a wide range of light conditions.

C) *S. sponferus* is found growing in abundance on the ocean's surface.

D) Some species of algae are discovered that do not need much light to grow.

14. A 30 mL sample of an unknown acid was titrated with 0.1M NaOH. The pH of the solution is shown on the graph below.

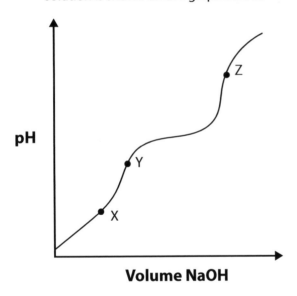

Volume NaOH

Which statement best explains the shape of the curve?

A) The acid is amphoteric.

B) The acid is polyprotic.

C) The reaction of the acid with the base is a double replacement reaction.

D) The reaction rate was increased using a catalyst.

15. In humans, which organ is not part of the endocrine system?

A) the stomach

B) the pancreas

C) the hypothalamus

D) the pineal gland

16. Which of the following processes will take place in both mitosis and meiosis?

A) separation of homologous chromatids

B) formation of new nuclei that each have half the number of chromosomes that exist in the parent nuclei

C) production of chiasma during synapsis

D) separation of duplicated sister chromatids

17. A man is on an airplane with a cabin pressure of 720 mm Hg and a temperature of 22 °C. He empties a flexible 0.5 L bottle and puts the cap back on. When he disembarks at the airport, where the pressure is 1 atm and the temperature is 24 °C, what will happen to the volume of his empty bottle?

A) It will increase.

B) It will decrease.

C) It will remain the same.

D) There is not enough information to determine what will happen.

18. A gas sample is heated so that the average kinetic energy of the particles in the sample doubles. Which of the following could describe the temperature change that occurred in the system?

A) 200 K to 400 K

B) 100°C to 50°C

C) 0 K to 100 K

D) 0°C to 100°C

19. Which of these processes is exothermic?

    A) freezing ice cubes

    B) baking a cake

    C) melting iron

    D) breaking up a gaseous diatom

20. Which of the following transformations would have an energy change equal in magnitude but opposite in sign?

    A) melting and vaporization

    B) sublimation and vaporization

    C) condensation and vaporization

    D) condensation and sublimation

21. The Haber-Bosch process uses the chemical reaction seen below to create ammonia out of nitrogen and hydrogen gas. At 500°C, the reaction goes to 82 percent completion. Which of the following could not be used to drive the reaction equilibrium further to the right?

    $N_2 + 3H_2 \rightarrow 2NH_3$

    A) increasing the temperature

    B) increasing the pressure

    C) adding a catalyst

    D) increasing the concentrations of nitrogen and hydrogen gas

22. The solubility of a compound is determined by many factors, including the presence of a similar ion in solution, the temperature, and in some cases, the partial pressure of the gas above the solution. Calcium hydroxide is a compound that dissolves relatively easily into water. However, calcium hydroxide's solubility can be decreased by the presence of similar ions in the solution.

    Which of the following methods could be used to increase the solubility of $Ca(OH)_2$ in ethanol?

    A) adding NAOH ions to the solution

    B) removing OH- ions from the solution

    C) adding more Ca(OH)2 to the solution

    D) stirring the solution vigorously

23. Which of the following molecules does not have an ionic bond?

    A) $FeCl_2$

    B) H_3PO_4

    C) KOH

    D) C_2H_6

24. The latent heat of vaporization of ammonia is about 1/20th that of water. If water and ammonia are both at their boiling points, which of the following statements is true?

    A) Ammonia will require 20 times more energy to turn into vapor compared with water.

    B) Ammonia will require 20 times more energy to see an increase of 1°C compared with water.

    C) Water will require 20 times more energy to turn into vapor compared with ammonia.

    D) Water will require 20 times more energy to see an increase of 1°C compared with ammonia.

25. Which equation is correctly balanced?

    A) $2\,AgNO_3 + 2\,NaOH \rightarrow Ag_2O + 2\,NaNO_3 + H_2O$

    B) $4\,AgNO_3 + 3\,NaOH \rightarrow Ag_2O + 2\,NaNO_3 + H_2O$

    C) $AgNO_3 + 2\,NaOH \rightarrow Ag_2O + 2\,NaNO_3 + H_2O$

    D) $2\,AgNO_3 + 2\,NaOH \rightarrow 2\,Ag_2O + 2\,NaNO_3 + H_2O$

26. In the following reaction, which species is being reduced?

    $2\,MnO_4^- + 5\,SO_3^{2-} + 6\,H^+ \rightarrow 2\,Mn^{2+} + 5\,SO_4^{2-} + 3\,H_2O$

    A) manganese

    B) sulfur

    C) oxygen

    D) hydrogen

CONTINUE

27. In the nuclear reaction shown below, what is the missing product, X?

$$^{11}_{5}B \rightarrow X + ^{4}_{2}He$$

- **A)** $^{9}_{5}B$
- **B)** $^{7}_{5}Li$
- **C)** $^{7}_{3}Li$
- **D)** $^{9}_{3}B$

28. Which of the following elements has the highest first ionization energy?

- **A)** sodium
- **B)** sulfur
- **C)** carbon
- **D)** argon

29. A catalyst is designed to:

- **A)** increase the amount of energy released during a reaction
- **B)** increase the amount of energy consumed during a reaction
- **C)** reduce the activation energy required for a reaction
- **D)** lower the entropy change that occurs during a reaction

30. The reaction of magnesium chloride and sodium sulfate follows the reaction below:

$$MgCl_2 + Na_2SO_4 \rightarrow MgSO_4 + 2NaCl$$

$$\Delta H = -17.2 \text{ kJ/mol}$$

Once the reaction has reached equilibrium, which of the following could be done to increase the rate of the reaction to the right?

- **A)** increase the concentration of salt
- **B)** mix the solution thoroughly
- **C)** heat the solution
- **D)** add more magnesium chloride

31. Which equation is correctly balanced?

- **A)** $NH_4NO_3 + \text{heat} \rightarrow N_2O + H_2O$
- **B)** $3NH_4NO_3 + \text{heat} \rightarrow 3N_2O + 2H_2O$
- **C)** $2NH_4NO_3 + \text{heat} \rightarrow 2N_2O + H_2O$
- **D)** $NH_4NO_3 + \text{heat} \rightarrow N_2O + 2H_2O$

32. In an enclosed container of gas, the pressure exerted on the walls of the container is due to what?

- **A)** the intermolecular forces of the gas
- **B)** the collision of gas molecules with the walls of the container
- **C)** the electronic repulsion of gas molecules away from each other
- **D)** the reaction taking place

33. The following graph shows the velocity of a moving object as a function of time during an interval of 3 seconds.

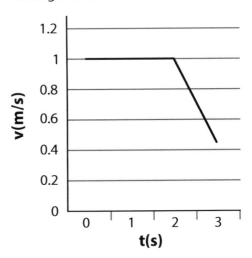

Which of the following statements concerning the motion of the object is true?

- **A)** The object remains still for the first 2 seconds and then starts to move backward.
- **B)** The acceleration of the object remains the same for the entire 3-second interval.
- **C)** The velocity of the object is zero for the first two seconds and then becomes negative.
- **D)** The acceleration of the object is zero for the first 2 seconds and then becomes negative.

34. A car travels with a constant speed of 40 miles per hour. If the car travels at this speed for 15 minutes, how far does the car travel in this time?

A) 0.375 miles

B) 2.7 miles

C) 10 miles

D) 40 miles

35. Which of the following statements concerning projectile motion is not true? (Note that any effects due to air resistance are neglected.)

A) The horizontal velocity of an object launched upward at an angle to the horizontal is constant.

B) The vertical acceleration of the object is positive while the object moves upward and negative while the object moves downward.

C) The vertical acceleration of the object is constant.

D) The vertical component of the object's velocity is zero at its highest point.

36. Consider a system of two objects. If both internal and external forces act on the system, and the net external force on the system is zero, which of the following statements must be true?

A) The internal forces cause a change in the net momentum of the system.

B) The momentum of one object changes while the other stays the same.

C) Both objects must be stationary.

D) The change in the net momentum of the system is zero.

37. A wave with a speed of 10 m/s is traveling on a string, causing each particle to oscillate with a period of 20 s. The wavelength of the wave is:

A) 0.5 meters

B) 2 meters

C) 200 meters

D) 300 meters

38. Which of the following statement is true concerning an object undergoing simple harmonic motion, such as a mass on the end of a spring?

A) The kinetic energy of the system is zero at the midpoint of the motion.

B) The speed of the mass is constant during the motion.

C) The kinetic energy of the system is maximum at the midpoint of the motion.

D) The potential energy of the system is maximum at the midpoint of the motion.

39. Consider an object acted on by only two forces as shown. If the magnitudes of F1 and F2 are equal, which of the following statements must be true?

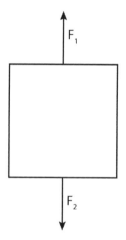

A) The velocity of the object must be zero.

B) The velocity of the object must be constant.

C) The velocity of the object must be increasing.

D) The velocity of the object must be decreasing.

CONTINUE

40. Why will using brighter headlights not help a driver see better in fog?

   A) The water droplets in fog have a high refractive index.

   B) Total internal reflection occurs in fog droplets.

   C) The water droplets absorb all the light.

   D) The water droplets reflect the light back toward the driver.

41. A bullet traveling horizontally hits a block placed on a smooth horizontal surface and gets embedded into it. Then the quantity that does not change is:

   A) linear momentum of the block

   B) kinetic energy of the block

   C) temperature of the block

   D) gravitational potential energy of the block

42. When a positive charge is taken from a low-potential region to a high-potential region, the electric potential energy:

   A) increases

   B) decreases

   C) remains constant

   D) may increase or decrease

43. A volcano that is low and flat to the ground and does not typically have large violent eruptions can be classified as what?

   A) plane volcano

   B) cinder cone

   C) shield volcano

   D) screen volcano

44. Which type of rock is created near or on the earth's surface?

   A) igneous rock

   B) sedimentary rock

   C) crustaceous rock

   D) metamorphic rock

45. The diagram below shows which type of plate boundary?

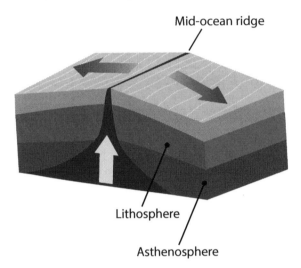

Mid-ocean ridge

Lithosphere

Asthenosphere

   A) transform

   B) translational

   C) divergent

   D) convergent

46. Which of these would not increase the amplitude of the tide on a shoreline?

   A) The shoreline is on the section of the earth closest to the moon.

   B) The shape of the coastline funnels water from a surrounding bay toward the shoreline.

   C) A strong wind blows off the water toward the shore.

   D) The friction created by shallow water moving along the ocean floor slows the flow of water.

47. The water cycle is the movement of water between organisms, the earth's surface, and the atmosphere. The main components of the water cycle are depicted below.

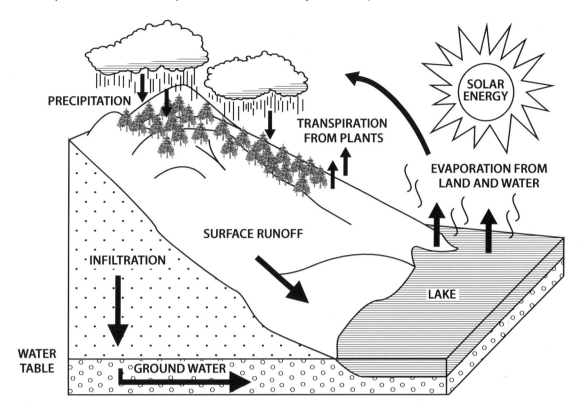

What of these could explain why the water level of a particular lake is lower than in previous years?

A) Abnormal weather patterns have created high levels of precipitation in surrounding areas.

B) Unseasonably high temperatures have melted large amounts of snow in the surrounding mountains.

C) A nearby factory has put measures in place to capture groundwater for use in manufacturing.

D) A farmer has cleared part of a forest and planted crops.

23

SOCIAL STUDIES PRACTICE TEST

Read the following passage carefully, and then answer questions 1 and 2.

The landmass of the United States doubled in 1803 with the purchase of the Louisiana Territory from France; this territory stretched from modern-day Louisiana on the Gulf of Mexico north through the Rocky Mountains to parts of what are today Montana and Minnesota. Thomas Jefferson, the president who brokered this deal, believed that the continued moral strength of the young nation depended on the availability of farmland and the possibilities of westward expansion. However, the sale of this land was not without controversy: American politicians of the time debated whether it was constitutional or prudent to increase the size of the nation so rapidly, and it's questionable whether France had legally obtained the land from Spain or had the right to sell it at all.

1. Which of the following is true about the Louisiana Purchase?

    A) It involved a transaction between Spain and the United States.

    B) It was universally considered to be a good idea.

    C) It included territory that would become multiple states in the U.S.

    D) It tripled the landmass area of the United States.

2. Based on the information in the passage, which of the following might be a reason for an American politician of 1803 to oppose the Louisiana Purchase?

    A) The Constitution did not stipulate whether the nation could be increased in size so rapidly.

    B) The price per acre of the land included was too high.

    C) Most of the soil in the regions of the Louisiana Territory was not good farmland.

    D) Giving citizens new areas to farm would strengthen the culture of the nation.

THE LAST FEW BUTTONS ARE ALWAYS THE HARDEST.

—Chapin in the St. Louis *Star*.

This cartoon was originally published in the *St. Louis Star* newspaper. Since 1807, only men had been legally allowed to vote in the United States. Suffragists, or activists for extending the right to vote to women, had been working for decades to overturn this. By the beginning of the 1900s, four states allowed women to vote at the state level. In 1918, President Woodrow Wilson began to support women's suffrage. In June of 1919, the legislature passed the Nineteenth Amendment, guaranteeing women the right to vote. However, thirty-six state legislatures had to ratify, or approve, the amendment before it could be official. This took until August of 1920.

3. During which of the following months is this cartoon most likely to have been published?

    A) June 1901

    B) August 1918

    C) June 1919

    D) March 1920

4. In the cartoon, what do the buttons represent?

    A) presidents who supported women's suffrage

    B) the number of amendments that needed to be passed

    C) states that are needed to ratify the Nineteenth Amendment

    D) steps in the process of finalizing a bill

Questions 5 – 7 refer to the following excerpt from *Common Sense*. Here, Paine describes the potential of America's military force:

Excerpt from *Common Sense*

BY THOMAS PAINE

No country on the globe is so happily situated, or so internally capable of raising a fleet as America. Tar, timber, iron, and cordage are her natural produce. We need go abroad for nothing. Whereas the Dutch, who make large profits by hiring out their ships of war to the Spaniards and Portuguese, are obliged to import most of their materials they use. We ought to view the building of a fleet as an article of commerce, it being the natural manufactory of this country. It is the best money we can lay out. A navy when finished is worth more than it cost. And is that nice point in national policy, in which commerce and protection are united. Let us build; if we want them not, we can sell; and by that means replace our paper currency with ready gold and silver…

In point of safety, ought we to be without a fleet? We are not the little people now, which we were sixty years ago; at that time we might have trusted our property in the streets, or fields rather; and slept securely without locks or bolts to our doors or windows. The case now is altered, and our methods of defense ought to improve with our increase of property. A common pirate, twelve months ago, might have come up the Delaware, and laid the city of Philadelphia under instant contribution, for what sum he pleased; and the same might have happened to other places. Nay, any daring fellow, in a brig of fourteen or sixteen guns might have robbed the whole continent, and carried off half a million of money. These are circumstances which demand our attention, and point out the necessity of naval protection.

Some, perhaps, will say, that after we have made it up with Britain, she will protect us. Can we be so unwise as to mean, that she shall keep a navy in our harbors for that purpose? Common sense will tell us, that the power which hath endeavored to subdue us, is of all others the most improper to defend us. Conquest may be affected under the pretense of friendship; and we after a long and brave resistance may be at last cheated into slavery. And if her ships are not to be admitted into our harbors, I would ask, how is she to protect us? A navy three or four thousand miles off can be of little use, and on sudden emergencies, none at all. Wherefore, if we must hereafter protect ourselves, why not do it for ourselves?

5. What does Thomas Paine indicate has changed over the past sixty years?

   A) Pirates are now more common.

   B) The American people now have much more property to protect.

   C) The relationship between America and Britain is now much friendlier.

   D) Guns have become more powerful, increasing the effectiveness of thieves.

6. The author most likely wanted America to produce a naval fleet to protect itself from

   A) Great Britain

   B) The Netherlands

   C) France

   D) Mexico

7. The author would most likely agree with which of the following points?

   A) America should maintain independence from Britain.

   B) Americans should attempt to return to a culture in which they could sleep without locking their doors.

   C) It's difficult to sell ships.

   D) It would be necessary to import ship-building materials to build the navy.

Questions 8 and 9 use information from the graph below:

AMERICAN IP INDEX

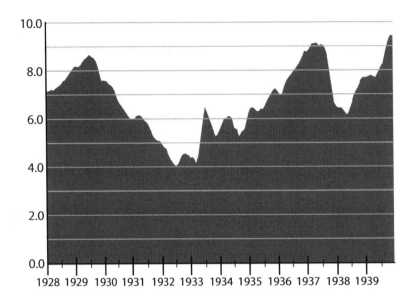

8. The longest period of decline in American manufacturing and mining occurred when?

    A) 1928 – 1929

    B) 1929 – 1932

    C) 1933 – 1935

    D) 1936 – 1938

9. Which of these most likely explains the drop in production in 1929?

    A) Demand for American-made goods dropped dramatically due to increases in foreign production.

    B) The United States Legislature introduced measures to increase domestic manufacturing.

    C) Panic in financial markets decreased the capital available to manufacturers.

    D) America's dominance in the automobile industry decreased its need to manufacture other goods.

Look at the map and answer question 10.

10. Based on the information in the map, which of the following conclusions is most likely?

   A) San Juan de Manapiare is one of the major centers of commerce in Venezuela.

   B) The majority of Venezuelans live in the northern part of the country.

   C) It's difficult to travel from Colombia to Venezuela by road.

   D) Colombia and Brazil frequently fight for control of territory in Venezuela.

Read the excerpt and answer question 11.

Article I, Section 3 of the United States Constitution:

The Senate of the United States shall be composed of two Senators from each State, chosen by the Legislature thereof for six Years; and each Senator shall have one Vote.

Immediately after they shall be assembled in Consequence of the first Election, they shall be divided as equally as may be into three Classes. The Seats of the Senators of the first Class shall be vacated at the Expiration of the second Year, of the second Class at the Expiration of the fourth Year, and of the third Class at the Expiration of the sixth Year, so that one third may be chosen every second Year; and if Vacancies happen by Resignation, or otherwise, during the Recess of the Legislature of any State, the Executive thereof may make temporary Appointments until the next Meeting of the Legislature, which shall then fill such Vacancies.

No Person shall be a Senator who shall not have attained to the Age of thirty Years, and been nine Years a Citizen of the United States, and who shall not, when elected, be an Inhabitant of that State for which he shall be chosen.

The Vice President of the United States shall be President of the Senate, but shall have no Vote, unless they are equally divided.

The Senate shall choose their other Officers, and also a President pro tempore, in the Absence of the Vice President, or when he shall exercise the Office of President of the United States.

The Senate shall have the sole Power to try all Impeachments. When sitting for that Purpose, they shall be on Oath or Affirmation. When the President of the United States is tried, the Chief Justice shall preside: And no Person shall be convicted without the Concurrence of two thirds of the Members present.

Judgment in Cases of Impeachment shall not extend further than to removal from Office, and disqualification to hold and enjoy any Office of honor, Trust or Profit under the United States: but the Party convicted shall nevertheless be liable and subject to Indictment, Trial, Judgment and Punishment, according to Law.

11. Of the following people, who would not be eligible to serve in the Senate today based on the information given?

   A) a thirty-year-old man

   B) a forty-two-year-old woman

   C) a person elected to serve as a senator for a state in which he does not live

   D) a person who obtained U.S. citizenship in the 1980s

Read the excerpt and answer questions 12 and 13.

Article I, Section 3 of the United States Constitution

The Senate shall have the sole power to try all impeachments. When sitting for that purpose, they shall be on oath or affirmation. When the President of the United States is tried, the Chief Justice shall preside: and no person shall be convicted without the concurrence of two thirds of the members present.

12. This section of the Constitution is an example of which principle?

   A) proportional representation

   B) freedom of speech

   C) the separation of church and state

   D) separation of powers

13. Which of the following best describes the vice president's role in the Senate?

   A) The vice president acts as a member of the Senate.

   B) The vice president presides over Senate sessions but is never allowed to vote.

   C) The vice president presides over the Senate during impeachment trials.

   D) The vice president presides over Senate sessions and breaks ties in Senate votes.

Read the excerpt and answer questions 14 and 15.

In 1913, the United States created the Federal Reserve System, partially in response to financial panics in the years prior. The Federal Reserve System is tasked with using monetary policy to help the United States weather economic fluctuations, maintain employment rates, and keep inflation to a predictable rate. While high-ranking members of the Federal Reserve Board are appointed by the president and confirmed by the Senate, the Federal Reserve is able to make decisions about monetary policy without approval by the branches of government.

14. Which of the following outcomes is prevented by giving the Federal Reserve System decision-making power independent of the branches of government?

   A) the Federal Reserve System using monetary policy to prevent high inflation

   B) the president of the United States appointing the chair of the Federal Reserve System

   C) the Senate influencing economic outcomes by setting monetary policy

   D) the Federal Reserve System preventing financial panics

15. Which of the following is not a situation in which the Federal Reserve System would be expected to act?

   A)   Parts of the country are experiencing dangerously high inflation rates.

   B)   A downturn in manufacturing causes an unexpected spike in unemployment.

   C)   A financial panic causes banks to close.

   D)   The Senate requests that funding for the military be increased.

Look at the chart and answer questions 16 – 18.

Significant inventions in textile production during the Industrial Revolution

YEAR	INVENTION	EFFECT ON PRODUCTIVITY
1733	**FLYING SHUTTLE**: A device that allows one worker to weave across a wide loom quickly.	This tool was estimated to have doubled the productivity of one weaver.
1764	**SPINNING JENNY**: A device that allows one worker to produce several spools of yarn at one time, using a frame operated by a wheel.	At first, workers could spin eight spools of yarn at once rather than one. As the technology improved, this increased to as many as 120 spools at once.
1764	**WATER FRAME**: Another device used for spinning multiple spools of thread at once, the water frame used power sufficient to produce high-quality threads.	With the introduction of the water frame, both the warp and the weft threads needed for making cotton cloth could now be produced by fully mechanized means.
1779	**SPINNING MULE**: This combined the technologies of the spinning jenny and the water frame, allowing higher-quality threads to be produced.	The cloth produced with the spinning mule was able to compete with higher-quality, more costly handmade fabrics.

16. Based on the chart, what was the main reason these inventions were introduced into textile production?

   A)   to increase the productivity of workers

   B)   to decrease the need to hire workers

   C)   to ease the burden on tired workers

   D)   to allow more workers to open their own textile factories

17. Each of these devices was invented in Great Britain. Which of the following is a likely effect these inventions had on that nation's economy?

   A)   British manufacturers profited by producing low-cost textiles that they sold overseas.

   B)   British manufacturers profited by producing textiles that were not affordable in other countries.

   C)   British manufacturers lost money by producing low-quality textiles that did not sell well.

   D)   British manufacturers profited by producing high-quality, high-cost textiles.

18. The inventions discussed in the chart explain which shifts in the lives of textile workers during the 1700s?

   A)   They faced more dangerous tasks and earned lower wages.

   B)   They became more productive and learned to use new machinery.

   C)   They earned higher wages but faced more dangerous conditions.

   D)   Their working conditions improved as they unionized.

Look at the poster and answer questions 19 and 20.

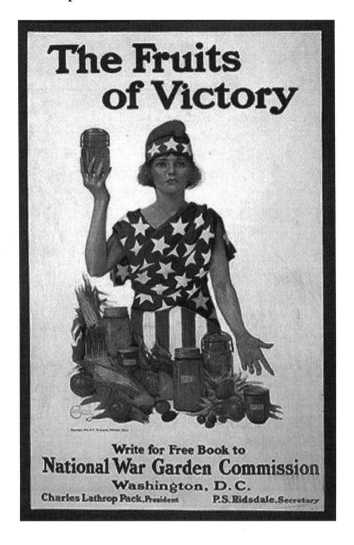

During World War I, food shortages became a problem in the United States and many other countries, as those who worked in agriculture enlisted in military service and food production regions in Europe became battlegrounds. To address food shortages domestically, the government encouraged citizens to plant their own vegetables at home or in public spaces such as parks.

Victory gardens came to the forefront again when the forced internment of over 100,000 Japanese Americans drastically reduced the agricultural capacity of the American West.

19. What was the purpose of the poster shown previously?

    A) to promote the idea of victory gardens

    B) to teach people how to plant a victory garden

    C) to encourage people to enlist in military service.

    D) to encourage healthy eating habits

20. During which period were Japanese Americans forced into internment camps?

    A) before World War I

    B) during World War I

    C) during the period between World War I and World War II

    D) during World War II

Look at the cartoon below and answer questions 21 and 22.

IN THE RUBBER COILS.

Scene—The Congo "Free" State.

In 1885, King Leopold of Belgium declared the Congo, the largest state in the African continent, to be his colony: the Congo Free State. The territory remained under his control until 1908, and during that time, Leopold used his power to brutally extract natural resources, including rubber, ivory, and mined minerals.

21. The snake in the cartoon above is depicting whom or what?

   A) the Belgian government

   B) King Leopold

   C) the rubber companies

   D) public outrage

→
CONTINUE

22. The artist who drew this cartoon likely believed that

    A) the Congolese people were suffering under King Leopold.

    B) people should boycott the rubber trade.

    C) the Congo Free State should not belong to Belgium.

    D) the Republic of the Congo could benefit economically from producing rubber.

Look at the chart below and answer questions 23 – 25.

Acts of Congress

YEAR	ACT	DESCRIPTION
1789	United States Constitution, Article III	Establishes that all crimes, with the exception of impeachment cases, must be tried by a jury in the state in which they were committed.
1791	Sixth Amendment of the Constitution (Bill of Rights)	Requires that each individual member of a jury be unbiased, or without preconceptions, toward the defendant. To ensure that bias does not exist, both the prosecution and the defense sides of a trial have the chance to interview prospective jurors and eliminate those whom they find to have a bias.
1968	Jury Selection and Service Act	A comprehensive reform of the jury selection process, this act made every district court in the U.S. compile names of potential jurors from voter registration lists or voting records. These lists could be supplemented by other means if they did not accurately reflect the demographics (age, race, gender) of the community.

23. Which of the following rights of those on trial was guaranteed by the Jury Selection and Service Act?

    A) The trial must occur in the state in which the crime was committed.

    B) The trial jury must be unbiased.

    C) The jury must be composed such that it reflects the demographics of the community.

    D) The defense has the opportunity to eliminate jurors whom they find to be biased before the trial begins.

24. The United States Declaration of Independence, adopted in 1776, denounced the British monarchy for often denying its subjects a trial by jury for accused crimes. Which of the following seeks to address this?

    A) Article III of the Constitution

    B) the Sixth Amendment of the Constitution (in the Bill of Rights)

    C) the Jury Selection and Service Act

    D) none of the above

25. Which of these best explains why the Jury Selection and Service Act was passed?

    A) to ensure that only capable individuals are assigned to juries

    B) to ensure that jurors do not allow their own prejudices to sway their decisions

    C) to ensure that only individuals who vote are able to serve on juries

    D) to ensure that minorities are not excluded from juries

Read the letters below and answer questions 26 and 27.

Letter 1 Dear Editor, I am concerned about the proposed free-trade agreement between the United States and the countries of the European Union. The North American Free Trade Agreement, between the United States, Canada, and Mexico, makes more sense to me because we are all neighbors and we do not produce the same types of goods, so there is less competition and more reason to trade. However in Germany for example, auto manufacturing is an important industry. If we remove the taxes from imported cars, fewer people will buy American-made cars because German cars will become cheaper than they are now. This will hurt our domestic industries. My son works in an auto plant, and if demand for American cars goes down, he could lose his job.	**Letter 2** Dear Editor, I am writing because I manage a small clothing business, and a free-trade agreement between the US and the EU would positively impact my bottom line. I design swimsuits and other garments, which are mostly manufactured in the Czech Republic due to its strong garment-manufacturing resources. When I ship the raw materials there and then when my vendors ship the finished products back to me, we are taxed twice, raising the prices of my clothes. Then, through online sales, we ship some clothes to countries in the EU—and are taxed again. Eliminating this triple tax means that my clothes will ultimately be cheaper for everyone. This must be true for many businesses, so a free-trade agreement would mean cheaper consumer goods for all.

26. The author of Letter 1 compares the proposed free-trade agreement with what?

    A) the American auto industry

    B) the global garment market

    C) the North American Free Trade Agreement

    D) the European Union

27. Which of the following accurately describes the production chain that the author of Letter 2 uses in his or her argument?

    A) Swimsuits are designed and manufactured in the Czech Republic and then shipped to the United States, where they are purchased and shipped to customers in countries in the European Union.

    B) Swimsuits are designed in the United States, manufactured in the European Union, and then shipped back to the United States, where they are sold or shipped to customers in the European Union.

    C) Swimsuits are designed in the United States, manufactured in the European Union, and then sold to customers in the European Union.

    D) Swimsuits are designed and manufactured in the United States, then shipped to customers in the Czech Republic and other countries in the European Union.

→

CONTINUE

Look at the chart and answer questions 28 and 29.

AUGUST 6, 1945	The United States bombs the Japanese cities Hiroshima and Nagasaki with atomic weapons during World War II.
MARCH 5, 1946	British Prime Minister Winston Churchill gives his famous speech warning of the "Iron Curtain" of communism falling across Europe, separating the Soviet Union and its satellites from the rest of Europe.
MARCH 12, 1946	U.S. President Harry Truman announces that the U.S. will give monetary aid to Greece and Turkey to prevent them from falling under Soviet control.
JUNE 5, 1947	U.S. Secretary of State George Marshall announces that the U.S. will give aid to all war-ravaged countries in Western Europe to prevent the spread of Soviet communism.

28. What event must have happened between August 6, 1945, and March 5, 1946?

    A) The United States tested its first atomic bomb.

    B) The Marshall Plan was announced.

    C) The Soviet Union began to exert influence over its satellite countries.

    D) World War II ended.

29. During the 1940s, what was the primary diplomatic means by which the United States worked to contain communism?

    A) constructing the Iron Curtain

    B) giving aid to other countries

    C) testing nuclear weapons

    D) declaring war on the Soviet Union

Read the excerpt and answer questions 30 and 31.

The World Bank was established in 1944 during the Bretton Woods Conference concerning international financial stability. The World Bank is intended to combat global poverty by assisting developing countries with loans for programs to benefit their citizens. In 1994 the World Bank, together with the International Monetary Fund, began a debt-relief program to help thirty-nine countries classified as heavily indebted and poor.

Critics of the World Bank say that its aid comes with overly stringent requirements: for example, to qualify for a World Bank loan, many countries in sub-Saharan Africa have undergone structural adjustment policies. These policies require countries' state-owned resources to be sold to private companies and their expensive government-run social programs to be cut. While it could be argued that structural adjustment policies are intended to be beneficial by stimulating economic growth, when they are implemented too quickly or without proper support they can actually trigger economic depressions instead.

30. What is the stated purpose of the World Bank?

    A) to implement structural adjustment policies

    B) to cancel out the debt of developing countries

    C) to combat global poverty

    D) to sell state-owned resources to private companies

31. Which of the following actions of the World Bank would a critic of the World Bank view as a harmful policy?

A) loaning 60 million dollars to Rwanda to improve access to electricity

B) giving Nicaragua a structural adjustment credit for selling state-owned assets to foreign investors

C) loaning money to Lebanon for the purpose of hiring unemployed young people in government roles

D) funding a program to enforce wastewater treatment regulations in industrialized areas of Vietnam

Read the excerpt and answer questions 32 – 35.

To ensure the peaceful development of nations, free from coercion, the United States has taken a leading part in establishing the United Nations. The United Nations is designed to make possible lasting freedom and independence for all its members. We shall not realize our objectives, however, unless we are willing to help free peoples to maintain their free institutions and their national integrity against aggressive movements that seek to impose upon them totalitarian regimes. This is no more than a frank recognition that totalitarian regimes imposed on free peoples, by direct or indirect aggression, undermine the foundations of international peace and hence the security of the United States.

The peoples of a number of countries of the world have recently had totalitarian regimes forced upon them against their will. The Government of the United States has made frequent protests against coercion and intimidation, in violation of the Yalta agreement, in Poland, Rumania, and Bulgaria. I must also state that in a number of other countries there have been similar developments.

At the present moment in world history nearly every nation must choose between alternative ways of life. The choice is too often not a free one.

One way of life is based upon the will of the majority, and is distinguished by free institutions, representative government, free elections, guarantees of individual liberty, freedom of speech and religion, and freedom from political oppression.

The second way of life is based upon the will of a minority forcibly imposed upon the majority. It relies upon terror and oppression, a controlled press and radio; fixed elections, and the suppression of personal freedoms.

I believe that it must be the policy of the United States to support free peoples who are resisting attempted subjugation by armed minorities or by outside pressures.

80th Cong. 171 (1947)(Statement of Harry Truman, President of the United States) March 12, 1947 (Truman Doctrine)

32. How does Truman differentiate between the two ways of life he discusses in his speech?

A) He describes one as better than the other.

B) He describes one as based on free institutions, speech, elections, religion, but politically oppressive, while the other is based on oppression, suppressed radio, press, and personal freedoms, but with some political freedoms.

C) He describes one free from political oppression and the other with only limited political freedoms.

D) He describes one as based on free institutions, speech, elections, religion, and freedom from political oppression, while the other is based on oppression, rigged elections, and suppressed radio, press, and personal freedoms.

CONTINUE

33. Read this sentence from the text.

This is no more than a frank recognition that totalitarian regimes imposed on free peoples, by direct or indirect aggression, undermine the foundations of international peace and hence the security of the United States.

In the context of the excerpt, how is this idea comparable with the Bush doctrine of preemption?

A) It argues that communism is a threat to U.S. security.

B) It states that the U.S. must protect its national sovereignty.

C) It argues that the U.S. must assist countries before they are taken over by totalitarian forces; otherwise, national security is at risk.

D) It argues that the U.S. must assist countries after they are taken over by totalitarian forces; otherwise, national security is at risk.

34. Read this excerpt from the text.

The peoples of a number of countries of the world have recently had totalitarian regimes forced upon them against their will. The Government of the United States has made frequent protests against coercion and intimidation, in violation of the Yalta agreement, in Poland, Rumania, and Bulgaria. I must also state that in a number of other countries there have been similar developments.

To what historical developments is Truman referring?

A) the occupation of the Sudetenland and Poland, among other European countries, by Hitler

B) the occupation of several Eastern European countries by Stalin

C) the construction of the Berlin Wall and the occupation of Poland, Romania, and Bulgaria by the U.S.S.R.

D) the construction of the Iron Curtain

35. When discussing the "two ways of life," what is Truman describing?

A) the differences between communism and democratic capitalism—that is, between the U.S. and the U.S.S.R.

B) the differences between communism and democratic totalitarianism—that is, between the U.S.S.R. and the European Union

C) the differences between communism and fascism—that is, between the U.S.S.R. and Nazi Germany

D) the differences between democratic capitalism and fascism—that is, between the U.S. and the U.S.S.R.

Read the excerpt and answer questions 36 and 37.

It's not true that the United States feels any land hunger or entertains any projects as regards the other nations of the Western Hemisphere save such as are for their welfare. All that this country desires is to see the neighboring countries stable, orderly, and prosperous. Any country whose people conduct themselves well can count upon our hearty friendship. If a nation shows that it knows how to act with reasonable efficiency and decency in social and political matters, if it keeps order and pays its obligations, it need fear no interference from the United States. Chronic wrongdoing, or an impotence which results in a general loosening of the ties of civilized society, may in America, as elsewhere, ultimately require intervention by some civilized nation, and in the Western Hemisphere the adherence of the United States to the Monroe

Doctrine may force the United States, however reluctantly, in flagrant cases of such wrongdoing or impotence, to the exercise of an international police power.

Theodore Roosevelt's Annual Message to Congress, December 6, 1904 (Roosevelt Corollary to the Monroe Doctrine)

36. What is Roosevelt saying about U.S. intentions in the Western Hemisphere?

    A) The United States will not intervene in domestic matters in Latin American countries.

    B) The United States will only intervene in domestic matters in Latin American countries upon request.

    C) The United States will intervene in Latin American countries when it sees fit.

    D) The United States will intervene in Latin American countries when it sees fit and may use force.

37. According to the Monroe Doctrine, the United States would view European interference in Latin America as a sign of aggression, consolidating U.S. influence in that region. What is different about the Roosevelt Corollary to the Monroe Doctrine?

    A) It stationed U.S. troops throughout Latin America.

    B) It strengthened commercial ties between the United States and Latin American countries.

    C) It limited diplomatic relations between Europe and Latin America.

    D) It provided for U.S. military intervention in Latin America.

Read the excerpt and answer questions 38–41.

Niger is a landlocked, sub-Saharan nation, whose economy centers on subsistence crops, livestock, and some of the world's largest uranium deposits. Agriculture contributes nearly 40% of GDP and provides livelihood for most of the population. The UN ranked Niger as the least developed country in the world in 2014 due to multiple factors such as food insecurity, lack of industry, high population growth, a weak educational sector, and few prospects for work outside of subsistence farming and herding. Since 2011 public debt has increased in part from a large loan financing a new uranium mine. The government relies on foreign donor resources for a large portion of its fiscal budget. The economy in recent years has been hurt by terrorist activity and kidnappings near its uranium mines and instability in Mali, and concerns about security have boosted fiscal spending on defense. Future growth may be sustained by exploitation of oil, gold, coal, and other mineral resources. Niger has sizable reserves of oil and oil production. Food insecurity and drought remain perennial problems for Niger, and the government plans to invest more in the agriculture sector, most notably irrigation. The mining sector may be affected by the government's attempt to renegotiate extraction rights contracts to increase royalty rates and reduce tax exemptions. Despite Niger's three-year $121 million IMF Extended Credit Facility agreement for years 2012-2015, formal private sector investment needed for economic diversification and growth remains a challenge, given the country's limited domestic markets, access to credit, and competitiveness.

Reprinted from the CIA World Factbook,
https://www.ciA)gov/library/publications/the-world-factbook/geos/ng.html

38. Given the information above, what is likely true about Niger?

    A) Rates of infant and child mortality are low.

    B) Rates of infant and child mortality are high.

    C) It's unlikely that Niger was formerly a European colony.

    D) Cities are growing in Niger.

39. Reasons for Niger's status as an LDC include all the following EXCEPT:

    A) its drought-prone geography and climate

    B) low levels of industrialization

    C) Niger's amount of mineral resources

    D) social insecurity

40. What would a demographer working in Niger likely study?

    A) how changes in the land and climate affect the movements of farmers and herders

    B) the push-and-pull factors driving Nigeriens into Niger's growing cities

    C) government monetary and debt policies

    D) the growing threats of kidnapping and violence near uranium mines

41. According to the reading, what is currently an important source of revenue for Niger?

    A) cattle

    B) uranium

    C) agriculture

    D) defense

Read the excerpt and answer questions 42 – 44.

Article 41

The Security Council may decide what measures not involving the use of armed force are to be employed to give effect to its decisions, and it may call upon the Members of the United Nations to apply such measures. These may include complete or partial interruption of economic relations and of rail, sea, air, postal, telegraphic, radio, and other means of communication, and the severance of diplomatic relations.

Article 42

Should the Security Council consider that measures provided for in Article 41 would be inadequate or have proved to be inadequate, it may take such action by air, sea or land forces as may be necessary to maintain or restore international peace and security. Such action may include demonstrations, blockade, and other operations by air, sea, or land forces of Members of the United Nations.

United Nations, Charter of the United Nations, 24 October 1945, 1 UNTS XVI, Chapter VII

42. According to Article 42, what action can the Security Council take to maintain international peace and security?

    A) It may impose embargoes on countries.

    B) It may force the General Assembly to take military action against countries.

    C) It may cut diplomatic relations with countries.

    D) It may take military action against countries.

43. What is the difference between the Security Council and the League of Nations?

    A) The Security Council can take military action to preserve international peace and security.

    B) The Security Council can compel countries to sever diplomatic ties to preserve international peace and security.

    C) The Security Council can take control of national military forces.

    D) The Security Council cannot take military action.

44. Read this sentence from the text.

These may include complete or partial interruption of economic relations and of rail, sea, air, postal, telegraphic, radio, and other means of communication, and the severance of diplomatic relations.

By taking these steps, the Security Council would likely be aiming for all the following outcomes EXCEPT:

A) to make the people suffer

B) to make the country change its policy

C) to encourage the country to negotiate

D) to avoid international military action

Read the excerpt and answer the questions that follow.

Four score and seven years ago our fathers brought forth, upon this continent, a new nation, conceived in liberty, and dedicated to the proposition that "all men are created equal."

Now we are engaged in a great civil war, testing whether that nation, or any nation so conceived, and so dedicated, can long endure.

Abraham Lincoln, the Gettysburg Address

45. Read this sentence from the passage.

Four score and seven years ago our fathers brought forth, upon this continent, a new nation, conceived in liberty, and dedicated to the proposition that "all men are created equal."

What was President Lincoln referring to here?

A) the Civil War

B) the American Revolution

C) the writing of the Constitution

D) the creation of the Bill of Rights

46. What statement would the author of this passage agree with?

A) The outcome of the Civil War would only impact the United States.

B) The Civil War would be the final battle for American independence.

C) The outcome of the Civil War would impact the future of any democracy based on equality.

D) The Civil War was a war for states' rights.

47. Why did President Lincoln speak at Gettysburg?

A) It was the site of a major Revolutionary War battle.

B) It was the site of an important debate about states' rights.

C) It was the site of a major Civil War battle.

D) It was the site of the signing of the Declaration of Independence.

24

ANSWER KEY

Mathematics

1.	D)	**26.**	B)
2.	B)	**27.**	D)
3.	B)	**28.**	C)
4.	C)	**29.**	C)
5.	C)	**30.**	$2.77
6.	A)	**31.**	B)
7.	300	**32.**	5
8.	D)	**33.**	A)
9.	B)	**34.**	B)
10.	B)	**35.**	C)
11.	C)	**36.**	A)
12.	0.25	**37.**	A)
13.	C)	**38.**	B)
14.	A)	**39.**	10
15.	C)	**40.**	C)
16.	D)	**41.**	D)
17.	5	**42.**	196
18.	C)	**43.**	C)
19.	D)	**44.**	C)
20.	C)	**45.**	$y = 3x + 4$
21.	C)	**46.**	B)
22.	C)		
23.	C)		
24.	C)		
25.	A)		

1. B)
2. A)
3. D)
4. D)
5. D)
6. A)
7. A)
8. C)
9. C)
10. The narrator, a young boy, is paid to look out for a fearsome, one-legged old man, a sailor who periodically comes to his family's inn and creates a tense, but thrilling, atmosphere. The old man is unpredictable, forceful, and even frightening, telling enthralling stories about his adventures at sea long ago and dominating the atmosphere. Despite scaring the locals and intimidating the innkeeper, the old man provides excitement in an otherwise dull town.
11. A)
12. A)
13. C)
14. Clearly, boy bands have remained an enduring part of American popular culture throughout the twentieth century, and their influence carries on into the twenty-first. Certain boy bands have been recognized as essential parts of rock and roll history around the world. Individual performers have begun their professional lives in boy bands and have moved on to very successful solo careers. From barbershop quartets to One Direction, the only "direction" for boy bands seems to be up.
15. Drop Area 1: C)

    Drop Area 2: A)

    Drop Area 3: B)

16. T.S. Eliot
17. Clive Bell
18. T.S. Eliot
19. T.S. Eliot
20. Clive Bell
21. D)
22. A)
23. C)
24. B)
25. A)
26. C)
27. A)
28. A)
29. B)
30. B)
31. nostalgic, loving, emotional
32. A)
33. D)
34. C)
35. D)
36. A)
37. B)
38. A)
39. B)
40. D)
41. D)
42. B)
43. A)
44. D)
45. 3
46. 2
47. 1

Sample Response (Keep in mind there is no one correct answer for these questions; the following are examples.)

"Analyze an Issue" #1

To be sure, extracting petroleum and natural gas requires hard choices and results in environmental damage. Around the world, oil and gas are obtained through drilling in deserts, off deep-sea platforms, and now through fracking, which can damage the earth and water resources. However, fossil fuels are essential to industry and the global economy. Oil and gas make it possible for the world to use electricity and transportation. Furthermore, the economic fate of millions is directly tied to the fossil fuels industry; the livelihoods of workers around the world, from roughnecks to office staff, depend on the oil and gas market. While oil and gas extraction can have negative consequences for the environment, it is too important to the global economy to limit exploration and production.

While oil and gas prices rise and fall, and the market can be unpredictable, there will be demand for fossil fuels for years to come. Rapidly growing countries like China, whose populations are beginning to demand products like automobiles, will require more petroleum than ever. Despite efforts to conserve energy and protect the environment, industrial production continues worldwide, including in countries with limited environmental protection laws in the developing world. Furthermore, international organizations like the World Trade Organization allow major corporations to sue countries in order to weaken environmental protection laws in favor of production. Fossil fuels power not only consumer goods like cars, but large-scale industrial production as well. Alternative sources of energy (like wind and solar power) do exist, but not on the same scale as oil and gas.

In addition, several countries located in oil-producing regions have become wealthy and powerful thanks to this natural resource. Saudi Arabia, Kuwait, the United Arab Emirates, Russia, Nigeria, Angola, Iran, and Iraq are just a few examples of major oil producers. Given the importance of oil to the world economy, the wealth of these countries helps make them important voices in regional and international affairs; moreover, oil wealth gives them the ability to form strategic alliances with world powers. It is unlikely that major oil producers would give up their substantial geostrategic power in favor of environmental protection.

In an ideal world, the global economy would flourish while the environment did the same. However, in order to make the most of natural resources, sacrifices are required. Perhaps environmental activism and new technology can help the international community find a way forward in order to safely extract the resources the global economy needs, and improve energy efficiency to make the most of those resources we already have.

Analyze an Issue #2

Violent storms are a huge risk to human life and property; they also have a strong impact on the economy, interfering with economic activity and sometimes damaging infrastructure. However, natural disasters are a fact of life on our planet, and it is impossible for economic development and growth to cease due to the possibility of a powerful storm. Still, rapid urban development is occurring in particularly storm-prone areas in Asia and even in North America, putting millions of people at risk. While the risks of a calamitous storm should never be underestimated, the solution is not to halt migration and slow economic growth, but to encourage investment in urban planning and public safety.

As discussed, centers of population in storm-prone areas in Indonesia, the Philippines, the United States East and Gulf Coasts, and elsewhere are indeed growing; natural resources and urban areas in these places are essential to local and national economies and even the global economy. During this time of change, especially in areas that are newly developing, opportunities for proper urban planning abound. Before growing urban areas get even larger, governments must take action to prevent the proliferation of slums, improve existing infrastructure to meet the needs of growing cities (or develop new infrastructure), and put policies into place for good urban management. Given the importance of these urban and industrial areas, especially for billion-dollar sectors like the oil and gas industry, there may even be opportunities for major companies to get involved in sponsoring urban development and safety in the economic zones and cities relevant to their interests around the world.

Furthermore, with economic growth also comes innovation and technology. Today, there are more opportunities than ever to develop products and procedures to ensure safety. From engineering to preparedness to emergency medical treatment, there are a plethora of approaches to storm readiness and flood control. Urban planning can take into account flooding and geographical impediments to emergency response time. There are more products on the market to help families survive for several days without help (for instance, water purifiers and generators). Governments, civic organizations, and NGOs could be involved in emergency preparedness efforts and enlisted to distribute preparedness items during storm seasons, especially to those poor and working people who are the most likely to be affected and who, according to the passage, would most likely be harmed. Using good technology and wise community coordination would ensure that vulnerable workers and their families are as safe as possible during storm season, so that they could benefit year-round from economic growth.

While storms and other natural disasters are and will remain a threat to human life, it is unrealistic to imagine that all economic activity will stop for the sake of safety. Thanks to economic growth and innovation, we can develop planning, technology, policy, and coordination to ensure the safety of communities as they drive the economic growth of those regions affected by major storms. That way, development can continue in as safe an environment as possible.

Science

1. B)	13. B)	25. A)	37. C)
2. A)	14. B)	26. A)	38. C)
3. A)	15. A)	27. C)	39. B)
4. C)	16. D)	28. D)	40. D)
5. B)	17. B)	29. C)	41. D)
6. C)	18. A)	30. D)	42. A)
7. B)	19. A)	31. D)	43. C)
8. C)	20. C)	32. B)	44. B)
9. D)	21. D)	33. D)	45. C)
10. C)	22. B)	34. C)	46. D)
11. D)	23. D)	35. B)	47. C)
12. C)	24. C)	36. D)	

Social Studies

1. C)	13. D)	25. D)	37. D)
2. A)	14. C)	26. C)	38. B)
3. D)	15. D)	27. B)	39. C)
4. C)	16. A)	28. C)	40. A)
5. B)	17. A)	29. B)	41. B)
6. A)	18. B)	30. C)	42. D)
7. A)	19. A)	31. B)	43. A)
8. B)	20. D)	32. D)	44. A)
9. C)	21. B)	33. C)	45. B)
10. B)	22. A)	34. B)	46. C)
11. C)	23. C)	35. A)	47. C)
12. D)	24. A)	36. D)	